PENGUIN REFERENCE

The Penguin Pocket Dictionary of Quotations

David Crystal was born in 1941 and spent the early years of his life in Holyhead, North Wales. He went to St Mary's College, Liverpool, and University College, London, where he read English and obtained his Ph.D. in 1966. He was a lecturer in linguistics at the universities of Bangor and Reading, becoming Professor of Linguistics at the University of Wales, Bangor. He is editor of *The Penguin Encyclopedia* and related publications, the former editor of the Cambridge family of general encyclopedias, compiler of several dictionaries, and author of publications on the theory and practice of reference works. He currently directs a company which manages a large reference database and which is developing systems for improving document classification and internet search. A past president of the Society of Indexers, in 2001 his book *Words on Words* (co-authored with Hilary Crystal) was awarded the Wheatley Medal for an outstanding index. In 1995 he was awarded the OBE for services to the English language.

THE PENGUIN POCKET DICTIONARY OF
QUOTATIONS

Edited by David Crystal

PENGUIN BOOKS

PENGUIN BOOKS

Published by the Penguin Group
Penguin Books Ltd, 80 Strand, London WC2R 0RL, England
Penguin Group (USA) Inc., 375 Hudson Street, New York, New York 10014, USA
Penguin Group (Canada), 10 Alcorn Avenue, Toronto, Ontario, Canada M4V 3B2
(a division of Pearson Penguin Canada Inc.)
Penguin Ireland, 25 St Stephen's Green, Dublin 2, Ireland (a division of Penguin Books Ltd)
Penguin Group (Australia), 250 Camberwell Road, Camberwell, Victoria 3124, Australia
(a division of Pearson Australia Group Pty Ltd)
Penguin Books India Pvt Ltd, 11 Community Centre, Panchsheel Park, New Delhi – 110 017, India
Penguin Group (NZ), cnr Airborne and Rosedale Roads, Albany, Auckland 1310, New Zealand
(a division of Pearson New Zealand Ltd)
Penguin Books (South Africa) (Pty) Ltd, 24 Sturdee Avenue, Rosebank 2196, South Africa

Penguin Books Ltd, Registered Offices: 80 Strand, London WC2R 0RL, England

www.penguin.com

First published 2005
1

Copyright © Crystal Reference Systems Ltd, 2005
All rights reserved

The moral right of the author has been asserted

Typeset by Tradespools, Frome, Somerset
Printed in England by Clays Ltd, St Ives plc

Except in the United States of America, this book is sold subject
to the condition that it shall not, by way of trade or otherwise, be lent,
re-sold, hired out, or otherwise circulated without the publisher's
prior consent in any form of binding or cover other than that in
which it is published and without a similar condition including this
condition being imposed on the subsequent purchaser

Contents

Acknowledgements

Crystal Reference

EDITOR
David Crystal

ASSOCIATE EDITOR
Peter Preston

EDITORIAL MANAGER
Hilary Crystal

DATABASE DEVELOPMENT
Ann Rowlands
Jan Thomas
Todd Warden Owen

DATABASE MANAGEMENT
Tony McNicholl
Philip Johnstone

CRYSTAL REFERENCE
ADMINISTRATION
Ian Saunders
Rob Phillips

Penguin Books

PUBLISHING DIRECTOR
Nigel Wilcockson

EDITORIAL ASSISTANCE
Ellie Smith

PRODUCTION
Andrew Henty

DESIGN
Richard Marston

TYPESETTING
Tradespools

Preface

What is a book of quotations for? For me, it is chiefly a pragmatic tool, which helps me solve two kinds of daily problem. In the first case, I am writing something or giving a talk, I want to include a quotation, and I need to be sure I get it right. In the second case, I am reading what someone else has written or said, I encounter a quotation, and I feel sure they have *not* got it right. Either way, I have to check – and in the absence of a personal library containing all the sources I need, a well-edited book of quotations solves my problem. (The Internet, incidentally, does not always do so: it contains millions of quotations, but these often include errors.)

A book of quotations is not compiled mechanically. It involves creative decision-making as does any work of art, and reflects the compiler's sources, reading, and interests. No two quotation-books are the same – though all share a common core of 'famous' quotations. They differ in terms of how much material they include from other languages, and whether they include contemporary observations, catch-phrases, song titles, nursery rhymes, and other items from our collective linguistic subconscious. Everyone knows the experience of hearing a fragment of a song from long ago and realizing that they can still remember the words. Are these quotations too?

For me, a quotation has to say something worth saying, to the extent that it has moved away from its original context and is found in contexts unintended or unimagined by its author. It is not a matter of semantic profundity – though many quotations are undoubtedly profoundly meaningful – but of pragmatic effect. We find a quotation useful or effective in making our point. We find we need them to answer a question, as in a crossword clue or panel game. In some cases we simply find them objects of beauty, in their use of language. In others, they are objects of enjoyment, making us marvel or laugh. But in all cases they are in some way self-contained, conveying a meaning or eliciting an effect which can be appreciated without reference to their text of origin. So yes, there are some song fragments in this book, but I have included them only when I know they have been used outside of their original musical setting.

Because of its use as a self- or other-checking device, the most important feature in a book of quotations is the index. If you half-remember a quotation, there is no way of knowing in advance which half is going to be remembered. So if you can't remember the author and want to look it up, you need to be able to find it through any of the salient words it contains. If your target is 'The better part of valour is discretion', and all you can recall is the word 'valour', then you need to find this word in the index. Similarly, someone who recalls 'discretion' needs to be able to find it from *that* starting-point. And if all you can remember is 'better part', the index should be able to help there too. It isn't just nouns that need to be indexed: the less central parts of speech can sometimes be important (adverbs such as *alone*, *never*, *once*, or prepositions such as *behind*). That is why a good index to a book of quotations is always as long as the quotation-section itself.

A further function of a book of quotations is browsing, and here it is important to know the order in which the items have been listed. In this anthology, the overall organization is author-by-author, from A to Z. Then, within an author, the quotations are numbered chronologically. But there are two exceptions. Books of quotations always contain large numbers of items from the Bible and Shakespeare, and in neither case can we be certain about chronology. So quotations from the former are here presented using the conventional sequencing of books in the Old and New Testaments; and quotations from Shakespeare are given play by play in alphabetical order.

David Crystal

Abelard, Peter (1079–1142). French ecclesiast and theologian

1 *Non enim facile de his, quos plurimum diligimus, turpitudinem suspicamur.*
We do not easily suspect evil of those whom we love most.
Historia Calamitatum (c.1132) ch. 6

Acheson, Dean (Gooderham) (1893–1971). American lawyer and politician

1 The first requirement of a statesman is that he be dull.
In the *Observer* 21 June 1970

2 A memorandum is written not to inform the reader but to protect the writer.
In the *Wall Street Journal* 8 September 1977

Acton, Lord (John Emerich Edward Dahlberg, 1st Baron Acton of Aldenham) (1834–1902). British historian

1 Power tends to corrupt and absolute power corrupts absolutely.
Letter to Bishop Mandell Creighton, 3 April 1887, in Louise Creighton *Life and Letters of Mandell Creighton* (1904) vol. 1, ch. 13

Adams, Abigail (1744–1818). Wife of John Adams, 2nd President of the USA

1 Remember all men would be tyrants if they could.
Letter to John Adams, 31 March 1776, in Butterfield et al. (eds.) *The Book of Abigail and John Adams* (1975) p. 121

2 Great necessities call out great virtues.
Letter to John Quincy Adams, 19 January 1780, in Butterfield et al. (eds.) *The Book of Abigail and John Adams* (1975) p. 253

Adams, Douglas (Noel) (1952–2001). English science-fiction writer

1 Don't Panic.
The Hitchhiker's Guide to the Galaxy (1979) preface; words written in large friendly letters on the cover of the Guide

2 The Answer to the Great Question Of … Life, the Universe and Everything … [is] Forty-two.
The Hitchhiker's Guide to the Galaxy (1979) ch. 27

3 So long, and thanks for all the fish.
Title of novel (1984)

Adams, Henry Brooks (1838–1918). American man of letters

1 A friend in power is a friend lost.
The Education of Henry Adams (1907) ch. 7

2 A teacher affects eternity; he can never tell where his influence stops.
The Education of Henry Adams (1907) ch. 20, 'Failure'

3 Morality is a private and costly luxury.
The Education of Henry Adams (1907) ch. 22

4 Practical politics consists in ignoring facts.
The Education of Henry Adams (1907) ch. 22

Adams, John (1735–1826). 2nd President of the USA

1 The happiness of society is the end of government.
Thoughts on Government (1776)

2 Fear is the foundation of most governments.
Thoughts on Government (1776)

3 I agree with you that in politics the middle way is none at all.
Letter to Horatio Gates, 23 March 1776

Adams, Sarah Flower (1805–48). English hymn-writer

1 Nearer, my God, to thee.
'Nearer My God to Thee' in W. G. Fox *Hymns and Anthems* (1841)

Adamson, Harold (1906–80). American songwriter

1 Comin' in on a wing and a pray'r.
Title of song (1943); comment made by the pilot of a damaged plane to ground control

Addison, Joseph (1672–1719). English poet, playwright and essayist

1 Music, the greatest good that mortals know,
And all of heaven we have below.
'A Song for St Cecilia's Day' (1694)

2 Poetic fields encompass me around,
And still I seem to tread on classic ground.
Letter from Italy (1704)

3 A perfect tragedy is the noblest production of human nature.
In the *Spectator* 1711, no. 39

4 Eternity! thou pleasing, dreadful thought!
Cato (1713) act 5, sc. 1, l. 1

5 Hunting is not a proper employment for a thinking man.
Quoted in Colin Jarman *The Guinness Dictionary of Sports Quotations* (1990)

Adenauer, Konrad (1876–1967). German statesman

1 A thick skin is a gift from God.
In the *New York Times* 30 December 1959

Adler, Polly (1900–62). American writer

1 A house is not a home.
Title of a book (1954)

Adorno, Theodor (1903–69). German social philosopher and musicologist

1 In psychoanalysis nothing is true except the exaggerations.
Negative Dialectics (1966)

Agate, James (1877–1947). English theatre critic

1 Long experience has taught me that in England nobody goes to the theatre unless he or she has bronchitis.
Attributed

2 A professional is a man who can do his job when he doesn't feel like it. An amateur is a man who can't do his job when he does feel like it.
Diary, 19 July 1945

Akins, Zoë (1886–1958). American poet and playwright

1 The Greeks had a word for it.
Title of play (1930)

Alan of Lille (Alanus de Insulis) (*c*.1114–1202). French writer and scholar

1 *Post nubila maxima, Phoebus.*
After the greatest clouds, the sun.
Liber Parabolarum (1175) ch. 1, l. 33

2 *Mille viae ducunt homines per sæcula Romam.*
Throughout the ages, a thousand roads lead to Rome.
Liber Parabolarum (1175) ch. 3, l. 56

Albee, Edward Franklin (1928–). American dramatist

1 Who's afraid of Virginia Woolf?
Title of play (1962)

Aldiss, Brian (Wilson) (1925–). English science-fiction writer and novelist

1 Science fiction is no more written for scientists than ghost stories are written for ghosts.
Penguin Science Fiction (1961) introduction

Aldrin, 'Buzz' (Edwin Eugene Aldrin Jnr) (1930–). American astronaut; second man on the moon

1 The Eagle has landed.
In *The Times* 21 July 1969, p. 1

Alexander, Cecil Frances (1818–95). Irish poet

1 All things bright and beautiful,
All creatures great and small,
All things wise and wonderful,
The Lord God made them all.
'All Things Bright and Beautiful' (1848)

2 The rich man in his castle,
The poor man at his gate,
God made them, high or lowly,
And ordered their estate.
'All Things Bright and Beautiful' (1848)

3 Once in royal David's city
Stood a lowly cattle-shed,
Where a mother laid her baby.
In a manger for his bed:
'Once in Royal David's City' (1848)

4 There is a green hill far away,
Without a city wall,
Where the dear Lord was crucified,
Who died to save us all.
'There is a Green Hill Far Away' (1848)

Alexander, Sir William (c.1567–1640). Scottish courtier and poet

1 The weaker sex, to piety more prone.
Of women. 'Doomsday', Fifth Hour (1637)

Alexander I (1777–1825). Tsar of Russia

1 Napoleon thinks that I am a fool, but he who laughs last laughs longest.
Letter to his sister, 8 October 1808

Algren, Nelson (1909–81). American novelist

1 A walk on the wild side.
Title of novel (1956)

2 Never play cards with a man called Doc. Never eat at a place called Mom's. And never, ever, no matter what else you do in your whole life, never sleep with anyone whose troubles are worse than your own.
In Newsweek 2 July 1956

Ali, Muhammad (formerly Cassius Clay) (1942–). American boxer

1 I am the greatest!
In the Louisville Times 16 November 1962

Allainval, Abbé d' (1700–53). French playwright

1 L'embarras des richesses.
The embarrassment of riches.
Title of comedy (1726)

Allen, Fred (John Florence Sullivan) (1895–1956). American humorist

1 Committee – a group of men who individually can do nothing but as a group decide that nothing can be done.
Attributed

Allen, Woody (Allen Stewart Konigsberg) (1935–). American film director, writer and actor

1 I think crime pays. The hours are good, you travel a lot.
Take the Money and Run (film, 1969)

2 Is sex dirty? Only if it's done right.
Everything You Always Wanted to Know about Sex (film, 1972)

3 My brain? It's my second favorite organ.
Sleeper (film, 1973, with Marshall Brickman)

4 If it turns out that there is a God, I don't think that he's evil. But the worst that you can say about him is that basically he's an under-achiever.
Love and Death (film, 1975)

5 It's not that I'm afraid to die. I just don't want to be there when it happens.
Death (1975) p. 63

6 I don't want to achieve immortality through my work … I want to achieve it through not dying.
Quoted in Eric Lax Woody Allen and His Comedy (1975) ch. 12

7 Don't knock masturbation. It's sex with someone I love.
Annie Hall (film, 1977, with Marshall Brickman)

Allingham, William (1824–89).
Irish poet

1 Up the airy mountain,
  Down the rushy glen,
  We daren't go a-hunting,
  For fear of little men.
  'The Fairies' (1850)

Ambrose, St (c.339–97 AD). Bishop
of Milan

1 *Ubi Petrus, ibi ergo ecclesia.*
  Where Peter is, there, accordingly,
  is the Church.
  Explanatio psalmi 40

**Amery, Leo(pold) Charles
Maurice Stennett** (1873–1955).
English Conservative politician

1 Cromwell said to the Long Parliament when he thought it was no longer fit to conduct the affairs of the nation, 'You have sat too long here for any good you have been doing. Depart, I say, and let us have done with you. In the name of God, go!'
  Remark addressed to Prime Minister Neville Chamberlain, House of Commons, 7 May 1940

Amis, Martin (Louis) (1949–).
English novelist, son of Kingsley
Amis

1 Most writers need a wound, either physical or spiritual.
  In the *Observer* 30 August 1987

Amis, Sir Kingsley (1922–95).
English novelist and poet

1 Women are really much nicer than men:
  No wonder we like them.
  'A Bookshop Idyll' (1956)

2 More will mean worse [of potential university students].
  In *Encounter* July 1960

3 Outside every fat man there was an even fatter man trying to close in.
  One Fat Englishman (1963) ch. 3

4 He was of the faith chiefly in the sense that the church he currently did not attend was Catholic.
  One Fat Englishman (1963) ch. 8

Anderson, Maxwell (1888–1959).
American playwright

1 But it's a long, long while
  From May to December;
  And the days grow short
  When you reach September.
  'September Song' (1938 song; music by Kurt Weill)

**Anderson, Maxwell and
Stallings, Lawrence** (1888–1959;
1894–1968). American playwrights

1 What price glory?
  Title of play (1924)

Anderson, Robert (Woodruff)
(1917–). American playwright

1 All you're supposed to do is every once in a while give the boys a little tea and sympathy.
  Tea and Sympathy (1957) act 1

Angell, Sir Norman (1872–1967).
English pacifist

1 The great illusion.
  Title of book (1910) on the futility of war

Angelou, Maya (Maya Johnson)
(1928–). Black American writer

1 Poetry is music written for the human voice.
  In *The Power of the Word*, Public Broadcasting Service, 15 September 1989

Anonymous – English

1 Sumer is icumen in,
  Lhude sing cuccu! (Summer is coming in, Loudly sings cuckoo)
  'Cuckoo Song' (c.1250)

2 The cloud of unknowing.
  Title of mystical prose work (fourteenth century)

3 Everyman, I will go with thee, and be thy guide,
  In thy most need to go by thy side.
  Everyman (c.1509–19) l. 522 (lines spoken by Knowledge)

4 Thirty days hath September,
  April, June, and November.
  Stevins MS (c.1555)

5 Greensleeves was all my joy,
Greensleeves was my delight,
'A new Courtly Sonnet of the Lady Greensleeves, to the new tune of 'Greensleeves',
in *A Handful of Pleasant Delights* (1584)

6 Please to remember the Fifth of
November,
Gunpowder, Treason and Plot.
Traditional rhyme on the Gunpowder Plot
(1605)

7 Matthew, Mark, Luke, and John,
The bed be blest that I lie on.
Traditional (the first two lines in Thomas
Ady *A Candle in the Dark*, 1656); also as: Bless
the bed that I lie on

8 The Campbells are comin'.
'The Campbells are comin' (*c*.1715). Possibly
originating in John Campbell, Duke of Ar-
gyll's attack on the Jacobite army at Sher-
iffmuir (1715)

9 In good King Charles's golden
days.
'The Vicar of Bray' in *British Musical Miscel-
lany* (1734) vol. 1

10 We hold these truths to be self-
evident, that all men are created
equal, that they are endowed by
their Creator with certain una-
lienable rights, that among these
are life, liberty and the pursuit of
happiness.
The American Declaration of Independence, 4 July 1776

11 The ministry of all the talents.
Ironic description of William Grenville's
coalition of 1806, in G. W. Cooke *The History
of Party* (1837) vol. 3, p. 460

12 Absence makes the heart grow
fonder.
In T. H. Bayly *Isle of Beauty* (revised edn,
1850)

13 John Brown's body lies a
mould'ring in the grave,
His soul is marching on.
Song (1861), variously attributed to Charles
Sprague Hall, Henry Howard Brownell and
Thomas Brigham Bishop, and inspired by
the hanging of abolitionist John Brown in
1859

14 O God, if there be a God, save my
soul, if I have a soul!
Soldier's prayer before the battle of Blenheim, quoted in John Henry Newman
Apologia pro Vita Sua (1864)

15 Please do not shoot the pianist. He
is doing his best.
Printed notice in a dancing saloon, in Oscar
Wilde *Impressions of America* 'Leadville'
(*c*.1882–3)

16 Miss Buss and Miss Beale
Cupid's darts do not feel.
Of the Headmistress of the North London
Collegiate School and the Principal of the
Ladies' College, Cheltenham, *c*.1884

17 Lizzie Borden took an axe
And gave her mother forty whacks;
When she saw what she had done
She gave her father forty-one!
Popular rhyme after the acquittal of Lizzie
Borden (1893) from the charge of murder-
ing her father and stepmother at Fall River,
Massachusetts in 1892

18 Every picture tells a story.
Advertisement for Doan's Backache Kidney
Pills (early 1900s)

19 We shall overcome.
Title of song from before the American Civil
War, adapted as a Baptist hymn ('I'll Overcome Some Day', 1901) by C. Albert Tindley,
and revived by various civil rights and
labour movements in the twentieth century

20 Give me a child for the first seven
years, and you may do what you
like with him afterwards.
Attributed Jesuit maxim, in *Lean's Collectanea* vol. 3 (1903) p. 472

21 The eternal triangle.
Book review title, in the *Daily Chronicle*
5 December 1907

22 All present and correct.
King's Regulations (Army) Report of the
Orderly Sergeant to the Officer of the Day

23 Your country needs you!
(1914) First use of British First World War
recruiting slogan

24 Are we downhearted? No!
Used by British soldiers during the First
World War

25 Mademoiselle from Armenteers,
  Hasn't been kissed for forty years,
  Hinky, dinky, parley-voo.
  Song from the First World War, variously
  attributed to Edward Rowland and to Harry
  Carlton

26 The man you love to hate.
  Advertising trail for Erich von Stroheim in
  the film *The Heart of Humanity* (1918)

27 From ghoulies and ghosties and
  long-leggety beasties
  And things that go bump in the
  night,
  Good Lord, deliver us!
  'The Cornish or West Country Litany', in
  Francis T. Nettleinghame *Polperro Proverbs
  and Others* (1926)

28 The bells of Hell go ting-a-ling-
  a-ling
  For you but not for me.
  'For You But Not For Me', in S. Louis Guir-
  aud (ed.) *Songs That Won the War* (1930)

29 We shall not be moved.
  Title of civil rights song (1931), from an
  earlier gospel hymn

30 It's that man again …!
  Headline in the *Daily Express* 2 May 1939; the
  acronym ITMA became the title of a BBC
  radio show, starring Tommy Handley, from
  September 1939

31 Walls have ears.
  Security slogan in the Second World War

32 Careless talk costs lives.
  Security slogan in the Second World War

33 *Nil carborundum illegitimi.*
  Cod Latin for 'Don't let the bastards grind you down'.
  Widely used during the Second World War;
  often quoted '*nil carborundum*'

34 Coughs and sneezes spread diseases.
  Health slogan in Second World War (1942)

35 Who dares wins.
  Motto of the British Special Air Service
  regiment, from 1942

36 It's a bird! It's a plane! It's Superman!
  Superman (US radio show, 1940s)

37 Ban the bomb.
  Used by US nuclear disarmament movement from 1953

38 Better red than dead.
  Slogan of nuclear disarmament campaign-
  ers, 1950s

39 The singer not the song.
  From a West Indian calypso; title of a novel
  by Audrey Erskine Lindop (1959)

40 Death [is] nature's way of telling
  you to slow down.
  American life insurance proverb, in *Newsweek* 25 April 1960, p. 70

41 That was the week that was.
  Title of satirical BBC TV series, from 1962

42 Not so much a programme, more a
  way of life!
  Title of BBC TV series, 1964

43 Black is beautiful.
  Slogan of American civil rights campaign-
  ers, 1960s

44 There's no such thing as a free
  lunch.
  Catchphrase in US economics from the
  1960s, associated with Milton Friedman

45 GIGO: Garbage in, garbage out.
  Popular saying when working with com-
  puters, from 1960s

46 Never again.
  Jewish Defence League, 1960s

47 Make love, not war.
  Flower Power movement, mid-1960s

48 Black power.
  US black civil rights slogan coined by Sto-
  kely Carmichael, 1966

49 Burn, baby, burn!
  Rioters' cry in Watts, California and Newark,
  New Jersey, quoted in *Time* 11 August 1967

50 Power to the people.
  Slogan of the Black Panther movement,
  from c.1968

51 When you've got it, flaunt it.
  Braniff Airlines slogan, 1969

52 Out of the closets and into the
  streets.
  US gay rights movement slogan, 1969

53 We came in peace for all mankind.
  Text of the plaque left on the moon by the
  first astronauts, 20 July 1969

54 Burn your bra!
  US feminists' slogan, 1970

55 Nice one, Cyril.
Slogan in TV advertisement for Wonderloaf, 1972; adopted in 1973 as a pop-song title addressed to Tottenham Hotspur left-back Cyril Knowles

56 Bigamy is having one husband too many. Monogamy is the same.
Epigraph in Erica Jong *Fear of Flying* (1973) ch. 1

57 Expletive deleted.
Recorded Presidential Conversations to the Committee on the Judiciary of the House of Representatives by President Richard M. Nixon 30 April 1974, appendix 1, p. 2

58 Just when you thought it was safe to go back in the water.
Advertising trail for *Jaws* 2 (film, 1978)

59 The future ain't what it used to be.
Anonymous Iowa farmer quoted by President Bush on NBC TV, 10 May 1987

60 No pain – no gain.
Bodybuilding motto

61 O ye'll tak' the high road, and I'll tak' the low road,
And I'll be in Scotland afore ye,
But me and my true love will never meet again,
On the bonnie, bonnie banks o' Loch Lomon'.
'The Bonnie Banks of Loch Lomond' (traditional song)

62 Let my people go.
'Go Down, Moses' (Negro spiritual)

Anonymous – French

1 *Liberté! Egalité! Fraternité!*
Freedom! Equality! Brotherhood!
Motto of the French Revolution, but of earlier origin

2 *Ils ne passeront pas.*
They shall not pass.
Slogan used by the French army defending Verdun (1916), variously attributed to Marshal Pétain and to General Robert Nivelle; also taken up by the Republicans in the Spanish Civil War in the form 'No pasarán!'; following Dolores Ibarruri's radio broadcast in Madrid, 19 July 1936; *Speeches and Articles 1936–68* (1938) p.7

Anonymous – German

1 *Ein Reich, ein Volk, ein Führer.*
One realm, one people, one leader.
Nazi Party slogan, early 1930s

2 *Arbeit macht frei.*
Work liberates.
Legend over the gates of the concentration camp at Auschwitz, Poland (1940)

3 *Vorsprung durch Technik.*
Progress through technology.
Advertising slogan for Audi motors (from 1986)

Anonymous – Greek

1 Know thyself.
Inscribed on the temple of Apollo at Delphi; Plato, in *Protagoras* 343 b, attributes the saying to the Seven Wise Men

Anonymous – Latin

1 *Ave Caesar, morituri te salutant.*
Hail Caesar, those who are about to die salute you.
Gladiators saluting the Roman Emperor, reported in Suetonius *Lives of the Caesars* 'Claudius' ch. 21

2 *Te Deum laudamus.*
We praise thee, God.
'Te Deum'; hymn variously attributed to St Ambrose, St Augustine or St Niceta in the third or fourth century

3 *Ave Maria, gratia plena, Dominus tecum.*
Hail Mary, full of grace, the Lord is with thee.
'Ave Maria', from the eleventh century

4 *Gaudeamus igitur,*
Juvenes dum sumus.
Let us then rejoice,
While we are young.
Medieval student song, known since 1267, and revised in the eighteenth century

5 *Sic transit gloria mundi.*
Thus passes the glory of the world.
Said during the coronation of a new Pope, known from the fourteenth century

6 *Tempora mutantur, et nos mutamur in illis.*
Times change, and we change with them.
In William Harrison *Description of Britain* (1577) bk 3, ch. 3, but known in various forms from earlier sources

7 *Si monumentum requiris, circumspice.*
If you seek a monument, gaze around.
Inscription in St Paul's Cathedral, London, attributed to the son of the architect, Sir Christopher Wren

8 *Per ardua ad astra.*
Through struggle to the stars.
Motto of the Mulvany family, quoted and translated by Rider Haggard in *The People of the Mist* (1894) ch. 1; still in use as motto of the RAF (from 1913)

9 *Citius, altius, fortius.*
Swifter, higher, stronger.
Motto of the Olympic Games, *c.*1908 (also attributed to Reverend Father Didon)

10 *Et in Arcadia ego.*
And I too in Arcadia.
Tomb inscription often depicted in classical paintings

11 *Nemo me impune lacessit.*
No one provokes me with impunity.
Motto of the Crown of Scotland and of all Scottish regiments

12 *Ad majorem Dei gloriam.*
To the greater glory of God.
Motto of the Society of Jesus

Anouilh, Jean (1910–87). French playwright

1 *La mort est belle. Elle seule donne à l'amour son vrai climat.*
Death is beautiful. It alone gives love its true habitat.
Eurydice (1942) act 4

2 *C'est bon pour les hommes de croire aux idées et de mourir pour elles.*
It is good for people to believe in ideas and die for them.
Antigone (1944)

3 *C'est plein de disputes, un bonheur.*
Happiness is full of strife.
Antigone (1944)

4 *Rien n'est vrai que ce qu'on ne dit pas.*
Nothing is true except that which is unsaid.
Antigone (1944)

5 *Dieu est avec tout le monde ... Et, en fin de compte, il est toujours avec ceux qui ont beaucoup d'argent et de grosses armées.*
God is on everyone's side ... And, in the last analysis, he is on the side of those with plenty of money and large armies.
L'Alouette (1953) p. 120

Anselm, St (1033–1109). Italian cleric, scholar and scholastic philosopher

1 *Neque enim quaero ut credem, sed credo ut intelligam.*
For I do not seek to understand so that I may believe; but I believe so that I may understand.
Proslogion (1078) ch. 1

Antheil, George (1900–59). American composer

1 Art cannot hold its breath too long without dying.
Bad Boy of Music (1945)

Anthony, Susan B(rownell) (1820–1906). American social reformer and women's suffrage leader

1 The true Republic: men, their rights and nothing more; women, their rights and nothing less.
On the front of her newspaper, *The Revolution* (1868–70)

Apollinaire, Guillaume (Wilhelm Apollinaris de Kostrowitzki) (1880–1918). French poet and author

1 *Avant tout, les artistes sont des hommes qui veulent devenir inhumains.*
Above all, artists are men who want to become inhuman.
Les Peintres cubistes; Méditations esthétiques (1913) 'Sur la peinture, 1'

Appleton, Thomas Gold (1812–84). American epigrammatist

1 Good Americans, when they die,
go to Paris.
In Oliver Wendell Holmes *The Autocrat of
the Breakfast Table* (1858) ch. 6

**Arabian Nights
Entertainments, or the
Thousand and one Nights**
A collection of Arabic stories

1 New lamps for old?
'The History of Aladdin'

2 Open Sesame!
'The History of Ali Baba'

Arbuthnot, John (1667–1735).
Scottish physician and
pamphleteer

1 Law is a bottomless pit.
The History of John Bull (1712), pamphlet title

Archimedes (*c.*287–212 BC). Greek
mathematician and inventor

1 Eureka! I've got it!
In Vitruvius Pollio *De Architectura* bk 9,
preface, sect. 10

Argenson, Marquis d' (René Louis
de Voyer d'Argenson) (1694–1757).
French politician and essayist

1 *Laisser-faire.*
No interference.
*Mémoires et Journal Inédit du Marquis d'Ar-
genson* (1858 edn) vol. 5, p. 364

Ariosto, Ludovico (1474–1533).
Italian poet and playwright

1 *Natura il fece, e poi roppe la stampa.*
Nature made him, and then broke
the mould.
Orlando Furioso (1532) canto 10, st. 84

Aristophanes (*c.*450–*c.*385 BC).
Athenian comic dramatist

1 How about 'Cloudcuckooland'?
Naming the capital city of the Birds in *The
Birds* (414 BC) l. 819

Aristotle (384–322 BC). Greek
philosopher

1 Human good turns out to be
activity of soul exhibiting excellence, and if there is more than one
sort of excellence, in accordance

with the best and most complete.
For one swallow does not make a
summer, nor does one day; and so
too one day, or a short time, does
not make a man blessed and happy.
Nicomachean Ethics bk 1, ch. 7, 1098

2 Man is by nature a political animal.
Politics bk 1, 1253a 2–3

3 Now a whole is that which has a
beginning, a middle, and an end.
Poetics ch. 7, referring to tragedy

Armistead, Lewis Addison (1777–
1863). Confederate general

1 Give them the cold steel, boys!
Attributed, during the American Civil War,
1863

Armstrong, Harry (1879–1951).
American songwriter

1 There's an old mill by the stream,
Nellie Dean.
'Nellie Dean' (1905 song)

Armstrong, John (1709–79).
Scottish poet and physician

1 He practised what he preached.
The Art of Preserving Health (1744) bk 4, l. 303

Armstrong, Louis (Satchmo)
(1900–71). American jazz trumpeter
and singer

1 All music is folk music. I ain't never
heard no horse sing a song.
Quoted in the *New York Times* 7 July 1971

Armstrong, Neil A(lden) (1930–).
American astronaut; first man on
the moon

1 That's one small step for [a] man,
one giant leap for mankind.
Remark having stepped on to the moon on
21 July 1969. Originally the 'a' had been lost
in the radio transmission.

Armstrong, Sir Robert (Baron Armstrong of Ilminster) (1927–). Head of the British Civil Service, 1981–7

1 It contains a misleading impression, not a lie. It was being economical with the truth.
Referring to a letter during the 'Spycatcher' trial, Supreme Court, New South Wales, in the *Daily Telegraph* 19 November 1986

Arnold, Matthew (1822–88). English poet and essayist

1 Not deep the Poet sees, but wide.
'Resignation' (1849) l. 214

2 France, famed in all great arts, in none supreme.
'To a Republican Friend – Continued' (1849)

3 All the live murmur of a summer's day.
'The Scholar-Gipsy' (1853) l. 20

4 Truth sits upon the lips of dying men.
'Sohrab and Rustum' (1853) l. 656

5 The men of culture are the true apostles of equality.
Culture and Anarchy (1869) ch. 1

6 The true meaning of religion is thus not simply morality, but morality touched by emotion.
Literature and Dogma (1873) ch. 1

7 Poetry is at bottom a criticism of life.
Essays in Criticism Second Series (1888) 'Wordsworth'

Arnold, Samuel James (1774–1852). English organist and composer

1 England, home and beauty.
'The Death of Nelson' (1811 song)

Arras, Jean d' (Jean Blondel) (fl. *c*.1375). French writer

1 *Bonté vaut mieux que beauté.*
Kindness is worth more than beauty.
Melusine (c.1393)

Asimov, Isaac (1920–92). Russian-born biochemist and science-fiction writer

1 The three fundamental Rules of Robotics … One, a robot may not injure a human being, or, through inaction, allow a human being to come to harm … Two … a robot must obey the orders given it by human beings except where such orders would conflict with the First Law … three, a robot must protect its own existence as long as such protection does not conflict with the First or Second Laws.
I, Robot (1950) 'Runaround'

Asquith, Margot (1864–1945). Scottish society figure and wit

1 She tells enough white lies to ice a wedding cake.
Of Lady Desborough. Quoted in the *Listener* 11 June 1953

2 The t is silent, as in Harlow.
Attributed riposte to Jean Harlow, who was having trouble pronouncing her first name

Astell, Mary (1668–1731). English poet and feminist

1 If all men are born free, how is it that all women are born slaves?
Some Reflections upon Marriage (1706 edn) preface

Astor, Nancy (Viscountess Astor) (1879–1964). British Conservative politician

1 I married beneath me, all women do.
In *Dictionary of National Biography* 1961–1970 (1981) p. 43

Atlas, Charles (1894–1972). American bodybuilder

1 You too can have a body like mine!
Advertising slogan c.1922

Attenborough, David (1926–). British naturalist and broadcaster

1 I am not over-fond of animals. I am merely astounded by them.
In the *Independent* 14 January 1995

Atwood, Margaret (Eleanor) (1939–). Canadian writer and poet

1 This above all, to refuse to be a
victim. Unless I can do that I am
nothing.
Surfacing (1972)

2 Mirrors
are the perfect lovers.
You are Happy (1974) 'Tricks with Mirrors'

Aubrey, John (1626–97). English
antiquary

1 How these curiosities would be
quite forgot, did not such idle fel-
lows as I am put them down.
Brief Lives (1693, published 1813) 'Venetia
Digby'

Auden, W(ystan) H(ugh) (1907–
73). English-born American poet

1 Private faces in public places
Are wiser and nicer
Than public faces in private places.
Orators (1932) dedication

2 A shilling life will give you all the
facts.
Title of poem (1936)

3 Look, stranger, at this island now
'Look, stranger, at this island now' (1936)

4 O what is that sound which so
thrills the ear
Down in the valley drumming,
drumming?
Only the scarlet soldiers, dear,
The soldiers coming.
'O what is that sound' (1936)

5 This is the Night Mail crossing the
Border,
Bringing the cheque and the postal
order.
'Night Mail' (1936) pt 1

6 Stop all the clocks, cut off the
telephone,
Prevent the dog from barking with
a juicy bone,
Silence the pianos and with muf-
fled drum
Bring out the coffin, let the
mourners come.
'Stop all the clocks', *Collected Poems* (1939)

7 We must love one another or die.
'September 1, 1939' (1940)

8 What instruments we have agree
The day of his death was a dark cold
day.
'In Memory of W. B. Yeats' (1940) pt 1

9 Art is born of humiliation.
In Stephen Spender *World Within World*
(1951) ch. 2

10 It is a sad fact about our culture that
a poet can earn much more money
writing or talking about his art
than he can by practising it.
The Dyer's Hand (1963) foreword

11 Some books are undeservedly forgotten; none are undeservedly
remembered.
The Dyer's Hand (1963) 'Reading'

12 Music is the best means we have of
digesting time.
Quoted in Robert Craft *Stravinsky: Chronicle
of a Friendship* (1972)

13 My face looks like a wedding-cake
left out in the rain.
Quoted in Humphrey Carpenter *W H Auden*
(1981) pt 2, ch. 6

Augustine of Hippo, St (AD 354–
430). Christian theologian

1 *Da mihi castitatem et continentiam,
sed noli modo.*
Give me chastity and continency –
but not yet!
Confessions (AD 397–8) bk 8, ch. 7

Augustus (63 BC–AD 14). First
Roman emperor

1 *Quintili Vare, legiones redde.*
Quintilius Varus, give me back my
legions.
In Suetonius *Lives of the Caesars* 'Divus Augustus' sect. 23

2 *Festina lente.*
Make haste slowly.
In Suetonius *Lives of the Caesars* 'Divus Au-
gustus' sect. 25

Austen, Jane (1775–1817). English
novelist

1 It is a truth universally acknow-
ledged, that a single man in possession of a good fortune, must be
in want of a wife.
Pride and Prejudice (1813) ch. 1

2 Happiness in marriage is entirely a matter of chance.
Pride and Prejudice (1813) ch. 6

3 One half of the world cannot understand the pleasures of the other.
Emma (1816) ch. 9

4 The sooner every party breaks up the better.
Emma (1816) ch. 25

5 Surprises are foolish things. The pleasure is not enhanced, and the inconvenience is often considerable.
Emma (1816) ch. 26

6 From politics, it was an easy step to silence.
Northanger Abbey (1818) ch. 14

Ayer, Sir A(lfred) J(ules) (1910–89). English philosopher

1 The traditional disputes of philosophers are, for the most part, as unwarranted as they are unfruitful.
Language, Truth and Logic (1936) ch. 1

2 But if science may be said to be blind without philosophy, it is true also that philosophy is virtually empty without science.
Language, Truth and Logic (1936) ch. 8

7 The history of England is emphatically the history of progress.
Essays Contributed to the Edinburgh Review (1843) vol. 2 'Sir James Mackintosh'

8 The reluctant obedience of distant provinces generally costs more than it [the territory] is worth.
Essays Contributed to the Edinburgh Review (1843) vol. 2 'The War of Succession in Spain'

9 Knowledge advances by steps, and not by leaps.
T. F. Ellis (ed.) *Miscellaneous Writings of Lord Macaulay* (1860) vol. 1 'History' (1828)

Babington, Thomas (1st Baron Macaulay) (1800–59). English essayist and historian

1 The object of oratory alone is not truth, but persuasion.
'Essay on Athenian Orators', in *Knight's Quarterly Magazine* August 1824

2 Perhaps no person can be a poet, or can even enjoy poetry, without a certain unsoundness of mind.
'Milton', in the *Edinburgh Review* August 1825

3 Every man who has seen the world knows that nothing is so useless as a general maxim.
'Machiavelli', in the *Edinburgh Review* March 1827

4 The gallery in which the reporters sit has become a fourth estate of the realm.
Essays Contributed to the Edinburgh Review (1843) vol. 1 'Hallam'

5 As civilization advances, poetry almost necessarily declines.
Essays Contributed to the Edinburgh Review (1843) vol. 1 'Milton'

6 We know no spectacle so ridiculous as the British public in one of its periodical fits of morality.
Essays Contributed to the Edinburgh Review (1843) vol. 1 'Moore's *Life of Lord Byron*'

Bacall, Lauren (1924–). American actress

1 I think your whole life shows in your face and you should be proud of that.
In the *Daily Telegraph*, 2 March 1988

Bach, Richard (1936–). American author, former military pilot

1 Heaven is not a place, and it is not a time. Heaven is being perfect.
Jonathan Livingston Seagull (1970)

Bacon, Francis (1st Baron Verulam and Viscount St Albans) (1561–1626). English lawyer, courtier, philosopher and essayist

1 Knowledge is power.
Meditationes sacrae (1597) 'De Haresibus' (Of Heresies)

2 Opportunity makes a thief.
'A Letter of Advice to the Earl of Essex …' (1598) in J. Spedding (ed.) *The Letters and Life of Francis Bacon* vol. 2 (1862) p. 99

3 If a man will begin with certainties, he shall end in doubts; but if he will be content to begin with doubts, he shall end in certainties.
The Advancement of Learning (1605) bk 1, ch. 5, sect. 8

4 It is not granted to man to love and to be wise.
The Advancement of Learning (1605) bk 2, preface, sect. 15

5 Antiquities are history defaced, or some remnants of history which have casually escaped the ship-wreck of time.
The Advancement of Learning (1605) bk 2, ch. 2, sect. 1

6 They are ill discoverers that think there is no land, when they can see nothing but sea.
The Advancement of Learning (1605) bk 2, ch. 7

7 A dance is a measured pace, as a verse is a measured speech.
The Advancement of Learning (1605) bk 2, ch. 16, sect. 5

8 *Quod enim mavult homo verum esse, id potius credit.*
For what a man would like to be true, that he more readily believes.
Novum Organum (1620) bk 1, aphorism 49

9 *Natura enim non imperatur, nisi parendo.*
For we cannot command Nature except by obeying her.
Novum Organum (1620) bk 1, aphorism 129

10 I would live to study, and not study to live.
'Memorial of Access to King James I' (c.1622), in *Letters, Speeches, Charges, Advices, etc. of Francis Bacon* (1763)

11 *Divitiae bona ancilla, pessima domina.*
Riches are a good handmaid, but the worst mistress.
De Dignitate et Augmentis Scientiarum (1623) bk 6, ch. 3, pt 3

12 *Silentium, stultorum virtus.*
Silence is the virtue of fools.
De Dignitate et Augmentis Scientiarum (1623) bk 6, ch. 3, pt 3

13 Prosperity is the blessing of the Old Testament, adversity is the blessing of the New.
Essays (1625) 'Of Adversity'

14 The virtue of prosperity, is temperance; the virtue of adversity, is fortitude.
Essays (1625) 'Of Adversity'

15 A little philosophy inclineth man's mind to atheism, but depth in philosophy bringeth men's minds about to religion.
Essays (1625) 'Of Atheism'

16 Virtue is like a rich stone, best plain set.
Essays (1625) 'Of Beauty'

17 There is no excellent beauty that hath not some strangeness in the proportion.
Essays (1625) 'Of Beauty'

18 Boldness is an ill keeper of promise.
Essays (1625) 'Of Boldness'

19 'If the hill will not come to Mahomet, Mahomet will go to the hill.'
Essays (1625) 'Of Boldness' (proverbially 'If the mountain will not come …')

20 There is in human nature generally more of the fool than of the wise.
Essays (1625) 'Of Boldness'

21 It is a strange desire to seek power and to lose liberty.
Essays (1625) 'Of Great Place'

22 Wives are young men's mistresses, companions for middle age, and old men's nurses.
Essays (1625) 'Of Marriage and the Single Life'

23 Nature is often hidden, sometimes overcome, seldom extinguished.
Essays (1625) 'Of Nature in Men'

24 New nobility is but the act of power, but ancient nobility is the act of time.
Essays (1625) 'Of Nobility'

25 Children sweeten labours, but they make misfortunes more bitter.
Essays (1625) 'Of Parents and Children'

26 The joys of parents are secret, and so are their griefs and fears.
Essays (1625) 'Of Parents and Children'

27 Age will not be defied.
Essays (1625) 'Of Regimen of Health'

28 A man that studieth revenge keeps his own wounds green.
Essays (1625) 'Of Revenge'

29 Money is like muck, not good except it be spread.
Essays (1625) 'Of Seditions and Troubles'

30 The remedy is worse than the disease.
Essays (1625) 'Of Seditions and Troubles'

31 Reading maketh a full man; conference a ready man; and writing an exact man.
Essays (1625) 'Of Studies'

32 There is a superstition in avoiding superstition.
Essays (1625) 'Of Superstition'

33 In all superstition wise men follow fools.
Essays (1625) 'Of Superstition'

34 What is truth? said jesting Pilate; and would not stay for an answer.
Essays (1625) 'Of Truth'

35 All colours will agree in the dark.
Essays (1625) 'Of Unity in Religion'

36 It is the wisdom of the crocodiles, that shed tears when they would devour.
Essays (1625) 'Of Wisdom for a Man's Self'

37 No man can tickle himself.
Sylva Sylvarum (published 1627), bk 8

38 Hope is a good breakfast, but it is a bad supper.
'Apophthegms contained in *Resuscitatio*' no. 36, in J. Spedding (ed.) *The Works of Francis Bacon* vol. 7 (1859)

Baden-Powell, Robert (1st Baron Baden-Powell) (1857–1941). English soldier; founder of the Boy Scouts, 1908

1 The scouts' motto is founded on my initials, it is: *Be Prepared*, which means, you are always to be in a state of readiness in mind and body to do your *duty*.
Scouting for Boys (1908) pt 1

Bagehot, Walter (1826–77). English economist and essayist

1 The Crown is, according to the saying, the 'fountain of honour'; but the Treasury is the spring of business.
The English Constitution (1867) 'The Cabinet'

2 Nations touch at their summits.
The English Constitution (1867) 'The House of Lords'

3 One of the greatest pains to human nature is the pain of a new idea.
Physics and Politics (1872) 'The Age of Discussion'

4 A constitutional statesman is in general a man of common opinion and uncommon abilities.
Biographical Studies (1881) 'The Character of Sir Robert Peel'

Bakunin, Mikhail Alekseyevich (1814–76). Russian anarchist

1 From each according to his faculties, to each according to his needs; that is what we wish, sincerely and energetically.
Anarchists' declaration (1870)

Baldwin, James (Arthur) (1924–87). American writer and civil rights activist

1 Anyone who has ever struggled with poverty knows how extremely expensive it is to be poor.
Nobody Knows My Name (1961) 'Fifth Avenue, Uptown: a letter from Harlem'

2 Money, it turned out, was exactly like sex, you thought of nothing else if you didn't have it and thought of other things if you did.
Esquire May 1961 'Black Boy looks at the White Boy'

Baldwin, Stanley (Earl Baldwin of Bewdley) (1867–1947). British Conservative politician and Prime Minister

1 A platitude is simply a truth repeated until people get tired of hearing it.
Speech, *Hansard* 29 May 1924, col. 727

2 There are three classes which need sanctuary more than others – birds, wild flowers, and Prime Ministers.
In the *Observer* 24 May 1925

3 The work of a Prime Minister is the loneliest job in the world.
Speech, 9 January 1927

Balfour, Arthur James (Earl of Balfour) (1848–1930). British Conservative politician and Prime Minister

1 I thought that he was a young man of promise, but it appears that he is a young man of promises.
Of Winston Churchill. Quoted in Churchill *My Early Life* (1930) ch. 17

Ballads

1 Old Uncle Tom Cobbleigh and all.
Old Uncle Tom Cobbleigh and all.
'Widdicombe Fair'

Balliett, Whitney (1926–). American writer

1 A bundle of biases held loosely together by a sense of taste.
Definition of a critic. *Dinosaurs in the Morning* (1962) introductory note

Balzac, Honoré de (1799–1850). French writer

1 *Le mariage doit incessamment combattre un monstre qui dévore tout: l'habitude.*
Marriage should always combat the monster that devours everything: habit.
Physiologie du mariage (1829)

2 *Un mari, comme un gouvernement, ne doit jamais avouer de faute.*
A husband, like a government, never needs to admit a fault.
Physiologie du mariage (1829)

3 *L'amour n'est pas seulement un sentiment, il est un art aussi.*
Love is not only a feeling; it is also an art.
La Recherche de l'absolu (1831)

4 *Le cœur d'une mère est un abîme au fond duquel se trouve toujours un pardon.*
A mother's heart is an abyss at the bottom of which there is always forgiveness.
La Femme de trente ans (1832)

5 *La passion est toute l'humanité. Sans elle, la religion, l'histoire, le roman, l'art seraient inutiles.*
Passion is all of humanity. Without it, religion, history, the novel and art would be useless.
La Comédie humaine (1842) foreword

6 *L'avarice commence où la pauvreté cesse.*
Greed begins where poverty ends.
Illusions perdues (1843) 'Les deux poètes'

Bankhead, Tallulah (1903–68). American actress

1 I'm as pure as the driven slush.
In the *Saturday Evening Post* 12 April 1947

2 Only good girls keep diaries. Bad girls don't have time.
Recalled on her death, 12 December 1968

Barach, Alvan Leroy (1895–1977). American physician

1 An alcoholic has been lightly defined as a man who drinks more than his own doctor.
In the *Journal of the American Medical Association* (1962) vol. 181, p. 393

Barham, R. H. ('Thomas Ingoldsby') (1788–1845). English clergyman

1 So put that in your pipe, my Lord Otto, and smoke it!
The Ingoldsby Legends (First Series, 1840) 'The Lay of St Odille'

Baring-Gould, Sabine (1834–1924). English clergyman

1 Onward, Christian soldiers,
Marching as to war,
With the cross of Jesus
Going on before.
'Onward, Christian Soldiers' (1864 hymn)

Barkley, Alben William (1877–1956). American lawyer and Democratic politician.

1 The best audience is intelligent, well-educated and a little drunk.
Recalled on his death, 30 April 1956

Barnard, Frederick R. (NA). American advertising executive.

1 One picture is worth ten thousand words.
Printers' Ink 10 March 1927

Barnes, Julian (Patrick) (1946–).
English novelist

1 You can have your cake and eat it:
the only trouble is you get fat.
Flaubert's Parrot (1984) ch. 7

2 Books are where things are
explained to you; life is where
things aren't … Books make sense
of life. The only problem is that the
lives they make sense of are other
people's lives, never your own.
Flaubert's Parrot (1984) ch. 13

3 Love is just a system for getting
someone to call you darling after
sex.
Talking It Over (1991) ch. 16

Barnum, Phineas T(aylor) (1810–
91). American showman

1 There's a sucker born every minute.
Attributed

Barrie, Sir J(ames) M(atthew)
(1860–1937). Scottish writer and
playwright

1 There are few more impressive
sights in the world than a Scotsman
on the make.
What Every Woman Knows (performed 1908,
published 1918) act 2

2 Every man who is high up loves to
think that he has done it all himself; and the wife smiles, and lets it
go at that. It's our only joke. Every
woman knows that.
What Every Woman Knows (performed 1908,
published 1918) act 4

3 To die will be an awfully big
adventure.
Peter Pan (1928) act 3

Barthes, Roland (1915–80). French
literary critic

1 *Tout refus du langage est une mort.*
Any refusal of language is a death.
Mythologies (1957) 'Le mythe, aujourd'hui'

Baruch, Bernard (Mannes)
(1870–1965). American financier
and presidential adviser

1 Let us not be deceived – we are
today in the midst of a cold war.
Speech to South Carolina Legislature, 16
April 1947, in the *New York Times* 17 April
1947, p. 21

2 To me old age is always fifteen years
older than I am.
In *Newsweek* 29 August 1955

3 Vote for the man who promises
least; he'll be the least disappoint-
ing.
In Meyer Berger *New York* (1960)

Barzun, Jacques (1907–). French-
born American scholar

1 Teaching is not a lost art, but the
regard for it is a lost tradition.
In *Newsweek* 5 December 1955

2 Whoever wants to know the heart
and mind of America had better
learn baseball.
Quoted in Michael Novak *The Joy of Sport*
(1976) pt 1

Bates, Katherine Lee (1859–1929).
American writer and educationist

1 America! America!
God shed His grace on thee
And crown thy good with
brotherhood
From sea to shining sea!
'America the Beautiful' (1893)

Baudelaire, Charles (1821–67).
French poet and critic

1 *Hypocrite lecteur, – mon semblable, –
mon frère.*
Hypocrite reader – my likeness –
my brother.
Les fleurs du mal (1857) 'Au Lecteur'

2 *Amer savoir, celui qu'on tire du voyage!*
Bitter is the knowledge gained in
travelling.
Les fleurs du mal (1857) 'Le Voyage'

3 *L'art moderne a une tendance essen-
tiellement démoniaque.*
Modern art tends towards the
demonic.
L'Art romantique (1869)

4 *Je ne comprends pas qu'une main pure puisse toucher un journal sans une convulsion de dégoût.*
I cannot imagine how a pure hand can touch a newspaper without disgust.
Mon cœur mis à nu (1887) pt 81

Baum, L. Frank (1856–1919). American writer

1 The road to the City of Emeralds is paved with yellow brick.
The Wonderful Wizard of Oz (1900) ch. 2 ('Follow the yellow brick road' in the 1939 film)

Beaumarchais, Pierre-Augustin Caron de (1732–99). French playwright

1 *De toutes les choses sérieuses, le mariage étant la plus bouffonne.*
Of all serious things, marriage is the most farcical.
Le Mariage de Figaro (1784) act 1, sc. 9

Beaumont, Francis and Fletcher, John (c.1584–1616; c.1578–1625). English playwrights

1 It is always good
When a man has two irons in the fire.
The Faithful Friends (1608) act 1

2 Kiss till the cow comes home.
The Scornful Lady (c.1610, published 1616) act 2, sc. 2

3 Those have most power to hurt us that we love.
The Maid's Tragedy (written 1610–11) act 5

Beaverbrook, Lord (Max Aitken, 1st Baron Beaverbrook) (1879–1964). Canadian-born British newspaper proprietor and Conservative politician

1 To whom must the praise be given? To the boys in the back rooms. They do not sit in the limelight. But they are the men who do the work.
In the *Listener* 27 March 1941

Beckett, Samuel (1906–89). Irish playwright, novelist and poet

1 We're waiting for Godot.
Waiting for Godot (1955) act 1

2 He can't think without his hat.
Waiting for Godot (1955) act 1

Bedford, Harry and Sullivan, Terry British songwriters

1 I'm a bit of a ruin that Cromwell knocked about a bit.
'It's a Bit of a Ruin that Cromwell Knocked about a Bit' (1920 song; written for Marie Lloyd)

Beecham, Sir Thomas (1879–1961). British conductor

1 A musicologist is a man who can read music but can't hear it.
(1930), quoted in H. Proctor-Gregg *Beecham Remembered* (1976)

2 Good music is that which penetrates the ear with facility and quits the memory with difficulty.
Television broadcast, 17 November 1953

3 Why do we have to have all these third-rate foreign conductors around – when we have so many second-rate ones of our own?
In L. Ayre *Wit of Music* (1966) p. 70

4 There are two golden rules for an orchestra: start together and finish together. The public doesn't give a damn what goes on in between.
In Harold Atkins and Archie Newman *Beecham Stories* (1978) p. 27

5 Like two skeletons copulating on a corrugated tin roof.
Describing the harpsichord, in Harold Atkins and Archie Newman *Beecham Stories* (1978) p. 34

6 The function of music is to release us from the tyranny of conscious thought.
Quoted in Harold Atkins and Archie Newman *Beecham Stories* (1978)

Beerbohm, Sir (Henry) Max(imilian) (1872–1956). English critic, essayist and caricaturist

1 Most women are not so young as they are painted.
The Yellow Book (1894) vol. 1, p. 67

2 Mankind is divisible into two great classes: hosts and guests.
And Even Now (1920) 'Hosts and Guests'

3 Only mediocrity can be trusted to be always at its best.
Quoted in S. N. Behrman *Conversations with Max* (1960); also attributed to Jean Giraudoux and W. Somerset Maugham

Beethoven, Ludwig van (1770–1827). German composer

1 The immortal god of harmony.
Of Bach. Letter to Christoph Breitkopf (1801)

2 I shall hear in heaven.
Attributed last words (1827)

Beeton, Mrs (née Isabella Mary Mayson) (1836–65). English writer on the domestic arts

1 A place for everything and everything in its place.
The Book of Household Management (1861) ch. 2, sect. 55

Behan, Brendan (1923–64). Irish playwright

1 When I came back to Dublin, I was courtmartialled in my absence and sentenced to death in my absence, so I said they could shoot me in my absence.
Hostage (1958) act 1

2 There's no such thing as bad publicity except your own obituary.
In Dominic Behan *My Brother Brendan* (1965) p. 158

Behn, Aphra (1640–89). English playwright, poet and novelist

1 Variety is the soul of pleasure.
The Rover pt 2 (1681) act 1

2 Money speaks sense in a language all nations understand.
The Rover pt 2 (1681) act 3

3 Love ceases to be a pleasure, when it ceases to be a secret.
The Lover's Watch (1686) 'Four o' Clock. General Conversation'

4 Faith, Sir, we are here to-day, and gone to-morrow.
The Lucky Chance (1686) act 4

Bell, (Arthur) Clive (Howard) (1881–1964). English critic

1 Art and Religion are, then, two roads by which men escape from circumstance to ecstasy.
Art (1914) pt 2, ch. 1

2 Comfort came in with the middle classes.
Civilization (1928) ch. 4

Belloc, Hilaire (1870–1953). British poet, essayist, novelist and Liberal politician

1 But as it is! … My language fails! Go out and govern New South Wales!
Cautionary Tales (1907) 'Lord Lundy'

2 Matilda told such Dreadful Lies, It made one Gasp and Stretch one's Eyes;.
Cautionary Tales (1907) 'Matilda'

3 And always keep a-hold of Nurse For fear of finding something worse.
Cautionary Tales (1907) 'Jim'

4 When I am dead, I hope it may be said:
'His sins were scarlet, but his books were read.'
'On His Books' (1923)

5 Do you remember an Inn, Miranda?
'Tarantella' (1923)

6 Like many of the Upper Class He liked the Sound of Broken Glass.
New Cautionary Tales (1930) 'About John'

Benchley, Robert (Charles) (1889–1945). American humorist

1 In America there are two classes of travel – first class, and with children.
Pluck and Luck (1925) p. 6

2 My only solution for the problem of habitual accidents … is to stay in bed all day. Even then, there is always the chance that you will fall out.
Chips Off the Old Benchley (1949) 'Safety Second'

3 It took me fifteen years to discover that I had no talent for writing, but I couldn't give it up because by that time I was too famous.
In Nathaniel Benchley *Robert Benchley* (1955) ch. 1

4 Streets flooded. Please advise.
Telegraph message to the US on arriving in Venice. Quoted in R. E. Drennan (ed.) *Wits End* (1973)

Benda, Julien (1867–1956). French philosopher and novelist

1 *La trahison des clercs.*
The treachery of the intellectuals.
Title of book (1927)

Benét, Stephen (Vincent) (1898–1943). American poet and novelist

1 Bury my heart at Wounded Knee.
'American Names' (1927)

Benn, Tony (Anthony Wedgwood Benn) (1925–). British Labour politician

1 A faith is something you die for; a doctrine is something you kill for; there is all the difference in the world.
In the *Observer* 16 April 1989

Bennard, George (1873–1958).

1 The old rugged cross.
'The Old Rugged Cross' (1913 hymn)

Bennett, Alan (1934–). English actor and playwright

1 Memories are not shackles, Franklin, they are garlands.
Forty Years On (1969) act 2

2 Standards are always out of date. That is what makes them standards.
Forty Years On (1969) act 2

3 I want a future that will live up to my past.
A Private Function (film, 1984)

4 The asylums of this country are full of the sound of mind disinherited by the out of pocket.
The Madness of George III (performed 1991)

Bennett, (Enoch) Arnold (1867–1931). English novelist

1 Englishmen act better than Frenchmen, and Frenchwomen better than Englishwomen.
Cupid and Commonsense (1909) preface

2 Being a husband is a whole-time job. That is why so many husbands fail. They cannot give their entire attention to it.
The Title (1918) act 1

3 Journalists say a thing that they know isn't true, in the hope that if they keep on saying it long enough it will be true.
The Title (1918) act 2

4 Pessimism, when you get used to it, is just as agreeable as optimism.
Things that have Interested Me (1921) 'Slump in Pessimism'

5 The price of justice is eternal publicity.
Things that have Interested Me (2nd series, 1923) 'Secret Trials'

Benson, A(rthur) C(hristopher) (1862–1925). English writer

1 Land of Hope and Glory, Mother of the Free.
'Land of Hope and Glory' written to be sung as the Finale to Elgar's *Coronation Ode* (1902)

Bentham, Jeremy (1748–1832). English philosopher and jurist

1 Every law is an evil, for every law is an infraction of liberty.
An Introduction to the Principles of Morals and Legislation (1789)

2 Natural rights is simple nonsense: natural and imprescriptible rights, rhetorical nonsense – nonsense upon stilts.
Anarchical Fallacies in J. Bowring (ed.) *Works* vol. 2 (1843) p. 501

3 The greatest happiness of the greatest number is the foundation of morals and legislation.
The Commonplace Book in J. Bowring (ed.) *Works* vol. 10 (1843) p. 142

Bentley, Edmund Clerihew
(1875–1956). English writer

1 The Art of Biography
Is different from Geography.
Geography is about Maps,
But Biography is about Chaps.
Biography for Beginners (1905) introduction

2 Sir Humphrey Davy
Abominated gravy.
He lived in the odium
Of having discovered Sodium.
Biography for Beginners (1905) 'Sir Humphrey Davy'

Bentley, Richard (1662–1742).
English classical scholar

1 It would be port if it could.
His judgement on claret, in R. C. Jebb
Bentley (1902) ch. 12

Benuzzi, Felice (1910–88). Italian
diplomat

1 To remember is far worse than to
forget.
On being a Prisoner of War. *No Picnic on
Mount Kenya* (1952)

Beresford, Lord Charles (1846–
1919). British Conservative
politician

1 Very sorry can't come. Lie follows
by post.
Telegram to the Prince of Wales, declining
a dinner invitation. Quoted in Ralph Nevill
The World of Fashion 1837–1922 (1923) ch. 5

Berger, John (Peter) (1926–).
English writer and art critic

1 The camera relieves us of the burden of memory.
In the *New Statesman* 17 August 1978

2 Photography, because it stops the
flow of life, is always flirting with
death.
In the *New Statesman* 22/29 December 1983

3 All painting is about the presence
of absence.
In the *New Statesman and Society* 15 July
1988

Bergson, Henri (1859–1941).
French philosopher

1 *L'élan vital.*
The vital spirit.
L'Evolution créatrice (1907) ch. 2 (section
title)

Berkeley, George (1685–1753).
Irish philosopher and Anglican
bishop

1 Truth is the cry of all, but the game
of the few.
Siris (1744) para. 368

Berlin, Irving (Israel Baline) (1888–
1989). American songwriter

1 The song is ended (but the melody
lingers on).
Title of song (1927)

2 I'm dreaming of a white Christmas,
Holiday Inn (film, 1942) 'White Christmas'

3 There's no business like show
business.
Annie Get Your Gun (film, 1946) title of song

Berlioz, Hector (1803–69). French
composer

1 Time is a great teacher but unfortunately it kills all its pupils.
Almanach des lettres françaises et étrangères,
11 May 1924

Bernanos, Georges (1888–1948).
French novelist and essayist

1 *Le désir de la prière est déjà une prière.*
The wish for prayer is already a
prayer.
Journal d'un curé de campagne (1936) ch. 2

2 *L'enfer, madame, c'est de ne plus ai-
mer.*
Hell, madam, is to love no more.
Journal d'un curé de campagne (1936) ch. 2

**Bernardin de Saint-Pierre,
Jacques-Henri** (1737–1814). French
novelist

1 *La solitude rétablit aussi bien les
harmonies du corps que celles de
l'âme.*

Solitude restores the harmonies of the body no less than those of the soul.
Paul et Virginie (1788)

Bernard of Chartres (d. *c.*1130). French divine and scholar

1 *Nanos gigantiun humeris insidentes.*
Dwarfs standing on the shoulders of giants.
(c.1128) Quoted in John of Salisbury *Metalogicon* (1159) bk 3, ch. 4

Berne, Eric (1910–70). American psychiatrist

1 Games people play: the psychology of human relationships.
Title of book (1964)

Berra, Yogi (Lawrence Peter) (1925–). American baseball player and coach

1 It ain't over 'til it's over.
Attributed

Berry, Chuck (Charles Edward Anderson) (1926–). American rock 'n' roll singer

1 Roll over Beethoven.
'Roll over Beethoven' (1956)

Berryman, John (John Allyn Smith) (1914–72). American poet and novelist

1 We must travel in the direction of our fear.
'A Point of Age' (1942)

Betjeman, Sir John (1906–84). English poet

1 Come, friendly bombs, and fall on Slough!
It isn't fit for humans now,
There isn't grass to graze a cow.
'Slough' (1937)

2 Miss J. Hunter Dunn, Miss J. Hunter Dunn,
Furnish'd and burnish'd by Aldershot sun.
'A Subaltern's Love-Song' (1945)

3 And is it true? And is it true,
This most tremendous tale of all,
Seen in a stained-glass window's hue,
A Baby in an ox's stall?
The Maker of the stars and sea
Become a Child on earth for me?
'Christmas' (1954)

4 Her sturdy legs were flannel-slack'd,
The strongest legs in Pontefract.
A Few Late Chrysanthemums, 'The Licorice Fields at Pontefract' (1954)

Bevan, Aneurin (1897–1960). British Labour politician

1 The language of priorities is the religion of Socialism.
Speech at Labour Party Conference in Blackpool, 8 June 1949, in *Report of the 48th Annual Conference* (1949) p. 172

2 I read the newspapers avidly. It is my one form of continuous fiction.
In *The Times* 29 March 1960

Bevin, Ernest (1881–1951). British Labour politician and trade unionist

1 The most conservative man in this world is the British Trade Unionist when you want to change him.
Speech, 8 September 1927, in *Report of Proceedings of the Trades Union Congress* (1927) p. 298

Bhagavadgita (*c.*150 BC–AD 150). Hindu poem

1 And do thy duty, even if it be humble, rather than another's, even if it be great. To die in one's duty is life; to live in another's is death.
Ch. 3, v. 35

Bible – Apocrypha (Authorized Version of 1611)

1 A faithful friend is the medicine of life.
Ecclesiasticus ch. 6, v. 16

2 When thou hast enough, remember the time of hunger.
Ecclesiasticus ch. 18, v. 25

3 Many have fallen by the edge of the sword: but not so many as have fallen by the tongue.
Ecclesiasticus ch. 28, v. 18

4 Let thy speech be short, comprehending much in few words; be as one that knoweth and yet holdeth his tongue.
Ecclesiasticus ch. 32, v. 8

5 Let us now praise famous men, and our fathers that begat us.
Ecclesiasticus ch. 44, v. 1

Bible – New Testament (Authorized Version of 1611)

1 Repent ye: for the kingdom of heaven is at hand.
St Matthew ch. 3, v. 2

2 The voice of one crying in the wilderness, Prepare ye the way of the Lord, make his paths straight.
St Matthew ch. 3, v. 3

3 Man shall not live by bread alone, but by every word that proceedeth out of the mouth of God.
St Matthew ch. 4, v. 4

4 The people which sat in darkness saw great light; and to them which sat in the region and shadow of death light is sprung up.
St Matthew ch. 4, v. 6

5 Thou shalt not tempt the Lord thy God.
St Matthew ch. 4, v. 7

6 Follow me, and I will make you fishers of men.
St Matthew ch. 4, v. 19

7 Blessed are the poor in spirit: for theirs is the kingdom of heaven.
Blessed are they that mourn: for they shall be comforted.
Blessed are the meek: for they shall inherit the earth.
Blessed are they which do hunger and thirst after righteousness: for they shall be filled.
Blessed are the merciful: for they shall obtain mercy.
Blessed are the pure in heart: for they shall see God.

Blessed are the peacemakers: for they shall be called the children of God.
St Matthew ch. 5, v. 3

8 Ye are the salt of the earth.
St Matthew ch. 5, v. 13

9 Ye are the light of the world.
St Matthew ch. 5, v. 14

10 And if thy right eye offend thee, pluck it out, and cast it from thee: for it is profitable for thee that one of thy members should perish, and not that thy whole body should be cast into hell.
St Matthew ch. 5, v. 29

11 Ye have heard that it hath been said, An eye for an eye, and a tooth for a tooth: But I say unto you, That ye resist not evil: but whosoever shall smite thee on thy right cheek, turn to him the other also.
St Matthew ch. 5, v. 38

12 Ye have heard that it hath been said, Thou shalt love thy neighbour, and hate thine enemy. But I say unto you, Love your enemies, bless them that curse you, do good to them that hate you, and pray for them which despitefully use you, and persecute you.
St Matthew ch. 5, v. 43

13 When thou doest alms, let not thy left hand know what thy right hand doeth.
St Matthew ch. 6, v. 3

14 After this manner therefore pray ye: Our Father which art in heaven, Hallowed be thy name.
Thy kingdom come. Thy will be done in earth, as it is in heaven.
Give us this day our daily bread.
And forgive us our debts, as we forgive our debtors.
And lead us not into temptation, but deliver us from evil: For thine is the kingdom, and the power, and the glory, for ever. Amen.
St Matthew ch. 6, v. 9

15 Lay up for yourselves treasures in heaven.
St Matthew ch. 6, v. 19

16 Where your treasure is, there will your heart be also.
St Matthew ch. 6, v. 21

17 No man can serve two masters … Ye cannot serve God and mammon.
St Matthew ch. 6, v. 24

18 Behold the fowls of the air: for they sow not, neither do they reap, nor gather into barns.
St Matthew ch. 6, v. 25

19 Consider the lilies of the field, how they grow; they toil not, neither do they spin:
And yet I say unto you, That even Solomon in all his glory was not arrayed like one of these.
St Matthew ch. 6, v. 28

20 Seek ye first the kingdom of God, and his righteousness; and all these things shall be added unto you.
St Matthew ch. 6, v. 33

21 Take therefore no thought for the morrow: for the morrow shall take thought for the things of itself. Sufficient unto the day is the evil thereof.
St Matthew ch. 6, v. 34

22 Judge not, that ye be not judged.
St Matthew ch. 7, v. 1

23 Why beholdest thou the mote that is in thy brother's eye, but considerest not the beam that is in thine own eye?
St Matthew ch. 7, v. 3

24 Neither cast ye your pearls before swine.
St Matthew ch. 7, v. 6

25 Ask, and it shall be given you; seek, and ye shall find; knock, and it shall be opened unto you.
St Matthew ch. 7, v. 7

26 Beware of false prophets, which come to you in sheep's clothing, but inwardly they are ravening wolves.
St Matthew ch. 7, v. 15

27 By their fruits ye shall know them.
St Matthew ch. 7, v. 20

28 But the children of the kingdom shall be cast out into outer darkness: there shall be weeping and gnashing of teeth.
St Matthew ch. 8, v. 12

29 Let the dead bury their dead.
St Matthew ch. 8, v. 22

30 Neither do men put new wine into old bottles.
St Matthew ch. 9, v. 17

31 The harvest truly is plenteous, but the labourers are few.
St Matthew ch. 9, v. 37

32 The very hairs of your head are all numbered.
St Matthew ch. 10, v. 30

33 Come unto me, all ye that labour and are heavy laden, and I will give you rest.
St Matthew ch. 11, v. 28

34 For my yoke is easy, and my burden is light.
St Matthew ch. 11, v. 30

35 He that is not with me is against me: and he that gathereth not with me scattereth abroad.
St Matthew ch. 12, v. 30

36 The tree is known by his fruit.
St Matthew ch. 12, v. 33

37 A prophet is not without honour, save in his own country, and in his own house.
St Matthew ch. 13, v. 57

38 And they say unto him, We have here but five loaves, and two fishes.
St Matthew ch. 14, v. 17

39 They be blind leaders of the blind. And if the blind lead the blind, both shall fall into the ditch.
St Matthew ch. 15, v. 14

40 Ye can discern the face of the sky; but can ye not discern the signs of the times?
St Matthew ch. 16, v. 3

41 Thou art Peter, and upon this rock I will build my church; and the gates of hell shall not prevail against it.
St Matthew ch. 16, v. 18

42 Get thee behind me, Satan.
St Matthew ch. 16, v. 23

43 If ye have faith as a grain of mustard seed, ye shall say unto this mountain, Remove hence to yonder place; and it shall remove; and nothing shall be impossible unto you.
St Matthew ch. 17, v. 20

44 Except ye be converted, and become as little children, ye shall not enter into the kingdom of heaven.
St Matthew ch. 18, v. 3

45 For where two or three are gathered together in my name, there am I in the midst of them.
St Matthew ch. 18, v. 20

46 Then came Peter to him, and said, Lord, how oft shall my brother sin against me, and I forgive him? till seven times? Jesus saith unto him, I say not unto thee, Until seven times: but, Until seventy times seven.
St Matthew ch. 18, v. 21

47 What therefore God hath joined together, let not man put asunder.
St Matthew ch. 19, v. 6

48 It is easier for a camel to go through the eye of a needle, than for a rich man to enter into the kingdom of God.
St Matthew ch. 19, v. 24

49 With men this is impossible; but with God all things are possible.
St Matthew ch. 19, v. 26

50 But many that are first shall be last; and the last shall be first.
St Matthew ch. 19, v. 30

51 So the last shall be first, and the first last: for many be called, but few chosen.
St Matthew ch. 20, v. 15

52 My house shall be called the house of prayer; but ye have made it a den of thieves.
St Matthew ch. 21, v. 13

53 For many are called, but few are chosen.
St Matthew ch. 22, v. 14

54 Render therefore unto Caesar the things which are Caesar's; and unto God the things that are God's.
St Matthew ch. 22, v. 21

55 Jesus said unto him, Thou shalt love the Lord Thy God with all thy heart, and with all thy soul, and with all thy mind. This is the first and great commandment. And the second is like unto it, Thou shalt love thy neighbour as thyself.
St Matthew ch. 22, v. 37

56 Ye are like unto whited sepulchres.
St Matthew ch. 23, v. 27

57 For nation shall rise against nation, and kingdom against kingdom.
St Matthew ch. 24, v. 7

58 Heaven and earth shall pass away, but my words shall not pass away.
St Matthew ch. 24, v. 35

59 Well done, thou good and faithful servant.
St Matthew ch. 25, v. 21

60 And he shall set the sheep on his right hand, but the goats on the left.
St Matthew ch. 25, v. 33

61 Thirty pieces of silver.
St Matthew ch. 26, v. 15

62 Jesus took bread, and blessed it, and brake it, and gave it to the disciples, and said, Take, eat; this is my body.
St Matthew ch. 26, v. 26

63 This night, before the cock crow, thou shalt deny me thrice.
St Matthew ch. 26, v. 34

64 What, could ye not watch with me one hour?
St Matthew ch. 26, v. 40

65 The spirit indeed is willing but the flesh is weak.
St Matthew ch. 26, v. 41

66 All they that take the sword shall perish with the sword.
St Matthew ch. 26, v. 52

67 The sabbath was made for man, and not man for the sabbath.
St Mark ch. 2, v. 27

68 If a house be divided against itself, that house cannot stand.
St Mark ch. 3, v. 25

69 My name is Legion: for we are many.
St Mark ch. 5, v. 9

70 For what shall it profit a man, if he shall gain the whole world, and lose his own soul?
St Mark ch. 8, v. 36

71 Lord, I believe; help thou mine unbelief.
St Mark ch. 9, v. 24

72 Suffer the little children to come unto me.
St Mark ch. 10, v. 14

73 And the angel came in unto her, and said, Hail, thou that art highly favoured, the Lord is with thee: blessed art thou among women.
St Luke ch. 1, v. 28

74 My soul doth magnify the Lord, And my spirit hath rejoiced in God my Saviour.
St Luke ch. 1, v. 46

75 She brought forth her firstborn son, and wrapped him in swaddling clothes, and laid him in a manger; because there was no room for them in the inn.
St Luke ch. 2, v. 7

76 Lord, now lettest thou thy servant depart in peace, according to thy word.
St Luke ch. 2, v. 29

77 Physician, heal thyself.
St Luke ch. 4, v. 23

78 And he said to them all, If any man will come after me, let him deny himself, and take up his cross daily, and follow me.
St Luke ch. 9, v. 23

79 And into whatsoever house ye enter, first say, Peace be to this house. And if the son of peace be there, your peace shall rest upon it: if not, it shall turn to you again.
St Luke ch. 10, v. 5

80 He passed by on the other side.
St Luke ch. 10, v. 31

81 Go, and do thou likewise.
St Luke ch. 10, v. 37

82 No man, when he hath lighted a candle, putteth it in a secret place, neither under a bushel, but on a candlestick, that they which come in may see the light.
St Luke ch. 11, v. 33

83 Friend, go up higher.
St Luke ch. 14, v. 10

84 For whosoever exalteth himself shall be abased; and he that humbleth himself shall be exalted.
St Luke ch. 14, v. 11

85 I have married a wife, and therefore I cannot come.
St Luke ch. 14, v. 20

86 Rejoice with me; for I have found my sheep which was lost.
St Luke ch. 15, v. 6

87 Bring hither the fatted calf, and kill it.
St Luke ch. 15, v. 23

88 The kingdom of God is within you.
St Luke ch. 17, v. 21

89 God be merciful to me a sinner.
St Luke ch. 18, v. 13

90 Not my will, but thine, be done.
St Luke ch. 22, v. 42

91 Father, forgive them: for they know not what they do.
St Luke ch. 23, v. 34

92 Why seek ye the living among the dead?
St Luke ch. 24, v. 5

93 In the beginning was the Word, and the Word was with God, and the Word was God.
St John ch. 1, v. 1

94 And the light shineth in darkness; and the darkness comprehended it not.
St John ch. 1, v. 5

95 And the Word was made flesh, and dwelt among us,
St John ch. 1, v. 14

96 Behold the Lamb of God, which taketh away the sin of the world.
St John ch. 1, v. 29

97 Can there any good thing come out of Nazareth?
St John ch. 1, v. 46

98 Mine hour is not yet come.
St John ch. 2, v. 4

99 But thou hast kept the good wine until now.
St John ch. 2, v. 10

100 Except a man be born again, he cannot see the kingdom of God.
St John ch. 3, v. 3

101 The wind bloweth where it listeth.
St John ch. 3, v. 8

102 Except ye see signs and wonders, ye will not believe.
St John ch. 4, v. 48

103 Rise, take up thy bed, and walk.
St John ch. 5, v. 8

104 I am the bread of life: he that cometh to me shall never hunger; and he that believeth on me shall never thirst.
St John ch. 6, v. 35

105 He that is without sin among you, let him first cast a stone at her.
St John ch. 8, v. 7

106 I am the light of the world: he that followeth me shall not walk in darkness, but shall have the light of life.
St John ch. 8, v. 12

107 I am the good shepherd: the good shepherd giveth his life for the sheep.
St John ch. 10, v. 11

108 I am the resurrection, and the life.
St John ch. 11, v. 25

109 Jesus wept.
St John ch. 11, v. 35

110 A new commandment I give unto you, That ye love one another; as I have loved you, that ye also love one another. By this shall all men know that ye are my disciples, if ye have love one to another.
St John ch. 13, v. 34

111 In my Father's house are many mansions.
St John ch. 14, v. 2

112 I am the way, the truth, and the life: no man cometh unto the Father, but by me.
St John ch. 14, v. 6

113 Peace I leave with you, my peace I give unto you.
St John ch. 14, v. 27

114 Greater love hath no man than this, that a man lay down his life for his friends.
St John ch. 15, v. 13

115 *Quo vadis?*
Where are you going?
St John ch. 16, v. 5

116 Pilate saith unto him, What is truth?
St John ch. 18, v. 38

117 *Ecce homo.*
Behold the man.
St John ch. 19, v. 5

118 What I have written I have written.
St John ch. 19, v. 22

119 My Lord and my God.
St John ch. 20, v. 28

120 For in him we live, and move, and have our being.
Acts of the Apostles ch. 17, v. 28

121 And suddenly there came a sound from heaven as of a rushing mighty wind, and it filled all the house where they were sitting.
And there appeared unto them cloven tongues like as of fire.
Acts of the Apostles ch. 2, v. 2

122 It is hard for thee to kick against the pricks.
Acts of the Apostles ch. 9, v. 5

123 God is no respecter of persons.
Acts of the Apostles ch. 10, v. 34

124 It is more blessed to give than to receive.
Acts of the Apostles ch. 20, v. 35

125 A law unto themselves.
Romans ch. 2, v. 14

126 For the wages of sin is death; but the gift of God is eternal life through Jesus Christ our Lord.
Romans ch. 6, v. 23

127 If God be for us, who can be against us?
Romans ch. 8, v. 31

128 Vengeance is mine; I will repay, saith the Lord.
Romans ch. 12, v. 19

129 Absent in body, but present in spirit.
1 Corinthians ch. 5, v. 3

130 Your body is the temple of the Holy Ghost.
1 Corinthians ch. 6, v. 19

131 The fashion of this world passeth away.
1 Corinthians ch. 7, v. 31

132 Though I speak with the tongues of men and of angels, and have not charity, I am become as sounding brass, or a tinkling cymbal.
1 Corinthians ch. 13, v. 1

133 For now we see through a glass, darkly; but then face to face.
1 Corinthians ch. 13, v. 12

134 And now abideth faith, hope, charity, these three; but the greatest of these is charity.
1 Corinthians ch. 13, v. 13

135 What advantageth it me, if the dead rise not? let us eat and drink; for tomorrow we die.
1 Corinthians ch. 15, v. 32

136 O death, where is thy sting? O grave, where is thy victory?
1 Corinthians ch. 15, v. 55

137 God loveth a cheerful giver.
2 Corinthians ch. 9, v. 7

138 For ye suffer fools gladly, seeing ye yourselves are wise.
2 Corinthians ch. 9, v. 19

139 There was given to me a thorn in the flesh, the messenger of Satan to buffet me.
2 Corinthians ch. 12, v. 7

140 Be not deceived; God is not mocked: for whatsoever a man soweth, that shall he also reap.
Galatians ch. 6, v. 7

141 Let not the sun go down upon your wrath.
Ephesians ch. 4, v. 26

142 Rejoice in the Lord alway: and again I say, Rejoice.
Philippians ch. 4, v. 4

143 The peace of God, which passeth all understanding, shall keep your hearts and minds through Christ Jesus.
Philippians ch. 4, v. 7

144 The love of money is the root of all evil.
1 Timothy ch. 6, v. 10

145 Fight the good fight of faith.
1 Timothy ch. 6, v. 12

146 Unto the pure all things are pure.
Titus ch. 1, v. 15

147 Faith without works is dead.
James ch. 2, v. 20

148 Ye have heard of the patience of Job.
James ch. 5, v. 11

149 Charity shall cover the multitude of sins.
1 Peter ch. 4, v. 8

150 I am Alpha and Omega, the beginning and the ending, saith the Lord.
Revelation ch. 1, v. 7

151 God shall wipe away all tears from their eyes.
Revelation ch. 7, v. 17

152 And I saw a new heaven and a new earth: for the first heaven and the first earth were passed away; and there was no more sea.
Revelation ch. 21, v. 1

153 The street of the city was pure gold.
Revelation ch. 21, v. 21

Bible – Old Testament (Authorized Version of 1611)

1 In the beginning God created the heaven and the earth. And the earth was without form, and void; and darkness was upon the face of the deep. And the Spirit of God moved upon the face of the waters. And God said, Let there be light: and there was light.
Genesis ch. 1, v. 1

2 And God said, Let us make man in our image, after our likeness.
Genesis ch. 1, v. 26

3 Male and female created he them.
Genesis ch. 1, v. 27

4 Be fruitful, and multiply.
Genesis ch. 1, v. 28

5 And on the seventh day God ended his work which he had made, and he rested on the seventh day from all his work which he had made.
Genesis ch. 2, v. 2

6 But of the tree of the knowledge of good and evil, thou shalt not eat of it: for in the day that thou eatest thereof thou shalt surely die.
Genesis ch. 2, v. 17

7 This is now bone of my bones, and flesh of my flesh: she shall be called Woman, because she was taken out of Man.
Genesis ch. 2, v. 23

8 Therefore shall a man leave his father and his mother, and shall cleave unto his wife: and they shall be one flesh.
Genesis ch. 2, v. 24

9 Now the serpent was more subtil than any beast of the field.
Genesis ch. 3, v. 1

10 For dust thou art, and unto dust shalt thou return.
Genesis ch. 3, v. 19

11 Am I my brother's keeper?
Genesis ch. 4, v. 9

12 And the Lord set a mark upon Cain.
Genesis ch. 4, v. 15

13 And Cain went out from the presence of the Lord, and dwelt in the land of Nod, on the east of Eden.
Genesis ch. 4, v. 16

14 There were giants in the earth in those days;
Genesis ch. 6, v. 4

15 There went in two and two unto Noah into the Ark, the male and the female.
Genesis ch. 7, v. 9

16 Therefore is the name of it called Babel; because the Lord did there confound the language of all the earth.
Genesis ch. 11, v. 5

17 But his wife looked back from behind him, and she became a pillar of salt.
Genesis ch. 19, v. 26

18 Esau selleth his birthright for a mess of potage.
Genesis ch. 25 (heading)

19 And he made him a coat of many colours.
Genesis ch. 37, v. 3

20 I have been a stranger in a strange land.
Exodus ch. 2, v. 22

21 A land flowing with milk and honey.
Exodus ch. 3, v. 8

22 I am that I am.
Exodus ch. 3, v. 14

23 Let my people go.
Exodus ch. 7, v. 16

24 It is the Lord's passover.
Exodus ch. 12, v. 11

25 I am the Lord thy God, which have brought thee out of the land of Egypt, out of the house of bondage.
Exodus ch. 20, v. 1

26 Thou shalt have no other gods before me.
Exodus ch. 20, v. 3

27 Thou shalt not take the name of the Lord thy God in vain.
Exodus ch. 20, v. 7

28 Remember the sabbath day, to keep it holy.
Exodus ch. 20, v. 8

29 Honour thy father and thy mother.
Exodus ch. 20, v. 12

30 Thou shalt not kill.
Exodus ch. 20, v. 13

31 Thou shalt not commit adultery.
Exodus ch. 20, v. 14

32 Thou shalt not steal.
Exodus ch. 20, v. 15

33 Thou shalt not bear false witness against thy neighbour.
Exodus ch. 20, v. 16

34 Thou shalt not covet thy neighbour's house, thou shalt not covet thy neighbour's wife, nor his manservant, nor his maidservant, nor his ox, nor his ass, nor any thing that is thy neighbour's.
Exodus ch. 20, v. 17

35 Eye for eye, tooth for tooth.
Exodus ch. 21, v. 23

36 Let him go for a scapegoat into the wilderness.
Leviticus ch. 16, v. 10

37 Thou shalt love thy neighbour as thyself.
Leviticus ch. 19, v. 18

38 What hath God wrought!
Numbers ch. 23, v. 23

39 Be sure your sin will find you out.
Numbers ch. 32, v. 23

40 For the Lord thy God is a jealous God.
Deuteronomy ch. 6, v. 15

41 Man doth not live by bread only, but by every word that proceedeth out of the mouth of the Lord doth man live.
Deuteronomy ch. 8, v. 3

42 He kept him as the apple of his eye.
Deuteronomy ch. 32, v. 10

43 Then said they unto him, Say now Shibboleth: and he said Sibboleth: for he could not frame to pronounce it right. Then they took him, and slew him.
Judges ch. 12, v. 6

44 Speak, Lord; for thy servant heareth.
1 Samuel ch. 3, v. 9

45 God save the king.
1 Samuel ch. 10, v. 24

46 A man after his own heart.
1 Samuel ch. 13, v. 14

47 Go, and the Lord be with thee.
1 Samuel ch. 17, v. 37

48 How are the mighty fallen!
2 Samuel ch. 1, v. 19

49 O Absalom, my son, my son!
2 Samuel ch. 18, v. 33

50 He girded up his loins, and ran before Ahab.
1 Kings ch. 18, v. 46

51 The Lord gave, and the Lord hath taken away; blessed be the name of the Lord.
Job ch. 1, v. 21

52 Wherefore then hast thou brought me forth out of the womb? Oh that I had given up the ghost, and no eye had seen me!
Job ch. 10, v. 18

53 Man that is born of a woman is of few days, and full of trouble.
He cometh forth like a flower, and is cut down: he fleeth also as a shadow, and continueth not.
Job ch. 14, v. 1

54 I have heard many such things: miserable comforters are ye all.
Job ch. 16, v. 1

55 I am escaped with the skin of my teeth.
Job ch. 19, v. 20

56 I know that my redeemer liveth.
Job ch. 19, v. 25

57 Out of the mouth of babes and sucklings hast thou ordained strength because of thine enemies, that thou mightest still the enemy and the avenger.
Psalms 8

58 The fool hath said in his heart, There is no God.
Psalms 14

59 The Lord is my shepherd; I shall not want. He maketh me to lie down in green pastures: he leadeth me beside the still waters. He restoreth my soul: he leadeth me in the paths of righteousness for his name's sake. Yea, though I walk through the valley of death, I will fear no evil: for thou art with me; thy rod and thy staff they comfort me. Thou preparest a table before me in the presence of mine enemies: thou anointest my head with oil; my cup runneth over. Surely goodness and mercy shall follow me all the days of my life: and I will dwell in the house of the Lord for ever.
Psalms 23

60 But the meek shall inherit the earth.
Psalms 37

61 Be still, and know that I am God.
Psalms 46

62 Oh that I had wings like a dove! for then would I fly away, and be at rest.
Psalms 55

63 The days of our years are threescore years and ten.
Psalms 90

64 They that go down to the sea in ships, that do business in great waters;
These see the works of the Lord, and his wonders in the deep.
Psalms 107

65 Out of the depths have I cried unto thee, O Lord. Lord, hear my voice: let thine ears be attentive to the voice of my supplications.
Psalms 130

66 By the rivers of Babylon, there we sat down, yea, we wept, when we remembered Zion.
Psalms 137

67 How shall we sing the Lord's song in a strange land?
Psalms 137

68 Wisdom hath builded her house, she hath hewn out her seven pillars.
Proverbs ch. 9, v. 1

69 In all labour there is profit.
Proverbs ch. 14, v. 23

70 Pride goeth before destruction, and an haughty spirit before a fall.
Proverbs ch. 16, v. 18

71 Where there is no vision, the people perish.
Proverbs ch. 29, v. 18

72 Vanity of vanities, saith the Preacher, vanity of vanities; all is vanity.
Ecclesiastes ch. 1, v. 2

73 And there is no new thing under the sun.
Ecclesiastes ch. 1, v. 8

74 All is vanity and vexation of spirit.
Ecclesiastes ch. 1, v. 14

75 He that increaseth knowledge increaseth sorrow.
Ecclesiastes ch. 1, v. 18

76 To every thing there is a season, and a time to every purpose under the heaven:
A time to be born, and a time to die; a time to plant, and a time to pluck up that which is planted;
A time to kill, and a time to heal; a time to break down, and a time to build up;
A time to weep, and a time to laugh; a time to mourn, and a time to dance;
A time to cast away stones, and a time to gather stones together; a

time to embrace, and a time to refrain from embracing;
A time to get, and a time to lose; a time to keep, and a time to cast away;
A time to rend, and a time to sew; a time to keep silence, and a time to speak;
A time to love, and a time to hate; a time of war, and a time of peace.
Ecclesiastes ch. 3, v. 1

77 God is in heaven, and thou upon earth: therefore let thy words be few.
Ecclesiastes ch. 5, v. 2

78 A man hath no better thing under the sun, than to eat, and to drink, and to be merry.
Ecclesiastes ch. 8, v. 15

79 The race is not to the swift, nor the battle to the strong.
Ecclesiastes ch. 9, v. 11

80 He that diggeth a pit shall fall into it.
Ecclesiastes ch. 10, v. 8

81 Cast thy bread upon the waters: for thou shalt find it after many days.
Ecclesiastes ch. 11, v. 1

82 Of making many books there is no end; and much study is a weariness of the flesh.
Ecclesiastes ch. 12, v. 12

83 I am the rose of Sharon, and the lily of the valleys.
Song of Solomon ch. 2, v. 1

84 Holy, holy, holy, is the Lord of hosts: the whole earth is full of his glory.
Isaiah ch. 6, v. 1

85 The people that walked in darkness have seen a great light: they that dwell in the land of the shadow of death, upon them hath the light shined.
Isaiah ch. 9, v. 2

86 For unto us a child is born, unto us a son is given: and the government shall be upon his shoulder: and his name shall be called Wonderful,

Counsellor, The mighty God, The everlasting Father, The Prince of Peace.
Isaiah ch. 9, v. 6

87 Let us eat and drink; for tomorrow we shall die.
Isaiah ch. 22, v. 13

88 The voice of him that crieth in the wilderness, Prepare ye the way of the Lord, make straight in the desert a highway for our God.
Isaiah ch. 40, v. 3

89 All we like sheep have gone astray.
Isaiah ch. 53, v. 5

90 He was cut off out of the land of the living.
Isaiah ch. 53, v. 8

91 Stand by thyself, come not near to me; for I am holier than thou.
Isaiah ch. 65, v. 5

92 Can the Ethiopian change his skin, or the leopard his spots?
Jeremiah ch. 13, v. 23

93 The fathers have eaten sour grapes, and the children's teeth are set on edge.
Ezekiel ch. 18, v. 2

94 Can these bones live?
Ezekiel ch. 37, v. 3

95 O ye dry bones, hear the word of the Lord.
Ezekiel ch. 37, v. 4

96 Beat your plowshares into swords, and your pruninghooks into spears: let the weak say, I am strong.
Joel ch. 3, v. 10

Bierce, Ambrose (Gwinett)
(1842–c.1914). American writer and journalist

1 Acquaintance, n. A person whom we know well enough to borrow from, but not well enough to lend to.
The Cynic's Word Book (1906). Retitled The Devil's Dictionary (1911)

2 Bore, n. A person who talks when you wish him to listen.
The Cynic's Word Book (1906). Retitled *The Devil's Dictionary* (1911)

3 Diplomacy, n. The patriotic art of lying for one's country.
The Cynic's Word Book (1906). Retitled *The Devil's Dictionary* (1911)

4 Egotist, n. A person of low taste, more interested in himself than in me.
The Cynic's Word Book (1906). Retitled *The Devil's Dictionary* (1911)

5 Marriage, n. The state or condition of a community consisting of a master, a mistress and two slaves, making in all, two.
The Cynic's Word Book (1906). Retitled *The Devil's Dictionary* (1911).

6 Prejudice, n. A vagrant opinion without visible means of support.
The Cynic's Word Book (1906). Retitled *The Devil's Dictionary* (1911)

Binyon, Laurence (1869–1943). English poet

1 They shall grow not old, as we that are left grow old.
Age shall not weary them, nor the years condemn.
At the going down of the sun and in the morning
We will remember them.
'For the Fallen' (1914)

2 Now is the time for the burning of the leaves.
'The Ruins' (1942)

Bismarck, Prince Otto (Edward Leopold) von (1815–98). Prussian statesman

1 The great questions of our day cannot be solved by speeches and majority votes but by iron and blood.
Speech to the Prussian Chamber, 30 September 1862; later changed to 'blood and iron'

2 *Die Politik ist die Lehre vom Möglichen.*
Politics is the art of the possible.
In conversation with Meyer von Waldeck, 11 August 1867, in H. Amelung *Bismarck-Worte* (1918) p. 19

3 If there is ever another war in Europe, it will come out of some damned silly thing in the Balkans.
Attributed deathbed remark (1898)

Blacker, Valentine (1728–1823). Anglo-Irish soldier

1 Put your trust in God, my boys, and keep your powder dry.
'Oliver's Advice', collected in E. Hayes *Ballads of Ireland* (1856) vol. 1, p. 192; also attributed to Oliver Cromwell

Blackstone, Sir William (1723–80). English jurist

1 The king never dies.
Commentaries on the Laws of England (1765) bk 1, ch. 7

2 That the king can do no wrong, is a necessary and fundamental principle of the English constitution.
Commentaries on the Laws of England (1765) bk 3, ch. 17

Blair, Tony (Anthony Charles Lynton Blair) (1953–). British Labour politician and Prime Minister

1 The state of Africa is a scar on the conscience of the world.
Labour Party Conference, 2 October 2001

Blake, William (1757–1827). English poet, painter, engraver and mystic

1 'Piper, pipe that song again!'
Songs of Innocence (1789) 'Introduction'

2 When the voices of children are heard on the green
And laughing is heard on the hill.
Songs of Innocence (1789) 'Nurse's Song'

3 Little lamb, who made thee?
Dost thou know who made thee?
Songs of Innocence (1789) 'The Lamb'

4 Then cherish pity, lest you drive an angel from your door.
Songs of Innocence (1789) 'Holy Thursday'

5 Energy is Eternal Delight.
The Marriage of Heaven and Hell (1790–3)
'The Voice of the Devil'

6 A fool sees not the same tree that a
wise man sees.
The Marriage of Heaven and Hell (1790–3)
'Proverbs of Hell'

7 My mother groaned! my father
wept.
Into the dangerous world I leapt:
Helpless, naked, piping loud;
Like a fiend hid in a cloud.
Songs of Experience (1794) 'Infant Sorrow'

8 Love seeketh not itself to please,
Nor for itself hath any care;
But for another gives its ease,
And builds a Heaven in Hell's des-
pair.
Songs of Experience (1794) 'The Clod and the
Pebble'

9 O Rose, thou art sick!
Songs of Experience (1794) 'The Sick Rose'

10 Did he who made the Lamb make
thee?
Songs of Experience (1794) 'The Tiger'

11 Tyger Tyger, burning bright,
In the forests of the night;
What immortal hand or eye,
Could frame thy fearful symmetry?
Songs of Experience (1794) 'The Tiger'

12 I was angry with my friend:
I told my wrath, my wrath did end.
I was angry with my foe:
I told it not, my wrath did grow.
Songs of Experience (1794) 'A Poison Tree'

13 To see a world in a grain of sand
And a heaven in a wild flower,
Hold infinity in the palm of your
hand
And eternity in an hour.
'Auguries of Innocence' (*c*.1803) l. 1

14 A robin red breast in a cage
Puts all Heaven in a rage.
'Auguries of Innocence' (*c*.1803) l. 5

15 Bring me my bow of burning gold:
Bring me my arrows of desire:
Bring me my spear: O clouds,
unfold!
Bring me my chariot of fire.
Milton (1804–8) preface 'And did those feet
in ancient time', st. 3

16 And did those feet in ancient time
Walk upon England's mountains
green?
Milton (1804–8) preface, st. 1

17 Till we have built Jerusalem
In England's green and pleasant
land.
Milton (1804–8) preface, st. 4

Bogart, John B. (1848–1921).
American journalist

1 When a dog bites a man, that is not
news, because it happens so often.
But if a man bites a dog, that is
news.
In F. M. O'Brien *The Story of the* [New York]
Sun (1918) ch. 10 (also attributed to Charles
A. Dana)

**Bolingbroke, Henry St John, 1st
Viscount** (1678–1751). English
statesman

1 They make truth serve as a stalking-
horse to error.
Letters on the Study and Use of History (1752)
no. 4, pt 1

Bonhoeffer, Dietrich (1906–45).
German Lutheran pastor and
theologian

1 If religion is only a garment of
Christianity – and even this garment has looked very different at
different times – then what is reli-
gionless Christianity?
Letter to Eberhardt Bethge, 30 April 1944,
collected in *Widerstand und Ergebung* (1951,
translated 1953)

2 Death is the supreme Festival on
the road to freedom.
Letter (1945), collected in *Widerstand und
Ergebung* (1951, translated 1953)

Book of Common Prayer (1662).

1 It is meet and right so to do.
Holy Communion Versicles and responses

2 Peace be to this house, and to all that dwell in it.
The Visitation of the Sick

3 And forgive us our trespasses, As we forgive them that trespass against us.
Morning Prayer The Lord's Prayer

4 Give peace in our time, O Lord.
Morning Prayer Versicle

5 Hear them, read, mark, learn, and inwardly digest them.
Of all the holy Scriptures. Collects, 2nd Sunday in Advent

6 The peace of God, which passeth all understanding, keep your hearts and minds in the knowledge and love of God, and of his Son Jesus Christ our Lord.
Holy Communion Blessing

7 If any of you know cause, or just impediment, why these two persons should not be joined together in holy Matrimony, ye are to declare it.
Solemnization of Matrimony The Banns

8 Dearly beloved, we are gathered together here in the sight of God, and in the face of this congregation, to join together this Man and this Woman in holy Matrimony.
Solemnization of Matrimony Exhortation

9 If any man can shew any just cause, why they may not lawfully be joined together, let him now speak, or else hereafter for ever hold his peace.
Solemnization of Matrimony Exhortation

10 Wilt thou have this Woman to thy wedded wife, to live together after God's ordinance in the holy estate of Matrimony? Wilt thou love her, comfort her, honour, and keep her in sickness and in health; and, forsaking all other, keep thee only unto her, so long as ye both shall live?
Solemnization of Matrimony Betrothal

11 I *N.* take thee *M.* to my wedded husband, to have and to hold from this day forward, for better for

worse, for richer for poorer, in sickness and in health, to love, cherish, and to obey, till death us do part, according to God's holy ordinance; and thereto I give thee my troth.
Solemnization of Matrimony Betrothal (the corresponding man's words include 'I plight thee my troth' and do not include 'to obey')

12 With this Ring I thee wed, with my body I thee worship, and with all my worldly goods I thee endow.
Solemnization of Matrimony Wedding ('All that I am I give to you, and all that I have I share with you' in *Alternative Service Book*)

13 Those whom God hath joined together let no man put asunder.
Solemnization of Matrimony Wedding

14 Man that is born of a woman hath but a short time to live, and is full of misery.
The Burial of the Dead First Anthem

15 In the midst of life we are in death.
The Burial of the Dead First Anthem

16 Forasmuch as it hath pleased Almighty God of his great mercy to take unto himself the soul of our dear brother here departed, we therefore commit his body to the ground; earth to earth, ashes to ashes, dust to dust; in sure and certain hope of the Resurrection to eternal life, through our Lord Jesus Christ;
The Burial of the Dead Interment

17 We therefore commit his body to the deep, to be turned into corruption, looking for the resurrection of the body (when the Sea shall give up her dead).
Forms of Prayer to be Used at Sea At the Burial of their Dead at Sea

18 Lift up your hearts.
Holy Communion Versicles and responses

Borges, Jorge Luis (1899–1986).
Argentinian writer

1 The Falklands thing was a fight
between two bald men over a
comb.
In *Time* 14 February 1983

Borrow, George (1803–81).
English writer

1 Life is very sweet, brother; who
would wish to die?
Lavengro (1851) ch. 25

2 Youth will be served, every dog has
his day, and mine has been a fine
one.
Lavengro (1851) ch. 92

Bosquet, Pierre (1810–61). French
general

1 *C'est magnifique, mais ce n'est pas la
guerre.*
It is magnificent, but it is not war.
On the charge of the Light Brigade at
Balaclava, 25 October 1854, in Cecil Wood-
ham-Smith *The Reason Why* (1953) ch. 12

Bossidy, John Collins (1860–1928).
American physician and poet

1 And this is good old Boston,
The home of the bean and the cod,
Where the Lowells talk to the Ca-
bots.
And the Cabots talk only to God.
Verse spoken at Holy Cross College alumni
dinner in Boston, Massachusetts, 1910, in
Springfield Sunday Republican 14 December
1924

Boucicault, Dion(ysus Lardner)
(Dionysius Lardner Boursiquot)
(*c.*1820–90). Irish playwright, actor
and director

1 Men talk of killing time, while time
quietly kills them.
London Assurance (1841) act 2, sc. 1

Boulton, Sir Harold Edwin (1859–
1935). British songwriter

1 Over the sea to Skye.
'Skye Boat Song' (1908)

Bourdillon, F(rancis) W(illiam)
(1852–1921). English poet

1 The night has a thousand eyes.
Among the Flowers (1878) 'Light'

Bowen, Elizabeth (1899–1973).
Anglo-Irish novelist

1 Fate is not an eagle, it creeps like a
rat.
The House in Paris (1935) pt 2, ch. 2

Boyer, Charles (1899–1978). French
actor

1 Come with me to the Casbah.
Line attributed to him as Pepe in the film
Algiers (1938), though never actually used
by him

Bradbury, Malcolm (Stanley)
(1932–2000). English novelist, critic
and teacher

1 I like the English. They have the
most rigid code of immorality in
the world.
Eating People Is Wrong (1959) ch. 5

2 The English are polite by telling
lies. The Americans are polite by
telling the truth.
Stepping Westward (1965) bk 2, ch. 5

Bradford, John (*c.*1510–55).
English Protestant martyr

1 But for the grace of God there goes
John Bradford.
On seeing a group of criminals being led to
their execution, in *Dictionary of National
Biography* (1917–) p. 1067 (usually quoted
'There but for the grace of God go I')

Bradley, F(rancis) H(erbert)
(1846–1924). English philosopher

1 The world is the best of all possible
worlds, and everything in it is a
necessary evil.
Appearance and Reality (1893) preface

Braque, Georges (1882–1963).
French painter

1 *L'Art est fait pour troubler, la Science
rassure.*
Art is meant to disturb, science
reassures.
Le Jour et la nuit: Cahiers 1917–52 p. 11

2 *La vérité existe; on n'invente que le mensonge.*
Truth exists; only lies are invented.
Le Jour et la nuit: Cahiers 1917–52 p. 20

Brecht, Bertolt (1898–1956). German playwright

1 *Und der Haifisch, der hat Zähne*
Und die trägt er im Gesicht
Und Macheath, der hat ein Messer
Doch das Messer sieht man nicht.
Oh, the shark has pretty teeth, dear,
And he shows them pearly white.
Just a jack-knife has Macheath, dear.
And he keeps it out of sight.
Die Dreigroschenoper (1928) prologue

2 *Erst kommt das Fressen, dann kommt die Moral.*
Food comes first, then morals.
Die Dreigroschenoper (1928) act 2, sc. 3

3 *Frieden, das ist nur Schlamperei, erst der Krieg schafft Ordnung.*
Peace is nothing but slovenliness, only war creates order.
Mutter Courage (1939) sc. 1

4 *Der Krieg findet immer einen Ausweg.*
War always finds a way.
Mutter Courage (1939) sc. 6

Brenan, Gerald (1894–1987). British travel writer and novelist

1 Those who have some means think that the most important thing in the world is love. The poor know that it is money.
Thoughts in a Dry Season (1978) p. 22

Breton, Nicholas (c.1545–1626). English writer and poet

1 We rise with the lark and go to bed with the lamb.
The Court and Country (1618) para. 8

Bridges, Robert (1844–1930). English poet

1 When men were all asleep the snow came flying,
In large white flakes falling on the city brown.
'London Snow' (1890)

Bright, John (1811–89). English Liberal politician and reformer

1 The angel of death has been abroad throughout the land; you may almost hear the beating of his wings.
On the effects of the war in the Crimea, in *Hansard* 23 February 1855, col. 1786

2 England is the mother of Parliaments.
Speech at Birmingham, 18 January 1865, in *The Times* 19 January 1865

3 The knowledge of the ancient languages is mainly a luxury.
Letter in *Pall Mall Gazette* 30 November 1886

Brillat-Savarin, (Jean) Anthelme (1755–1826). French jurist and gastronome

1 *Dis-moi ce que tu manges, je te dirai ce que tu es.*
Tell me what you eat and I will tell you what you are.
Physiologie du goût (1825) 'Aphorismes pour servir de prolégomènes' no. 4

2 *C'est aussi de tous les arts celui qui nous a rendu le service le plus important pour la vie civile.*
It is also of all arts the one which has done the most to advance the cause of civilization.
Of cooking. *Physiologie du goût* (1825) pt 1 ch. 27, sect. 123

Bronowski, Jacob (1908–74). Polish-born British mathematician, poet and humanist.

1 No science is immune to the infection of politics and the corruption of power.
In *The Listener* (1971)

2 The essence of science: ask an impertinent question, and you are on the way to a pertinent answer.
The Ascent of Man (1973) ch. 4

Brontë, Charlotte (1816–55). English novelist

1 Reader, I married him.
Jane Eyre (1847) ch. 38

Brooke, Rupert (Chawner)
(1887–1915). English poet

1 If I should die, think only this of
me:
That there's some corner of a for-
eign field
That is for ever England.
'The Soldier' (1914)

2 They love the Good; they worship
Truth;
They laugh uproariously in youth;
(And when they get to feeling old,
They up and shoot themselves, I'm
told).
'The Old Vicarage, Grantchester' (1915)

3 Stands the Church clock at ten to
three?
And is there honey still for tea?
'The Old Vicarage, Grantchester' (1915)

Brooks, Mel (Melvin Kaminsky)
(1926–). American director, writer
and actor

1 If you've got it, flaunt it.
The Producers (1968)

**Broun, (Matthew) Heywood
Campbell** (1888–1939). American
journalist, humorist and novelist

1 The tragedy of life is not that man
loses, but that he almost wins.
Pieces of Hate, and Other Enthusiasms (1922)
'Sport for Art's Sake'

Brown, Lew (Louis Brownstein)
(1893–1958). American songwriter

1 Life is just a bowl of cherries.
Title of song (1931)

Browne, Sir Thomas (1605–82).
English writer and physician

1 All things are artificial, for nature is
the art of God.
Religio Medici (1643) pt 1, sect. 16

2 To believe only in possibilities, is
not faith, but mere Philosophy.
Religio Medici (1643) pt 1, sect. 48

3 There is no road or ready way to
virtue.
Religio Medici (1643) pt 1, sect. 55

4 It is the common wonder of all
men, how among so many millions
of faces, there should be none alike.
Religio Medici (1643) pt 2, sect. 1

5 We all labour against our own cure,
for death is the cure of all diseases.
Religio Medici (1643) pt 2, sect. 9

6 The long habit of living indispo-
seth us for dying.
Hydriotaphia (Urn Burial, 1658) ch. 5

7 Generations pass while some trees
stand, and old families last not
three oaks.
Hydriotaphia (Urn Burial, 1658) ch. 5

8 Man is a noble animal, splendid in
ashes, and pompous in the grave.
Hydriotaphia (Urn Burial, 1658) ch. 5

9 There is no antidote against the
opium of time.
Hydriotaphia (Urn Burial, 1658) ch. 5

10 Life is a pure flame, and we live by
an invisible sun within us.
Hydriotaphia (Urn Burial, 1658) ch. 5

Browning, Elizabeth Barrett
(1806–61). English poet

1 Colours seen by candle-light
Will not look the same by day.
'The Lady's Yes' (1844)

2 How do I love thee? Let me count
the ways.
Sonnets from the Portuguese (1850) no. 43

Browning, Robert (1812–89).
English poet

1 Measure your mind's height by the
shade it casts!
Paracelsus (1835) pt 3, l. 821

2 Still more labyrinthine buds the
rose.
Sordello (1840) bk 1, l. 476

3 God's in his heaven –
All's right with the world!
Pippa Passes (1841) pt 1, l. 221

4 'You're wounded!' 'Nay,' the soldier's pride
Touched to the quick, he said:

'I'm killed, Sire!' And his chief beside,
Smiling the boy fell dead.
'Incident of the French Camp' (1842) st. 5

5 Rats!
They fought the dogs and killed the cats,
And bit the babies in the cradles.
'The Pied Piper of Hamelin' (1842) st. 2

6 That's my last Duchess painted on the wall,
Looking as if she were alive.
'My Last Duchess' (1842) l. 1

7 Oh, to be in England
Now that April's there.
'Home-Thoughts, from Abroad' (1845)

8 I sprang to the stirrup, and Joris, and he;
I galloped, Dirck galloped, we galloped all three.
'How they brought the Good News from Ghent to Aix' (1845) l. 1

9 Oppression makes the wise man mad.
Luria (1846) act 4, l. 16

10 Ah, did you once see Shelley plain,
And did he stop and speak to you,
And did you speak to him again?
How strange it seems, and new!
'Memorabilia' (1855)

11 What of soul was left, I wonder,
when the kissing had to stop?
'A Toccata of Galuppi's' (1855) st. 14

12 Dear dead women, with such hair, too – what's become of all the gold
Used to hang and brush their bosoms? I feel chilly and grown old.
'A Toccata of Galuppi's' (1855) st. 15

13 Who knows but the world may end tonight?
'The Last Ride Together' (1855) st. 2

14 It was roses, roses, all the way.
'The Patriot' (1855)

15 Do I carry the moon in my pocket?
Men and Women (1855) 'Master Hugues of Saxe–Gotha'

16 A man can have but one life and one death,
One heaven, one hell.
'In a Balcony' (1855) l. 13

17 Stung by the splendour of a sudden thought.
'A Death in the Desert' (1864) l. 59

18 Faultless to a fault.
The Ring and the Book (1868–9) bk 9, l. 1175

19 Ignorance is not innocence but sin.
The Inn Album (1875) canto 5

Browning, Sir Frederick (1896–1965). British soldier

1 I think we might be going a bridge too far.
Expressing reservations about the Arnhem 'Market Garden' operation to Field Marshal Montgomery on 10 September 1944, in R. E. Urquhart *Arnhem* (1958) p. 4

Buchan, John (1st Baron Tweedsmuir) (1875–1940). Scottish novelist and statesman

1 It's a great life if you don't weaken.
Mr Standfast (1919) ch. 5

2 An atheist is a man who has no invisible means of support.
In H. E. Fosdick *On Being a Real Person* (1943) ch. 10

Buck, (Eu)Gene (Edward) and Ruby, Herman (1885–1957; 1891–1959). American songwriters

1 That Shakespearian rag, –
Most intelligent, very elegant.
'That Shakespearian Rag' (1912 song)

Buck, Pearl (née Sydenstricker) (1892–1973). American novelist

1 Every great mistake has a halfway moment, a split second when it can be recalled and perhaps remedied.
What America Means To Me (1943) ch. 10

Bucke, Richard Maurice (1837–1902). Canadian psychiatrist and author

1 Cosmic consciousness.
Paper read to the American Medico-Psychological Association, Philadelphia, 18 May 1894

Buffon, Comte de (George-Louis Leclerc) (1707–88). French naturalist

1 *Ces choses sont hors de l'homme, le style est l'homme même.*
These things [subject matter] are external to the man; style is the man.
Discours sur le style (address given to the Académie Française, 25 August 1753)

2 *Le génie n'est qu'une plus grande aptitude à la patience.*
Genius is only a greater aptitude for patience.
In Hérault de Séchelles *Voyage à Montbar* (1803) p. 15

Bulwer-Lytton, Edward George (1st Baron Lytton) (1803–73). British novelist and politician

1 Beneath the rule of men entirely great
The pen is mightier than the sword.
Richelieu (1839) act 2, sc. 2, l. 307

Bunn, Alfred 'Poet' (c.1796–1860). English theatrical manager and librettist

1 I dreamed that I dwelt in marble halls
With vassals and serfs at my side.
The Bohemian Girl (1843) act 2 'The Gipsy Girl's Dream'

Buñuel, Luis (1900–83). Spanish film director

1 *Grâce à Dieu, je suis toujours athée.*
Thanks be to God, I am still an atheist.
In *Le Monde* 16 December 1959

2 *Le charme discret de la bourgeoisie.*
The discreet charm of the bourgeoisie.
Title of film (1972)

Bunyan, John (1628–88). English writer and Nonconformist preacher

1 As I walked through the wilderness of this world.
The Pilgrim's Progress (1678) pt 1, opening words

2 The name of the slough was Despond.
The Pilgrim's Progress (1678) pt 1, p. 12

3 It beareth the name of Vanity-Fair, because the town where 'tis kept, is lighter than vanity.
The Pilgrim's Progress (1678) pt 1, p. 72

4 Hanging is too good for him, said Mr Cruelty.
The Pilgrim's Progress (1678) pt 1, p. 79

5 So I awoke, and behold it was a dream.
The Pilgrim's Progress (1678) pt 1, p. 133

6 One leak will sink a ship, and one sin will destroy a sinner.
The Pilgrim's Progress (1684) pt 2, p. 168

7 Who would true valour see,
Let him come hither.
The Pilgrim's Progress (1684) pt 2, p. 247

8 To be a pilgrim.
The Pilgrim's Progress (1684) pt 2, p. 247

Burgess, Anthony (John Anthony Burgess Wilson) (1917–93). English novelist and critic

1 A clockwork orange.
Title of novel (1962)

2 The possession of a book becomes a substitute for reading it.
In the *New York Times Book Review* 4 December 1966

3 Music says nothing to the reason: it is a kind of closely structured nonsense.
In the *Observer* 23 July 1989

Burgon, John William (1813–88). English clergyman; Dean of Chichester from 1876

1 A rose-red city – half as old as Time!
Petra (1845) l. 131

Burke, Edmund (1729–97). Irish-born statesman and man of letters

1 Custom reconciles us to everything.
On the Sublime and Beautiful (1757) pt 4, sect. 18

2 Laws, like houses, lean on one
another.
A Tract on the Popery Laws (planned c.1765)
ch. 3, pt 1 in *The Works* vol. 5 (1812)

3 The greater the power, the more
dangerous the abuse.
Speech on the Middlesex Election, 7 February 1771, in *The Speeches* (1854) p. 357

4 Falsehood has a perennial spring.
On American Taxation (1775) p. 30

5 The concessions of the weak are the
concessions of fear.
On Conciliation with America (1775) p. 7

6 Freedom and not servitude is the
cure of anarchy; as religion, and
not atheism, is the true remedy for
superstition.
On Conciliation with America (1775) p. 40

7 Parties must ever exist in a free
country.
On Conciliation with America (1775) p. 59

8 Slavery they can have anywhere. It
is a weed that grows in every soil.
On Conciliation with America (1775) p. 61

9 Liberty too must be limited in order
to be possessed.
Letter to the Sheriffs of Bristol (1777) p. 55

10 Individuals pass like shadows; but
the commonwealth is fixed and
stable.
Speech, *Hansard* 11 February 1780, col. 48

11 The people are the masters.
Speech, *Hansard* 11 February 1780, col. 67

12 Bad laws are the worst sort of tyranny.
Speech at Bristol, previous to the Late Election
(1780)

13 He was not merely a chip off the old
block, but the old block itself.
Commenting on William Pitt the Younger's
maiden speech in the House of Commons,
26 February 1781

14 An event has happened, upon
which it is difficult to speak, and
impossible to be silent.
Speech, 5 May 1789, in E. A. Bond (ed.)
Speeches … in the Trial of Warren Hastings
(1859) vol. 2, p. 109

15 The age of chivalry is gone. – That
of sophisters, economists, and cal-
culators, has succeeded; and the
glory of Europe is extinguished for
ever.
Reflections on the Revolution in France (1790)

16 Man is by his constitution a religious animal; atheism is against
not only our reason, but our
instincts.
Reflections on the Revolution in France (1790)

17 Superstition is the religion of feeble
minds.
Reflections on the Revolution in France (1790)

18 Good order is the foundation of all
good things.
Reflections on the Revolution in France (1790)

19 Those who attempt to level never
equalize.
Reflections on the Revolution in France (1790)

20 Society is indeed a contract … it
becomes a partnership not only
between those who are living, but
between those who are living,
those who are dead, and those who
are to be born.
Reflections on the Revolution in France (1790)

21 Our patience will achieve more
than our force.
Reflections on the Revolution in France (1790)

22 Kings will be tyrants from policy
when subjects are rebels from
principle.
Reflections on the Revolution in France (1790)

23 Tyrants seldom want pretexts.
Letter to a Member of the National Assembly
(1791) p. 25

24 You can never plan the future by
the past.
Letter to a Member of the National Assembly
(1791) p. 73

25 Old religious factions are volcanoes
burnt out.
Speech on the Petition of the Unitarians, 11
May 1792, in *The Works* vol. 5 (1812)

26 To innovate is not to reform.
A Letter to a Noble Lord (1796) p. 20

27 Never, no never, did Nature say one
thing and Wisdom say another.
*Third Letter ... on the Proposals for Peace with
the Regicide Directory* (1797) p. 30

28 It is necessary only for the good
man to do nothing for evil to triumph.
Attributed

Burke, Johnny (1908–64).
American songwriter

1 Like Webster's dictionary, we're
Morocco bound.
Title song in *Road to Morocco* (film, 1942)

Burney, Fanny (Mme d'Arblay)
(1752–1840). English novelist and
diarist

1 A little alarm now and then keeps
life from stagnation.
Camilla (1796) bk 3, ch. 11

Burns, John (1858–1943). British
Liberal politician

1 The Thames is liquid history.
In the *Daily Mail* 25 January 1943

Burns, Robert (1759–96). Scottish
poet

1 Gie me ae spark o' Nature's fire,
That's a' the learning I desire.
'Epistle to J. L[aprai]k' (1786) st. 13

2 Wee, sleekit, cow'rin', tim'rous
beastie,
'To a Mouse' (1786)

3 The best laid schemes o' mice an'
men
Gang aft a-gley.
'To a Mouse' (1786)

4 Green grow the rashes, O.
'Green Grow the Rashes' (1787)

5 Great chieftain o' the puddin'-race!
'To a Haggis' (1787)

6 A man's a man for a' that.
'For a' that and a' that' (1790)

7 Ye banks and braes o' bonny Doon,
'The Banks o' Doon' (1792)

8 And I will luve thee still, my Dear,
Till a' the seas gang dry.
'A Red, Red rose' (1794)

9 Should auld acquaintance be for-
got
And never brought to mind?
'Auld Lang Syne' (1796)

10 Gin a body meet a body
Comin thro' the rye,
'Comin thro' the rye' (1796)

11 O, my Luve's like a red, red rose
That's newly sprung in June.
'A Red Red Rose' (1794)

12 An' Charlie he's my darling, my
darling, my darling,
Charlie he's my darling, the young
Chevalier.
'Charlie he's my darling' (1796) chorus

13 Liberty's in every blow!
Let us do – or die!!!
'Robert Bruce's March to Bannockburn'
(1799)

Burroughs, Edgar Rice (1875–
1950). American novelist

1 Tarzan of the Apes.
Title of story (1912)

Burroughs, William S(eward)
(1914–97). American writer

1 You can't fake quality any more
than you can fake a good meal.
The Western Lands (1987) ch. 2

2 Nothing exists until or unless it is
observed. An artist is making
something exist by observing it.
Painting and Guns (1992) 'The Creative
Observer'

Burt, Benjamin Hapgood (1880–
1950). American songwriter

1 When you're all dressed up and no
place to go.
Title of song (1913)

Burton, Nat (fl. 1940s). American
songwriter

1 There'll be bluebirds over the white
cliffs of Dover.
'The White Cliffs of Dover' (1941 song)

Burton, Robert ('Democritus
Junior') (1577–1640). English
clergyman and scholar

1 All poets are mad.
The Anatomy of Melancholy (1621–51) 'Democritus to the Reader'

2 A loose, plain, rude writer … I call a spade a spade.
The Anatomy of Melancholy (1621–51) 'Democritus to the Reader'

3 The gods are well pleased when they see great men contending with adversity.
The Anatomy of Melancholy (1621–51) pt 2, sect. 3, member 1, subsect. 1

4 What is a ship but a prison?
The Anatomy of Melancholy (1621–51) pt 2, sect. 3, member 4, subsect. 1

5 One religion is as true as another.
The Anatomy of Melancholy (1621–51) pt 3, sect. 4, member 2, subsect. 1

Busenbaum, Hermann (1600–68). German theologian

1 *Cum finis est licitus, etiam media sunt licita.*
The end justifies the means.
Medulla Theologiae Moralis (1650); literally 'When the end is allowed, the means also are allowed'

Bush, George (1924–). 41st President of the USA

1 Read my lips: no new taxes.
Campaign pledge on taxation, in the *New York Times* 19 August 1988

Bush, George W. (1946–). 43rd President of the USA

1 States like these … constitute an axis of evil, arming to threaten the peace of this world.
State of the Union address, in *Newsweek* 11 February 2002

Butler, Nicholas Murray (1862–1947). President of Columbia University, 1901–45

1 An expert is one who knows more and more about less and less.
Commencement address at Columbia University (attributed)

Butler, R(ichard) A(usten) (Baron Butler of Saffron Walden) (1902–82). British Conservative politician

1 Politics is the art of the possible.
The Art of the Possible (1971)

Butler, Samuel (1612–80). English poet

1 He knew what's what, and that's as high
As metaphysic wit can fly.
Hudibras pt 1 (1663), canto 1, l. 149

2 Learning, that cobweb of the brain, Profane, erroneous, and vain.
Hudibras pt 1 (1663), canto 3, l. 1339

3 She that with poetry is won
Is but a desk to write upon.
Hudibras pt 2 (1664), canto 1, l. 591

4 Love is a boy, by poets styled, Then spare the rod, and spoil the child.
Hudibras pt 2 (1664), canto 1, l. 843

5 Oaths are but words, and words but wind.
Hudibras pt 2 (1664), canto 2, l. 107

6 For, those that fly, may fight again, Which he can never do that's slain.
Hudibras pt 3 (1678), canto 3, l. 243

7 He that complies against his will
Is of his own opinion still.
Hudibras pt 3 (1678), canto 3, l. 547

8 For Justice, though she's painted blind,
Is to the weaker side inclined.
Hudibras pt 3 (1678), canto 3, l. 709

Butler, Samuel (1835–1902). English writer

1 A hen is only an egg's way of making another egg.
Life and Habit (1877) ch. 8

2 All animals, except man, know that the principal business of life is to enjoy it.
The Way of All Flesh (1903) ch. 19

3 'Tis better to have loved and lost than never to have loved at all.
The Way of All Flesh (1903) ch. 67

4 It was very good of God to let Carlyle and Mrs Carlyle marry one
another and so make only two
people miserable instead of four.
*Letters between Samuel Butler and Miss E. M.
A. Savage 1871–1885 (1935)* 21 November 1884

5 Life is one long process of getting
tired.
Notebooks (1912) ch. 1

6 All progress is based upon a universal innate desire on the part of
every organism to live beyond its
income.
Notebooks (1912) ch. 1

7 The history of art is the history of
revivals.
Notebooks (1912) ch. 8

8 An apology for the Devil: It must be
remembered that we have only
heard one side of the case. God has
written all the books.
Notebooks (1912) ch. 14

9 Justice is being allowed to do
whatever I like.
Injustice is whatever prevents my
doing it.
Notebooks (1912) ch.14

10 To live is like to love – all reason is
against it, and all healthy instinct
for it.
Notebooks (1912) ch. 14

Byrom, John (1692–1763). English
poet

1 Christians, awake!
Hymn (c.1750)

Byron, Lord (George Gordon, 6th
Baron Byron) (1788–1824). English
poet

1 The petrifications of a plodding
brain.
English Bards and Scotch Reviewers (1809)
l. 416

2 A land of meanness, sophistry, and
mist.
'The Curse of Minerva' (1812) l. 138 (of
Scotland)

3 Fair Greece! sad relic of departed
worth!
Childe Harold's Pilgrimage (1812–18) canto 2,
st. 76

4 Oh Rome! my country! city of the
soul!
Childe Harold's Pilgrimage (1812–18) canto 4,
st. 78

5 Of its own beauty is the mind dis-
eased.
Childe Harold's Pilgrimage (1812–18) canto 4,
st. 122

6 While stands the Coliseum, Rome
shall stand;
When falls the Coliseum, Rome
shall fall;
And when Rome falls – the World.
Childe Harold's Pilgrimage (1812–18) canto 4,
st. 145

7 The Assyrian came down like the
wolf on the fold,
And his cohorts were gleaming in
purple and gold.
'The Destruction of Sennacherib' (1815) st. 1

8 The glory and the nothing of a
name.
'Churchill's Grave' (1816)

9 So, we'll go no more a-roving
'So we'll go no more a-roving' (written 1817)

10 Married, charming, chaste, and
twenty-three.
Don Juan (1819–24) canto 1, st. 59

11 What men call gallantry, and gods
adultery,
Is much more common where the
climate's sultry.
Don Juan (1819–24) canto 1, st. 63

12 Pleasure's a sin, and sometimes
sin's a pleasure.
Don Juan (1819–24) canto 1, st. 133

13 There's nought, no doubt, so much
the spirit calms
As rum and true religion.
Don Juan (1819–24) canto 2, st. 34

14 Let us have wine and women,
mirth and laughter,
Sermons and soda-water the day
after.
Don Juan (1819–24) canto 2, st. 178

15 Think you, if Laura had been Petrarch's wife,
He would have written sonnets all his life?
Don Juan (1819–24) canto 3, st. 8

16 The isles of Greece, the isles of Greece!
Where burning Sappho loved and sung.
Don Juan (1819–24) canto 3, st. 86 (1)

17 There is a tide in the affairs of women,
Which taken at the flood, leads – God knows where.
Don Juan (1819–24) canto 6, st. 2

18 And, after all, what is a lie? 'Tis but The truth in masquerade.
Don Juan (1819–24) canto 11, st. 37

19 Now hatred is by far the longest pleasure;
Men love in haste, but they detest at leisure.
Don Juan (1819–24) canto 13, st. 4

20 The English winter – ending in July, To recommence in August.
Don Juan (1819–24) canto 13, st. 42

21 'Tis strange – but true; for truth is always strange;
Stranger than fiction.
Don Juan (1819–24) canto 14, st. 101

22 There's music in the sighing of a reed;
There's music in the gushing of a rill;
There's music in all things, if men had ears:
Their earth is but an echo of the spheres.
Don Juan (1819–24) canto 15, st. 5

23 Sorrow is knowledge.
Manfred (1817) act 1, sc. 1, l. 10

24 I am ashes where once I was fire.
'To the Countess of Blessington' (written 1823)

25 I awoke one morning and found myself famous.
On the instantaneous success of *Childe Harold*, in Thomas Moore *Letters and Journals of Lord Byron* (1830) vol. 1, p. 346

Cabell, James Branch (1879–1958). American novelist and essayist

1 The optimist proclaims that we live in the best of all possible worlds; and the pessimist fears this is true.
The Silver Stallion (1926) bk 4, ch. 26

Caecus, Appius Claudius (4c–3c BC). Roman statesman and lawgiver

1 *Faber est suae quisque fortunae.*
Each man is the architect of his own fate.
Sallust Ad Caesarem Senem de Re Publica Oratio ch. 1, sect. 2

Caesar, Irving (1895–1996). American songwriter

1 Just tea for two and two for tea.
'Tea for Two' (1925 song)

Caesar, Julius (100–44 BC). Roman general and statesman

1 *Gallia est omnis divisa in partes tres.*
Gaul as a whole is divided into three parts.
De Bello Gallico bk 1, sect. 1

2 *Iacta alea est.*
The die is cast.
At the crossing of the Rubicon, from Suetonius *Lives of the Caesars* 'Divus Julius' sect. 32

3 Caesar's wife must be above suspicion.
Attributed

4 *Veni, vidi, vici.*
I came, I saw, I conquered.
Inscription displayed in Caesar's Pontic triumph, according to Suetonius *Lives of the Caesars* 'Divus Julius' sect. 37, and elsewhere

5 *Et tu, Brute?*
You too, Brutus?
Traditional rendering of Suetonius *Lives of the Caesars* 'Divus Julius' sect 82

Cain, James M(allahan) (1892–1977). American novelist

1 The postman always rings twice.
Title of novel (1934)

Calverley, C(harles) S(tuart) (born Blayds) (1831–84). English writer

1 Life is with such all beer and skittles.
'Contentment' (1872)

Campbell, Jane Montgomery (1817–78). English hymn-writer

1 We plough the fields, and scatter
The good seed on the land.
'We plough the fields, and scatter' (1861 hymn); translated from the German of Matthias Claudius (1740–1815)

Campbell, Mrs Patrick (Beatrice Stella Tanner) (1865–1940). English actress

1 It doesn't matter what you do in the bedroom as long as you don't do it in the street and frighten the horses.
In Daphne Fielding *The Duchess of Jermyn Street* (1964) ch. 2

Campbell, Thomas (1777–1844). Scottish poet

1 O leave this barren spot to me!
Spare, woodman, spare the beechen tree.
'The Beech-Tree's Petition' (1800)

2 To-morrow let us do or die!
'Gertrude of Wyoming' (1809) pt 3, st. 37

3 Now Barabbas was a publisher.
Attributed, in Samuel Smiles *A Publisher and his Friends: Memoir and Correspondence of the late John Murray* (1891) vol. 1, ch. 14

Campion, Thomas (1567–1620).
English physician, poet and
composer

1 There is a garden in her face,
Where roses and white lilies grow,
A heavenly paradise is that place,
Wherein all pleasant fruits do flow.
There cherries grow, which none
may buy
Till 'Cherry ripe!' themselves do
cry.
Fourth Book of Airs (1617) 'There is a Garden
in her Face'

Camus, Albert (1913–60). French
novelist, playwright and essayist

1 *Intellectuel = celui qui se dédouble.*
An intellectual is someone whose
mind watches itself.
Carnets, 1935–42 (1962)

2 *Il y a dans les hommes plus de choses à
admirer que de choses à mépriser.*
There are more things to admire in
people than to despise.
La Peste (1947)

3 *Toutes les révolutions modernes ont
abouti à un renforcement de l'État.*
All modern revolutions have ended
in a reinforcement of the State.
L'Homme révolté (1951)

4 *Tout révolutionnaire finit en oppres-
seur ou en hérétique.*
Every revolutionary ends as an
oppressor or a heretic.
L'Homme révolté (1951)

5 *Vous savez ce qu'est le charme: une
manière de s'entendre répondre oui
sans avoir posé aucune question claire.*
You know what charm is: a way of
getting the answer yes without
having asked any clear question.
La Chute (1956)

6 *Nous nous confions rarement à ceux
qui sont meilleurs que nous.*
We seldom confide in those who
are better than ourselves.
La Chute (1956)

Canning, George (1770–1827).
British Tory politician and Prime
Minister

1 But of all plagues, good Heaven,
thy wrath can send,
Save me, oh, save me, from the
candid friend.
'New Morality' (1821) l. 207

2 I called the New World into existence, to redress the balance of the
Old.
Speech on the affairs of Portugal, in *Hansard*
12 December 1826, col. 397

Capote, Truman (1924–84).
American novelist

1 I don't care what anybody says
about me as long as it isn't true.
Quoted in David Frost *The Americans* (1970)
'When Does A Writer Become A Star'

2 Great fury, like great whisky,
requires long fermentation.
Music for Chameleons (1980) 'Handcarved
Coffins'

Cardus, Sir Neville (1889–1975).
English critic and journalist

1 Cricket more than any other game
is inclined towards sentimentalism
and cant.
Quoted in Sir Rupert Hart-Davis *Cardus on
Cricket* (1977)

Carew, Thomas (c.1595–1640).
English poet and courtier

1 Here lies a king, that ruled as he
thought fit
The universal monarchy of wit.
'An Elegy upon the Death of Dr John
Donne' (1640)

Carey, George (1935–). English
Anglican churchman, Archbishop
of Canterbury (1991–2002)

1 We must recall that the Church is
always one generation away from
extinction.
Working Party Report, *Youth A Part* (1996)
foreword

Carlyle, Thomas (1795–1881). Scottish historian and political philosopher

1 No man who has once heartily and wholly laughed can be altogether irreclaimably bad.
Sartor Resartus (1833) bk 1, ch. 4

2 Be not the slave of words.
Sartor Resartus (1833) bk 1, ch. 8

3 Language is called the garment of thought: however, it should rather be, language is the flesh-garment, the body, of thought.
Sartor Resartus (1833) bk 1, ch. 11

4 The everlasting No.
Sartor Resartus (1833) bk 2, ch. 7 (title)

5 Hope ushers in a Revolution – as earthquakes are preceded by bright weather.
History of the French Revolution (1837) vol. 1, bk 2, ch. 1

6 A whiff of grapeshot.
History of the French Revolution (1837) vol. 1, bk 5, ch. 3

7 History, a distillation of rumour.
History of the French Revolution (1837) vol. 1, bk 7, ch. 5

8 France was long a despotism tempered by epigrams.
History of the French Revolution (1837) vol. 3, bk 7, ch. 7

9 History is the essence of innumerable biographies.
Critical and Miscellaneous Essays (1838) 'On History'

10 A well-written Life is almost as rare as a well-spent one.
Critical and Miscellaneous Essays (1838) 'Jean Paul Friedrich Richter'

11 Silence is deep as Eternity; speech is shallow as Time.
Critical and Miscellaneous Essays (1838) 'Sir Walter Scott'

12 History is philosophy teaching by experience.
Critical and Miscellaneous Essays (1838) 'History'

13 A good book is the purest essence of a human soul.
Speech in support of the London Library, 24 June 1840, in F. Harrison *Carlyle and the London Library* (1907) p. 66

14 Worship is transcendent wonder.
On Heroes, Hero-Worship, and the Heroic (1841) 'The Hero as Divinity'

15 The true University of these days is a collection of books.
On Heroes, Hero-Worship, and the Heroic (1841) 'The Hero as Man of Letters'

16 Captains of industry.
Past and Present (1843) bk 4, ch. 4 (title)

17 Nature admits no lie.
Latter-Day Pamphlets (1850) no. 5

Carnegie, Dale (1888–1955). American writer and lecturer

1 How to win friends and influence people.
Title of book (1936)

Carroll, Lewis (Charles Lutwidge Dodgson) (1832–98). English writer and logician

1 'What is the use of a book', thought Alice, 'without pictures or conversations?'
Alice's Adventures in Wonderland (1865) ch. 1

2 'Curiouser and curiouser!' cried Alice.
Alice's Adventures in Wonderland (1865) ch. 2

3 'You are old, Father William,' the young man said
Alice's Adventures in Wonderland (1865) ch. 5

4 'Then you should say what you mean,' the March Hare went on. 'I do,' Alice hastily replied; 'at least – at least I mean what I say – that's the same thing, you know.'
Alice's Adventures in Wonderland (1865) ch. 7

5 Take care of the sense, and the sounds will take care of themselves.
Alice's Adventures in Wonderland (1865) ch. 9

6 Everything's got a moral, if only you can find it.
The Duchess. *Alice's Adventures in Wonderland* (1865) ch. 9

7 'Twas brillig, and the slithy toves
Did gyre and gimble in the wabe;
All mimsy were the borogoves,
And the mome raths outgrabe.
Through the Looking-Glass (1872) ch. 1

8 The Walrus and the Carpenter
Were walking close at hand;
They wept like anything to see
Such quantities of sand.
Tweedledee. *Through the Looking-Glass*
(1872) ch. 4

9 'The time has come,' the Walrus
said,
'To talk of many things:
Of shoes – and ships – and sealing
wax –
Of cabbages – and kings –
And why the sea is boiling hot –
And whether pigs have wings.'
Through the Looking-Glass (1872) ch. 4

10 The rule is, jam to-morrow and jam
yesterday – but never jam today.
Through the Looking-Glass (1872) ch. 5

11 'When *I* use a word,' Humpty
Dumpty said in a rather scornful
tone, 'it means just what I choose it
to mean – neither more nor less.'
Through the Looking-Glass (1872) ch. 6

12 It's as large as life, and twice as
natural!
Through the Looking-Glass (1872) ch. 7

13 The Lion and the Unicorn were
fighting for the crown:
The Lion beat the Unicorn all
round the town.
Through the Looking-Glass (1872) ch. 7

14 He's an Anglo-Saxon Messenger –
and those are Anglo-Saxon atti-
tudes.
Through the Looking-Glass (1872) ch. 7

15 What I tell you three times is true.
The Hunting of the Snark (1876) 'Fit the First:
The Landing'

16 But oh, beamish nephew, beware
of the day,
If your Snark be a Boojum!
The Hunting of the Snark (1876) 'Fit the Third:
The Baker's Tale'

Carruth, William Herbert (1859–
1924). American educator, editor
and poet

1 Some call it evolution,
And others call it God.
'Each in His Own Tongue' (1908)

Carter, Angela (Olive) (1940–92).
English novelist and essayist

1 Solitude and melancholy, that is a
woman's life.
The Passion of New Eve (1977) ch. 9

2 He was a man with a great future
behind him, already.
Wise Children (1991) ch. 3

3 She looked like a million dollars, I
must admit, even if in well-used
notes.
Wise Children (1991) ch. 5

Carter, Sydney (1915–2004).
English folk-song writer

1 Dance then wherever you may be,
I am the Lord of the Dance, said he.
'Lord of the Dance' (1967)

Cartier-Bresson, Henri (1908–
2004). French photographer and
artist

1 The decisive moment.
Title of book (1952)

Cartwright, John (1740–1824).
English political reformer

1 One man shall have one vote.
The People's Barrier Against Undue Influence
(1780) ch. 1 'Principles, maxims, and primary
rules of politics' no. 68

Casson, Sir Hugh (Maxwell)
(1910–99). English architect and
artist

1 Architecture cannot be understood
without some knowledge of the
society it serves.
An Introduction to Victorian Architecture
(1948)

Castro, Fidel (1927–). Cuban
revolutionary and President

1 *La historia me absolverá.*
History will absolve me.
Title of propaganda pamphlet (1953)

Cather, Willa Sibert (1873–1947).
American novelist, poet and
journalist

1 The dead might as well speak to the
living as the old to the young.
One of Ours (1922) bk 2, ch. 6

2 Oh, the Germans classify, but the
French arrange.
Death Comes to the Archbishop (1927) pro-
logue

3 Most of the basic material a writer
works with is acquired before the
age of fifteen.
Quoted in René Rapin *Willa Cather* (1930)

4 Religion and art spring from the
same root and are close kin. Economics and art are strangers.
In *Commonweal* 17 April 1936

Cato the Elder (Marcus Porcius
Cato, 'the Censor') (234–149 BC).
Roman statesman, orator and
writer

1 *Delenda est Carthago.*
Carthage must be destroyed.
In Pliny the Elder *Naturalis Historia* bk 15,
ch. 74

Catullus (Gaius Valerius Catullus)
(c.84–c.54 BC). Roman poet

1 *Otium et reges prius et beatas perdidit
urbes.*
Often has leisure ruined great kings
and fine cities.
Carmina no. 51

Cavendish, Margaret (Duchess of
Newcastle) (c.1624–74). English
woman of letters

1 Marriage is the grave or tomb of
wit.
Plays (1662) 'Nature's Three Daughters' pt 2,
act 5, sc. 20

Cellini, Benvenuto (1500–71).
Italian goldsmith and sculptor

1 The difference between a painting
and sculpture is the difference
between a shadow and the thing
which casts it.
Letter to Benedetto Varchi (1547)

Cervantes, Miguel de (1547–1616).
Spanish novelist

1 *El Caballero de la Triste Figura.*
The Knight of the Doleful Coun-
tenance.
Don Quixote (1605) pt 1, ch. 19

2 *La mejor salsa del mundo es el ham-
bre.*
Hunger is the best sauce in the
world.
Don Quixote (1605) pt 2, ch. 5

3 *Para todo hay remedio, si no es para la
muerte.*
There's a remedy for everything
except death.
Don Quixote (1605) pt 2, ch. 10

4 *Digo, paciencia y barajar.*
What I say is, patience, and shuffle
the cards.
Don Quixote (1605) pt 2, ch. 23

Chalmers, Patrick (Reginald)
(1872–1942). English writer and
banker

1 What's lost upon the roundabouts
we pulls up on the swings!
Green Days and Blue Days (1912) 'Roundabouts and Swings'

Chamberlain, Joseph (1836–1914).
British Liberal politician

1 In politics, there is no use looking
beyond the next fortnight.
In A. J. Balfour *Chapters of Autobiography*
(1930) ch. 16, letter from Balfour to 3rd
Marquess of Salisbury, 24 March 1886

2 The day of small nations has long
passed away. The day of Empires
has come.
Speech at Birmingham, 12 May 1904, in *The
Times* 13 May 1904

Chamberlain, Neville (1869–
1940). British Conservative
politician and Prime Minister

1 In war, whichever side may call
itself the victor, there are no winners, but all are losers.
Speech at Kettering, 3 July 1938, in *The Times*
4 July 1938

2 This is the second time in our history that there has come back from Germany to Downing Street peace with honour. I believe it is peace for our time.
Speech from 10 Downing Street, 30 September 1938, in *The Times* 1 October 1938

Chandler, Raymond (1888–1959). American writer

1 It was a blonde. A blonde to make a bishop kick a hole in a stained glass window.
Farewell, My Lovely (1940) ch. 13

2 She gave me a smile I could feel in my hip pocket.
Farewell, My Lovely (1940) ch. 18

3 A dead man is the best fall guy in the world. He never talks back.
The Long Good-Bye (1953) ch. 10

Chanel, Gabrielle (known as Coco) (1883–1971). French couturier

1 Nature gives you the face you have when you are twenty. Life shapes the face you have at thirty. But it is up to you to earn the face you have at fifty.
Quoted in Marcel Haedrich *Coco Chanel: Her Life, Her Secrets* (1972) ch. 1

2 Fashion is architecture: it is a matter of proportions.
Quoted in Marcel Haedrich *Coco Chanel: Her Life, Her Secrets* (1972) ch. 1

Chapman, George (c.1559–1634). English scholar, poet and playwright

1 Man is a torch borne in the wind.
Bussy D'Ambois (1607–8) act 1, sc. 1

2 I am ashamed the law is such an ass.
Revenge for Honour (published posthumously, 1654) act 3, sc. 2

3 They're only truly great who are truly good.
Revenge for Honour (published posthumously, 1654) act 5, sc. 2, last line

Chargaff, Erwin (1905–2002). Czech-born American biochemist

1 What counts … in science is to be not so much the first as the last.
In *Science* (1971) vol. 172

Charles, Prince (Charles Philip Arthur George, Prince of Wales) (1948–). Heir apparent to the British throne

1 A monstrous carbuncle on the face of a much-loved and elegant friend.
On the proposed extension to the National Gallery, London; speech to the Royal Institute of British Architects, 30 May 1984, in *The Times* 31 May 1984

Charles I (1600–49). King of England, Scotland and Ireland from 1625

1 Never make a defence or apology before you be accused.
Letter to Lord Wentworth, 3 September 1636, in Sir Charles Petrie (ed.) *Letters of King Charles I* (1935)

2 I see all the birds are flown.
In the House of Commons, 4 January 1642, after attempting to arrest the Five Members: *Hansard Parliamentary History to the year 1803* vol. 2 (1807) col. 1010

Charles II (1630–85). King of England, Scotland and Ireland from 1660

1 This is very true: for my words are my own, and my actions are my ministers'.
Reply to Lord Rochester's epitaph on him, in *Thomas Hearne: Remarks and Collections* (1885–1921) 17 November 1706

2 Let not poor Nelly starve.
Of Nell Gwyn, his mistress, in Bishop Gilbert Burnet *History of My Own Time* (1724) vol. 1, bk 3, p. 609

Charles V (1500–58). Holy Roman Emperor, 1519–56; King of Spain from 1516

1 To God I speak Spanish, to women Italian, to men French, and to my horse – German.
Attributed

Charron, Pierre (1541–1603). French philosopher and theologian

1 *La vraie science et le vrai étude de l'homme, c'est l'homme.*
The true science and study of man is man.
De la Sagesse (1601) bk 1, preface

Chase, Edna Woolman (1877–1954). American fashion journalist, editor of *Vogue*

1 Fashion can be bought. Style one must possess.
Always in Vogue (1954) ch. 12

Chaucer, Geoffrey (c.1343–1400). English poet

1 Whan that Aprill with his shoures soote
The droghte of March hath perced to the roote.
The Canterbury Tales 'The General Prologue' l. 1

2 Thanne longen folk to goon on pilgrimages.
The Canterbury Tales 'The General Prologue' l. 9

3 He was a verray, parfit gentil knyght.
The Canterbury Tales 'The General Prologue' l. 72

4 He was as fressh as is the month of May.
The Canterbury Tales 'The General Prologue' l. 92

5 And Frenssh she spak ful faire and fetisly,
After the scole of Stratford atte Bowe,
For Frenssh of Parys was to hire unknowe.
The Canterbury Tales 'The General Prologue' l. 122

6 And gladly wolde he lerne and gladly teche.
The Canterbury Tales 'The General Prologue' l. 308

7 Trouthe is the hyeste thyng that man may kepe.
The Canterbury Tales 'The Franklin's Tale' l. 1479

8 The bisy larke, messager of day.
The Canterbury Tales 'The Knight's Tale' l. 1491

9 Mordre wol out; that se we day by day.
The Canterbury Tales 'The Nun's Priest's Tale' l. 3052

10 Thou shalt make castels thanne in Spayne
And dreme of joye, all but in vayne.
The Romaunt of the Rose l. 2573

11 That lyf so short, the craft so long to lerne,
Th'assay so hard, so sharp the conquerynge.
The Parliament of Fowls l. 1

12 Oon ere it herde, at tother out it wente.
Troilus and Criseyde bk 4, l. 434

13 For tyme ylost may nought recovered be.
Troilus and Criseyde bk 4, l. 1283

14 Go, litel bok, go, litel myn tragedye.
Troilus and Criseyde bk 5, l. 1786

Chekhov, Anton (1860–1904). Russian playwright and short-story writer

1 Medicine is my lawful wife and literature is my mistress. When I get tired of one I spend the night with the other.
Letter to A. S. Suvorin, 11 September 1888, in L. S. Friedland (ed.) *Anton Chekhov: Letters on the Short Story …* (1964)

2 Brevity is the sister of talent.
Letter to Alexander Chekhov, 11 April 1889, in L. S. Friedland (ed.) *Anton Chekhov: Letters on the Short Story …* (1964)

3 Women can't forgive failure.
The Seagull (1896) act 2

4 A woman can become a man's friend only in the following stages – first an acquaintance, next a mistress, and only then a friend.
Uncle Vanya (1897) act 2

Chesterfield, Lord (Philip Dormer Stanhope, 4th Earl of Chesterfield) (1694–1773). English writer and politician

1 Whatever is worth doing at all is worth doing well.
Letters to his Son (1774) 10 March 1746

2 The knowledge of the world is only to be acquired in the world, and not in a closet.
Letters to his Son (1774) 4 October 1746

3 An injury is much sooner forgotten than an insult.
Letters to his Son (1774) 9 October 1746

4 I recommend to you to take care of minutes: for hours will take care of themselves.
Letters to his Son (1774) 6 November 1747

5 Advice is seldom welcome; and those who want it the most always like it the least.
Letters to his Son (1774) 29 January 1748

6 Speak of the moderns without contempt, and of the ancients without idolatry.
Letters to his Son (1774) 27 February 1748

7 Idleness is only the refuge of weak minds.
Letters to his Son (1774) 20 July 1749

8 The chapter of knowledge is a very short, but the chapter of accidents is a very long one.
Letter to Solomon Dayrolles, 16 February 1753, in M. Maty (ed.) *Miscellaneous Works* vol. 2 (1778) no. 79

9 In scandal, as in robbery, the receiver is always thought as bad as the thief.
Advice to his Son (1775) 'Rules for Conversation: Private Scandal'

10 Cunning is the dark sanctuary of incapacity.
Letters ... to his Godson and Successor (1890)

11 Religion is by no means a proper subject of conversation in a mixed company.
Letters ... to his Godson and Successor (1890)

12 The pleasure is momentary, the position ridiculous, and the expense damnable.
On sex (attributed)

Chesterton, G(ilbert) K(eith) (1874–1936). English essayist, novelist and poet

1 Literature is a luxury; fiction is a necessity.
The Defendant (1901) 'A Defence of Penny Dreadfuls'

2 There is no such thing on earth as an uninteresting subject; the only thing that can exist is an uninterested person.
Heretics (1905) ch. 3

3 Charity is the power of defending that which we know to be indefensible. Hope is the power of being cheerful in circumstances which we know to be desperate.
Heretics (1905) ch. 12

4 A good novel tells us the truth about its hero; but a bad novel tells us the truth about its author.
Heretics (1905) ch. 15

5 Bigotry may be roughly defined as the anger of men who have no opinions.
Heretics (1905) ch. 20

6 An adventure is only an inconvenience rightly considered. An inconvenience is only an adventure wrongly considered.
All Things Considered (1908) 'On Running after One's Hat'

7 Poets do not go mad; but chess players do.
Orthodoxy (1908) ch. 2

8 Thieves respect property. They merely wish the property to become their property that they may more perfectly respect it.
The Man who was Thursday (1908) ch. 4

9 The night we went to Birmingham by way of Beachy Head.
'The Rolling English Road' (1914)

10 The rolling English drunkard made the rolling English road.
'The Rolling English Road' (1914)

11 The rich are the scum of the earth in every country.
The Flying Inn (1914) ch. 15

12 Strong gongs groaning as the guns boom far,
Don John of Austria is going to the war.
'Lepanto' (1915)

13 Smile at us, pay us, pass us; but do not quite forget. For we are the people of England, that never have spoken yet.
'The Secret People' (1915)

14 Democracy means government by the uneducated, while aristocracy means government by the badly educated.
In the *New York Times* 1 February 1931, pt 5, p. 1

15 Am in Market Harborough. Where ought I to be?
Attributed

Christiansen, Arthur (1904–63). British journalist

1 Show me a contented newspaper editor and I will show you a bad newspaper.
Headlines all my Life (1961) ch. 15

Christopher, Warren (1925–). American lawyer and government official

1 Sometimes you have to learn how to give the right answer to the wrong question.
In *US News and World Report* 19 December 1994

Chuang-tzu (Zhuangzi) (*c*.369–286 BC). Chinese philosopher

1 I do not know whether I was then a man dreaming I was a butterfly, or whether I am now a butterfly dreaming I am a man.
Chuang Tzu (1889) ch. 2 (translated by H. A. Giles)

Churchill, Charles (1731–64). English poet

1 So much they talked, so very little said.
The Rosciad (1761) l. 550

2 A joke's a very serious thing.
The Ghost (1763) bk 4, l. 1386

3 Be England what she will,
With all her faults, she is my country still.
The Farewell (1764) l. 27

Churchill, Lord Randolph (1849–94). British Conservative politician

1 Ulster will fight; Ulster will be right.
Public letter, 7 May 1886, in R. F. Foster *Lord Randolph Churchill* (1981) p. 258

2 An old man in a hurry.
On Gladstone, in an address to the electors of South Paddington, 19 June 1886; in W. S. Churchill *Lord Randolph Churchill* (1906) vol. 2, p. 491

Churchill, Sir Winston (Leonard Spencer) (1874–1965). British statesman, Prime Minister and writer

1 Dictators ride to and fro upon tigers which they dare not dismount. And the tigers are getting hungry.
Letter, 11 November 1937, in *Step by Step* (1939) p. 186

2 I cannot forecast to you the action of Russia. It is a riddle wrapped in a mystery inside an enigma.
Radio broadcast, 1 October 1939, in *Into Battle* (1941) p. 131

3 I have nothing to offer but blood, toil, tears and sweat.
Speech, *Hansard* 13 May 1940, col. 1502

4 We shall fight on the beaches, we shall fight on the landing grounds, we shall fight in the fields and in the streets, we shall fight in the hills; we shall never surrender.
Speech, *Hansard* 4 June 1940, col. 796

5 Let us therefore brace ourselves to our duty, and so bear ourselves that, if the British Commonwealth

and its Empire lasts for a thousand years, men will still say, 'This was their finest hour.'
Speech, *Hansard* 18 June 1940, col. 60

6 Never in the field of human conflict was so much owed by so many to so few.
Speech, *Hansard* 20 August 1940, col. 1166 (on British airmen)

7 Here is the answer which I will give to President Roosevelt … Give us the tools and we will finish the job.
Radio broadcast, 9 February 1941, in *Complete Speeches* (1974) vol. 6, p. 6350

8 Now this is not the end. It is not even the beginning of the end. But it is, perhaps, the end of the beginning.
Speech at the Mansion House, London, 10 November 1942, in *The End of the Beginning* (1943) p. 214 (on the Battle of Egypt)

9 There is no finer investment for any community than putting milk into babies.
Radio broadcast, 21 March 1943, in *Complete Speeches* (1974) vol. 7, p. 6761

10 The empires of the future are the empires of the mind.
Speech at Harvard, 6 September 1943, in *Onwards to Victory* (1944) p. 238

11 From Stettin in the Baltic to Trieste in the Adriatic an iron curtain has descended across the Continent.
Speech at Westminster College, Fulton, Missouri, 5 March 1946, in *Complete Speeches* (1974) vol. 7, p. 7290; the phrase 'iron curtain' had previously been used by others

12 This is the sort of English up with which I will not put.
In Ernest Gowers *Plain Words* (1948) 'Troubles with Prepositions'

13 In war: resolution. In defeat: defiance. In victory: magnanimity. In peace: goodwill.
The Second World War vol. 1 (1948) epigraph

14 I am ready to meet my maker. Whether my maker is ready for the ordeal of meeting me is another matter.
Speech, November 1949

15 Talking jaw is better than going to war.
Speech at White House, 26 June 1954, in the *New York Times* 27 June 1954, p. 1, usually quoted as 'To jaw-jaw is always better than to war-war'

16 In defeat unbeatable: in victory unbearable.
Of Viscount Montgomery, in Edward Marsh *Ambrosia and Small Beer* (1964) ch. 5

17 The ability to foretell what is going to happen tomorrow, next week, next month, and next year. And to have the ability afterwards to explain why it didn't happen.
Describing the qualifications desirable in a prospective politician, in B. Adler *Churchill Wit* (1965) p. 4

18 Scientists should be on tap, but not on top.
Quoted in Randolph S. Churchill *Twenty-One Years* (1965)

19 There, but for the grace of God, goes God.
Of Sir Stafford Cripps (attributed)

Cibber, Colley (1671–1757). English playwright

1 Perish the thought!
Richard III (1700) act 5

Cicero (Marcus Tullius Cicero) (106–43 BC). Roman orator and statesman

1 *Sed nescio quo modo nihil tam absurde dici potest quod non dicatur ab aliquo philosophorum.*
There is nothing so absurd but some philosopher has said it.
De Divinatione bk 2, ch. 119

2 *Salus populi suprema est lex.*
The good of the people is the chief law.
De Legibus bk 3, ch. 8

3 *Summum bonum.*
The highest good.
De Officiis bk 1, ch. 5

4 *Mens cuiusque is est quisque.*
The spirit is the true self.
De Republica bk 6, ch. 26

5 *O tempora, O mores!*
Oh, the times! Oh, the manners!
In Catilinam Speech 1, ch. 1

6 *Civis Romanus sum.*
I am a Roman citizen.
In Verrem Speech 5, ch. 147

7 *Silent enim leges inter arma.*
Laws are silent in time of war.
Pro Milone ch. 11

8 *Cui bono?*
Who benefits?
Pro Roscio Amerino ch. 84 and *Pro Milone*
ch. 12, sect. 32, quoting L. Cassius Longinus
Ravilla

Clare, John (1793–1864). English
poet

1 The present is the funeral of the
past,
And man the living sepulchre of
life.
'The present is the funeral of the past'
(written 1845)

2 Untroubling and untroubled
where I lie
The grass below, above, the vaulted
sky.
'I Am' (1848)

Clarke, Arthur C(harles) (1917–).
British author

1 Overhead without any fuss the
stars were going out.
'The Nine Billion Names of God' (1958)

2 When a distinguished but elderly
scientist states that something is
possible, he is almost certainly
right. When he states that something is impossible; he is very
probably wrong.
Profiles of the Future (1962)

Claudel, Paul (1868–1955). French
dramatist, poet and diplomat

1 A cocktail is to a glass of wine as
rape is to love.
Quoted by William Grimes in 'The American
Cocktail', *Americana* December 1992

Clemenceau, Georges (1841–
1929). French politician and Prime
Minister

1 *La guerre, c'est une chose trop grave
pour la confier à des militaires.*
War is too serious a matter to
entrust to military men.
Attributed to Clemenceau, but also to
others

2 We have won the war. Now we
have to win the peace – and that
may be more difficult.
Quoted in David R. Watson *George Clemenceau; A Political Biography* (1974)

Clough, Arthur Hugh (1819–61).
English poet

1 'Tis better to have fought and lost,
Than never to have fought at all.
'Peschiera' (1854)

2 Say not the struggle naught availeth.
'Say not the struggle naught availeth' (1855)

3 Thou shalt not kill; but need'st not
strive
Officiously to keep alive.
'The Latest Decalogue' (1862)

Cockburn, Alison (née
Rutherford) (1713–94). Scottish poet
and songwriter

1 For the flowers of the forest are a'
wade away.
'The Flowers of the Forest' (1765); *wade*
weeded

Cocteau, Jean (1889–1963). French
playwright and film director

1 *Le pire drame pour un poète, c'est
d'être admiré par malentendu.*
The worst tragedy for a poet is to be
admired through being misunderstood.
Le Rappel à l'ordre (1926) 'Le Coq et l'Arle-
quin' p. 20

2 *La poésie est une religion sans espoir.*
Poetry is a religion with no hope.
Journal d'un inconnu (1953) 'De l'invisibilité'

Coke, Sir Edward (1552–1634).
English jurist

1 For a man's house is his castle.
*The Third Part of the Institutes of the Laws of
England* (1628) ch. 73, p. 162

Coleridge, Samuel Taylor (1772–1834). English poet, critic and philosopher

1 It is an ancient Mariner,
And he stoppeth one of three.
'The Rime of the Ancient Mariner' (1798) pt 1

2 As idle as a painted ship
Upon a painted ocean.
'The Rime of the Ancient Mariner' (1798) pt 2

3 Water, water, everywhere,
Nor any drop to drink.
'The Rime of the Ancient Mariner' (1798) pt 2

4 Alone, alone, all, all alone,
Alone on a wide wide sea
And never a saint took pity on
My soul in agony.
'The Rime of the Ancient Mariner' (1798) pt 4

5 We were a ghastly crew.
'The Rime of the Ancient Mariner' (1798) pt 5

6 Like one, that on a lonesome road
Doth walk in fear and dread,
And having once turned round
walks on,
And turns no more his head;
Because he knows, a frightful fiend
Doth close behind him tread.
'The Rime of the Ancient Mariner' (1798) pt 6

7 He prayeth well, who loveth well
Both man and bird and beast.
He prayeth best, who loveth best
All things both great and small.
'The Rime of the Ancient Mariner' (1798) pt 7

8 A sadder and a wiser man,
He rose the morrow morn.
'The Rime of the Ancient Mariner' (1798) pt 7

9 This lime-tree bower my prison!
'This Lime-Tree Bower my Prison' (1800) l. 1

10 I may not hope from outward
forms to win
The passion and the life, whose
fountains are within.
'Dejection: an Ode' (1802) st. 3

11 O Lady! we receive but what we
give,
And in our life alone does Nature
live.
'Dejection: an Ode' (1802) st. 4

12 But oh! each visitation
Suspends what nature gave me at
my birth,
My shaping spirit of imagination.
'Dejection: an Ode' (1802) st. 6

13 What is an Epigram? a dwarfish
whole,
Its body brevity, and wit its soul.
'Epigram' (1809)

14 In Xanadu did Kubla Khan
A stately pleasure-dome decree:
Where Alph, the sacred river, ran
Through caverns measureless to
man
Down to a sunless sea.
'Kubla Khan' (1816)

15 It was a miracle of rare device,
A sunny pleasure-dome with caves
of ice.
'Kubla Khan' (1816)

16 A damsel with a dulcimer
In a vision once I saw.
'Kubla Khan' (1816)

17 For he on honey-dew hath fed,
And drunk the milk of Paradise.
'Kubla Khan' (1816)

18 The dwarf sees farther than the
giant, when he has the giant's
shoulder to mount on.
The Friend (1818) vol. 2 'On the Principles of
Political Knowledge'

19 Prose = words in their best order; –
poetry = the *best* words in the best
order.
Table Talk (1835) 12 July 1827

20 Farce is nearer tragedy in its essence
than comedy is.
Table Talk (1835), entry for 25 August 1833

Collins, Charles (fl. 1910–20).
English songwriter

1 Any old iron, any old iron,
Any any old old iron?
'Any Old Iron' (1911 song, with E. A. Sheppard and Fred Terry); the second line usually sung 'Any any any old iron?'

2 My old man said, 'Follow the van,
Don't dilly-dally on the way!'
'Don't Dilly-Dally on the Way' (1919 song,
with Fred Leigh); popularized by Marie
Lloyd

Collins, William (1721–59). English poet

1 How sleep the brave, who sink to rest,
By all their country's wishes blest!
'Ode Written in the Year 1746' (1748)

Colton, Charles Caleb (c.1780–1832). English clergyman and writer

1 When you have nothing to say, say nothing.
Lacon (1820) vol. 1, no. 183

2 Imitation is the sincerest form of flattery.
Lacon (1820) vol. 1, no. 217

3 If you would be known, and not know, vegetate in a village; if you would know, and not be known, live in a city.
Lacon (1820) vol. 1, no. 334

Comden, Betty and Green, Adolph (1919– ; 1915–).

1 The party's over, it's time to call it a day.
'The Party's Over' (1956); music by Jule Styne

Compton-Burnett, Dame Ivy (1892–1969). English novelist

1 As regards plots I find real life no help at all. Real life seems to have no plots.
Orion (1945) no. 1, 'A Conversation'

2 There is more difference within the sexes than between them.
Mother and Son (1955) ch. 10

Comte, Auguste Isidore Marie Françoise (1798–1857). French social scientist and mathematician

1 To understand a science it is necessary to know its history.
Système de Politique positive (*Positive Philosophy*) (1851–4)

Congreve, William (1670–1729). English playwright

1 Eternity was in that moment.
The Old Bachelor (1693) act 4, sc. 7

2 Thus grief still treads upon the heels of pleasure:
Married in haste, we may repent at leisure.
The Old Bachelor (1693) act 5, sc. 1

3 She lays it on with a trowel.
The Double Dealer (1694) act 3, sc. 10

4 See how love and murder will out.
The Double Dealer (1694) act 4, sc. 6

5 Music has charms to sooth a savage breast.
The Mourning Bride (1697) act 1, sc. 1

6 Heaven has no rage, like love to hatred turned,
Nor Hell a fury, like a woman scorned.
The Mourning Bride (1697) act 3, sc. 8

7 Beauty is the lover's gift.
The Way of the World (1700) act 2, sc. 4

8 Love's but the frailty of the mind,
When 'tis not with ambition joined.
The Way of the World (1700) act 3, sc. 12

9 Music alone with sudden charms can bind
The wand'ring sense, and calm the troubled mind.
'Hymn to Harmony' (c.1701)

Connell, James M. (1852–1929). Irish socialist songwriter

1 Then raise the scarlet standard high!
Within its shade we'll live or die.
Tho' cowards flinch and traitors sneer,
We'll keep the red flag flying here.
'The Red Flag' (1889) in H. E. Piggott *Songs that made History* (1937) ch. 6

Connolly, Cyril (1903–74). English writer

1 Life is a maze in which we take the wrong turning before we have learnt to walk.
The Unquiet Grave (1944) pt 1

2 The civilization of one epoch becomes the manure of the next.
The Unquiet Grave (1944) pt 2

3 Imprisoned in every fat man a thin one is wildly signalling to be let out.
The Unquiet Grave (1944) pt 2

4 Civilization is an active deposit which is formed by the combustion of the Present with the Past.
The Unquiet Grave (1944) pt 2

Conrad, Joseph (Josef Teodor Konrad Nalecz Korzeniowski) (1857–1924). Polish-born English novelist

1 Liberty of the imagination should be the most precious possession of a novelist.
'Books' (1905)

2 The terrorist and the policeman both come from the same basket.
The Secret Agent (1907) ch. 4

3 Some kind of moral discovery should be the object of every tale.
Under Western Eyes (1911) prologue

Constable, John (1776–1837). English painter

1 There is nothing ugly; *I never saw an ugly thing in my life*: for let the form of an object be what it may, – light, shade, and perspective will always make it beautiful.
In C. R. Leslie *Memoirs of the Life of John Constable* (1843) ch. 17

2 When I set down to make a sketch from nature, the first thing I try to do is to forget that I have ever seen a picture.
Quoted in C. R. Leslie *Memoirs of the Life of John Constable* (1843)

Constant, Benjamin (Henri Benjamin Constant de Rebecque) (1767–1834). French novelist, political philosopher and politician

1 *L'art pour l'art, sans but, car tout but dénature l'art.*
Mais l'art atteint un but qu'il n'a pas.
Art for art's sake, with no purpose, for any purpose perverts art.
But art achieves a purpose which is not its own.
Journal intime 11 February 1804, in *Revue Internationale* 10 January 1887, p. 96

Constantine the Great (AD *c.*288–337). Roman emperor from AD 306

1 *In hoc signo vinces.*
In this sign shalt thou conquer.
Traditional form of Constantine's vision (AD 312), reported in Greek – [By this, conquer] – in Eusebius *Life of Constantine* bk 1, ch. 28

Cook, Dan American sports editor

1 The opera ain't over 'til the fat lady sings.
In the *Washington Post* 3 June 1978

Cook, Peter (1937–94). English comedian

1 I go to the theatre to be entertained. I don't want to see plays about rape, sodomy and drug addiction – I can get all that at home.
Comedy routine, 1962

Cooke, (Alfred) Alistair (1908–2004). English-born American journalist and broadcaster

1 Canned music is like audible wallpaper.
Quoted in David Pickering *Brewer's Twentieth Century Music* (1994)

Coolidge, Calvin (1872–1933). 30th President of the USA

1 The chief business of the American people is business.
Speech in Washington, 17 January 1925, in the *New York Times* 18 January 1925, p. 19

Cooper, James Fenimore (1789–1851). American writer

1 The tendency of democracies is, in all things, to mediocrity.
The American Democrat (1838) 'On the Disadvantages of Democracy'

2 Individuality is the aim of political liberty.
The American Democrat (1838) 'Individuality'

3 The press, like fire, is an excellent servant, but a terrible master.
The American Democrat (1838) 'On the Press'

Corneille, Pierre (1606–84). French playwright

1 *A vaincre sans péril, on triomphe sans gloire.*
When there is no peril in the fight, there is no glory in the triumph.
Le Cid (1637) act 2, sc. 2

2 *Un premier mouvement ne fut jamais un crime.*
A first impulse was never a crime.
Horace (1640) act 5, sc. 3

Cory, William (born Johnson) (1823–92). English poet; assistant master at Eton College

1 Jolly boating weather.
'Eton Boating Song' in *Eton Scrap Book* (1865)

Coubertin, Baron Pierre de (1863–1937). French sportsman and educationist

1 *L'important dans la vie ce n'est point le triomphe mais le combat; l'essentiel ce n'est pas d'avoir vaincu mais de s'être bien battu.*
The important thing in life is not the victory but the contest; the essential thing is not to have won but to have fought well.
Speech at a government banquet in London, 24 July 1908, in T. A. Cook *Fourth Olympiad* (1909) p. 793

Coué, Emile (1857–1926). French psychologist

1 *Tous les jours, à tous points de vue, je vais de mieux en mieux.*
Every day, in every way, I am getting better and better.
In *De la suggestion et de ses applications* (1915) p. 17

Coupland, Douglas (1961–). Canadian novelist

1 Generation X
From the title of his novel *Generation X: Tales for an Accelerated Culture*

Coward, Noël (1899–1973). English playwright, actor, composer and singer

1 Poor little rich girl.
'Poor Little Rich Girl' (1925 song)

2 I'll see you again,
Whenever spring breaks through again.
'I'll See You Again' (1929 song)

3 Mad dogs and Englishmen
Go out in the midday sun.
'Mad Dogs and Englishmen' (1931 song)

4 Mad about the boy.
'Mad about the Boy' (1932 song)

5 Don't put your daughter on the stage, Mrs Worthington.
'Mrs Worthington' (1935 song)

6 Don't let's be beastly to the Germans
When our Victory is ultimately won.
'Don't Let's Be Beastly to the Germans' (1943 song)

Cowley, Abraham (1618–67). English poet and essayist

1 Life is an incurable disease.
'To Dr Scarborough' (1656) st. 6

Cowley, Hannah (née Parkhouse) (1743–1809). English playwright

1 Vanity, like murder, will out.
The Belle's Stratagem (1780) act 1, sc. 4

Cowper, William (1731–1800). English poet

1 God moves in a mysterious way
His wonders to perform.
Olney Hymns (1779) 'Light Shining out of Darkness'

2 Could he with reason murmur at his case,
Himself sole author of his own disgrace?
'Hope' (1782) l. 316

3 Toll for the brave –
The brave! that are no more:
All sunk beneath the wave,
Fast by their native shore.
'On the Loss of the Royal George' (written 1782)

4 The disencumbered Atlas of the state.
'Retirement' (1782) l. 394 (of the statesman)

5 Pernicious weed! whose scent the fair annoys,
Unfriendly to society's chief joys.
'Conversation' (1782) l. 251 (on tobacco)

6 Truth lies somewhere, if we knew but where.
'Hope' (1782) l. 423

7 I am monarch of all I survey.
'Verses Supposed to be Written by Alexander Selkirk' (1782)

8 Our severest winter, commonly called the spring.
Letter to Rev. William Unwin, 8 June 1783

9 The poplars are felled, farewell to the shade
And the whispering sound of the cool colonnade.
'The Poplar-Field' (written 1784)

10 God made the country, and man made the town.
The Task (1785) bk 1 'The Sofa' l. 749

11 England, with all thy faults I love thee still.
The Task (1785) bk 2 'The Timepiece' l. 206

12 Variety's the very spice of life,
That gives it all its flavour.
The Task (1785) bk 2 'The Timepiece' l. 606

13 Knowledge is proud that he has learned so much;
Wisdom is humble that he knows no more.
The Task (1785) bk 6 'The Winter Walk at Noon' l. 96

14 Nature is but a name for an effect,
Whose cause is God.
The Task (1785) bk 6 'The Winter Walk at Noon' l. 223

15 John Gilpin was a citizen
Of credit and renown.
'John Gilpin' (1785) l. 1

Crabbe, George (1754–1832).
English poet

1 The murmuring poor, who will not fast in peace.
'The Newspaper' (1785) l. 158

2 With awe, around these silent walks I tread;
These are the lasting mansions of the dead.
'The Library' (1808) l. 105

3 The face the index of a feeling mind.
Tales of the Hall (1819) 'Lady Barbara' l. 124

4 Secrets with girls, like loaded guns with boys,
Are never valued till they make a noise.
Tales of the Hall (1819) 'The Maid's Story' l. 84

Crane, Stephen (1871–1900).
American writer

1 The red badge of courage.
Title of novel (1895)

Crashaw, Richard (c.1612–49).
English poet

1 I would be married, but I'd have no wife,
I would be married to a single life.
'On Marriage' (1646)

Crisp, Quentin (1908–99). English writer

1 Life was a funny thing that happened to me on the way to the grave.
The Naked Civil Servant (1968) ch. 18

2 An autobiography is an obituary in serial form with the last instalment missing.
The Naked Civil Servant (1968) ch. 29

Crompton, Richmal (Richmal Crompton Lamburn) (1890–1969).
English author of books for children

1 I'll thcream and thcream and thcream till I'm thick.
Still – William (1925) ch. 8 (Violet Elizabeth)

Cromwell, Oliver (1599–1658).
English soldier, politician and
general

1 You have sat too long here for any
good you have been doing. Depart,
I say, and let us have done with
you. In the name of God, go!
Addressing the Rump Parliament, 20 April
1653 (oral tradition; quoted by Leo Amery,
Hansard 7 May 1940, col. 1150)

2 Mr Lely, I desire you would use all
your skill to paint my picture truly
like me, and not flatter me at all;
but remark all these roughnesses,
pimples, warts, and everything as
you see me; otherwise I will never
pay a farthing for it.
In Horace Walpole *Anecdotes of Painting in
England* vol. 3 (1763) ch. í (commonly
quoted 'warts and all')

3 Cruel necessity.
On the execution of Charles I, in Joseph
Spence *Anecdotes* (1820) p. 286

Cummings, Edward Estlin (e e
cummings) (1894–1962). American
poet

1 a politician is an arse upon which
everyone has sat except a man.
1 × 1 (1944) no. 10

2 anyone lived in a pretty how town
(with up so floating many bells
down)
spring summer autumn winter
he sang his didn't he danced his did
50 poems (1949) no. 29

Cunningham, Allan (1784–1842).
Scottish poet

1 A wet sheet and a flowing sea,
A wind that follows fast
And fills the white and rustling sail
And bends the gallant mast.
'A Wet Sheet and a Flowing Sea' (1825)

Cupitt, Don (1934–). English
radical theologian

1 A belief is made religious, not so
much by its content, as rather by
the way it is held.
The Sea of Faith (1984)

2 Christmas is the Disneyfication of
Christianity
In the *Independent* 19 December 1996

Curie, Marie (Marya Sklodowska)
(1867–1934). Polish-born French
chemist

1 In science, we must be interested in
things, not in persons.
Quoted in Eve Curie *Madame Curie* (1937)
ch. 16

Curran, John Philpot (1750–1817).
Irish judge

1 The condition upon which God
hath given liberty to man is eternal
vigilance.
Speech on the right of election of the Lord
Mayor of Dublin, 10 July 1790, in Thomas
Davis (ed.) *Speeches* (1845) p. 94

Cyprian, St (Thascius Caecilius
Cyprianus) (*c.*200–258 AD). Christian
martyr and Father of the Church

1 *Habere non potest Deum patrem qui
ecclesiam non habet matrem.*
He cannot have God for his father
who has not the church for his
mother.
De Ecclesiae Catholicae Unitate (251) ch. 6

Dafoe, John W(esley) (1866–1944). Canadian publisher and editor

1 There are only two kinds of government, the scarcely tolerable and the absolutely unbearable.
Quoted in Murray Donnelly *Dafoe of the Free Press* (1968)

Dalí, Salvador (1904–89). Spanish painter, graphic artist and sculptor

1 I do not paint a portrait to look like the subject, rather does the person grow to look like his portrait.
Quoted in Esar *A Treasury of Humorous Quotations* (1951)

2 *Le surréalisme, c'est moi.*
I am surrealism.
Quoted in Saranne Alexandrian *Surrealist Art* (1970) ch. 5

Dana, Charles Anderson (1819–97). American newspaper editor

1 Get the news, get all the news, and nothing but the news.
The Art of Newspaper Making (1888) 'The Modern American Newspaper'

Daniel, Samuel (1562–1619). English poet and playwright

1 Unless above himself he can Erect himself, how poor a thing is man!
'To the Lady Margaret, Countess of Cumberland' (1594)

Dante Alighieri (1265–1321). Italian poet

1 *Nel mezzo del cammin di nostra vita.*
Midway along the path of our life.
Divina Commedia 'Inferno' canto 1, l. 1

2 *Lasciate ogni speranza voi ch'entrate!*
Abandon all hope, you who enter!
Divina Commedia 'Inferno' canto 3, l. 1 (inscription at the entrance to Hell)

3 *Non ragioniam di lor, ma guarda, e passa.*
Let us not speak of them, but look, and pass on.
Divina Commedia 'Inferno' canto 3, l. 51

4 *Il gran rifiuto.*
The great refusal.
Divina Commedia 'Inferno' canto 3, l. 60

Danton, Georges Jacques (1759–94). French revolutionary

1 *De l'audace, et encore de l'audace, et toujours de l'audace!*
Boldness, and again boldness, and always boldness!
Speech to the Legislative Committee of General Defence, 2 September 1792, in *Le Moniteur* 4 September 1792

Darion, Joe (1917–2001). American songwriter

1 Dream the impossible dream.
'The Quest' (1965 song)

Darnell, Bill (c.1940–). Canadian ecologist and activist

1 Make it a *green* peace.
Quoted in Robert Hunter *Warriors of the Rainbow* (1979)

Darwin, Charles (1809–82). English natural historian

1 I have called this principle, by which each slight variation, if useful, is preserved, by the term of Natural Selection.
On the Origin of Species (1859) ch. 3

2 The expression often used by Mr Herbert Spencer of the Survival of the Fittest is more accurate [than 'Struggle for Existence'], and is sometimes equally convenient.
On the Origin of Species (1869 edn) ch. 3

3 Man with all his noble qualities … still bears in his bodily frame the indelible stamp of his lowly origin.
The Descent of Man (1871) closing words

4 A mathematician is a blind man in a dark room looking for a black cat which isn't there.
Quoted in John D. Barrow *Pie in the Sky, Counting, Thinking and Being* (1992)

Darwin, Sir Francis (1848–1925). English botanist; son of Charles Darwin

1 In science the credit goes to the man who convinces the world, not to the man to whom the idea first occurs.
Eugenics Review April 1914 'Francis Galton'

D'Avenant, Charles (1656–1714). English playwright and political economist

1 Custom, that unwritten law, By which the people keep even kings in awe.
Circe (1677) act 2, sc. 3

Davies, Ray(mond Douglas) (1944–). British songwriter and rock musician

1 A dedicated follower of fashion.
'Dedicated Follower of Fashion' (1966)

Davies, Robertson (1913–95). Canadian writer

1 The ideal companion in bed is a good book.
Interview in J. Madison Davis (ed.) *Conversations with Robertson Davies* (1989)

Davies, Sir John (1569–1626). English poet

1 This wondrous miracle did Love devise,
For dancing is love's proper exercise.
'Orchestra, or a Poem of Dancing' (1596) st. 18

2 Skill comes so slow, and life so fast doth fly,
We learn so little and forget so much.
'Nosce Teipsum' (1599) st. 19

Davies, W(illiam) H(enry) (1871–1940). Welsh poet

1 It was the Rainbow gave thee birth, And left thee all her lovely hues.
'Kingfisher' (1910)

2 What is this life if, full of care, We have no time to stand and stare.
'Leisure' (1911)

Davis, Bette (Ruth Elizabeth Davis) (1908–89). American film actress

1 She's the original good time who was had by all.
On an anonymous starlet (attributed)

Davis, Steve (1957–). English snooker player

1 Billiards is very similar to snooker, except there are only three balls and no one watches it.
(1988) Quoted in Colin Jarman *The Guinness Dictionary of Sports Quotations* (1990)

Davis Jnr, Sammy (1925–90). American jazz musician, actor, dancer and comedian

1 Being a star has made it possible for me to get insulted in places where the average Negro could never hope to go and get insulted.
Yes I Can (1965) pt 3, ch. 23

Davison, Emily (Wilding) (1872–1913). English militant suffragette

1 Rebellion against tyrants is obedience to God.
Comment on uncompleted census return (1911), quoted in Gertrude Colmore *The Life of Emily Wilding Davison* (1913)

Dawkins, Richard (1941–). British zoologist

1 The selfish molecules known as genes.
The Selfish Gene (1976) ch. 2

2 [Natural selection] has no vision, no foresight, no sight at all. If it can be said to play the role of watchmaker in nature, it is the *blind* watchmaker.
The Blind Watchmaker (1986) ch. 1

de Beauvoir, Simone (1908–86). French novelist and feminist

1 *On ne naît pas femme: on le devient.*
One is not born a woman: one becomes one.
Le Deuxième Sexe (1949) vol. 2, pt 1, ch. 1

Defoe, Daniel (1660–1731). English novelist and journalist

1 We loved the doctrine for the teacher's sake.
'Character of the late Dr S. Annesley' (1697)

2 The best of men cannot suspend their fate:
The good die early, and the bad die late.
'Character of the late Dr S. Annesley' (1697)

3 Wherever God erects a house of prayer,
The Devil always builds a chapel there;
And 'twill be found, upon examination,
The latter has the largest congregation.
The True-Born Englishman (1701) pt 1, l. 1

4 And of all plagues with which mankind are curst,
Ecclesiastic tyranny's the worst.
The True-Born Englishman (1701) pt 2, l. 299

5 The good of subjects is the end of kings.
The True-Born Englishman (1701) pt 2, l. 313

6 Nature has left this tincture in the blood,
That all men would be tyrants if they could.
The History of the Kentish Petition (1712–13) addenda, l. 11

7 My man Friday.
Robinson Crusoe (1719, ed. J. D. Crowley, 1972) p. 207

8 Necessity makes an honest man a knave.
The Serious Reflections of Robinson Crusoe (1720) ch. 2

9 Vice came in always at the door of necessity, not at the door of inclination.
Moll Flanders (1721, ed. G. A. Starr, 1971) p. 128

Degas, (Hilaire Germain) Edgar (1834–1917). French artist

1 *L'art n'augmente pas, il se répète.*
Art does not expand, it repeats itself.
Letter to Paul Frölich, 27 November 1872

2 *Le dessin n'est pas la forme, il est la manière de voir la forme.*
Drawing is not the form; it is the way of seeing the form.
In P. Valéry *Degas, danse, dessin* (1938)

de Gaulle, Charles (1890–1970). French general and President

1 *La France a perdu une bataille! Mais la France n'a pas perdu la guerre!*
France has lost a battle! But France has not lost the war!
Proclamation, 18 June 1940

2 *Comment voulez-vous gouverner un pays qui a deux cent quarante-six variétés de fromage?*
How can you govern a country which has 246 varieties of cheese?
In Ernest Mignon *Les Mots du Général* (1962) p. 57

3 *Vive Le Québec Libre.*
Long Live Free Quebec.
Speech in Montreal, 24 July 1967, in *Discours et messages* (1970) p. 192

Dekker, Thomas (1570–1641). English playwright

1 Golden slumbers kiss your eyes,
Smiles awake you when you rise.
Patient Grissil (1603) act 4, sc. 2

de Kooning, Willem (1904–). Dutch-born American painter

1 Flesh was the reason why oil painting was invented.
In *Bulletin* (1980) Pittsburgh International Museum

Delacroix, (Ferdinand Victor) Eugène (1798–1863). French painter

1 Painters who are not colourists produce illumination and not painting.
The Journal of Eugène Delacroix (1852)

de la Mare, Walter (1873–1956). English poet and novelist

1 'Is there anybody there?' said the Traveller,
Knocking on the moonlit door.
'The Listeners' (1912)

DeLillo, Don (1936–). American novelist

1 I've come to think of Europe as a hardcover book, America as the paperback version.
The Names (1982) ch. 1

2 Tourism is the march of stupidity.
The Names (1982) ch. 3

Deniehy, Daniel Henry (1828–65). Australian lawyer, politician, orator and writer

1 A Bunyip Aristocracy.
Quoted in *The Australian Dictionary of Biography* (1853) vol. 4

Dennis, John (1657–1734). English critic, poet and playwright

1 Damn them, see how the rascals use me! They will not let my play run, but they steal my thunder!
After hearing his new thunder effects used at a performance of *Macbeth*, following the early withdrawal of one of his own plays; in William S. Walsh *A Handy-Book of Literary Curiosities* (1893) p. 1052

Descartes, René (1596–1650). French philosopher and mathematician

1 The reading of good books is like a conversation with the best men of past centuries.
Le Discours de la méthode (1637) pt 1

2 *Je pense, donc je suis.*
I think, therefore I am.
Le Discours de la méthode (1637) pt 4 (usually quoted as 'Cogito, ergo sum')

Destouches, Philippe Néricault (1680–1754). French playwright

1 *Les absents ont toujours tort.*
The absent are always in the wrong.
L'Obstacle imprévu (1717) act 1, sc. 6

Dewar, Sir James (1842–1923). Scottish physicist

1 Minds are like parachutes. They only function when they are open.
Attributed

Diana, Princess of Wales (1961–97).

1 There were three of us in this marriage, so it was a bit crowded.
Of her marriage to Charles, Prince of Wales and his relationship with Camilla Parker-Bowles. BBC *Panorama* broadcast, 20 November 1995

Dick, Philip K(indred) (1928–82). American science-fiction writer

1 Reality is that which, when you stop believing in it, doesn't go away.
Quoted in introduction to *I Hope I Shall Arrive Soon* (1986)

Dickens, Charles (1812–70). English novelist

1 Poverty and oysters always seem to go together.
(Sam Weller) *Pickwick Papers* (1837) ch. 22

2 He had but one eye, and the popular prejudice runs in favour of two.
(Mr Squeers) *Nicholas Nickleby* (1839) ch. 4

3 All is gas and gaiters.
(The Gentleman in the Small-clothes) *Nicholas Nickleby* (1839) ch. 49

4 Please, sir, I want some more.
(Oliver) *Oliver Twist* (1839) ch. 2

5 Known by the *sobriquet* of 'The artful Dodger'.
Oliver Twist (1839) ch. 8

6 'Hard,' replied the Dodger. 'As nails,' added Charley Bates.
Oliver Twist (1839) ch. 9

7 'If the law supposes that,' said Mr Bumble ... 'the law is a ass – a idiot.'
(Bumble) *Oliver Twist* (1839) ch. 51

8 Polly put the kettle on, we'll all have tea.
(Grip) *Barnaby Rudge* (1841) ch. 17

9 'Bah,' said Scrooge. 'Humbug!'
A Christmas Carol (1843) stave 1

10 'God bless us every one!' said Tiny Tim, the last of all.
A Christmas Carol (1843) stave 3

11 Affection beaming in one eye, and calculation shining out of the other.
(Mrs Todgers) *Martin Chuzzlewit* (1844) ch. 8

12 Here's the rule for bargains: 'Do other men, for they would do you.' That's the true business precept.
(Jonas Chuzzlewit) *Martin Chuzzlewit* (1844) ch. 11

13 Barkis is willin'.
(Barkis) *David Copperfield* (1850) ch. 5

14 Annual income twenty pounds, annual expenditure nineteen nineteen six, result happiness. Annual income twenty pounds, annual expenditure twenty pounds ought and six, result misery.
(Mr Micawber) *David Copperfield* (1850) ch. 12

15 We are so very 'umble.
(Uriah Heep) *David Copperfield* (1850) ch. 17

16 Accidents will occur in the best-regulated families.
(Mr Micawber) *David Copperfield* (1850) ch. 28

17 'Not to put too fine a point upon it' – a favourite apology for plain-speaking with Mr Snagsby.
Bleak House (1853) ch. 11

18 The one great principle of the English law is, to make business for itself.
Bleak House (1853) ch. 39

19 It was the best of times, it was the worst of times.
A Tale of Two Cities (1859) bk 1, ch. 1

20 It is a far, far better thing that I do, than I have ever done; it is a far, far better rest that I go to, than I have ever known.
(Sydney Carton) *A Tale of Two Cities* (1859) bk 3, ch. 15

21 A literary man – *with* a wooden leg.
(Mr Boffin, of Silas Wegg) *Our Mutual Friend* (1865) bk 1, ch. 5

22 I think … that it is the best club in London.
Mr Tremlow's description of the House of Commons. *Our Mutual Friend* (1865) bk 2, ch. 3

Dickinson, Emily (1830–86). American poet

1 Because I could not stop for Death – He kindly stopped for me.
'Because I could not stop for Death' (c.1863)

2 A word is dead
When it is said,
Some say.
I say it just
Begins to live
That day.
Complete Poems, no. 1212

Dickinson, John (1732–1808). American revolutionary statesman

1 Then join hand in hand, brave Americans all –
By uniting we stand, by dividing we fall.
'The Liberty Song' (1768)

Diderot, Denis (1713–84). French writer and critic

1 *Le génie se sent; mais il ne s'imite point.*
Genius is felt, but it is not imitated.
Discours sur la poésie dramatique (1758)

2 *L'esprit de l'escalier.*
Staircase wit.
That is, the witty reply that comes to mind after leaving the company, while descending the stairs. *Paradoxe sur le Comédien* (1773–8, published 1830)

Dietz, Howard (1896–1983).
American writer and lyricist

1 That's entertainment.
The Band Wagon (film, 1953)

Dillard, Annie (1945–). American
writer

1 I think the dying pray at the last
not please but thank you as a guest
thanks his host at the door.
Pilgrim at Tinker Creek (1974) ch. 15

Dillon, Wentworth (4th Earl of
Roscommon) (c.1633–85). Irish poet
and critic

1 Choose an author as you choose a
friend.
Essay on Translated Verse (1684) l. 96

2 Immodest words admit of no defence,
For want of decency is want of
sense.
Essay on Translated Verse (1684) l. 113

Dimnet, Ernest (1866–1954).
French priest, writer and lecturer

1 Architecture, of all the arts, is the
one which acts the most slowly,
but the most surely, on the soul.
What We Live By (1932) pt 2, ch. 12

Diogenes of Sinope (c.410–c.320
BC). Greek Cynic philosopher and
moralist

1 I am looking for an honest man.
Reply when asked why he was wandering
the streets of Athens during the day with a
lantern

Dionysius of Halicarnassus
(fl. 30–7 BC). Greek historian,
resident in Rome from 30 BC

1 History is philosophy from
examples.
Ars Rhetorica ch. 11, sect. 2

Disney, Walt (1901–66). American
animator and film producer

1 Fancy being remembered around
the world for the invention of a
mouse!
Disney's World (1985)

D'Israeli, Isaac (1766–1848). British
literary historian; father of
Benjamin Disraeli

1 There is an art of reading, as well as
an art of thinking, and an art of
writing.
The Literary Character (1795) ch. 11

Disraeli, Benjamin (1st Earl of
Beaconsfield) (1804–81). British
Conservative politician, Prime
Minister and novelist

1 Time is the great physician.
Henrietta Temple (1837) bk 6, ch. 9

2 No Government can be long secure
without a formidable Opposition.
Coningsby (1844) bk 2, ch. 1

3 Youth is a blunder; Manhood a
struggle; Old Age a regret.
Coningsby (1844) bk 3, ch. 1

4 Man is only truly great when he
acts from the passions.
Coningsby (1844) bk 4, ch. 13

5 Little things affect little minds.
Sybil (1845) bk 3, ch. 2

6 The Youth of a Nation are the
trustees of Posterity.
Sybil (1845) bk 6, ch. 13

7 Protection is not a principle, but an
expedient.
Speech, *Hansard* 17 March 1845, col. 1023

8 That fatal drollery called a representative government.
Tancred (1847) bk 2, ch. 13

9 Justice is truth in action.
Speech, *Hansard* 11 February 1851, col. 412

10 England does not love coalitions.
Speech, *Hansard* 16 December 1852,
col. 1666

11 Finality is not the language of politics.
Speech, *Hansard* 28 February 1859, col. 998

12 Colonies do not cease to be colonies because they are independent.
Speech, *Hansard* 5 February 1863, col. 81

13 Party is organized opinion.
Speech at Oxford, 25 November 1864, in *The
Times* 26 November 1864

14 Is man an ape or an angel? Now I
am on the side of the angels.
Speech at Oxford, 25 November 1864, in *The
Times* 26 November 1864

15 Assassination has never changed
the history of the world.
Speech, *Hansard* 1 May 1865, col. 1246

16 London: a nation, not a city.
Lothair (1870) ch. 27

17 You know who the critics are? The
men who have failed in literature
and art.
Lothair (1870) ch. 35

18 Increased means and increased
leisure are the two civilizers of
man.
Speech at Manchester, 3 April 1872, in *The
Times* 4 April 1872

19 A University should be a place of
light, of liberty, and of learning.
Speech, *Hansard* 11 March 1873, col. 1814

20 Upon the education of the people
of this country the fate of this
country depends.
Speech, *Hansard* 15 June 1874, col. 1618

21 Lord Salisbury and myself have
brought you back peace – but a
peace I hope with honour.
Speech on returning from the Congress of
Berlin, 16 July 1878, in *The Times* 17 July 1878

22 Never complain and never explain.
In J. Morley *Life of William Ewart Gladstone*
(1903) vol. 1, p. 123

23 I have climbed to the top of the
greasy pole.
On becoming Prime Minister, in W. Monypenny and G. Buckle *Life of Benjamin Disraeli*
vol. 4 (1916) ch. 16

24 When I want to read a novel, I write
one.
In W. Monypenny and G. Buckle *Life of
Benjamin Disraeli* vol. 6 (1920) ch. 17

25 There are three kinds of lies: lies,
damned lies and statistics.
Attributed to Disraeli in Mark Twain *Autobiography* (1924) vol. 1, p. 246

26 I never deny; I never contradict; I
sometimes forget.
Said to Lord Esher of his relations with
Queen Victoria, in Elizabeth Longford *Victoria R. I.* (1964) ch. 27

Doctorow, E(dgar) L(awrence)
(1931–). American novelist

1 There is no longer any such thing
as fiction or non-fiction; there's
only narrative.
In the *New York Times Book Review* 27 January 1988

Donleavy, J(ames) P(atrick)
(1926–). Irish-American novelist

1 When you don't have any money,
the problem is food. When you
have money, it's sex. When you
have both it's health.
The Ginger Man (1955) ch. 5

Donne, John (1572–1631). English
poet and divine

1 On a huge hill,
Cragged, and steep, Truth stands,
and he that will
Reach her, about must, and about
must go.
Satire no. 3 (1594–5) l. 79

2 Love built on beauty, soon as
beauty, dies.
Elegies 'The Anagram' (c.1595)

3 I sing the progress of a deathless
soul.
'The Progress of the Soul' (1601) st. 1

4 Great Destiny the commissary of
God.
'The Progress of the Soul' (1601) st. 4

5 At the round earth's imagined
corners, blow
Your trumpets, angels.
Holy Sonnets (1609) no. 4 (ed. J. Carey, 1990)

6 Death be not proud, though some
have called thee
Mighty and dreadful, for thou art
not so.
Holy Sonnets (1609) no. 6 (ed. J. Carey, 1990)

7 One short sleep past, we wake
eternally,
And death shall be no more; Death
thou shalt die.
Holy Sonnets (1609) no. 6 (ed. J. Carey, 1990)

8 Batter my heart, three-personed
God.
Holy Sonnets (1609) no. 10 (ed. J. Carey,
1990)

9 And new philosophy calls all in doubt.
An Anatomy of the World: The First Anniversary (1611) l. 205

10 She, she is dead; she's dead; when thou know'st this,
Thou know'st how dry a cinder this world is.
An Anatomy of the World: The First Anniversary (1611) l. 427

11 Think then, my soul, that death is but a groom,
Which brings a taper to the outward room.
Of the Progress of the Soul: The Second Anniversary (1612) l. 85

12 But I do nothing upon my self, and yet I am mine own executioner.
Devotions Upon Emergent Occasions (1624) Meditation no. 12

13 No man is an Island, entire of it self; every man is a piece of the Continent, a part of the main.
Devotions upon Emergent Occasions (1624) 'Meditation no. 17'

14 And therefore never send to know for whom the bell tolls; it tolls for thee.
Devotions upon Emergent Occasions (1624) 'Meditation no. 17'

15 The world is a great volume, and man the index of that book.
'Sermon preached at the Funeral of Sir William Cockayne' 12 December 1626

16 All other things, to their destruction draw,
Only our love hath no decay;
This, no tomorrow hath, nor yesterday,
Running it never runs from us away,
But truly keeps his first, last, everlasting day.
Songs and Sonnets 'The Anniversary' (1633)

17 Come live with me, and be my love,
And we will some new pleasures prove.
Songs and Sonnets 'The Bait' (1633)

18 For God's sake hold your tongue, and let me love.
Songs and Sonnets 'The Canonization' (1633)

19 Go, and catch a falling star,
Get with child a mandrake root,
Tell me, where all past years are,
Or who cleft the Devil's foot.
Songs and Sonnets 'Song: Go and catch a falling star' (1633)

20 I wonder by my troth, what thou, and I
Did, till we loved, were we not weaned till then?
Songs and Sonnets 'The Good-Morrow' (1633)

21 And now good morrow to our waking souls,
Which watch not one another out of fear.
Songs and Sonnets 'The Good-Morrow' (1633)

22 I long to talk with some old lover's ghost,
Who died before the god of love was born.
Songs and Sonnets 'Love's Deity' (1633)

23 'Tis the year's midnight, and it is the day's.
Songs and Sonnets 'A Nocturnal upon St Lucy's Day' (1633)

24 As virtuous men pass mildly away,
And whisper to their souls, to go.
Songs and Sonnets 'A Valediction: Forbidding Mourning' (1633)

25 Nature's great masterpiece, an Elephant.
Songs and Sonnets 'The Progress of the Soul' (c.1595–1605) st. 39 (1633)

26 Busy old fool, unruly sun,
Why dost thou thus,
Through windows, and through curtains call on us?
Must to thy motions lovers' seasons run?
Songs and Sonnets 'The Sun Rising' (1633)

27 I am two fools, I know,
For loving, and for saying so
In whining poetry.
Songs and Sonnets 'The Triple Fool' (1633)

Dorman-Smith, Sir Reginald
(1899–1977). British Conservative politician

1 Let 'Dig for Victory' be the motto of every one with a garden and of every able-bodied man and woman capable of digging an allotment in their spare time.
Radio broadcast, 3 October 1939, in *The Times* 4 October 1939

Dostoevsky, Fedor (1821–81).
Russian novelist

1 If the devil doesn't exist, but man has created him, he has created him in his own image and likeness.
The Brothers Karamazov (1879–80) bk 5, ch. 4

2 So long as man remains free he strives for nothing so incessantly and so painfully as to find someone to worship.
The Brothers Karamazov (1879–80) bk 5, ch. 5

Douglas, (George) Norman
(1868–1952). Scottish writer

1 You can tell the ideals of a nation by its advertisements.
South Wind (1917) ch. 6

2 Education is a state-controlled manufactory of echoes.
How About Europe? (1929)

3 To find a friend one must close one eye. To keep him – two.
Alamanc (1941)

Douglas, Lord Alfred (1870–1945).
Poet and intimate of Oscar Wilde

1 I am the Love that dare not speak its name.
'Two Loves' (1896)

Dowson, Ernest (1867–1900).
English poet

1 They are not long, the days of wine and roses.
'Vitae Summa Brevis' (1896)

Doyle, Sir Arthur Conan (1859–1930). Scottish-born writer and physician

1 It is a mistake to confound strangeness with mystery.
A Study in Scarlet (1887) ch. 7

2 Our ideas must be as broad as Nature if they are to interpret Nature.
A Study in Scarlet (1887) ch. 7

3 Where there is no imagination there is no horror.
A Study in Scarlet (1887) ch. 5

4 I never make exceptions. An exception disproves the rule.
The Sign of Four (1890) ch. 2

5 How often have I said to you that when you have eliminated the impossible, whatever remains, *however improbable*, must be the truth?
The Sign of Four (1890) ch. 6

6 It is quite a three-pipe problem, and I beg that you won't speak to me for fifty minutes.
The Adventures of Sherlock Holmes (1892) 'The Red-Headed League'

7 You see, but you do not observe.
The Adventures of Sherlock Holmes (1892) 'Scandal in Bohemia'

8 It has long been an axiom of mine that the little things are infinitely the most important.
The Adventures of Sherlock Holmes (1892) 'A Case of Identity'

9 Depend upon it, there is nothing so unnatural as the commonplace.
The Adventures of Sherlock Holmes (1892) 'A Case of Identity'

10 'Excellent,' I cried. 'Elementary,' said he.
The Memoirs of Sherlock Holmes (1894) 'The Crooked Man'; the words 'Elementary, my dear Watson' are not in any book by Conan Doyle

11 Mediocrity knows nothing higher than itself, but talent instantly recognizes genius.
The Valley of Fear (1915) ch. 1

12 Of all ruins that of a noble mind is the most deplorable.
His Last Bow (1917) 'The Dying Detective'

Drake, Sir Francis (*c.*1540–96).
English sailor and explorer

1 The singeing of the King of Spain's
Beard.
On the expedition to Cadiz, 1587, in Francis
Bacon *Considerations touching a War with
Spain* (1629)

2 There is plenty of time to win this
game, and to thrash the Spaniards
too.
Attributed, in *Dictionary of National Biography* (1917–) vol. 5, p. 1342

Drayton, Michael (1563–1631).
English poet

1 Thus when we fondly flatter our
desires,
Our best conceits do prove the
greatest liars.
The Barons' Wars (1603) canto 6, st. 94

2 Fair stood the wind for France.
To the Cambro-Britons (1619) 'Agincourt'

Dryden, John (1631–1700). English
poet, critic and playwright

1 And love's the noblest frailty of the
mind.
The Indian Emperor (1665) act 2, sc. 2

2 Repentance is the virtue of weak
minds.
The Indian Emperor (1665) act 3, sc. 1

3 By viewing nature, nature's handmaid art,
Makes mighty things from small
beginnings grow.
Annus Mirabilis (1667) st. 155

4 For secrets are edged tools,
And must be kept from children
and from fools.
Sir Martin Mar-All (1667) act 2, sc. 2

5 A thing well said will be wit in all
languages.
An Essay of Dramatic Poesy (1668)

6 All delays are dangerous in war.
Tyrannic Love (1669) act 1, sc. 1

7 I am as free as nature first made man,
Ere the base laws of servitude
began,
When wild in woods the noble
savage ran.
The Conquest of Granada (1670) pt 1, act 1,
sc. 1

8 So poetry, which is in Oxford made
An art, in London only is a trade.
'Prologue to the University of Oxon … at
the Acting of *The Silent Woman*' (1673)

9 None would live past years again,
Yet all hope pleasure in what yet
remain.
Aureng-Zebe (1675) act 4, sc. 1

10 In pious times, ere priestcraft did
begin,
Before polygamy was made a sin.
Absalom and Achitophel (1681) pt 1, l. 1

11 Plots, true or false, are necessary
things,
To raise up commonwealths and
ruin kings.
Absalom and Achitophel (1681) pt 1, l. 83

12 Great wits are sure to madness near
allied,
And thin partitions do their
bounds divide.
Absalom and Achitophel (1681) pt 1, l. 150

13 The people's prayer, the glad divi-
ner's theme,
The young men's vision and the
old men's dream!
Absalom and Achitophel (1681) pt 1, l. 238

14 All empire is no more than power
in trust.
Absalom and Achitophel (1681) pt 1, l. 411

15 Better one suffer, than a nation
grieve.
Absalom and Achitophel (1681) pt 1, l. 416

16 Beware the fury of a patient man.
Absalom and Achitophel (1681) pt 1, l. 1005

17 There is a pleasure sure,
In being mad, that none but mad-
men know!
The Spanish Friar (1681) act 1, sc. 1

18 Bold knaves thrive without one
grain of sense,
But good men starve for want of
impudence.
Constantine the Great (1684) epilogue

19 By education most have been mis-
led.
The Hind and the Panther (1687) pt 3, l. 389

20 From harmony, from heavenly
harmony
This universal frame began:
From harmony to harmony.
Through all the compass of the
notes it ran,
The diapason closing full in Man.
A Song for St Cecilia's Day (1687) st. 1

21 What passion cannot Music raise
and quell?
A Song for St Cecilia's Day (1687) st. 2

22 The trumpet shall be heard on
high,
The dead shall live, the living die,
And Music shall untune the sky.
A Song for St Cecilia's Day (1687) 'Grand
Chorus'

23 War is the trade of kings.
King Arthur (1691) act 2, sc. 2

24 Thou tyrant, tyrant Jealousy,
Thou tyrant of the mind!
Love Triumphant (1694) act 3, sc. 1 'Song of
Jealousy'

25 None but the brave deserves the
fair.
Alexander's Feast (1697) l. 4

26 Arms, and the man I sing, who,
forced by fate,
And haughty Juno's unrelenting
hate,
Expelled and exiled, left the Trojan
shore.
Translation of Virgil *Aeneid* (*Aeneis*, 1697) bk
1, l. 1

27 She hugged the offender, and for-
gave the offence.
Cymon and Iphigenia (1700) l. 367

28 Thoughts, such as they are, come
crowding in so fast upon me, that
my only difficulty is to choose or

reject; to run them into verse or to
give them the other harmony of
prose.
Fables Ancient and Modern (1700) preface

29 But love's a malady without a cure.
Palamon and Arcite (1700) bk 2, l. 110

30 Repentance is but want of power to
sin.
Palamon and Arcite (1700) bk 3, l. 813

Dubin, Al (1891–1945). Swiss-born
American lyricist

1 You're getting to be a habit with
me.
Title of song in *Forty-Second Street* (film,
1932)

2 We're in the money.
From the song 'We're in the Money' in *Gold
Diggers of 1933* (film, 1933)

3 I only have eyes for you.
Title of song in *Dames* (film, 1934)

4 Come on along and listen to
The Lullaby of Broadway.
From the song 'Lullaby of Broadway' in *Gold
Diggers of 1935* (film, 1935)

Dudek, Louis (1918–2001).
Canadian poet and aphorist

1 Intellectually, most people never
wash. They never free their minds
of the accumulated rubbish of
centuries.
Collected in *Notebooks 1960–1994* (1994)

Duffield, George (1818–88).
American Presbyterian minister

1 Stand up! – stand up for Jesus!
'Stand Up, Stand Up for Jesus' (1858 hymn)

Duhamel, Georges (1884–1966).
French novelist

1 *Je respecte trop l'idée de Dieu pour le
rendre responsable d'un monde aussi
absurde.*
I have too much respect for the idea
of God to make it responsible for
such an absurd world.
Le Désert de Bièvres (1937)

Dumas, Alexandre ('Dumas fils')
(1824–95). French writer

1 All generalizations are dangerous,
  even this one.
  Attributed

2 *Cherchons la femme.*
  Let us look for the woman.
  Les Mohicans de Paris (1854–5) *passim*;
  attributed to Joseph Fouché (1763–1820) in
  the form '*Cherchez la femme*'

3 *Tous pour un, un pour tous.*
  All for one, one for all.
  Les Trois Mousquetaires (1844) ch. 9

Du Maurier, Dame Daphne
(1907–89). English novelist

1 Last night I dreamt I went to
  Manderley again.
  Rebecca (1938) ch. 1

Dunbar, Paul Lawrence (1872–
1906). American poet

1 I know why the caged bird sings!
  'Sympathy' st. 3 (adopted by Maya Angelou
  as the title of her autobiography, 1969)

Durocher, Leo (1906–91).
American baseball coach

1 All nice guys. They'll finish last.
  Nice guys. Finish last.
  Comment made at a practice ground, July
  1946: in *Nice Guys Finish Last* (as the remark
  generally is quoted, 1975) pt 1, p. 14

Dury, Ian (1942–2000). British rock
singer and songwriter

1 Sex 'n' drugs 'n' rock 'n' roll.
  Title of song (1977)

Dworkin, Andrea (1946–2005).
American feminist and writer

1 Seduction is often difficult to dis-
  tinguish from rape. In seduction,
  the rapist bothers to buy a bottle of
  wine.
  Letters from a War Zone (1988)

Dyer, John (NA). English poet

1 And he that will this health deny,
  Down among the dead men let him
  lie.
  'Down among the Dead Men' (*c*.1700)

Dyer, Sir Edward (d. 1607). English
poet

1 My mind to me a kingdom is.
  'In praise of a contented mind' (1588).
  Attributed

Dylan, Bob (Robert Zimmerman)
(1941–). American singer and
songwriter

1 How many roads must a man walk
  down
  Before you can call him a man? …
  The answer, my friend, is blowin'
  in the wind,
  The answer is blowin' in the wind.
  'Blowin' in the Wind' (1962 song)

2 For the times they are a-changin'!
  'The Times They Are A-Changing' (1964
  song)

3 Hey! Mr Tambourine Man, play a
  song for me.
  'Mr Tambourine Man' (1965 song)

Edison, Thomas Alva (1847–1931). American inventor

1 Genius is one per cent inspiration, ninety-nine per cent perspiration.
Said *c.*1903, in *Harper's Monthly Magazine* September 1932

Edmonds, John Maxwell (1875–1958). English classicist

1 When you go home, tell them of us and say,
'For your tomorrows these gave their today.'
Inscriptions Suggested for War Memorials (1919)

Edward III (1312–77). King of England (from 1327)

1 *Honi soit qui mal y pense.*
Evil be to him that evil thinks.
Motto of the Order of the Garter; said to have been uttered by Edward when adjusting the Countess of Salisbury's garter, which had slipped down (*c.*1348)

Edwards, Oliver (1711–91). English lawyer

1 I have tried too in my time to be a philosopher; but, I don't know how, cheerfulness was always breaking in.
In James Boswell *Life of Samuel Johnson* (1934 edn) vol. 3, p. 305 (17 April 1778)

Einstein, Albert (1879–1955). German-born theoretical physicist

1 *Raffiniert ist der Herrgott, aber boshaft ist er nicht.*
God is subtle but he is not malicious.
Remark made at Princeton University, May 1921, in R. W. Clark *Einstein* (1973) ch. 14

2 *Jedenfalls bin ich überzeugt, dass der nicht würfelt.*
At any rate, I am convinced that *He* [God] does not play dice.
Letter to Max Born, 4 December 1926; in *Einstein und Born Briefwechsel* (1969) p. 130

3 I never think of the future. It comes soon enough.
Interview, given on the *Belgenland*, December 1930

4 Science without religion is lame, religion without science is blind.
Science, Philosophy and Religion: a Symposium (1941) ch. 13

5 Science can only state what is, not what should be.
Out of my Later Years (1950)

6 The man of science is a poor philosopher.
Out of my Later Years (1950)

7 The whole of science is nothing more than a refinement of everyday thinking.
Out of my Later Years (1950)

8 The most incomprehensible thing about the world is that it is comprehensible.
In *Life Magazine* (1950)

9 Nationalism is an infantile sickness. It is the measles of the human race.
In Helen Dukas and Banesh Hoffman *Albert Einstein, the Human Side* (1979) p. 38

10 Equations are more important to me, because politics is for the present, but an equation is something for eternity.
In Stephen Hawking *A Brief History of Time* (1988) p. 178

Eliot, George (Mary Ann Evans)
(1819–80). English novelist

1 In every parting there is an image
of death.
Scenes of Clerical Life (1858) 'Amos Barton'
ch. 10

2 Our deeds determine us, as much as
we determine our deeds.
Adam Bede (1859) ch. 29

3 If art does not enlarge men's sym-
pathies, it does nothing morally.
Letter to Charles Bray, 5 July 1859, in G. S.
Haight (ed.) *The George Eliot Letters* vol. 3
(1954) p. 111

4 Anger and jealousy can no more
bear to lose sight of their objects
than love.
The Mill on the Floss (1860) bk 1, ch. 10

5 The dead level of provincial existence.
The Mill on the Floss (1860) bk 5, ch. 3

6 The happiest women, like the
happiest nations, have no history.
The Mill on the Floss (1860) bk 6, ch. 3

7 There is no private life which has
not been determined by a wider
public life.
Felix Holt (1866) ch. 3

8 There's many a one who would be
idle if hunger didn't pinch him; but
the stomach sets us to work.
Felix Holt (1866) ch. 30

9 'Abroad', that large home of ruined
reputations.
Felix Holt (1866) epilogue

10 Among all forms of mistake,
prophecy is the most gratuitous.
Middlemarch (1871–2) bk 1, ch. 10

11 A difference of taste in jokes is a
great strain on the affections.
Daniel Deronda (1876) bk 2, ch. 15

Eliot, T(homas) S(tearns) (1888–
1965). American-born English poet,
critic and playwright

1 Let us go then, you and I,
When the evening is spread out
against the sky
Like a patient etherized upon a
table.
'The Love Song of J. Alfred Prufrock' (1917)

2 I am not Prince Hamlet, nor was
meant to be.
'The Love Song of J. Alfred Prufrock' (1917)

3 In the room the women come and
go
Talking of Michelangelo.
'The Love Song of J. Alfred Prufrock' (1917)

4 I have measured out my life with
coffee spoons.
'The Love Song of J. Alfred Prufrock' (1917)

5 I have seen the eternal Footman
hold my coat, and snicker.
'The Love Song of J. Alfred Prufrock' (1917)

6 I grow old … I grow old …
I shall wear the bottoms of my
trousers rolled.
Shall I part my hair behind? Do I
dare to eat a peach?
I shall wear white flannel trousers,
and walk upon the beach.
I have heard the mermaids singing,
each to each.
I do not think that they will sing to
me.
'The Love Song of J. Alfred Prufrock' (1917)

7 Webster was much possessed by
death
And saw the skull beneath the skin.
'Whispers of Immortality' (1919)

8 Thoughts of a dry brain in a dry
season.
'Gerontion' (1920)

9 Immature poets imitate; mature
poets steal.
The Sacred Wood (1920) 'Philip Massinger'

10 April is the cruellest month,
breeding
Lilacs out of the dead land, mixing
Memory and desire, stirring
Dull roots with spring rain.
The Waste Land (1922) pt 1

11 The Chair she sat in, like a bur-
nished throne,
Glowed on the marble.
The Waste Land (1922) pt 2

12 I think we are in rats' alley
Where the dead men lost their
bones.
The Waste Land (1922) pt 2

13 O the moon shone bright on Mrs
Porter
And on her daughter
They wash their feet in soda water.
The Waste Land (1922) pt 3

14 I, Tiresias, though blind, throbbing
between two lives,
Old man with wrinkled female
breasts.
The Waste Land (1922) pt 3

15 Sweet Thames, run softly till I end
my song,
The Waste Land (1922) pt 3

16 We are the hollow men
We are the stuffed men.
'The Hollow Men' (1925)

17 This is the way the world ends
Not with a bang but a whimper.
'The Hollow Men' (1925)

18 A cold coming we had of it.
'Journey of the Magi' (1927)

19 Our literature is a substitute for
religion, and so is our religion.
Selected Essays (1932) 'A Dialogue on Dramatic Poetry' (1928)

20 Genuine poetry can communicate
before it is understood.
Dante (1929)

21 Because I do not hope to turn
again.
Ash-Wednesday (1930) pt 1

22 I gotta use words when I talk to
you.
Sweeney Agonistes (1932) 'Fragment of an
Agon'

23 Birth, and copulation, and death.
That's all the facts when you come
to brass tacks.
Sweeney Agonistes (1932) 'Fragment of an
Agon'

24 The last temptation is the greatest
treason:
To do the right deed for the wrong
reason.
Murder in the Cathedral (1935) pt 1

25 Yet we have gone on living,
Living and partly living.
Murder in the Cathedral (1935) pt 1

26 Time present and time past
Are both perhaps present in time
future,
And time future contained in time
past.
Four Quartets 'Burnt Norton' (1935) pt 1

27 At the still point of the turning
world.
Four Quartets 'Burnt Norton' (1935) pt 2

28 In my beginning is my end.
Four Quartets 'East Coker' (1940) pt 1

29 That was a way of putting it – not
very satisfactory:
A periphrastic study in a worn-out
poetical fashion,
Leaving one still with the intoler-
able wrestle
With words and meanings.
Four Quartets 'East Coker' (1940) pt 2

30 The houses are all gone under the
sea.
The dancers are all gone under the
hill.
Four Quartets 'East Coker' (1940) pt 2

31 I do not know much about gods;
but I think that the river
Is a strong brown god – sullen,
untamed and intractable.
Four Quartets 'The Dry Salvages' (1941) pt 1

32 Since our concern was speech, and
speech impelled us
To purify the dialect of the tribe
And urge the mind to aftersight
and foresight.
Four Quartets 'Little Gidding' (1942) pt 2

Elizabeth, Queen (the Queen Mother) (1900–2002). Queen Consort of George VI

1 The Princesses would never leave without me and I couldn't leave without the King, and the King will never leave.
On the suggestion that the royal family be evacuated during the Blitz, in Penelope Mortimer *Queen Elizabeth* (1986) ch. 25

2 I'm glad we've been bombed. It makes me feel I can look the East End in the face.
To a London policeman, 13 September 1940

Elizabeth I (1533–1603). Queen of England and Ireland from 1558

1 I know I have the body of a weak and feeble woman, but I have the heart and stomach of a king, and of a king of England too.
Speech to the troops at Tilbury on the approach of the Armada, 1588, in Lord Somers *A Third Collection of Scarce and Valuable Tracts* (1751) p. 196

Elizabeth II (1926–). Queen of Great Britain and Northern Ireland

1 In the words of one of my more sympathetic correspondents, it has turned out to be an 'annus horribilis'.
Speech at Guildhall, London, 24 November 1992

Ellis, Henry Havelock (1859–1939). English sexologist

1 All civilization has from time to time become a thin crust over a volcano of revolution.
Little Essays of Love and Virtue (1922)

Eluard, Paul (1895–1952). French poet

1 *Ce qui a été compris n'existe plus.*
What has been understood no longer exists.
'Le Miroir d'un moment' (1926)

2 *Adieu tristesse*
Bonjour tristesse.
Tu es inscrite dans les lignes du plafond.
Farewell sadness

Good-day sadness.
You are inscribed in the lines of the ceiling.
'A peine défigurée' (1932)

Emerson, Ralph Waldo (1803–82). American philosopher and poet

1 There is properly no history; only biography.
Essays (1841) 'History'

2 The faith that stands on authority is not faith.
Essays (1841) 'The Over-Soul'

3 To be great is to be misunderstood.
Essays (1841) 'Self-Reliance'

4 Nothing great was ever achieved without enthusiasm.
Essays (1841) 'Circles'

5 A friend may well be reckoned the masterpiece of nature.
Essays (1841) 'Friendship'

6 All mankind love a lover.
Essays (1841) 'Love'

7 The dice of God are always loaded.
Essays (1841) 'Compensation'

8 The reward of a thing well done is to have done it.
'New England Reformers', lecture to the Society, 3 March 1844

9 To fill the hour – that is happiness.
Essays. Second Series (1844) 'Experience'

10 The years teach much which the days never know.
Essays. Second Series (1844) 'Experience'

11 Language is fossil poetry.
Essays. Second Series (1844) 'The Poet'

12 Every hero becomes a bore at last.
Representative Men (1850) 'Uses of Great Men'

13 Art is a jealous mistress.
The Conduct of Life (1860) 'Wealth'

14 We are born believing. A man bears beliefs as a tree bears apples.
The Conduct of Life (1860) 'Worship'

15 The louder he talked of his honour, the faster we counted our spoons.
The Conduct of Life (1860) 'Worship'

16 What is a weed? A plant whose
virtues have not been discovered.
Fortune of the Republic (1878) p. 3

Empson, Sir William (1906–84).
English poet and literary critic

1 Seven types of ambiguity.
Title of book (1930)

Ephron, Nora (1941–). American
screenwriter

1 I'll have what she's having.
When Harry Met Sally (film, 1989)

Epstein, Julius J. (1909–2000).
American screenwriter

1 Of all the gin joints in all the towns
in all the world, she walks into
mine.
Humphrey Bogart in *Casablanca* (film, 1942,
with Philip Epstein and Howard Koch)

2 If she can stand it, I can. Play it!
Humphrey Bogart in *Casablanca* (film, 1942,
with Philip Epstein and Howard Koch);
usually misquoted as 'Play it again, Sam';
earlier in the film Ingrid Bergman says, 'Play
it, Sam. Play *As Time Goes By*'

3 Here's looking at you, kid.
Humphrey Bogart in *Casablanca* (film, 1942,
with Philip Epstein and Howard Koch)

4 I'm no good at being noble, but it
doesn't take much to see that the
problems of three little people
don't amount to a hill of beans in
this crazy world.
Humphrey Bogart in *Casablanca* (film, 1942,
with Philip Epstein and Howard Koch)

5 If that plane leaves the ground and
you're not with him, you'll regret
it. Maybe not today, maybe not
tomorrow, but soon and for the rest
of your life.
Humphrey Bogart in *Casablanca* (film, 1942,
with Philip Epstein and Howard Koch)

6 Major Strasser has been shot.
Round up the usual suspects.
Claude Rains in *Casablanca* (film, 1942, with
Philip Epstein and Howard Koch)

Erasmus (Desiderius Erasmus)
(*c*.1469–1536). Dutch Christian
humanist

1 *In regione caecorum rex est luscus.*
In the country of the blind the one-
eyed man is king.
Adages bk 3, century 4, no. 96

Euclid (fl. *c*.300 BC). Greek
mathematician

1 Which was to be proved.
Elementa bk 1, proposition 5 and *passim*
(usually quoted in Latin: 'Quod erat de-
monstrandum')

Everett, David (1769–1813).
American lawyer and writer

1 Large streams from little fountains
flow,
Tall oaks from little acorns grow.
'Lines Written for a School Declamation'
(aged seven)

Fadiman, Clifton (1904–99).
American writer, literary critic and
lecturer

1 Poetry in a bottle.
Of wine. In *Manhattan Inc.* July 1985

Farjeon, Eleanor (1881–1965).
English writer for children

1 Morning has broken
Like the first morning,
Blackbird has spoken
Like the first bird.
Children's Bells (1957) 'A Morning Song (for
the First Day of Spring)'

Farquhar, George (1678–1707).
Irish playwright

1 Crimes, like virtues, are their own
rewards.
The Inconstant (1702) act 4, sc. 2

2 My Lady Bountiful.
The Beaux' Stratagem (1707) act 1, sc. 1

3 There is no scandal like rags, nor
any crime so shameful as poverty.
The Beaux' Stratagem (1707) act 1, sc. 1

4 No woman can be a beauty without
a fortune.
The Beaux' Stratagem (1707) act 2, sc. 2

Faulkner, William (1897–1962).
American novelist

1 The writer's only responsibility is
to his art.
In *Paris Review* Spring 1956, p. 30

2 An artist is a creature driven by
demons.
Interview in *Paris Review* Spring 1956

3 A man shouldn't fool with booze
until he's fifty; then he's a damn
fool if he doesn't.
In James M. Webb and A. Wigfall Green
William Faulkner of Oxford (1965) p. 110

Fawkes, Guy (1570–1606).
Conspirator in the Gunpowder
Plot, 1605

1 A desperate disease requires a dangerous remedy.
6 November 1605

Ferber, Edna (1887–1968).
American writer

1 Mother knows best.
Title of story (1923)

Ferdinand I (1503–64). Holy
Roman Emperor from 1558

1 *Fiat justitia et pereat mundus.*
Let justice be done, though the
world perish.
Motto. *See* Johannes Manlius *Locorum
Communium Collectanea* (1563) vol. 2 'De
Lege: Octatum Praeceptum'

Fermat, Pierre de (1601–65).
French lawyer, mathematician and
founder of number theory

1 To divide a cube into two other
cubes, a fourth power or in general
any power whatever into two
powers of the same denomination
above the second is impossible,
and I have assuredly found an
admirable proof of this, but the
margin is too narrow to contain it.
Scribbled note in the margins of his copy of
Diophantus' *Arithmetica* (Fermat's Last
Theorem)

Fern, Fanny (née Willis) (1811–72).
American writer

1 The straightest road to a man's
heart is through his palate.
*Fern Leaves from Fanny's Port-Folio, Second
Series* (1854) 'Hungry Husbands'; usually
quoted as 'The way to a man's heart is
through his stomach.'

Feuerbach, Ludwig (1804–72). German philosopher

1 *Der Mensch ist, was er isst.*
Man is what he eats.
In Jacob Moleschott *Lehre der Nahrungs-mittel: Für das Volk* (1850) 'Advertisement'

Fielding, Henry (1707–54). English novelist and playwright

1 Love and scandal are the best sweeteners of tea.
Love in Several Masques (1728) act 4, sc. 11

2 All Nature wears one universal grin.
Tom Thumb the Great (1731) act 1, sc. 1

3 And a-hunting we will go.
Don Quixote in England (1734) act 2, sc. 5 'A-Hunting We Will Go'

4 I am as sober as a Judge.
Don Quixote in England (1734) act 3, sc. 14

5 Public schools are the nurseries of all vice and immorality.
Joseph Andrews (1742) bk 3, ch. 5

6 One fool at least in every married couple.
Amelia (1751) bk 9, ch. 4

Fields, Dorothy (1905–74). American songwriter

1 Just direct your feet
To the sunny side of the street.
'On the Sunny Side of the Street' (1930 song)

Fields, W. C. (William Claude Dukenfield) (1879–1946). American comedian

1 It ain't a fit night out for man or beast.
The Fatal Glass of Beer (1932)

2 Anybody who hates children and dogs can't be all bad.
Attributed

Fisher, H(erbert) A(lbert) L(aurens) (1856–1940). English historian

1 Purity of race does not exist. Europe is a continent of energetic mongrels.
A History of Europe (1935) ch. 1

Fisher, John Arbuthnot (Baron Fisher) (1841–1920). British admiral

1 Never contradict
Never explain
Never apologize.
Letter to *The Times*, 5 September 1919

2 Yours till Hell freezes.
Attributed to Fisher, but not original

Fisher, Marve (NA). American songwriter

1 I want an old-fashioned house
With an old-fashioned fence
And an old-fashioned millionaire.
'An Old-Fashioned Girl' (1954 song)

Fitzgerald, Edward (1809–83). English scholar and poet

1 Here with a loaf of bread beneath the bough,
A flask of wine, a book of verse – and Thou.
The Rubáiyát of Omar Khayyám (1859) st. 11; 'A book of verses underneath the bough, / A jug of wine, a loaf of bread – and Thou', in 4th edn (1879) st. 12

2 Alas, that spring should vanish with the rose!
The Rubáiyát of Omar Khayyám (1859) st. 72

3 Taste is the feminine of genius.
Letter to J. R. Lowell, October 1877, in A. M. and A. B. Terhune (eds.) *Letters of Edward Fitzgerald* (1980) vol. 4, p. 79

Fitzgerald, F(rancis) Scott (Key) (1896–1940). American novelist

1 Personality is an unbroken series of successful gestures.
The Great Gatsby (1925) ch. 1

2 Mostly, we authors repeat ourselves – that's the truth.
'One Hundred False Starts', in the *Saturday Evening Post* 4 March 1933

3 No grand idea was ever born in a conference, but a lot of foolish ideas have died there.
Edmund Wilson (ed.) *The Crack-Up* (1945) 'Note-Books E'

4 Show me a hero and I will write you
a tragedy.
Edmund Wilson (ed.) *The Crack-Up* (1945)
'Note-Books E'

Fitzsimmons, Bob (Robert
Fitzsimmons) (1862–1917). New
Zealand boxer

1 The bigger they are, the further
they have to fall.
In the *Brooklyn Daily Eagle* 11 August 1900

**Flanders, Michael and Swann,
Donald** (1922–75; 1923–). English
songwriters

1 Mud! Mud! Glorious mud!
Nothing quite like it for cooling the
blood.
'The Hippopotamus' (1952)

2 Eating people is wrong!
'The Reluctant Cannibal' (1956 song);
adopted as the title of a novel (1959) by
Malcolm Bradbury

Flaubert, Gustave (1821–80).
French novelist

1 *Le style c'est la vie! C'est le sang même
de la pensée!*
Style is life! It is the very life-blood
of thought!
Letter to Louise Colet, 7 September 1853, in
M. Nadeau (ed.) *Correspondence 1853–56*
(1964)

Flecker, James Elroy (1884–1915).
English poet

1 For lust of knowing what should
not be known,
We take the Golden Road to Sa-
markand.
The Golden Journey to Samarkand (1913) pt 1,
'Epilogue'

Fleming, Ian (1908–64). English
novelist

1 From Russia with love.
Title of novel (1957)

2 A medium Vodka dry Martini –
with a slice of lemon peel. Shaken
and not stirred.
Dr No (1958) ch. 14

Fletcher, Phineas (1582–1650).
English clergyman and poet

1 Love's tongue is in the eyes.
Piscatory Eclogues (1633) no. 5, st. 13

Florian, Jean-Pierre Claris de
(1755–94). French writer and poet

1 *Plaisir d'amour ne dure qu'un
moment,
Chagrin d'amour dure toute la vie.*
Love's pleasure lasts but a moment;
Love's sorrow lasts all through life.
Célestine (1784)

Florio, John (c.1553–1625). English
lexicographer; translator of
Montaigne's essays

1 England is the paradise of women,
the purgatory of men, and the hell
of horses.
Second Frutes (1591) ch. 12

Fo, Dario (1926–). Italian
playwright and actor-manager

1 *Non si paga, non si paga.*
We won't pay, we won't pay.
Play title (1974), translated into English in
1981 as *Can't pay? Won't pay!*

Foley, J. (1906–70). British
songwriter

1 Old soldiers never die,
They simply fade away.
'Old Soldiers Never Die' (1920 song)

Ford, Gerald (1909–). 38th
President of the USA (1974–77)

1 If the government is big enough to
give you everything you want, it is
big enough to take away everything you have.
John F. Parker *If Elected* (1960)

Ford, Henry (1863–1947). American
car manufacturer

1 History is more or less bunk. It's
tradition. We don't want tradition.
We want to live in the present and
the only history that is worth a
tinker's damn is the history we
make today.
In the *Chicago Tribune* 25 May 1916 (interview with Charles N. Wheeler)

2 Any colour – so long as it's black.
On the choice of colour for the Model T
Ford, in Allan Nevins *Ford* (1957) vol. 2, ch. 15

3 My name is on the building.
His standard reason for having the last
word; recalled on his death

Ford, John (c.1586–c.1640). English
playwright

1 Busy opinion is an idle fool.
'Tis Pity She's a Whore (1633) act 5, sc. 3

2 Of one so young, so rich in nature's
store,
Who could not say, 'tis pity she's a
whore?
'Tis Pity She's a Whore (1633) act 5, sc. 6

Ford, Lena Guilbert (1870–1916).
American poet

1 Keep the Home-fires burning,
'Till the Boys Come Home!' (1914 song);
music by Ivor Novello

Forgy, Howell (1908–83).
American naval chaplain

1 Praise the Lord and pass the
ammunition.
At Pearl Harbor, 7 December 1941; in the
New York Times 1 November 1942 (later the
title of a song by Frank Loesser, 1942)

Forster, E(dward) M(organ)
(1879–1970). English novelist and
critic

1 A room with a view.
Title of novel (1908)

2 To trust people is a luxury in which
only the wealthy can indulge; the
poor cannot afford it.
Howards End (1910) ch. 5

3 Only connect! … Only connect the
prose and the passion, and both
will be exalted, and human love
will be seen at its height.
Howards End (1910) ch. 22

4 Death destroys a man: the idea of
death saves him.
Howards End (1910) ch. 27

5 Works of art, in my opinion, are the
only objects in the material universe to possess internal order, and

that is why, though I don't believe
that only art matters, I do believe in
Art for Art's sake.
Two Cheers for Democracy (1951) 'Art for Art's
Sake'

Foster, Stephen (Collins) (1826–
64). American songwriter

1 Way down upon the Swanee River.
'The Old Folks at Home' (1851)

2 I dream of Jeanie with the light
brown hair.
'Jeanie with the Light Brown Hair' (1854)

3 Beautiful dreamer, wake unto me.
'Beautiful Dreamer' (1864 song)

France, Anatole (Jacques Anatole
François Thibault) (1844–1924).
French novelist, poet and essayist

1 *Le livre est l'opium de l'Occident.*
Books are the opium of the West.
La Vie littéraire (1892) preface

Francis of Assisi, St (1181–1226).
Founder of the Franciscan Order

1 Make me an instrument of Your
peace!
'Prayer of St Francis' (attributed)

Franklin, Benjamin (1706–90).
American statesman, writer and
scientist

1 To lengthen thy Life, lessen thy
Meals.
Poor Richard's Almanack, June 1733

2 He that drinks fast, pays slow.
Poor Richard's Almanack August 1733

3 Necessity never made a good bargain.
Poor Richard's Almanack, April 1735

4 Remember that time is money.
Advice to a Young Tradesman (1748)

5 He that lives upon hope will die
fasting.
Poor Richard's Almanac (1758) preface

6 Here Skugg
Lies snug
As a bug
In a rug.
Letter to Georgiana Shipley on the death of
her squirrel, 26 September 1772, in W. B.
Willcox (ed.) *Papers of Benjamin Franklin*
vol. 19 (1975) p. 302 (*skugg* squirrel)

7 Man is a tool-making animal.
In James Boswell *Life of Samuel Johnson* (1934
edn) vol. 3, p. 245 (7 April 1778)

8 There never was a good war, or a
bad peace.
Letter to Josiah Quincy, 11 September 1783,
in *Works* (1882) vol. 10, p. 11

9 In this world nothing can be said to
be certain, except death and taxes.
Letter to Jean Baptiste Le Roy, 13 November
1789, in *Works of Benjamin Franklin* (1817)
ch. 6

Freed, Arthur (Arthur Grossman)
(1894–1973). American producer
and lyricist

1 Singin' in the rain.
'Singin' in the Rain' featured in *Hollywood
Revue of 1929*

Freeman, Edward (Augustus)
(1823–92). English historian

1 History is past politics, and politics
is present history.
Methods of Historical Study (1886)

Frelang, Fritz (born Isadore
Frelang) (1906–95). American
cartoon director

1 That's all folks!
Porky Pig's sign-off for Warner Brothers'
Looney Tunes

Freud, Sigmund (1856–1939).
Austrian psychiatrist, originator of
psychoanalysis

1 The interpretation of dreams is the
royal road to a knowledge of the
unconscious activities of the mind.
The Interpretation of Dreams (2nd edn, 1909)
ch. 7, sect. E (often quoted 'Dreams are the
royal road to the unconscious')

Friedman, Milton (1912–).
American economist

1 There is no such thing as a free
lunch.
Lecture (1973)

Friedrich, Caspar David (1774–
1840). German painter

1 The artist should not only paint
what he sees before him, but also
what he sees within him. If, however, he sees nothing within him,
then he should also omit to paint
that which he sees before him.
Quoted in *Caspar David Friedrich 1774–1840*,
Tate Gallery (1972)

Fromm, Erich (1900–80).
American philosopher and
psychologist

1 Immature love says 'I love you
because I need you'. Mature love
says 'I need you because I love you'.
The Art of Loving (1956)

Frost, Robert (1874–1963).
American poet

1 Two roads diverged in a wood,
and I –
I took the one less travelled by,
And that has made all the differ-
ence.
'The Road Not Taken' (1916)

2 The woods are lovely, dark and
deep.
But I have promises to keep,
And miles to go before I sleep.
'Stopping by Woods on a Snowy Evening'
(1923)

3 I have been one acquainted with
the night.
'Acquainted with the Night' (1928)

4 An unromantic poet is a self-con-
tradiction.
Letter to Louis Untermeyer, 6 June 1930

5 Writing a poem is discovering.
In the *New York Times* 7 November 1955

6 Poetry is a way of taking life by the
throat.
In Elizabeth S. Sergeant *Robert Frost* (1960)
ch. 18

7 Forgive, O Lord, my little jokes on
Thee
And I'll forgive Thy great big one
on me.
'Cluster of Faith' (1962)

Fry, Christopher (Christopher
Harris) (1907–). English playwright

1 The lady's not for burning.
Play title (1949), later altered by Margaret
Thatcher to 'The lady's not for turning' at
the Conservative Party Conference, 1980

Fuentes, Carlos (1928–). Mexican
novelist and playwright

1 What America does best is to
understand itself.
What it does worst is to understand
others.
In *Time* 16 June 1986

Fuller, R(ichard) Buckminster
(1895–1983). American architect,
inventor and philosopher

1 I am a passenger on the spaceship,
Earth.
Operating Manual for Spaceship Earth (1969)
ch. 1

Fuller, Thomas (1608–61). English
preacher and historian

1 Anger is one of the sinews of the
soul.
The Holy State and the Profane State bk 3 'Of
Anger'

2 Bacchus hath drowned more men
than Neptune.
Gnomologia no. 830

3 Borrowed garments never fit well.
Gnomologia no. 1008

4 Fine cloth is never out of fashion.
Gnomologia no. 1537

5 Good clothes open all doors.
Gnomologia no. 1705

Fuseli, Henry (1741–1825). Swiss-
born painter and writer

1 Selection is the invention of the
landscape painter.
Aphorisms on Art (1789) number 237 (published 1831)

Fyffe, Will (1885–1947). Scottish
comedian, singer and actor

1 I belong to Glasgow
Dear old Glasgow town!
'I Belong to Glasgow' (1921) chorus

Fyleman, Rose (1877–1957). English
writer for children

1 There are fairies at the bottom of
our garden!
Fairies and Chimneys (1918) 'The Fairies' (first
published in *Punch* 23 May 1917)

Galbraith, J(ohn) K(enneth)
(1908–). American economist
1 Politics is not the art of the possible. It consists in choosing between the disastrous and the unpalatable.
Letter to President Kennedy, 2 March 1962, in *Ambassador's Journal* (1969) p. 312

2 Trickle-down theory – the less than elegant metaphor that if one feeds the horse enough oats, some will pass through to the road for the sparrows.
The Culture of Contentment (1992)

Galileo Galilei (1564–1642). Italian astronomer and physicist
1 *Eppur si muove.*
But it does move.
Attributed to Galileo after his recantation that the earth moves around the sun, in 1632

Galsworthy, John (1867–1933). English novelist and playwright
1 Death being contrary to their principles, they took precautions against it.
The Man of Property (1906) pt 1, ch. 1

Gandhi, Mohandas Karamchand (known as Mahatma) (1869–1948). Indian nationalist leader

1 What do I think of Western civilization? I think that it would be a good idea.
Attributed

Garbo, Greta (Greta Lovisa Gustafsson) (1905–90). Swedish film actress
1 I want to be alone.
Grand Hotel (film, 1932)

Gardner, Ed (1901–63). American radio comedian
1 Opera is when a guy gets stabbed in the back and, instead of bleeding, he sings.
Duffy's Tavern (US radio programme, 1940s)

Garrick, David (1717–79). English actor-manager
1 Heart of oak are our ships,
Heart of oak are our men.
Harlequin's Invasion (1759) 'Heart of Oak' (song)

Gaskell, Elizabeth (1810–65). English novelist
1 A man … is *so* in the way in the house!
Cranford (1853) ch. 1

2 That kind of patriotism which consists in hating all other nations.
Sylvia's Lovers (1863) ch. 1

Gautier, Théophile (1811–72). French poet, novelist and critic.
1 *L'orgueil sort du cœur le jour où l'amour y entre.*
Pride leaves the heart the moment love enters it.
Mademoiselle de Maupin (1835).

Gay, John (1685–1732). English poet and playwright
1 All in the Downs the fleet was moored,
The streamers waving in the wind,
When black-eyed Susan came aboard.
'Sweet William's Farewell to Black-Eyed Susan' (1720)

2 They'll tell thee, sailors, when
away,
In ev'ry port a mistress find.
'Sweet William's Farewell to Black-Eyed
Susan' (1720)

3 She who has never loved, has never
lived.
The Captives (1724) act 2, sc. 2

4 Whence is thy learning? Hath thy
toil
O'er books consumed the midnight oil?
Fables (1727) introduction l. 15

5 Those who in quarrels interpose,
Must often wipe a bloody nose.
Fables (1727) 'The Mastiffs' l. 1

6 How, like a moth, the simple maid
Still plays around the flame!
The Beggar's Opera (1728) act 1, sc. 4, air 4

7 The comfortable estate of widow-
hood, is the only hope that keeps
up a wife's spirits.
The Beggar's Opera (1728) act 1, sc. 10

8 If with me you'd fondly stray
Over the hills and far away.
The Beggar's Opera (1728) act 1, sc. 13, air 16

9 Youth's the season made for joys;
Love is then our duty.
The Beggar's Opera (1728) act 2, sc. 4, air 22

10 From wine what sudden friendship
springs!
Fables (1738) 'The Squire and his Cur' l. 4

11 That politician tops his part,
Who readily can lie with art.
Fables (1738) 'The Squire and his Cur' l. 27

Gay, Noel (Richard Moxon
Armitage) (1898–1954). British
songwriter

1 I'm leaning on a lamp-post at the
corner of the street.
'Leaning on a Lamp-Post' (1937); sung by
George Formby in the film *Father Knew Best*

Geldof, Bob and Ure, Midge
(1954–; 1953–). Irish rock musician;
Scottish rock musician

1 Do they know it's Christmas?
Title of song (1984)

Genet, Jean (1910–86). French
playwright, author and poet

1 *Ce qu'il nous faut, c'est la haine.
D'elle naîtront nos idées.*
Hatred is what we need. Ideas are
born from hatred.
Les Nègres (1958) epigraph

George, Daniel (Daniel George
Bunting) (1890–1967). English writer

1 O Freedom, what liberties are taken
in thy name!
The Perpetual Pessimist (1963) p. 58

George V (1865–1936). King of
Great Britain and Ireland from 1910

1 How's the Empire?
To his private secretary on the morning of
his death. *See* Kenneth Rose *King George V*
(1983) ch. 10

Gerety, Frances (1916–99).
copywriter at N. W. Ayer
advertising agency

1 A diamond is forever.
De Beers Consolidated Mines advertising
slogan, April 1947

**Gerhardie, William
(Alexander)** (1895–1977). English
novelist

1 There are as many fools at a university as anywhere … But their
folly, I admit, has a certain stamp –
the stamp of university training, if
you like. It is trained folly.
Polyglots (1925) ch. 7

Gershwin, Ira (Israel Gershowitz)
(1896–1983). US lyricist

1 I got rhythm.
Girl Crazy (1930) 'I Got Music' (music by
George Gershwin)

2 A foggy day in London Town.
Damsel in Distress (1937) 'A Foggy Day'
(music by George Gershwin)

3 Nice work if you can get it,
And you can get it if you try.
Damsel in Distress (1937) 'Nice Work If You
Can Get It' (music by George Gershwin)

4 They can't take that away from me!
Shall We Dance? (1937) 'They Can't Take That Away from Me' (music by George Gershwin)

5 You say potato and I say po-tah-to
You say tomato and I say to-mah-to...
Let's call the whole thing off!
Shall We Dance? (1937) 'Let's Call the Whole Thing Off'

6 Our love is here to stay.
The Goldwyn Follies (1938) 'Love is Here to Stay' (music by George Gershwin)

Getty, Jean Paul (1892–1976). American industrialist

1 If you can actually count your money, then you are not really a rich man.
In the *Observer* 3 November 1957

Giacosa, Giuseppe and Illica, Luigi (1847–1906; 1857–1919). Italian librettists

1 *Che gelida manina.*
Your tiny hand is frozen.
La Bohème (1896) act 1; music by Puccini (Rodolfo to Mimi)

Gibbon, Edward (1737–94). English historian

1 The principles of a free constitution are irrecoverably lost, when the legislative power is nominated by the executive.
The Decline and Fall of the Roman Empire (1776–88) ch. 3

2 History ... is, indeed, little more than the register of the crimes, follies, and misfortunes of mankind.
The Decline and Fall of the Roman Empire (1776–88) ch. 3

3 Corruption, the most infallible symptom of constitutional liberty.
The Decline and Fall of the Roman Empire (1776–88) ch. 21

4 My English text is chaste, and all licentious passages are left in the obscurity of a learned language.
Memoirs of My Life (1796) ch. 8 (parodied as 'decent obscurity' in the *Anti-Jacobin*, 1797–8)

Gibbons, Stella (1902–89). English novelist

1 Something nasty in the woodshed.
Cold Comfort Farm (1932) ch. 10

Gibran, Kahlil (1883–1931). Syrian writer and painter

1 Work is love made visible.
The Prophet (1923) 'On Work'

2 An exaggeration is a truth that has lost its temper.
Sand and Foam (1926) p. 59

Gide, André (Paul Guillaume) (1869–1951). French writer

1 *La sagesse n'est pas dans la raison, mais dans l'amour.*
Wisdom comes not from reason but from love.
Les Nourritures terrestres (1897) pt 1

Gilbert, W. S. (Sir William Schwenck Gilbert) (1836–1911). English writer of comic and satirical verse

1 What, never?
No, never!
What, *never*?
Hardly ever!
HMS Pinafore (1878) act 1

2 And so do his sisters, and his cousins and his aunts!
HMS Pinafore (1878) act 1

3 In short, in matters vegetable, animal, and mineral,
I am the very model of a modern Major-General.
The Pirates of Penzance (1879) act 1

4 When constabulary duty's to be done,
A policeman's lot is not a happy one.
The Pirates of Penzance (1879) act 2

5 Man is Nature's sole mistake!
Princess Ida (1884) act 2

6 A wandering minstrel I –
A thing of shreds and patches.
The Mikado (1885) act 1

7 I've got a little list.
The Mikado (1885) act 1

8 Three little maids from school are
we.
The Mikado (1885) act 1

9 Awaiting the sensation of a short,
sharp shock.
The Mikado (1885) act 1

10 My object all sublime
I shall achieve in time –
To let the punishment fit the
crime.
The Mikado (1885) act 2

11 On a tree by a river a little tom-tit
Sang 'Willow, titwillow, titwillow!'
The Mikado (1885) act 2

12 The flowers that bloom in the
spring,
Tra la.
The Mikado (1885) act 2

13 Take a pair of sparkling eyes.
The Gondoliers (1889) act 2

Gill, (Arthur) Eric (Rowton)
(1882–1940). English artist, type
designer and writer

1 The artist is not a special kind of
man but every man a special kind
of artist.
Art (1934) introduction

Ginsberg, Allen (1926–97).
American poet

1 What if someone gave a war &
Nobody came?
Life would ring the bells of Ecstasy
and Forever be Itself again.
The Fall of America (1973) 'Graffiti 12th
Cubicle Men's Room Syracuse Airport'

Gladstone, W(illiam) E(wart)
(1809–98). British Liberal politician
and Prime Minister

1 Finance is, as it were, the stomach
of the country, from which all the
other organs take their tone.
Article on finance, 1858, in H. C. G. Matthew
Gladstone 1809–1874 (1986) ch. 5

2 My mission is to pacify Ireland.
On receiving news that he was to form his
first cabinet, 1 December 1868, in H. C. G.
Matthew *Gladstone 1809–1874* (1986) ch. 5

3 We have been borne down in a
torrent of gin and beer.
Letter to his brother, 6 February 1874, in
John Morley *Life of William Ewart Gladstone*
(1903) vol. 2, ch. 14

**Gloucester, William Henry, 1st
Duke of** (1743–1805)

1 Another damned, thick, square
book! Always scribble, scribble,
scribble! Eh! Mr Gibbon?
In Henry Best *Personal and Literary Memorials* (1829) p. 68 (also attributed to the Duke
of Cumberland and King George III)

Godard, Jean-Luc (1930–). French
film director

1 *La photographie, c'est la vérité. Le
cinéma: la vérité vingt-quatre fois par
seconde.*
Photography is truth. The cinema
is truth twenty-four times per second.
Le Petit Soldat (film, 1960)

2 'Movies should have a beginning, a
middle and an end,' harrumphed
French film maker Georges Franju
… 'Certainly,' replied Jean-Luc
Godard. 'But not necessarily in that
order.'
In *Time* 14 September 1981

Goering, Hermann (1893–1946).
German Nazi leader

1 I herewith commission you to carry
out all preparations with regard to
… a *total solution* of the Jewish
question in those territories of
Europe which are under German
influence.
Instructions to Heydrich, 31 July 1941, in W.
L. Shirer *The Rise and Fall of the Third Reich*
(1962) bk 5, ch. 27

Goethe, Johann Wolfgang von
(1749–1832). German poet, novelist
and playwright

1 *Es bildet ein Talent sich in der Stille,
Sich ein Charakter in dem Strom der
Welt.*

Talent develops in quiet places,
character in the full current of
human life.
Torquato Tasso (1790) act 1, sc. 2

2 *Du musst herrschen und gewinnen,*
Oder dienen und verlieren,
Leiden oder triumphieren
Amboss oder Hammer sein.
You must be master and win, or
serve and lose, grieve or triumph,
be the anvil or the hammer.
Der Gross-Cophta (1791) act 2

3 *Es irrt der Mensch, so lang er strebt.*
Man will err while yet he strives.
Faust pt 1 (1808) 'Prolog im Himmel'

4 *Ich bin der Geist der stets verneint.*
I am the spirit that always denies.
Faust pt 1 (1808) 'Studierzimmer'

5 *Der Aberglaube ist die Poesie des Le-*
bens.
Superstition is the poetry of life.
Maximen und Reflexionen (1819) 'Literatur
und Sprache' no. 908

6 *Das Erste und Letzte, was vom Genie*
gefordert wird, ist Wahrheitsliebe.
The first and the last thing
demanded of genius is the love of
truth.
Sprüche in Prosa, Maximen und Reflexionen
(1819) pt 6

7 *Die Tat ist alles, nichts der Ruhm.*
The deed is all, the glory nothing.
Faust pt 2 (1832) 'Hochgebirg'

Goldberg, Isaac (1887–1938).
American writer and critic

1 Diplomacy is to do and say
The nastiest thing in the nicest
way.
The Reflex October 1927, p. 77

Goldsmith, Oliver (1730–74).
Anglo-Irish poet and playwright

1 The true use of speech is not so
much to express our wants as to
conceal them.
The Bee no. 3 (20 October 1759) 'On the Use
of Language'

2 Laws grind the poor, and rich men
rule the law.
The Traveller (1764) l. 386

3 The man recovered of the bite,
The dog it was that died.
'Elegy on the Death of a Mad Dog' (1766);
second line also the title of a play by Tom
Stoppard

4 When lovely woman stoops to folly
The Vicar of Wakefield (1766) ch. 29

5 Sweet Auburn, loveliest village of
the plain.
The Deserted Village (1770) l. 1

6 How happy he who crowns in
shades like these,
A youth of labour with an age of
ease.
The Deserted Village (1770) l. 99

7 Well had the boding tremblers
learned to trace
The day's disasters in his morning
face;
Full well they laughed with counterfeited glee,
At all his jokes, for many a joke had
he.
The Deserted Village (1770) l. 197

8 And still they gazed, and still the
wonder grew,
That one small head could carry all
he knew.
The Deserted Village (1770) l. 211

9 In all the silent manliness of grief.
The Deserted Village (1770) l. 384

10 Let schoolmasters puzzle their
brain,
With grammar, and nonsense, and
learning,
Good liquor, I stoutly maintain,
Gives genius a better discerning.
She Stoops to Conquer (1773) act 1, sc. 1
'Song'

11 The very pink of perfection.
She Stoops to Conquer (1773) act 1

12 The first blow is half the battle.
She Stoops to Conquer (1773) act 2

13 This is Liberty-Hall, gentlemen.
She Stoops to Conquer (1773) act 2

14 But there's no love lost between
us.
She Stoops to Conquer (1773) act 4

Goldwyn, Sam (Schmuel Gelbfisz)
(1882–1974). Polish-born American
film producer

1 Gentlemen, include me out.
On resigning from the Motion Picture Producers and Distributors of America, 1933; in
Michael Freedland *The Goldwyn Touch*
(1986) ch. 10

2 A verbal contract isn't worth the
paper it is written on.
In Alva Johnston *The Great Goldwyn* (1937)
ch. 1

3 Any man who goes to a psychiatrist
should have his head examined.
In Norman Zierold *Moguls* (1969) ch. 3

4 I'll give you a definite maybe.
Attributed

Gore, Al (Albert Gore Jr) (1948–).
American Vice-President 1993–
2001

1 I am Al Gore, and I used to be the
next president of the United States
of America.
Newsweek 19 March 2001

Gosse, Sir Edmund (1849–1928).
English poet and man of letters

1 A sheep in sheep's clothing.
Of the 'woolly-bearded poet' Sturge
Moore, in F. Greenslet *Under the Bridge*
(1943) ch. 10

Grahame, Kenneth (1859–1932).
Scottish writer

1 There is *nothing* – absolutely nothing – half so much worth doing as
simply messing about in boats.
The Wind in the Willows (1908) ch. 1

Grant, Ulysses S(impson) (1822–
85). American soldier and 18th
President of the USA

1 I only know two tunes. One of
them is 'Yankee Doodle', and the
other isn't.
Attributed

Graves, John Woodcock (1795–
1886). British huntsman and
songwriter

1 D'ye ken John Peel with his coat so
grey?
'John Peel' (1820)

Graves, Robert (1895–1985).
English poet

1 Far away is close at hand.
'Song of Contrariety' (1923)

2 Goodbye to all that.
Title of autobiography (1929)

3 To be a poet is a condition rather
than a profession.
Response to a questionnaire from the editor
of *Horizon* (1946)

4 In love as in sport, the amateur
status must be strictly maintained.
Occupation: Writer (1950) 'Lars Porsena'

5 If there's no money in poetry, nei-
ther is there poetry in money.
Speech at London School of Economics, 6
December 1963

Gray, John (1951–). American
writer

1 Men are from Mars, women are
from Venus.
Title of book (1992)

Gray, Thomas (1716–71). English
poet

1 The language of the age is never the
language of poetry.
Letter to Richard West, 8 April 1742, in H. W.
Starr (ed.) *Correspondence of Thomas Gray*
(1971) vol. 1

2 Since sorrow never comes too late,
And happiness too swiftly flies.
Ode on a Distant Prospect of Eton College
(1747) l. 96

3 Where ignorance is bliss,
'Tis folly to be wise.
Ode on a Distant Prospect of Eton College
(1747) l. 99

4 Nor all, that glisters, gold.
'Ode on the Death of a Favourite Cat' (1748)

5 The untaught harmony of spring.
'Ode on the Spring' (1748) l. 5

6 The curfew tolls the knell of parting
day,
The lowing herd wind slowly o'er
the lea,
The ploughman homeward plods
his weary way,
And leaves the world to darkness
and to me.
Elegy Written in a Country Churchyard (1751)
l. 1

7 And drowsy tinklings lull the distant folds.
Elegy Written in a Country Churchyard (1751)
l. 8

8 Beneath those rugged elms, that
yew-tree's shade,
Where heaves the turf in many a
mouldering heap,
Each in his narrow cell for ever laid,
The rude forefathers of the hamlet
sleep.
Elegy Written in a Country Churchyard (1751)
l. 13

9 The short and simple annals of the
poor.
Elegy Written in a Country Churchyard (1751)
l. 32

10 The paths of glory lead but to the
grave.
Elegy Written in a Country Churchyard (1751)
l. 36

11 Full many a flower is born to blush
unseen,
And waste its sweetness on the
desert air.
Elegy Written in a Country Churchyard (1751)
l. 55

12 Some mute inglorious Milton here
may rest.
Elegy Written in a Country Churchyard (1751)
l. 59

13 Far from the madding crowd's
ignoble strife.
Elegy Written in a Country Churchyard (1751)
l. 73

14 A youth to fortune and to fame
unknown.
Elegy Written in a Country Churchyard (1751)
l. 118

Greeley, Horace (1811–72).
American founder and editor of the
New York Tribune

1 Go West, young man.
Hints toward Reforms (1850)

Green, Hannah (Joanne
Greenberg) (1932–). American
novelist

1 I never promised you a rose garden.
Title of novel (1964)

Greene, Graham (1904–91).
English novelist

1 There is always one moment in
childhood when the door opens
and lets the future in.
The Power and the Glory (1940) pt 1, ch. 1

2 Evil ran like malaria in his veins.
The Power and the Glory (1940) pt 3, ch. 1

3 If only it were possible to love
without injury – fidelity isn't
enough.
The Quiet American (1955) pt 2, ch. 3

4 Fame is a powerful aphrodisiac.
In the *Radio Times* 10 September 1964

5 An autobiography is only 'a sort of
life' – it may contain less errors of
fact than a biography, but it is of
necessity even more selective: it
begins later and it ends prema-
turely.
A Sort of Life (1971) preface

6 Writing is a form of therapy.
Ways of Escape (1980) ch. 9

7 The world is not black and white.
More like black and grey.
Quoted in 'Sayings of the Year', the
Observer December 1982

Greene, Robert (c.1560–92).
English poet and playwright

1 Ah! what is love! It is a pretty thing,
As sweet unto a shepherd as a king.
'The Shepherd's Wife's Song' (1590)

Greenspan, Alan (1926–).
American financier and economist

1 The buck starts here.
Sign on his desk; quoted in Bob Woodward
The Agenda (1994)

Gregory the Great (AD C.540–604). Pope from 590

1 *Non Angli sed Angeli.*
Not Angles but Angels.
Oral tradition. *See* Bede *Historia Ecclesiastica* bk 2, sect. 1

Grenfell, Joyce (née Phipps) (1910–79). English comedienne

1 George – don't do that.
Catchphrase from one of her comic monologues, and title of her autobiography (1977)

Grey, Sir Edward (Viscount Grey of Fallodon) (1862–1933). British Liberal politician

1 The lamps are going out all over Europe; we shall not see them lit again in our lifetime.
25 Years (1925) vol. 2, ch. 18 (on the eve of the First World War)

Gurney, Dorothy Frances (1858–1932). English poet and hymn-writer

1 One is nearer God's Heart in a garden
Than anywhere else on earth.
'God's Garden' (1913)

Guthrie, Woody (Woodrow Wilson Guthrie) (1912–67). American folksinger and songwriter

1 This land was made for you and me.
'This Land is Your Land' (1956 song)

Haggard, Rider (Sir Henry Rider Haggard) (1856–1925). English writer

1 She who must be obeyed.
She (1887) ch. 6 and *passim*

Hahnemann, C(hristian) F(riedrich) S(amuel) (1755–1843). German physician; founder of homeopathy

1 *Similia similibus curantur.*
Like cures like.
Motto of homeopathic medicine, although not found in this form in Hahnemann's writings

Halifax, 1st Marquis of (George Savile) (1633–95). English statesman and essayist

1 Anger is never without an argument, but seldom with a good one.
Political, Moral, and Miscellaneous Thoughts and Reflections (1750) 'Of Anger'

2 Malice is of a low stature, but it hath very long arms.
Political, Moral, and Miscellaneous Thoughts and Reflections (1750) 'Of Malice and Envy'

3 Men are not hanged for stealing horses, but that horses may not be stolen.
Political, Moral, and Miscellaneous Thoughts and Reflections (1750) 'Of Punishment'

Hall, Joseph (1574–1656). English bishop

1 Perfection is the child of Time.
Works (1625) p. 670

Halm, Friedrich (Baron von Münch-Bellinghausen) (1806–71). German playwright

1 Two souls with but a single thought,
Two hearts that beat as one.
Der Sohn der Wildnis (1842) act 2 *ad fin.*
(translated by Maria Lovell as *Ingomar the Barbarian*, 1854)

Hamilton, Sir William (1788–1856). Scottish metaphysician

1 Truth, like a torch, the more it's shook it shines.
Discussions on Philosophy (1852) title page (epigram)

Hammerstein II, Oscar (1895–1960). American songwriter

1 Ol' man river.
Showboat (1927) 'Ol' Man River' (music by Jerome Kern)

2 When I grow too old to dream
Your love will live in my heart.
The Night is Young (1935)

3 You are the promised kiss of springtime.
'All the Things You Are' (1940)

4 As you walk through the storm,
Hold your head up high,
And don't be afraid of the dark,
Carousel, 'You'll Never Walk Alone' (1945);
later (1963) given a pop version by Gerry and the Pacemakers and adopted as a club song by Liverpool Football Club

5 The hills are alive with the sound of music.
The Sound of Music (1959)

Hankey, Kate (1834–1911). English evangelist

1 Tell me the old, old story.
'Tell me the old, old story' (1867 hymn)

Hanrahan, Brian (1949–). British journalist

1 I counted them all out and I
counted them all back.
On the number of British aeroplanes (which
he was not permitted to disclose) joining
the raid on Port Stanley in the Falkland
Islands; BBC broadcast report, 1 May 1982,
in *Battle for the Falklands* (1982) p. 21

Harbach, Otto (1873–1963).
American songwriter

1 When a lovely flame dies,
Smoke gets in your eyes.
'Smoke Gets in your Eyes' (1933) (music by
Jerome Kern)

Harburg, E(dgar) Y(ip) (1898–
1981). American songwriter

1 Brother can you spare a dime?
Title of song (1932)

2 Somewhere over the rainbow.
The Wizard of Oz (1939) 'Over the Rainbow'

3 It's that Old Devil Moon in your
eyes.
Finian's Rainbow (1946) 'Old Devil Moon'

Hardy, Thomas (1840–1928).
English novelist and poet

1 A lover without indiscretion is no
lover at all.
The Hand of Ethelberta (1876) ch. 20

2 It had a lonely face, suggesting
tragical possibilities.
The Return of the Native (1878) bk 1, ch. 1
(Egdon Heath)

3 'Justice' was done, and the
President of the Immortals (in
Aeschylean phrase) had ended his
sport with Tess.
Tess of the D'Urbervilles (1891) ch. 59

4 A novel is an impression, not an
argument.
Tess of the D'Urbervilles (5th edn, 1892)
preface

5 War makes rattling good history;
but Peace is poor reading.
The Dynasts (1904) pt 1, act 2, sc. 5

6 Yes; quaint and curious war is!
You shoot a fellow down
You'd treat if met where any bar is,
Or help to half-a-crown.
'The Man he Killed' (1909)

7 What of the faith and fire within us
Men who march away?
'Men Who March Away' (1914)

8 Yonder a maid and her wight
Come whispering by:
War's annals will cloud into night
Ere their story die.
'In Time of "The Breaking of Nations"'
(1917)

Hargreaves, W(illiam) F. (1846–
1919). British songwriter

1 I'm Burlington Bertie
I rise at ten thirty.
'Burlington Bertie from Bow' (1915 song)

Harington, Sir John (1561–1612).
English writer and courtier

1 Treason doth never prosper, what's
the reason?
For if it prosper, none dare call it
treason.
Epigrams (1618) bk 4, no. 5

Harkness, Richard Long (1907–
1977). American radio and
television news commentator

1 A group of the unwilling, picked
from the unfit, to do the unnecessary.
Definition of a committee. In the *New York
Herald Tribune* 15 June 1960

Harlech, Lord (David Ormsby
Gore) (1918–85). British Ambassador
to Washington, 1961–5

1 Britain will be honoured by his-
torians more for the way she dis-
posed of an empire than for the
way in which she acquired it.
In the *New York Times* 28 October 1962, sect.
4, p. 11

Harlow, Jean (Harlean Carpentier)
(1911–37). American actress

1 Excuse me while I slip into something more comfortable.
Line delivered in *Hell's Angels* (1930)

Harris, Joel Chandler (1848–1908). American writer

1 Bred en bawn in a brier-patch!
Uncle Remus: His Songs and His Sayings (1880) 'How Mr. Rabbit Was Too Sharp for Mr. Fox'

Harris, Rolf (1930–). Australian entertainer and artist

1 Tie me kangaroo down, sport.
Title of song, 1950s

Hart, Lorenz (1895–1943). American songwriter

1 That's why the lady is a tramp.
Babes in Arms (1937) 'The Lady is a Tramp' (music by Richard Rodgers)

2 Bewitched, bothered, and bewildered am I.
Pal Joey (1941) 'Bewitched' (music by Richard Rodgers)

Hartley, L(eslie) P(oles) (1895–1972). English novelist

1 The past is a foreign country: they do things differently there.
The Go-Between (1953) prologue

Haskins, Minnie Louise (1875–1951). English author and educationist

1 And I said to the man who stood at the gate of the year:
'Give me a light that I may tread safely into the unknown.'
And he replied:
'Go out into the darkness and put your hand into the hand of God.
That shall be to you better than light and safer than a known way.'
Desert, 'God Knows' (1908); quoted by King George VI, Christmas address, 25 December 1939

Hawker, R(obert) S(tephen) (1803–75). English clergyman and poet

1 And shall Trelawny die?
'The Song of the Western Men' (referring to the imprisonment by James II, in 1688, of Bishop Trelawny of Bristol)

Hawking, Stephen (William) (1942–). British theoretical physicist

1 God not only plays dice. He also sometimes throws the dice where they cannot be seen.
In *Nature* (1975) vol. 257

2 If we find the answer to that [why it is that we and the universe exist], it would be the ultimate triumph of human reason – for then we would know the mind of God.
A Brief History of Time (1988) ch. 11

Hawthorne, Nathaniel (1804–64). American novelist

1 We sometimes congratulate ourselves at the moment of waking from a troubled dream: it may be so the moment after death.
The American Notebooks (c.1836) ch. 1

Hay, Ian (John Hay Beith) (1876–1952). Scottish novelist and playwright

1 What do you mean, funny? Funny-peculiar or funny ha-ha?
The Housemaster (1938) act 3

Hayes, J. Milton (1884–1940). British writer

1 There's a one-eyed yellow idol to the north of Khatmandu,
There's a little marble cross below the town,
There's a broken-hearted woman tends the grave of Mad Carew,
And the Yellow God forever gazes down.
The Green Eye of the Yellow God (1911)

Hazlitt, William (1778–1830). English essayist

1 Fashion constantly begins and ends in the two things it abhors most, singularity and vulgarity.
'On Fashion', in the *Scots Magazine* (1818)

2 The love of liberty is the love of others; the love of power is the love of ourselves.
Political Essays (1819) 'The Times Newspaper'

3 A nickname is the heaviest stone that the devil can throw at a man.
Sketches and Essays (1839) 'Nicknames'

4 The greatest offence against virtue is to speak ill of it.
Sketches and Essays (1839) 'On Cant and Hypocrisy'

5 Rules and models destroy genius and art.
Sketches and Essays (1839) 'On Taste'

Healey, Denis Winston (Baron Healey) (1917–). British Labour politician

1 That part of his speech was rather like being savaged by a dead sheep.
Responding to a speech by Chancellor of the Exchequer Sir Geoffrey Howe, House of Commons, June 1988

Heaney, Seamus (1939–). Irish poet

1 My passport's green.
No glass of ours was ever raised To toast *The Queen*.
Open Letter (Field Day pamphlet no. 2, 1983) p. 9, criticizing the editors of *The Penguin Book of Contemporary British Poetry* for including him among its authors

Hearst, William Randolph (1863–1951). American newspaper proprietor

1 You furnish the pictures and I'll furnish the war.
Telegram to the artist Frederic Remington at the beginning of the Spanish–American War in Cuba, March 1898

Hegel, Georg Wilhelm Friedrich (1770–1831). German idealist philosopher

1 Poetry is the universal art of the spirit.
Introduction to Aesthetics (1842, translated by T. M. Knox, 1979) p. 89

2 Political genius consists in identifying oneself with a principle.
Constitution of Germany

Heine, Heinrich (1797–1856). German poet

1 *Dort, wo man Bücher Verbrennt, verbrennt man auch am Ende Menschen.*
Wherever books will be burned, men also, in the end, are burned.
Almansor (1823) l. 245

2 *Auf Flügeln des Gesanges.*
On wings of song.
Title of song (1823)

3 *Dieu me pardonnera, c'est son métier.*
God will pardon me, it is His trade.
On his deathbed, in Alfred Meissner *Heinrich Heine. Erinnerungen* (1856) ch. 5

Heisenberg, Werner (1901–76). German physicist

1 An expert is someone who knows some of the worst mistakes that can be made in his subject and who manages to avoid them.
Der Teil und das Ganze (1969), trans. by A. J. Pomerans as *Physics and Beyond* (1971) ch. 17

Heller, Joseph (1923–99). American novelist

1 There was only one catch and that was Catch-22, which specified that a concern for one's own safety in the face of dangers that were real and immediate was the process of a rational mind.
Catch-22 (1961) ch. 5

Hellman, Lillian (Florence) (1907–84). American playwright

1 If I had to give young writers advice, I would say don't listen to writers talking about writing or themselves.
In the *New York Times* 21 February 1960

Helvétius (Claude Arien Helvétius) (1715–71). French philosopher

1 *L'éducation nous faisait ce que nous sommes.*
Education made us what we are.
De l'esprit (1758) 'Discours 3' ch. 30

Hemans, Felicia (neé Browne)
(1793–1835). English poet

1 The boy stood on the burning deck
Whence all but he had fled.
'Casabianca' (1849)

2 The stately homes of England,
How beautiful they stand!
'The Homes of England' (1849)

Hemingway, Ernest (1899–1961).
American novelist

1 A man's got to take a lot of punishment to write a really funny
book.
Letter, 6 December 1924

2 Don't you like to write letters? I do
because it's such a swell way to
keep from working and yet feel
you've done something.
Letter to F. Scott Fitzgerald, 1 July 1925

3 About morals, I know only that
what is moral is what you feel good
after and what is immoral is what
you feel bad after.
Death in the Afternoon (1932) ch. 1

4 Madame, all stories, if continued
far enough, end in death, and he is
no true story-teller who would
keep that from you.
Death in the Afternoon (1932) ch. 11

5 No classic resembles any previous
classic, so do not be discouraged.
Advice to young writers, in McCall's, May
1956

6 Once writing has become your
major vice and greatest pleasure
only death can stop it.
Interview in the Paris Review, spring 1958

7 I always try to write as good as the
best picture that was ever painted.
Quoted in the Saturday Review, 9 May 1964

8 Paris is a movable feast.
A Movable Feast (1964) epigraph

Henley, W(illiam) E(rnest)
(1849–1903). English poet and
playwright

1 In the fell clutch of circumstance,
I have not winced nor cried aloud:
Under the bludgeonings of chance
My head is bloody but unbowed.
'Invictus' (1888) collected in In Hospital
(1903)

2 I am the master of my fate:
I am the captain of my soul.
'Invictus. In Memoriam R.T.H.B.' (1888)

Henri IV (of Navarre) (1553–1610).
King of France from 1589

1 The wisest fool in Christendom.
Of James I of England; attributed both to
Henri IV and Sully (French original not
known)

Henry, Patrick (1736–99).
American statesman

1 Give me liberty, or give me death!
Speech in Virginia Convention, 23 March
1775, in William Wirt Patrick Henry (1818) sect.
4, p. 123

Henry, Philip (1631–96). English
clergyman

1 All this, and heaven too!
In Matthew Henry Life of Mr Philip Henry
(1698) ch. 5

Henry II (1133–89). King of England
from 1154

1 Will no one rid me of this turbulent
priest?
Of Thomas Becket, Archbishop of Canterbury, murdered in Canterbury Cathedral,
December 1170. Oral tradition

Hepworth, Barbara (1903–75).
English sculptor

1 There is an inside and an outside to
every form.
A Pictorial Autobiography (1970)

Heraclitus (c.540–c.480 BC). Greek
philosopher

1 You can't step twice into the same
river.
In Plato Cratylus 402a

Herbert, George (1593–1633).
English poet and clergyman

1 I struck the board, and cried, 'No more.
I will abroad.'
'The Collar' (1633)

2 The God of love my Shepherd is.
'The 23rd Psalm' (1633)

3 Sweet day, so cool, so calm, so bright,
The bridal of the earth and sky.
'Virtue' (1633)

4 Love bade me welcome.
'Love: Love bade me welcome' (1633)

5 'You must sit down,' says Love, 'and taste my meat.'
So I did sit and eat.
'Love: Love bade me welcome' (1633)

6 Only a sweet and virtuous soul,
Like seasoned timber, never gives;
But though the whole world turn to coal,
Then chiefly lives.
'Virtue' (1633)

7 My crooked winding ways, wherein I live.
'A Wreath' (1633)

8 A broken Altar, Lord, thy servant rears,
Made of a heart, and cemented with tears.
'The Altar' (1633)

9 Joy, I did lock thee up; but some bad man
Hath let thee out again.
'The Bunch of Grapes' (1633)

10 He that makes a good war makes a good peace.
Outlandish Proverbs (1640) no. 420

11 He that lives in hope danceth without music.
Outlandish Proverbs (1640) no. 1006

12 Music helps not the toothache.
Jacula Prudentum (1640)

13 God's mill grinds slow, but sure.
Jacula Prudentum (1651)

14 He that will learn to pray, let him go to sea.
Jacula Prudentum (1651)

Herbert, Sir A(lan) P(atrick)
(1890–1971). English writer and politician

1 Well, fancy giving money to the Government!
Might as well have put it down the drain.
Fancy giving money to the Government!
Nobody will see the stuff again.
'Too Much!' (1931)

2 People must not do things for fun. We are not here for fun. There is no reference to fun in any Act of Parliament.
Uncommon Law (1935) 'Is it a Free Country?'

3 The critical period in matrimony is breakfast-time.
Uncommon Law (1935) 'Is Marriage Lawful?'

4 Nothing is wasted, nothing is in vain:
The seas roll over but the rocks remain.
Tough at the Top (operetta c.1949)

Herrick, Robert (1591–1674). English poet and clergyman

1 But ne'er the rose without the thorn.
'The Rose' (1647)

2 Cherry-ripe, ripe, ripe, I cry,
Full and fair ones; come and buy.
'Cherry-Ripe' (1648)

3 Love is a circle that doth restless move
In the same sweet eternity of love.
'Love What It Is' (1648)

4 Fair daffodils, we weep to see
You haste away so soon.
'To Daffodils' (1648)

5 Gather ye rosebuds while ye may.
'To the Virgins, to Make Much of Time' (1648)

Hesse, Hermann (1877–1962). German novelist and poet

1 If you hate a person, you hate something in him that is part of yourself. What isn't part of ourselves doesn't disturb us.
Demian (1919)

Hewart, Gordon (Viscount Hewart) (1870–1943). British lawyer and politician

1 Justice should not only be done, but should manifestly and undoubtedly be seen to be done.
Rex. v Sussex Justices, 9 November 1923, in *Law Reports King's Bench Division* (1924) vol. 1, p. 259

Heyward, Du Bose (1885–1940). American songwriter

1 Summer time an' the livin' is easy.
Porgy and Bess (1935) 'Summertime' (with Ira Gershwin; music by George Gershwin)

Hickson, William Eward (1803–70). British educator and writer on singing

1 If at first you don't succeed, Try, try again.
'Try and Try Again' (1857)

Higley, Brewster (1823–1911). American songwriter

1 Oh give me a home where the buffalo roam,
Where the deer and the antelope play,
Where seldom is heard a discouraging word
And the skies are not cloudy all day.
'Home on the Range' (c.1873)

Hill, Joe (Joel Hägglund) (1879–1915). American labour leader and songwriter

1 You will eat, by and by, In that glorious land above the sky;
Work and pray, live on hay,
You'll get pie in the sky when you die.
Songs of the Workers (1911) 'Preacher and the Slave'

Hill, Pattie S. (1868–1946). American educationist

1 Happy birthday to you.
Title of song (1935); music by Mildred J. Hill

Hill, Rowland (1744–1833). English clergyman

1 He did not see any reason why the devil should have all the good tunes.
In E. W. Broome *The Rev. Rowland Hill* (1881) ch. 7

Hillary, Sir Edmund (1919–). New Zealand mountaineer

1 Well, we knocked the bastard off!
On conquering Mount Everest, 1953

Hillebrand, Fred (1893–1963).

1 Home James, and don't spare the horses.
Title of song (1934)

Hillingdon, Lady (1857–1940).

1 When I hear his steps outside my door I lie down on my bed, close my eyes, open my legs, and think of England.
Journal 1912, in J. Gathorne-Hardy *The Rise and Fall of the British Nanny* (1972) ch. 3

Hippocrates (c.460 BC–c.370 BC). Greek physician

1 Science is the father of knowledge, but opinion breeds ignorance.
The Canon vol. 4 (trans. by John Chadwick)

2 Life is short, the art long.
Aphorisms sect. 1, para. 1 (trans. by W. H. S. Jones) and often quoted 'Ars longa, vita brevis'

Hirsch Jr, E(ric) D(onald) (1928–). American educational reformer

1 Cultural literacy is the oxygen of social intercourse.
Cultural Literacy: What Every American Needs to Know (1987) introduction

Hitchcock, Sir Alfred (Joseph) (1899–1980). English film director

1 Television has brought back murder into the home – where it belongs.
In the *Observer* 19 December 1965

2 The more successful the villain, the more successful the picture.
Quoted in François Truffaut *Hitchcock* (1968)

Hitler, Adolf (1889–1945). German dictator

1 *Die breite Masse eines Volkes … fällt einer grossen Lüge leichter zum Opfer als einer kleinen.*
The broad mass of a nation … will more easily fall victim to a big lie than to a small one.
Mein Kampf (1925) vol. 1, ch. 10

2 *Die Nacht der langen Messer.*
The night of the long knives.
Phrase given to the massacre of Ernst Roehm and his associates by Hitler on 29–30 June 1934, though taken from an early Nazi marching song; later associated with Harold Macmillan's Cabinet dismissals of 13 July 1962

3 *Wer in Europa die Brandfackel des Krieges erhebt, kann nur das Chaos wünschen.*
Whoever lights the torch of war in Europe can wish for nothing but chaos.
Speech in the Reichstag, Berlin, 21 May 1935

Hobbes, Thomas (1588–1679).
English political philosopher

1 Words are wise men's counters, they do but reckon by them: but they are the money of fools.
Leviathan (1651) pt 1, ch. 4

2 Science is the knowledge of consequences and the dependence of one fact upon another.
Leviathan (1651), pt 1, ch. 5

3 They that approve a private opinion, call it opinion; but they that mislike it, heresy: and yet heresy signifies no more than private opinion.
Leviathan (1651) pt 1, ch. 11

4 No arts; no letters; no society; and which is worst of all, continual fear and danger of violent death; and the life of man, solitary, poor, nasty, brutish, and short.
Leviathan (1651) pt 1, ch. 13

Hodgson, Ralph (1871–1962).
English poet

1 Time, you old gipsy man,
Will you not stay,
Put up your caravan
Just for one day?
'Time, You Old Gipsy Man' (1917)

Hoffman, August Heinrich
(Hoffman von Fallersleben) (1798–1874). German poet

1 *Deutschland über alles.*
Germany above all.
Title of poem (1841)

Hoffnung, Gerard (1925–59).
English humorist

1 Standing among savage scenery, the hotel offers stupendous revelations. There is a French widow in every bedroom, affording delightful prospects.
Supposedly quoting a letter from a Tyrolean landlord; in a speech at the Oxford Union, 4 December 1958

Hogarth, William (1697–1764).
English painter and engraver

1 Simplicity, without variety, is wholly insipid.
The Analysis of Beauty (1753)

Holbach, Paul Henri, Baron d'
(1723–89). French philosopher

1 *L'art n'est que la Nature agissante à l'aide des instruments qu'elle a faits.*
Art is only Nature operating with the aid of the instruments she has made.
Système de la Nature (1780 edn) pt 1, ch. 1

Holland, Henry Scott (1847–1918).
English theologian and preacher

1 Death is nothing at all; it does not count. I have only slipped away into the next room.
Sermon preached on Whitsunday 1910, in *Facts of the Faith* (1919) 'The King of Terrors'

Hollweg, Theobald von Bethmann (1856–1921). Chancellor of Germany, 1909–17

1 Just for a word 'neutrality' – a word which in wartime has so often been disregarded – just for a scrap of

paper, Great Britain is going to make war on a kindred nation who desires nothing better than to be friends with her.
Summary of a report by Sir E. Goschen to Sir Edward Grey in *British Documents on Origins of the War 1898–1914* (1926) vol. 11, p. 351

Holmes, John H. (1879–1964). American Unitarian minister

1 This universe is not hostile, nor yet is it friendly. It is simply indifferent.
The Sensible Man's View of Religion (1932) ch. 4

Holmes, Oliver Wendell (1809–94). American physician, poet and essayist

1 A moment's insight is sometimes worth a life's experience.
The Autocrat of the Breakfast Table (1857–8) ch. 1

2 A thought is often original, though you have uttered it a hundred times.
The Autocrat of the Breakfast Table (1857–8) ch. 1

3 Put not your trust in money, but put your money in trust.
The Autocrat of the Breakfast Table (1857–8) ch. 2

4 Knowledge and timber shouldn't be much used till they are seasoned.
The Autocrat of the Breakfast Table (1857–8) ch. 6

5 Nothing is so common-place as to wish to be remarkable.
The Autocrat of the Breakfast Table (1857–8) ch. 12

6 We must have a weak spot or two in a character before we can love it much.
The Professor at the Breakfast Table (1858–9) ch. 3

7 Apology is only egotism wrong side out.
The Professor at the Breakfast Table (1858–9) ch. 6

8 Fashion is only the attempt to realize Art in living forms and social intercourse.
The Professor at the Breakfast Table (1858–9) ch. 6

9 It is the province of knowledge to speak and it is the privilege of wisdom to listen.
The Poet at the Breakfast Table (1872) ch. 10

Homer (8c BC). Greek epic poet

1 Winged words.
The Iliad bk 1, l. 201 and elsewhere

2 Like that of leaves is a generation of men.
The Iliad bk 6, l. 146

3 Smiling through her tears.
The Iliad bk 6, l. 484

4 It is no shame for a man to die fighting for his country.
The Iliad, bk 15, l. 496

5 It lies in the lap of the gods.
The Iliad bk 17, l. 514 and elsewhere

6 Rosy-fingered dawn.
The Odyssey bk 2, l. 1 and elsewhere

Honegger, Arthur (1892–1955). Franco-Swiss composer

1 The modern composer is a madman who persists in manufacturing an article which nobody wants.
I am a Composer (1951)

2 The public doesn't want new music: the main thing it demands of a composer is that he be dead.
I am a Composer (1951)

Hood, Thomas (1799–1845). English poet and humorist

1 I remember, I remember,
The house where I was born,
The little window where the sun
Came peeping in at morn.
'I Remember' (1826)

2 It was a childish ignorance,
But now 'tis little joy
To know I'm farther off from heav'n
Than when I was a boy.
'I Remember' (1826).

3 They went and told the sexton, and
The sexton tolled the bell.
'Faithless Sally Brown' (1826)

Hoover, Herbert (1874–1964). 31st
President of the USA

1 Older men declare war. But it is
youth who must fight and die.
Speech at the Republican National Convention, Chicago, 27 June 1944, in *Addresses upon the American Road* (1946) p. 254

2 All men are equal before a fish.
(1951) Quoted in Colin Jarman *The Guinness Dictionary of Sports Quotations* (1990)

3 Honour is not the exclusive property of any political party.
In *Christian Science Monitor* 21 May 1964

Hope, Anthony (Sir Anthony Hope
Hawkins) (1863–1933). English
novelist

1 Economy is going without something you do want in case you
should, some day, want something
you probably won't want.
The Dolly Dialogues (1894) no. 12

2 Bourgeois … is an epithet which
the riff-raff apply to what is
respectable, and the aristocracy to
what is decent.
The Dolly Dialogues (1894) no. 17

3 His foe was folly and his weapon
wit.
Inscription on W. S. Gilbert's memorial on
the Victoria Embankment, London, 1915

Hope, Bob (1903–2003). American
comedian

1 A bank is a place that will lend you
money if you can prove that you
don't need it.
In Alan Harrington *Life in the Crystal Palace*
(1959) 'The Tyranny of Farms'

Hopkins, Gerard Manley (1844–
89). English poet and priest

1 The world is charged with the
grandeur of God.
'God's Grandeur' (written 1877)

2 Glory be to God for dappled things.
'Pied Beauty' (written 1877)

3 I caught this morning morning's
minion, kingdom of daylight's
dauphin, dapple-dawn-drawn
Falcon.
'The Windhover' (written 1877)

4 My heart in hiding
Stirred for a bird, – the achieve of,
the mastery of the thing!
'The Windhover' (written 1877)

5 O let them be left, wildness and
wet;
Long live the weeds and the wilderness yet.
'Inversnaid' (written 1881)

6 Not, I'll not, carrion comfort, Despair, not feast on thee.
'Carrion Comfort' (written 1885)

Hopper, Edward (1882–1967).
American painter

1 A nation's art is greatest when it
most reflects the character of its
people.
Quoted in Anatole Broyard *Aroused by Books*
(1974)

Horace (Quintus Horatius Flaccus)
(65–8 BC). Roman poet

1 *Inceptis gravibus plerumque et magna
professis
Purpureus, late qui splendeat, unus et
alter.
Adsuitur pannus.*
Works of serious purpose and
grand promises often have a purple
patch or two stitched on, to shine
far and wide.
Ars Poetica l. 14

2 *Si vis me flere, dolendum est
Primum ipsi tibi.*
If you want me to weep, you must
first feel grief yourself.
Ars Poetica l. 102

3 *Indignor quandoque bonus dormitat
Homerus.*
I'm aggrieved when sometimes
even excellent Homer nods.
Ars Poetica l. 359

4 *Ut pictura poesis.*
A poem is like a painting.
Ars Poetica l. 361

5 *Ira furor brevis est.*
Anger is a short madness.
Epistles bk 1, no. 2, l. 62

6 *Omnem crede diem tibi diluxisse supremum.*
Believe each day that has dawned is your last.
Epistles bk 1, no. 4, l. 13

7 *O imitatores, servum pecus.*
O imitators, you slavish herd.
Epistles bk 1, no. 19, l. 19

8 *Scribimus indocti doctique poemata passim.*
Skilled or unskilled, we all scribble poems.
Epistles bk 2, no. 1, l. 117.

9 *Atque inter silvas Academi quaerere verum.*
And seek for truth in the groves of Academe.
Epistles bk 2, no. 2, l. 45

10 *Vitae summa brevis spem nos vetat incohare longam.*
Life's short span forbids us to enter on far-reaching hopes.
Odes bk 1, no. 4, l. 15

11 *Nil desperandum.*
Never despair.
Odes bk 1, no. 7, l. 27

12 *Carpe diem, quam minimum credula postero.*
Seize the day, put no trust in the future.
Odes bk 1, no. 11, l. 7

13 *Dulce et decorum est pro patria mori.*
Sweet and honourable it is to die for one's country.
Odes bk 3, no. 2, l. 13

14 *Exegi monumentum aere perennius.*
I have erected a monument more lasting than bronze.
Odes bk 3, no. 30, l. 1

15 *Est modus in rebus.*
There is moderation in everything.
Satires bk 1, no. 1, l. 106

16 *Hoc genus omne.*
All that tribe.
Satires bk 1, no. 2, l. 2

Housman, A(lfred) E(dward)
(1859–1936). English poet

1 Loveliest of trees, the cherry now
Is hung with bloom along the bough.
A Shropshire Lad (1896) no. 2

2 And silence sounds no worse than cheers
After dying has stopped the ears.
A Shropshire Lad (1896) no. 19

3 What are those blue remembered hills,
What spires, what farms are those?
A Shropshire Lad (1896) no. 40

4 And malt does more than Milton can
To justify God's ways to man.
A Shropshire Lad (1896) no. 62

5 I, a stranger and afraid
In a world I never made.
Last Poems (1922) no. 12

6 Life, to be sure, is nothing much to lose;
But young men think it is, and we were young.
More Poems (1936) no. 36

Howe, Julia Ward (1819–1910).
American Unitarian lay preacher

1 Mine eyes have seen the glory of the coming of the Lord.
'Battle Hymn of the Republic' (1862)

Howell, James (c.1593–1666).
Anglo-Welsh man of letters

1 One hair of a woman can draw more than a hundred pair of oxen.
Familiar Letters (1645–55) bk 2, no. 4

Howitt, Mary (née Botham) (1799–1888). English writer for children

1 'Will you walk into my parlour?' said a spider to a fly.
'The Spider and the Fly' (1834)

Hoyle, Sir Fred (1915–2001). British astrophysicist

1 Space isn't remote at all. It's only an hour's drive away if your car could go straight upwards.
In the *Observer* 9 September 1979

Hubbard, Elbert (Green) (1859–1915). American writer, editor and printer

1 Never explain – your friends do not need it and your enemies will not believe you anyway.
The Motto Book (1907) p. 31

2 Life is just one damned thing after another.
Philistine December 1909, p. 32 (often attributed to Frank Ward O'Malley)

3 Little minds are interested in the extraordinary; great minds in the commonplace.
Thousand and One Epigrams (1911)

4 One machine can do the work of fifty ordinary men. No machine can do the work of one extraordinary man.
Thousand and One Epigrams (1911)

5 Editor: a person employed by a newspaper, whose business it is to separate the wheat from the chaff, and to see that the chaff is printed.
The Roycroft Dictionary (1914) p. 46

Hughes, Jimmy, Lake, Frank and Stillman, Al (fl. 1940s). British songwriters

1 Bless 'em all! Bless 'em all! The long and the short and the tall.
'Bless 'Em All' (1940 song)

Hughes, Thomas (1822–96). English lawyer, politician and writer

1 It's more than a game. It's an institution.
Tom Brown's Schooldays (1857) pt 2, ch. 7 (of cricket)

Hugo, Victor (Marie) (1802–85). French poet, playwright and novelist

1 *La vérité de l'art ne saurait jamais être ... la réalité absolue. L'art ne peut donner la chose même.*
The truth of art should never be ... *absolute reality.* Art should not show the thing itself.
Cromwell (1827) preface

2 *Mêlez toute votre âme à la création!*
Involve all of your soul in creation!
Les Feuilles d'automne (1831) no. 38, 'Pan'

3 *Le drame tient de la tragédie par la peinture des passions et de la comédie par la peinture des caractères. Le drame est la troisième grande forme de l'art.*
In drama, tragedy paints the passions and comedy paints characters. Drama is the third great form of art.
Ruy Blas (1838) preface

4 *Sous l'habit d'un valet, les passions d'un roi.*
Beneath the clothing of a manservant, the passions of a king.
Ruy Blas (1838) act 1, sc. 3

5 *Dieu s'est fait homme; Soit! Le diable s'est fait femme.*
God made himself a man. So be it! The devil made himself a woman.
Ruy Blas (1838) act 2, sc. 5

6 *On résiste à l'invasion des armées; on ne résiste pas à l'invasion des idées.*
A stand can be made against invasion by an army; no stand can be made against invasion by an idea.
Histoire d'un crime (written 1851–2, published 1877) pt 5, sect. 10

7 *Le mot, c'est le Verbe, et le Verbe, c'est Dieu.*
The word is the Verb, and the Verb is God.
Contemplations (1856) bk 1, no. 8

8 *Cette cloison qui nous sépare du mystère des choses et que nous appelons la vie.*
Life is a screen which separates us from the mystery of things.
Les Misérables (1862) vol. 1, bk 1, ch. 2

9 *Ce génie particulier de la femme qui comprend l'homme mieux que l'homme ne se comprend.*
A woman's particular talent is to understand a man better than he understands himself.
Les Misérables (1862) vol. 1, bk 1, ch. 9

10 *Les livres sont des amis froids et sûrs.*
Books are cold and certain friends.
Les Misérables (1862) vol. 1, bk 5, ch. 3

11 *Personne ne garde un secret comme un enfant.*
No one keeps a secret like a child.
Les Misérables (1862) vol. 2, bk 7, ch. 8

12 *Respirer Paris, cela conserve l'âme.*
To inhale Paris preserves the soul.
Les Misérables (1862) vol. 3, bk 1, ch. 6

13 *Le premier symptôme de l'amour vrai chez un jeune homme, c'est la timidité, chez une jeune fille, c'est la hardiesse.*
The first symptom of true love in a young man is timidity; in a young woman, it is boldness.
Les Misérables (1862) vol. 4, bk 3, ch. 6

14 *Le dix-neuvième siècle est grand, mais le vingtième sera heureux.*
The nineteenth century is great, but the twentieth will be happy.
Les Misérables (1862) vol. 5, bk 1, ch. 4

15 Science says the first word on everything and the last word on nothing.
Things of the Infinite (translated by L. O'Rourke, 1907)

Hume, David (1711–76). Scottish philosopher

1 It is not, therefore, reason, which is the guide of life, but custom.
A Treatise of Human Nature (1739) abstract

2 Money ... is none of the wheels of trade: it is the oil which renders the motion of the wheels more smooth and easy.
Essays: Moral and Political (1741–2) 'Of Money'

3 The heart of man is made to reconcile the most glaring contradictions.
Essays, Moral, Political, and Literary (ed. T. H. Green and T. H. Grose, 1875) 'Of the Parties of Great Britain' (1741–2)

4 Art may make a suit of clothes; But nature must produce a man.
Essays, Moral, Political, and Literary (ed. T. H. Green and T. H. Grose, 1875) 'The Epicurean' (1741)

5 All the objects of human reason or enquiry may naturally be divided into two kinds, to wit, *Relations of Ideas*, and *Matters of Fact*.
An Enquiry Concerning Human Understanding (1748) sect. 4, pt 1

6 A wise man proportions his belief to the evidence.
An Enquiry Concerning Human Understanding (1748) sect. 10, pt 1

7 Beauty is no quality in things themselves. It exists merely in the mind which contemplates them.
Essays, Moral, Political, and Literary (ed. T. H. Green and T. H. Grose, 1875) 'Of the Standard of Taste' (1757)

Hunt, G. W. (1829–1904). British composer, lyricist and painter

1 We don't want to fight, but by Jingo if we do,
We've got the ships, we've got the men, we've got the money too!
Music hall song (1878), inspired by a speech by Disraeli threatening Russia with war

Hunt, Lamar (1932–). American owner of the Kansas City Chiefs American football club

1 My definition of utter waste is a coachload of lawyers going over a cliff, with three empty seats.
Quoted in Colin Jarman *The Guinness Dictionary of Sports Quotations* (1990)

Hunt, Leigh (1784–1859). English poet and essayist

1 The two divinest things this world has got,
A lovely woman in a rural spot!
'The Story of Rimini' (1816) canto 3, l. 257

2 Stolen sweets are always sweeter,
Stolen kisses much completer,
Stolen looks are nice in chapels,
Stolen, stolen, be your apples.
'Song of Fairies Robbing an Orchard' (1830)

3 Poetry, in the most comprehensive application of the term, I take to be the flower of any kind of experience, rooted in truth, and issuing forth into beauty.
The Story of Rimini (1832 edn) preface

4 The pretension is nothing; the performance everything. A good apple is better than an insipid peach.
The Story of Rimini (1832) preface to revised edition

Hupfeld, Herman (1894–1951). American songwriter

1 You must remember this, a kiss is still a kiss,
A sigh is just a sigh.
'As Time Goes By' (1931 song)

Hussein, Saddam (1937–). President of Iraq 1979–2003

1 The mother of battles.
Popular interpretation of his description of the approaching Gulf War, given in a speech in Baghdad, 6 January 1991

Hutcheson, Francis (1694–1746). Scottish philosopher

1 Wisdom denotes the pursuing of the best ends by the best means.
An Inquiry into the Original of our Ideas of Beauty and Virtue (1725) treatise 1, sect. 5

Hutchins, Robert M. (1899–1977). American educationist

1 Whenever I feel like exercise, I lie down until the feeling passes.
Quoted in Colin Jarman *The Guinness Dictionary of Sports Quotations* (1990)

Huxley, Aldous (Leonard) (1894–1963). English novelist and essayist

1 The proper study of mankind is books.
Crome Yellow (1921) ch. 28

2 There are few who would not rather be taken in adultery than in provincialism.
Antic Hay (1923) ch. 10

3 Facts do not cease to exist because they are ignored.
Proper Studies (1927) 'Note on Dogma'

4 That all men are equal is a proposition to which, at ordinary times, no sane human being has ever given his assent.
Proper Studies (1927) 'The Idea of Equality'

5 Several excuses are always less convincing than one.
Point Counter Point (1928) ch. 1

6 A bad book is as much of a labour to write as a good one; it comes as sincerely from the author's soul.
Point Counter Point (1928) ch. 13

7 There is no substitute for talent. Industry and all the virtues are of no avail.
Point Counter Point (1928) ch. 13

8 Too much consistency is as bad for the mind as it is for the body. Consistency is contrary to nature, contrary to life. The only completely consistent people are the dead.
Do What You Will (1929) 'Wordsworth in the Tropics'

9 After silence, that which comes nearest to expressing the inexpressible is music.
Music At Night (1931)

10 Official dignity tends to increase in inverse ratio to the importance of the country in which the office is held.
Beyond the Mexique Bay (1934)

11 Chastity – the most unnatural of all the sexual perversions.
Eyeless in Gaza (1936) ch. 27

12 There's only one corner of the universe you can be certain of improving, and that's your own self.
Time Must Have a Stop (1945) ch. 7

13 Most human beings have an infinite capacity for taking things for granted.
'Variations on a Philosopher' (1950)

14 We participate in a tragedy; at a comedy we only look.
The Devils of Loudun (1952) ch. 11

15 The most distressing thing that can happen to a prophet is to be proved wrong. The next most distressing thing is to be proved right.
'Brave New World Revisited' (1956) in *Esquire*

Huxley, T(homas) H(enry) (1825–95). English biologist

1 It is the customary fate of new truths to begin as heresies and to end as superstitions.
Science and Culture and Other Essays (1881) 'The Coming of Age of the Origin of Species'

2 Logical consequences are the scarecrows of fools and the beacons of wise men.
Science and Culture and Other Essays (1881) 'On the Hypothesis that Animals are Automata'

3 I am too much of a sceptic to deny the possibility of anything.
Letter to Herbert Spencer, 22 March 1886, in Leonard Huxley *Life and Letters of Thomas Henry Huxley* (1900) vol. 2, ch. 8

4 The great tragedy of Science – the slaying of a beautiful hypothesis by an ugly fact.
Collected Essays (1893–4) 'Biogenesis and Abiogenesis'

5 Science is nothing but trained and organized common sense.
Collected Essays (1893–4) 'The Method of Zadig'

Ibarruri, Dolores ('La Pasionaria')
(1895–1989). Spanish Communist
leader

1 *No pasarán.*
They shall not pass.
Radio broadcast, Madrid, 19 July 1936, in
Speeches and Articles 1936–38 (1938) p. 7

Ibn Battuta (1304–68). Arab
traveller and geographer

1 Never to travel any road a second
time.
Travels in Asia and Africa 1325–1354 (translated by H. A. R. Gibb, 1929)

Ibsen, Henrik Johan (1828–1906).
Norwegian playwright

1 Castles in the air – they are so easy
to take refuge in. And so easy to
build, too.
The Master Builder (1892) act 3

2 In a consumer society there are
inevitably two kinds of slaves: the
prisoners of addiction and the
prisoners of envy.
Tools for Conviviality (1973) ch. 3

Illich, Ivan (1926–2002). Austrian-
born American social critic

1 In both rich and poor nations
consumption is polarized while
expectation is equalized.
Celebration of Awareness (1970) ch. 12

Inge, William Ralph (1860–1954).
English writer and Dean of St Paul's

1 The aim of education is the knowledge not of facts but of values.
'The Training of the Reason' in A. C. Benson
(ed.) *Cambridge Essays on Education* (1917)
ch. 2

2 To become a popular religion, it is
only necessary for a superstition to
enslave a philosophy.
Idea of Progress (Romanes Lecture delivered
at Oxford, 27 May 1920) p. 9

3 The enemies of freedom do not
argue; they shout and they shoot.
The End of an Age (1948) ch. 4

4 The effect of boredom on a large
scale in history is underestimated.
The End of an Age (1948) ch. 6

5 A nation is a society united by a
delusion about its ancestry and by a
common hatred of its neighbours.
Sagittarius and George (1931)

**Ingres, Jean Auguste
Dominique** (1780–1867). French
painter

1 *Le dessin est la probité de l'art.*
Drawing is the true test of art.
Pensées d'Ingres (1922) p. 70

Ionesco, Eugène (1912–94). French
playwright

1 *Tu ne prévois les événements que
lorsqu'ils sont déjà arrivés.*
You can only predict things after
they have happened.
Le Rhinocéros (1959) act 3

Irving, Washington (1783–1859).
American writer

1 Whenever a man's friends begin to
compliment him about looking
young, he may be sure that they
think he is growing old.
Bracebridge Hall (1822) 'Bachelors'

Ising, Rudolf C. (1903–92). American film producer and director

1 That's all folks!
Porky Pig's sign-off line for Warner Brothers' *Looney Tunes*; recalled on his death in the *New York Times*, 23 July 1992

Issigonis, Sir Alec (Alexander Arnold Constantine) (1906–88). Turkish-born British car designer

1 Styling is designing for obsolescence.
Recalled on his death; quoted in the *Australian* 5 October 1988

2 A camel is a horse designed by a committee.
On his dislike of working in teams, in the *Guardian* 14 January 1991 'Notes and Queries' (attributed)

1 The land of my fathers, how fair is thy fame.
Land of my Fathers (1856)

James, Henry (1843–1916). American-born British novelist

1 Cats and monkeys – monkeys and cats – all human life is there!
The Madonna of the Future (1879) vol. 1, p. 59 ('All human life is there' became the slogan of the *News of the World* during the late 1950s)

2 It takes a great deal of history to produce a little literature.
Hawthorne (1879) ch. 1

3 There are few hours in life more agreeable than the hour dedicated to the ceremony known as afternoon tea.
The Portrait of a Lady (1881) ch. 1

4 An Englishman's never so natural as when he's holding his tongue.
Isabel Archer. *The Portrait of a Lady* (1881) ch. 10

5 The time-honoured bread-sauce of the happy ending.
Theatricals, Second Series (1894–5) preface

6 The Story is just the spoiled child of art.
The Ambassadors (1909 edn) preface

7 The deep well of unconscious cerebration.
The American (1909 edn) preface

8 The fatal futility of Fact.
The Spoils of Poynton (1909 edn) preface

9 In art economy is always beauty.
Preface for revised New York edition of *The Altar of the Dead* (1909, first published 1895)

Jackson, Jesse (Louis) (1941–). American clergyman and Democratic politician

1 My constituency is the desperate, the damned, the disinherited, the disrespected, and the despised.
Speech at the Democratic National Convention, San Francisco, 17 July 1984

Jacobs, Joe (1896–1940). American boxing manager

1 We was robbed!
After Jack Sharkey beat Max Schmeling (whom Jacobs managed) in the heavyweight title fight, 21 June 1932; in Peter Heller *In This Corner* (1975) p. 44

Jagger, Mick and Richard, Keith (1943–; 1943–). English rock musicians

1 I can't get no satisfaction.
Title of song (1965)

James, Alice (1848–92). American diarist

1 I suppose one has a greater sense of intellectual degradation after an interview with a doctor than from any human experience.
Diary entry, 27 September 1890

James, Evan (1809–1878). Welsh Bard

James, William (1842–1910). American philosopher and psychologist

1 Man lives by science as well as bread.
Vivisection (1875)

2 There is no more miserable human being than one in whom nothing is habitual but indecision.
The Principles of Psychology (1890) ch. 4

3 Metaphysics means nothing but an unusually obstinate effort to think clearly.
The Principles of Psychology (1890) ch. 6

4 The aim of science is always to reduce complexity to simplicity.
The Principles of Psychology (1890) ch. 9

5 The baby, assailed by eyes, ears, nose, skin, and entrails at once, feels it all as one great blooming, buzzing confusion.
The Principles of Psychology (1890) ch. 13

6 The art of being wise is the art of knowing what to overlook.
The Principles of Psychology (1890) ch. 22

7 Sobriety diminishes, discriminates, and says no; drunkenness expands, unites, and says yes.
The Varieties of Religious Experience (1902) 'Mysticism'

8 There is no worse lie than a truth misunderstood by those who hear it.
The Varieties of Religious Experience (1902) p. 355

James I (James VI of Scotland) (1566–1625). King of Scotland from 1567 and England from 1603

1 A custom loathsome to the eye, hateful to the nose, harmful to the brain, dangerous to the lungs, and in the black, stinking fume thereof, nearest resembling the horrible Stygian smoke of the pit that is bottomless.
A Counterblast to Tobacco (1604)

2 I will govern according to the common weal, but not according to the common will.
December, 1621, in J. R. Green *History of the English People* vol. 3 (1879) bk 7, ch. 4

Janowitz, Tama (1957–). American writer

1 With publicity comes humiliation.
In the *International Herald Tribune*, 8 September 1992

Jarry, Alfred (1873–1907). French playwright and humorist

1 *La mort n'est que pour les médiocres.*
Death is only for the mediocre.
Gestes et opinions du Docteur Faustroll Pataphysicien (1898) vol. 8, pt 37

Jay, Sir Antony (Rupert) (1930–). English writer and television producer

1 The bigger the organization, the fewer the jobs worth doing.
Management and Machiavelli (1967)

Jefferson, Thomas (1743–1826). 3rd President of the USA

1 We hold these truths to be sacred and undeniable; that all men are created equal and independent, that from that equal creation they derive rights inherent and inalienable, among which are the preservation of life, and liberty, and the pursuit of happiness.
'Rough Draft' of the American Declaration of Independence, in J. P. Boyd et al. *Papers of Thomas Jefferson* vol. 1 (1950) p. 423

2 A little rebellion now and then is a good thing.
Letter to James Madison, 30 January 1787, in *Papers of Thomas Jefferson* vol. 11 (1955) p. 93

Jerome, Jerome K(lapka) (1859–1927). English humorous novelist and playwright

1 It is impossible to enjoy idling thoroughly unless one has plenty of work to do.
Idle Thoughts of an Idle Fellow (1886) 'On Being Idle'

2 Love is like the measles; we all have to go through it.
Idle Thoughts of an Idle Fellow (1886) 'On Being in Love'

Jerrold, Douglas (1803–57). English playwright and journalist

1 Religion's in the heart, not in the knees.
The Devil's Ducat (1830) act 1, sc. 2

Joad, C(yril) E(dwin) M(itchinson) (1891–1953). English philosopher

1 It all depends what you mean by ...
Answering questions on *The Brains Trust* (formerly *Any Questions*), BBC radio (1941–8)

Johnson, Lyndon B(aines) (1908–73). 36th President of the USA

1 You let a bully come into your front yard, and the next day he'll be on your porch.
In *Time* April 1964

Johnson, Philander Chase (1866–1939).

1 Cheer up! the worst is yet to come!
In *Everybody's Magazine* May 1920

Johnson, Philip (Cortelyou) (1906–2005). American architect

1 Surely architecture is the organization for pleasure of enclosed space.
'The Seven Crutches of Architecture', talk to students, School of Architectural Design, Harvard University, 7 December 1954

2 The automobile is the greatest catastrophe in the entire history of City architecture.
'The Town and the Automobile or the Pride of Elm Street' (1955) published in *Writings* (1979)

3 Architecture is the art of how to waste space.
In the *New York Times* 27 December 1964, p. 9

Johnson, Samuel (Dr Johnson) (1709–84). English poet, critic, lexicographer and conversationalist

1 A generous and elevated mind is distinguished by nothing more certainly than an eminent degree of curiosity.
Dedication of his English translation of Fr J. Lobo's *Voyage to Abyssinia* (1735)

2 No place affords a more striking conviction of the vanity of human hopes, than a public library.
The Rambler no. 106 (23 March 1751)

3 This man [Lord Chesterfield] I thought had been a Lord among wits; but, I find, he is only a wit among Lords.
Boswell *Life* vol. 1 (1754)

4 Every quotation contributes something to the stability or enlargement of the language.
A Dictionary of the English Language (1755) preface (on citations of usage in a dictionary)

5 *Lexicographer.* A writer of dictionaries, a harmless drudge.
A Dictionary of the English Language (1755)

6 *Oats.* A grain, which in England is generally given to horses, but in Scotland supports the people.
A Dictionary of the English Language (1755)

7 *Patron.* Commonly a wretch who supports with insolence, and is paid with flattery.
A Dictionary of the English Language (1755)

8 *Pension.* Pay given to a state hireling for treason to his country.
A Dictionary of the English Language (1755)

9 Ignorance, madam, pure ignorance.
Boswell *Life* vol. 1 on Johnson being asked why he had defined *pastern* as the 'knee' of a horse (1755)

10 If a man does not make a new acquaintance as he advances through life, he will soon find himself left alone. A man, Sir, should keep his friendship in constant repair.
Boswell *Life* vol. 1 (1755)

11 The only end of writing is to enable the readers better to enjoy life, or better to endure it.
A Free Enquiry (1757, ed. D. Greene, 1984)

12 When two Englishmen meet, their first talk is of the weather.
The Idler no. 11 (24 June 1758)

13 Promise, large promise, is the soul of an advertisement.
The Idler no. 40 (20 January 1759)

14 Marriage has many pains, but celibacy has no pleasures.
Rasselas (1759) ch. 26

15 Example is always more efficacious than precept.
Rasselas (1759) ch. 26

16 Integrity without knowledge is weak and useless, and knowledge without integrity is dangerous and dreadful.
Rasselas (1759) ch. 41

17 A man ought to read just as inclination leads him; for what he reads as a task will do him little good.
Boswell *Life* vol. 1 (14 July 1763)

18 Notes are often necessary, but they are necessary evils.
Plays of William Shakespeare ... (1765) preface (Yale edn, p. 111)

19 It was not for me to bandy civilities with my Sovereign.
Boswell *Life* vol. 2 (February 1767)

20 It matters not how a man dies, but how he lives. The act of dying is not of importance, it lasts so short a time.
Boswell *Life* vol. 2 (26 October 1769)

21 The triumph of hope over experience.
Boswell *Life* vol. 2 (1770) of a man who remarried immediately after the death of a wife with whom he had been unhappy

22 Every man has a lurking wish to appear considerable in his native place.
Boswell *Life* vol. 2 letter to Sir Joshua Reynolds, 17 July 1771

23 Every man has, some time in his life, an ambition to be a wag.
In Joyce Hemlow (ed.) *Journals and Letters of Fanny Burney* vol. 1 (1972) p. 182

24 Grief is a species of idleness.
Letter to Mrs Thrale, 17 March 1773, in R. W. Chapman (ed.) *Letters of Samuel Johnson* (1952) vol. 1

25 Read over your compositions, and where ever you meet with a passage which you think is particularly fine, strike it out.
Boswell *Life* vol. 2 (30 April 1773) quoting a college tutor

26 I am always sorry when any language is lost, because languages are the pedigree of nations.
In Boswell *Tour to the Hebrides* (1785) 18 September 1773

27 The greatest part of a writer's time is spent in reading, in order to write: a man will turn over half a library to make one book.
Boswell *Life* vol. 2 (6 April 1775)

28 Patriotism is the last refuge of a scoundrel.
Boswell *Life* vol. 2 (7 April 1775)

29 Knowledge is of two kinds. We know a subject ourselves, or we know where we can find information upon it.
Boswell *Life* vol. 2 (18 April 1775)

30 We would all be idle if we could.
Boswell *Life* vol. 3 (3 April 1776)

31 No man but a blockhead ever wrote, except for money.
Boswell *Life* vol. 3 (5 April 1776)

32 Depend upon it, Sir, when a man knows he is to be hanged in a fortnight, it concentrates his mind wonderfully.
Boswell *Life* vol. 3 (19 September 1777) on the execution of Dr Dodd

33 When a man is tired of London, he is tired of life; for there is in London all that life can afford.
Boswell *Life* vol. 3 (20 September 1777)

34 Worth seeing, yes; but not worth going to see.
Boswell *Life* vol. 3 (12 October 1779) on the Giant's Causeway

35 If you are idle, be not solitary; if you are solitary, be not idle.
Boswell *Life* vol. 3, letter to Boswell, 27 October 1779

36 The great source of pleasure is variety. Uniformity must tire at last, though it be uniformity of excellence.
Lives of the English Poets (1779–81) 'Butler'

37 Language is the dress of thought.
Lives of the English Poets (1779–81) 'Cowley'

38 The father of English criticism.
Lives of the English Poets (1779–81) 'Dryden'

39 Every man has a right to utter what he thinks truth, and every other man has a right to knock him down for it. Martyrdom is the test.
Boswell *Life* vol. 4 (1780)

40 Classical quotation is the *parole* of literary men all over the world.
Boswell *Life* vol. 4 (8 May 1781)

41 Sir, there is no settling the point of precedency between a louse and a flea.
On the relative merits of two minor poets.
Quoted in Boswell *Life* vol. 4 (1783)

42 Sir, I have found you an argument; but I am not obliged to find you an understanding.
Boswell *Life* vol. 4 (June 1784)

43 Sir, I look upon every day to be lost, in which I do not make a new acquaintance.
Boswell *Life* vol. 4 (November 1784)

44 What is written without effort is in general read without pleasure.
In William Seward *Biographia* (1799) p. 260

45 Love is the wisdom of the fool and the folly of the wise.
In William Cooke *Life of Samuel Foote* (1805) vol. 2, p. 154

46 Of all noises I think music the least disagreeable.
Quoted in *The Morning Chronicle*, 1816

Jolson, Al (Asa Yoelson) (1886–1950). American singer

1 You think that's noise – you ain't heard nuttin' yet!
In a café, before an encore, after having had his applause drowned out by the din from a building site; in Martin Abramson *The Real Story of Al Jolson* (1950) p. 12 (later the title of a Jolson song, 1919, in the form 'You Ain't Heard Nothing Yet')

Jones, James (1921–77). American writer

1 From here to eternity.
Title of novel (1951)

Jong, Erica (née Mann) (1942–). American novelist and poet

1 Gossip is the opiate of the oppressed.
Fear of Flying (1973) ch. 6

2 Advice is what we ask for when we already know the answer but wish we didn't.
How To Save Your Own Life (1977) 'A Day in the Life …'

Jonson, Ben (c.1573–1637). English playwright and poet

1 I do honour the very flea of his dog.
Every Man in His Humour (1598) act 4, sc. 2

2 Ramp up my genius, be not retrograde;
But boldly nominate a spade a spade.
The Poetaster (1601) act 5, sc. 1

3 Calumnies are answered best with silence.
Volpone (1605) act 2, sc. 2

4 Fortune, that favours fools.
The Alchemist (1610) prologue

5 Drink to me only with thine eyes, And I will pledge with mine.
'To Celia' (1616)

6 Thou hadst small Latin, and less Greek.
'To the Memory of … Shakespeare' (1623)

7 He was not of an age, but for all time!
'To the Memory of … Shakespeare' (1623)

8 Sweet Swan of Avon!
'To the Memory of … Shakespeare' (1623)

Jowett, Benjamin (1817–93). English classicist; Master of Balliol College, Oxford, from 1870

1 One man is as good as another until he has written a book.
In Evelyn Abbott and Lewis Campbell (eds.) *Life and Letters of Benjamin Jowett* (1897) vol. 1, p. 248

Joyce, James (1882–1941). Irish novelist

1 Once upon a time and a very good time it was.
A Portrait of the Artist as a Young Man (1916) ch. 1

2 Greater love than this, he said, no
man hath that a man lay down his
wife for his friend.
Ulysses (1922) p. 375

3 And yes I said yes I will Yes.
Ulysses (1922) p. 732

Julian of Norwich (1343–after
1416). English anchoress

1 Sin is behovely, but all shall be well
and all shall be well and all manner
of thing shall be well.
Revelations of Divine Love (the long text)
ch. 27, Revelation 13

Jung, Carl Gustav (1875–1961).
Swiss psychiatrist

1 The pendulum of the mind oscil-
lates between sense and nonsense,
not between right and wrong.
Memories, Dreams and Reflections (1962)
ch. 5

2 Every form of addiction is bad, no
matter whether the narcotic be
alcohol or morphine or idealism.
Memories, Dreams and Reflections (1962)
ch. 12

3 Show me a sane man and I will cure
him for you.
Quoted in the *Observer* 19 July 1975

Juvenal (Decimus Iunius Iuvenalis)
(AD *c*.60–*c*.130). Roman satirist

1 ... *Omnia Romae*
Cum pretio.
Everything in Rome has its price.
Satires no. 3, l. 183

2 *Rara avis in terris nigroque simillima
cycno.*
A rare bird on this earth, like
nothing so much as a black swan.
Satires no. 6, l. 165

3 *'Pone seram, cohibe.' Sed quis custo-
diet ipsos
Custodes? Cauta est et ab illis incipit
uxor.*
'Bolt her in, keep her indoors.' But
who is to guard the guards themselves? Your wife is prudent and
begins with them.
Satires no. 6, l. 347

4 *Orandum est ut sit mens sana in cor-
pore sano.*
You should pray to have a sound
mind in a sound body.
Satires no. 10, l. 356

Kafka, Franz (1883–1924). Czech novelist and short-story writer

1 *Es ist oft besser, in Ketten als frei zu sein.*
It is often safer to be in chains than to be free.
Der Prozess (1925, *The Trial*)

Kandinsky, Wassily (1866–1944). Russian-born painter and writer on art

1 Every work of art is the child of its time, often it is the mother of our emotions.
Concerning the Spiritual in Art (1912)

Kant, Immanuel (1724–1804). German philosopher

1 *Aus so krummen Holze, als woraus der Mensch gemacht ist, kann nichts ganz Gerades gezimmert werden.*
Out of the crooked timber of humanity, no straight thing can ever be made.
Idee zu einer allgemeinen Geschichte in weltbürgerlicher Absicht (1784) prop. 6

2 *Glückseligkeit ist nicht ein Ideal der Vernunft, sondern der Einbildung-straft.*
Happiness is not an ideal of reason but of imagination.
Grundlegung zur Metaphysik der Sitten (1785) sect. 2 (translated by T. K. Abbott)

Karr, Alphonse (1808–90). French novelist and journalist

1 *Plus ça change, plus c'est la même chose.*
The more things change, the more they are the same.
Les Guêpes January 1849 (6th series, 1859) p. 305

Kaufman, George S(imon) (1889–1961). American playwright, director and journalist

1 God finally caught his eye.
Epitaph for a deceased waiter. Quoted in Jon Winokur *The Portable Curmudgeon* (1987)

2 There was scattered laughter in the rear of the theatre, leading to the belief that somebody was telling jokes back there.
Play review

Kaufmann, Christoph (1753–95). German man of letters

1 *Sturm und Drang.*
Storm and stress.
Title originally suggested for a Romantic drama of the American War of Independence by the German playwright F. M. Klinger (1775)

Keats, John (1795–1821). English poet

1 Silent, upon a peak in Darien.
'On First Looking into Chapman's Homer' (1817)

2 Much have I travelled in the realms of gold,
And many goodly states and kingdoms seen.
'On First Looking into Chapman's Homer' (1817)

3 O for a life of sensations rather than of thoughts!
Letter to Benjamin Bailey, 22 November 1817, in H. E. Rollins (ed.) *Letters of John Keats* (1958) vol. 1

4 If poetry comes not as naturally as leaves to a tree it had better not come at all.
Letter to John Taylor, 27 February 1818

5 A thing of beauty is a joy for ever.
Endymion (1818) bk 1, l. 1

6 Scenery is fine – but human nature is finer.
Letter to Benjamin Bailey, 13 March 1818, in H. E. Rollins (ed.) *Letters of John Keats* (1958) vol. 1

7 There are four seasons in the mind of man.
'The Human Seasons' (1819)

8 St Agnes' Eve – Ah, bitter chill it was!
The owl, for all his feathers, was a-cold.
'The Eve of St Agnes' (1820) st. 1

9 And soft adorings from their loves receive
Upon the honeyed middle of the night.
'The Eve of St Agnes' (1820) st. 6

10 A poor, weak, palsy-stricken, churchyard thing.
'The Eve of St Agnes' (1820) st. 18

11 And the long carpets rose along the gusty floor.
'The Eve of St Agnes' (1820) st. 40

12 The sedge has withered from the lake
And no birds sing!
'La belle dame sans merci' (1820) st. 1

13 ... La belle dame sans merci
Thee hath in thrall.
'La belle dame sans merci' (1820) st. 10

14 Love in a hut, with water and a crust,
Is – Love, forgive us! – cinders, ashes, dust.
'Lamia' (1820) pt 2, l. 1

15 That purple-linèd palace of sweet sin.
'Lamia' (1820) pt 2, l. 31

16 Philosophy will clip an Angel's wings.
'Lamia' (1820) pt 2, l. 234

17 Thou still unravished bride of quietness,
Thou foster-child of silence and slow time.
'Ode on a Grecian Urn' (1820) st. 1

18 Heard melodies are sweet, but those unheard
Are sweeter; therefore, ye soft pipes, play on.
'Ode on a Grecian Urn' (1820) st. 2

19 For ever panting, and for ever young.
'Ode on a Grecian Urn' (1820) st. 3

20 'Beauty is truth, truth beauty,' – that is all
Ye know on earth, and all ye need to know.
'Ode on a Grecian Urn' (1820) st. 5

21 My heart aches, and a drowsy numbness pains
My sense, as though of hemlock I had drunk.
'Ode to a Nightingale' (1820) st. 1

22 Where youth grows pale, and spectre-thin, and dies.
'Ode to a Nightingale' (1820) st. 3

23 Already with thee! tender is the night.
'Ode to a Nightingale' (1820) st. 4

24 Darkling I listen; and, for many a time
I have been half in love with easeful Death.
'Ode to a Nightingale' (1820) st. 6

25 Thou wast not born for death, immortal bird!
'Ode to a Nightingale' (1820) st. 7

26 Forlorn! the very word is like a bell
To toll me back from thee to my sole self!
'Ode to a Nightingale' (1820) st. 8

27 Was it a vision, or a waking dream?
Fled is that music: – do I wake or sleep?
'Ode to a Nightingale' (1820) st. 8

28 Season of mists and mellow fruit-fulness.
'To Autumn' (1820) st. 1

29 Where are the songs of Spring? Ay, where are they?
Think not of them, thou hast thy music too.
'To Autumn' (1820) st. 3

30 Here lies one whose name was writ in water.
Epitaph for himself, in Richard Monckton Milnes *Life, Letters and Literary Remains of John Keats* (1848) vol. 2, p. 91

Keillor, (Gary Edward) Garrison
(1942–). American humorous writer and broadcaster

1 Where all the women are strong, all the men are good-looking, and all the children are above average.
Of the fictional mid-Western town Lake Wobegon, created in *A Prairie Home Companion* (from 1974)

Kelman, James (1946–). Scottish novelist

1 My culture and my language have the right to exist, and no one has the authority to dismiss that.
Speech at the Booker Prize award ceremony, 11 October 1994

Kempis, St Thomas à (*c.*1380–1471). German monk and author

1 *Vere magnus est, qui magnam habet caritatem.*
He is truly great who has great charity.
De Imitatione Christi (*c.*1413) bk 1, ch. 4, sect. 6

2 *Quam cito transit gloria mundi.*
How quickly the glory of the world passes.
De Imitatione Christi (*c.*1413) bk 1, ch. 4, sect. 6

3 *Homo proponit, sed Deus disponit.*
Man proposes, but God disposes.
De Imitatione Christi (*c.*1413) bk 1, ch. 19, sec. 2

4 *Hodie homo est: et cras non comparet. Cum autem sublatus fuerit ab oculis: etiam cito transit a mente.*
Today the man is here; tomorrow he is gone. And when he is 'out of sight', quickly also is he out of mind.
De Imitatione Christi (*c.*1413) bk 1, ch. 23, sect. 1

5 *Si libenter crucem portas, portabit te.*
If you bear your cross willingly, it will bear you.
De Imitatione Christi (*c.*1413) bk 2, ch. 12, sect. 5

6 *De duobos malis minus est semper eligendum.*
Of two evils the lesser should always be chosen.
De Imitatione Christi (*c.*1413) bk 3, ch. 12, sect. 2

Kennedy, John F(itzgerald)
(1917–63). 35th President of the USA

1 Let us never negotiate out of fear. But let us never fear to negotiate.
Inaugural address, 20 January 1961

2 And so, my fellow Americans: ask not what your country can do for you – ask what you can do for your country. My fellow citizens of the world: ask not what America will do for you, but what together we can do for the freedom of man.
Inaugural address, 20 January 1961

3 Mankind must put an end to war or war will put an end to mankind.
Address to the United Nations, 25 September 1961

4 The rights of every man are diminished when the rights of one man are threatened.
On sending the National Guard to ensure peaceful integration at the University of Alabama. Address to the nation, 11 June 1963

5 *Ich bin ein Berliner.*
I am a Berliner.
Speech in West Berlin, 26 June 1963, in the *New York Times* 27 June 1963

Kennedy, Joseph Patrick (1888–1969). American businessman and diplomat

1 Don't get mad, get even.
Attributed

Kennedy, Robert F(rancis)
(1925–68). American politician

1 Courage is the most important attribute of a lawyer.
Speech at the University of San Francisco Law School, 29 September 1962

2 One fifth of the people are against everything all the time.
In the *Observer* May 1964

Kerouac, Jack (1922–69).
American novelist

1 The beat generation.
Early use in *Playboy* June 1959, p. 32

Kesey, Ken (Elton) (1935–2001).
American novelist

1 One flew over the cuckoo's nest.
Title of novel (1962), from a traditional rhyme

Kethe, William (d. 1594). Scottish Calvinist

1 All people that on earth do dwell, Sing to the Lord with cheerful voice.
'All people that on earth do dwell' in *Fourscore and Seven Psalms of David* (Geneva, 1561; later known as the Geneva Psalter)

Key, Francis Scott (1779–1843).
American lawyer and poet

1 O say, can you see, by the dawn's early light,
What so proudly we hailed at the twilight's last gleaming –,
Whose broad stripes and bright stars, through the clouds of the fight,
O'er the ramparts we watched were so gallantly streaming?
And the rocket's red glare, the bombs bursting in air,
Gave proof through the night that our flag was still there;
O say, does that star-spangled banner yet wave
O'er the land of the free, and the home of the brave?
'The Star-Spangled Banner' (1814), originally published as 'The Defence of Fort M'Henry' in the *Baltimore Patriot* 20 September

Khrushchev, Nikita Sergeyevich (1894–1971). Soviet politician

1 Those who wait for the USSR to reject Communism must wait until a shrimp learns to whistle.
Speech in Moscow, 17 September 1955

2 Politicians are the same all over. They promise to build a bridge even where there is no river.
Press conference, New York, October 1960

Kierkegaard, Sören (Aabye) (1813–55). Danish philosopher and religious thinker

1 Without risk there is no faith.
Concluding Unscientific Postscript (1846) bk 2, pt 2, ch. 2

Kilmer, Joyce (1886–1918).
American poet

1 I think that I shall never see A poem lovely as a tree.
'Trees' (1914)

Kilvert, Francis (1840–79). English clergyman and diarist

1 Of all noxious animals, too, the most noxious is a tourist. And of all tourists the most vulgar, ill-bred, offensive and loathsome is the British tourist.
W. Plomer (ed.) *Selections from the Diary of the Rev. Francis Kilvert* (1938–40) 5 April 1870

King, Benjamin Franklin (1857–94). American poet

1 Nowhere to go but out, Nowhere to come but back.
'The Pessimist'

King, Martin Luther Jr (1929–68).
American civil rights leader

1 He who passively accepts evil is as much involved in it as he who helps to perpetuate it.
Strides Towards Freedom (1958)

2 Injustice anywhere is a threat to justice everywhere.
Letter from Birmingham jail, Alabama, 16 April 1963

3 I have a dream. I have a dream that my four little children will one day live in a nation where they will not

be judged by the colour of their skin but by the content of their character.
Washington civil rights rally, 15 June 1963

4 If a man hasn't discovered something he will die for, he isn't fit to live.
Speech in Detroit, 23 June 1963

5 I've been to the mountain top. I've looked over, and I've seen the promised land. I may not get there with you, but I want you to know tonight that we as a people will get to the promised land.
Speech at Memphis, the day before he was assassinated, 3 April 1968

6 Love is the only force capable of transforming an enemy into a friend.
Attributed

King, Stoddard (1889–1933).
British songwriter

1 There's a long, long trail awinding Into the land of my dreams.
'There's a Long, Long Trail' (1913 song)

Kingsley, Charles (1819–75).
English writer and clergyman

1 Young blood must have its course, lad,
And every dog his day.
The Water Babies (1863) 'Young and Old'

Kipling, Rudyard (1865–1936).
English writer and poet

1 The man who would be king.
Title of story (1888)

2 Down to Gehenna or up to the Throne,
He travels fastest who travels alone.
The Story of the Gadsbys (1888), 'L'Envoi'; the poem was later renamed 'The Winners' (1912)

3 Oh, East is East, and West is West, and never the twain shall meet,
Till earth and sky stand presently at God's great Judgement seat.
'The Ballad of East and West' (1889)

4 On the road to Mandalay,
Where the flyin'-fishes play.
'Mandalay' (1890)

5 There are nine and sixty ways of constructing tribal lays,
And – every – single – one – of – them – is – right!
'In the Neolithic Age' (1892)

6 Four things greater than all things are, –
Women and Horses and Power and War.
'The Ballad of the King's Jest' (1892)

7 'It's clever, but is it Art?'
'The Conundrum of the Workshops' (1892)

8 You're a better man than I am, Gunga Din!
'Gunga Din' (1892)

9 A man-cub is a man-cub, and he must learn *all* the Law of the Jungle.
The Jungle Book (1894) 'Kaa's Hunting'

10 Such boasting as the Gentiles use, Or lesser breeds without the Law.
'Recessional' (1897)

11 Lord God of Hosts, be with us yet, Lest we forget – lest we forget!
'Recessional' (1897)

12 Little Friend of all the World.
Kim (1901) ch. 1 (Kim's nickname)

13 He walked by himself, and all places were alike to him.
Just So Stories (1902) 'The Cat that Walked by Himself'

14 (Boots – boots – boots – boots – movin' up and down again!)
'Boots' (1903)

15 Sussex by the sea!
'Sussex' (1903)

16 Brandy for the Parson,
'Baccy for the Clerk.
Puck of Pook's Hill (1906) 'A Smuggler's Song'

17 If you can keep your head when all about you
Are losing theirs and blaming it on you …
Rewards and Fairies (1910) 'If –'

18 You'll be a Man, my son!
Rewards and Fairies (1910) 'If –'

19 If any question why we died,
Tell them, because our fathers lied.
'Common Form' (1919)

20 Their Name Liveth for Evermore.
Proposal for the text to be carved over the lists of the dead in the Commonwealth war cemeteries after World War 1 (1919)

21 The female of the species is more deadly than the male.
'The Female of the Species' (1919)

Kissinger, Henry (Alfred)
(1923–). American academic and statesman

1 We lost sight of one of the cardinal maxims of guerrilla war: the guerrilla wins if he does not lose. The conventional army loses if it does not win.
On the Vietnam War. In *Foreign Affairs* January 1969

2 Power is the great aphrodisiac.
In the *New York Times* 19 January 1971, p. 12

3 We are the President's men.
In M. and B. Kalb *Kissinger* (1974) ch. 7

4 Every civilization that has ever existed has ultimately collapsed.
In the *New York Times* 13 October 1974

5 There can't be any crisis next week. My schedule is already full.
In *Time* January 1977

6 The statesman's duty is to bridge the gap between his nation's experience and his vision.
Years of Upheaval (1982)

7 The nice thing about being a celebrity is that when you bore people, they think that it's their fault.
Quoted in *Reader's Digest* April 1985

Klee, Paul (1874–1940). Swiss painter and graphic artist

1 The worst state of affairs is when science begins to concern itself with art.
Collected in *The Notebooks of Paul Klee* (1906, published 1957)

2 *Kunst gibt nicht das Sichtbare wieder, sondern macht sichtbar.*
Art does not reproduce the visible; rather it makes visible.
'Creative Credo' (1920), in *Inward Vision* (1958)

Knight, Charles and Lyle, Kenneth British songwriters

1 Are we downhearted?
No!
'Here we are! Here we are again!!' (1914 song)

Knox, John (c.1513–72). Scottish Protestant reformer

1 The Monstrous Regiment of Women.
Part of a pamphlet title, *The First Blast of the Trumpet Against the Monstrous Regiment of Women* (1558)

2 *Un homme avec Dieu est toujours dans la majorité.*
One man with God is always a majority.
Attributed inscription on the Reformation Monument, Geneva

Knox, Ronald (1888–1957). English writer and Roman Catholic priest

1 There once was a man who said, 'God
Must think it exceedingly odd
If he finds that this tree
Continues to be
When there's no one about in the Quad.'
In Langford Reed *Complete Limerick Book* (1924), to which came the anonymous reply: 'Dear Sir, / Your astonishment's odd: / I am always about in the Quad. / And that's why the tree / Will continue to be, / Since observed by / Yours faithfully, / God.'

2 A loud noise at one end and no sense of responsibility at the other.
Definition of a baby (attributed)

Koehler, Ted (1894–1973). American songwriter

1 Stormy weather.
'Stormy Weather' (1933 song); music by Harold Arlen

Koestler, Arthur (1905–83). Hungarian-born British writer

1 One may not regard the world as a sort of metaphysical brothel for emotions.
Darkness at Noon (1940) 'The Second Hearing' pt 7

2 Creativity in science could be described as the act of putting two and two together to make five.
The Act of Creation (1964)

Kraus, Karl (1874–1936). Austrian critic, publisher, and dramatist

1 A historian is often only a journalist facing backwards.
Aphorism collected in Heinrich Fischer (ed.) *Beim Wort genommen* (1955); translated by Harry Zohn in *Half-truths and one-and-a-half truths* (1986)

2 One ought to acknowledge the significance for mankind of the simultaneous invention of gunpowder and printer's ink.
Aphorism collected in Heinrich Fischer (ed.) *Beim Wort genommen* (1955); translated by Harry Zohn in *Half-truths and one-and-a-half truths* (1986)

Krishnamurti, Jiddu (1895–1986). Indian spiritual philosopher

1 Religion is the frozen thought of men out of which they build temples.
In the *Observer* 22 April 1928 'Sayings of the Week'

Kronecker, Leopold (1823–91). German mathematician

1 *Die ganze Zahl schuf der liebe Gott, alles Ubrige ist Menschenwerk.*
God made the integers, man made the rest.
Quoted in F. Cajori *A History of Mathematics* (1919)

Kronenberger, Louis (1904–80). American writer, lecturer and critic

1 The trouble with our age is that it is all signpost and no destination.
Company Manners (1954) 'The Spirit of The Age'

Kronsberg, Jeremy Joe American screenwriter

1 Every which way but loose.
Title of film (1978) starring Clint Eastwood

Krutch, Joseph (Wood) (1893–1970). American author, teacher and critic

1 A tragic writer does not have to believe in God, but he must believe in man.
The Modern Temper (1929) 'The Tragic Fallacy'

2 The most serious charge which can be brought against New England is not Puritanism but February.
The Twelve Seasons (1949) 'February'

3 Cats seem to go on the principle that it never does any harm to ask for what you want.
The Twelve Seasons (1949) 'February'

Kuhn, Maggie (1905–95). American writer and social reformer

1 The ultimate indignity is to be given a bedpan by a stranger who calls you by your first name.
In the *Observer* 20 August 1978

Kundera, Milan (1929–). Czech novelist

1 The unbearable lightness of being.
Title of novel (1984)

Kurosawa, Akira (1910–98). Japanese film director

1 The Japanese see self-assertion as immoral and self-sacrifice as the sensible course to take in life.
Something Like an Autobiography (1982)

Kurz, Mordecai (1934–). American economist

1 There is only one truth, and many opinions. Therefore, most people are wrong most of the time.
In *Fortune* 3 April 1985

Küng, Hans (1928–). Swiss Roman Catholic theologian

1 A Church which abandons the truth abandons itself.
Die Kirche (1967)

Kyd, Thomas (1558–94. English playwright

1 Where words prevail not, violence prevails;
But gold doth more than either of them both.
The Spanish Tragedy (c.1592) act 2, sc. 1, l. 110

2 What outcries pluck me from my naked bed?
The Spanish Tragedy (c.1592) act 2, sc. 5, l. 1

3 For what's a play without a woman in it?
The Spanish Tragedy (c.1592) act 4, sc. 1, l. 97

La Bruyère, Jean de (1645–96).
French moralist

1 *Tout est dit, et l'on vient trop tard
depuis plus de sept mille ans qu'il y a
des hommes et qui pensent.*
Everything has been said. After
seven thousand years of human
thought, we have come too late.
Les Caractères ou les mœurs de ce siècle (1688)
'Des ouvrages de l'esprit'

2 *C'est un métier que de faire un livre,
comme de faire une pendule: il faut
plus que de l'esprit pour être auteur.*
Making a book is a craft, as is
making a clock; it takes more than
wit to become an author.
Les Caractères ou les mœurs de ce siècle (1688)
'Des ouvrages de l'esprit'

3 *Le temps, qui fortifie les amitiés, af-
faiblit l'amour.*
Time, which strengthens friend-
ships, weakens love.
Les Caractères ou les mœurs de ce siècle (1688)
'Du cœur'

4 *L'amour et l'amitié s'excluent l'un
l'autre.*
Love and friendship exclude one
another.
Les Caractères ou les mœurs de ce siècle (1688)
'Du cœur'

5 *L'amour qui naît subitement est le
plus long à guérir.*
Love which strikes suddenly takes
the longest to cure.
Les Caractères ou les mœurs de ce siècle (1688)
'Du cœur'

6 *Si la vie est misérable, elle est pénible à
supporter; si elle est heureuse, il est
horrible de la perdre. L'un revient à
l'autre.*
If life is miserable, it is difficult to
endure; if it is happy, it is horrible
to lose. They come to the same
thing.
Les Caractères ou les mœurs de ce siècle (1688)
'De l'homme'

7 *A parler humainement, la mort a un
bel endroit, qui est de mettre fin à la
vieillesse.*
To speak humanely, death has a
useful function: it puts an end to
old age.
Les Caractères ou les mœurs de ce siècle (1688)
'De l'homme'

8 *Les enfants n'ont ni passé ni avenir, et,
ce qui ne nous arrive guère, ils jouis-
sent du présent.*
Children have neither past nor
future. They live in the present,
something which rarely happens
to us.
Les Caractères ou les mœurs de ce siècle (1688)
'De l'homme'

9 *L'impossibilité où je suis de prouver
que Dieu n'est pas me découvre son
existence.*
The impossibility I find myself in to
prove that God does not exist
proves to me his existence.
Les Caractères ou les mœurs de ce siècle (1688)
'Des esprits forts'

**Laclos, Pierre-Ambroise
Choderlos de** (1741–1803). French
artillery officer and writer

1 *J'avoue bien que l'argent ne fait pas le
bonheur; mais il faut avouer aussi
qu'il le facilite beaucoup.*

I will admit that money does not bring happiness, but it must also be admitted that it facilitates much.
Les Liaisons dangereuses (1782) letter 104

2 *Pour les hommes, l'infidélité n'est pas l'inconstance.*
For men, infidelity is not inconstancy.
Les Liaisons dangereuses (1782) letter 134

Lady Chudleigh, Mary (née Leigh) (1656–1710). English poet

1 Wife and Servant are the same,
But only differ in the name.
Poems (1703) 'To the Ladies'

La Fayette, Marie Madeleine (Pioche de La Vergne) (1634–93). French novelist

1 *L'amour était toujours mêlé aux affaires et les affaires à l'amour.*
Love has always mixed with politics and politics with love.
La Princesse de Clèves (1678)

2 *On persuade aisément une vérité agréable.*
It is easy to persuade one with an agreeable truth.
La Princesse de Clèves (1678)

3 *La honte est la plus violente de toutes les passions.*
Shame is the most violent of all the passions.
La Princesse de Clèves (1678)

La Fontaine, Jean de (1621–95). French poet and moralist

1 *Il accusait toujours les miroirs d'être faux.*
He was always blaming mirrors for being untrue.
Fables (1668) pt 1, 'L'Homme et son image'

2 *Plutôt souffrir que mourir,
C'est la devise des hommes.*
Rather suffer than die, that is the motto of men
Fables (1668) pt 1, 'La Mort et le bûcheron'

3 *C'est double plaisir de tromper le trompeur.*
It is doubly pleasing to trick the trickster.
Fables pt 2 (1668) 'Le Coq et le renard'

4 *En toute chose il faut considérer la fin.*
One must consider the end in everything.
Fables (1668) pt 3, 'Le Renard et le bouc'

5 *Aide-toi, le ciel t'aidera.*
Help yourself, and heaven will help you.
Fables (1668) pt 6 'Le Chartier embourbé'

6 *Sur les ailes du Temps la tristesse s'envole.*
Grief is carried off by the wings of Time.
Fables (1668) pt 6, 'La Jeune Veuve'

7 *Tout est mystère dans l'Amour.*
Everything about Love is a mystery.
Fables (1668) pt 12, 'L'Amour et la folie'

8 *Tous chemins vont à Rome.*
All roads lead to Rome.
Fables (1668) pt 12, 'Le Juge arbitre, l'hospitalier, et le solitaire'

Lamb, Charles (1775–1834). English writer

1 Nothing puzzles me more than time and space; and yet nothing troubles me less, as I never think about them.
Letter to Thomas Manning, 2 January 1806

2 In everything that relates to science, I am a whole Encyclopedia behind the rest of the world.
Essays of Elia (1823) 'The Old and the New Schoolmaster'

3 Not many sounds in life, and I include all urban and rural sounds, exceed in interest a knock at the door.
Essays of Elia (1823) 'Valentine's Day'

4 The human species, according to the best theory I can form of it, is composed of two distinct races, *the men who borrow*, and *the men who lend*.
Essays of Elia (1823) 'The Two Races of Men'

5 Credulity is the man's weakness, but the child's strength.
Essays of Elia (1823) 'Witches, and Other Night-Fears'

6 Newspapers always excite curiosity. No one ever lays one down without a feeling of disappointment.
Essays of Elia (1823) 'Detached Thoughts of Books and Reading'

7 [A pun] is a pistol let off at the ear; not a feather to tickle the intellect.
Last Essays of Elia (1833) 'Popular Fallacies' no. 9

Lamb, Lady Caroline (1785–1828). Wife of William Lamb, 2nd Viscount Melbourne

1 Mad, bad, and dangerous to know.
Writing of Byron in her journal after their first meeting in 1812; in Elizabeth Jenkins *Lady Caroline Lamb* (1932) ch. 6

Lamb, William (2nd Lord Melbourne) (1779–1848). British Whig politician and Prime Minister

1 God help the Minister that meddles with art!
In Lord David Cecil *Lord M* (1954) ch. 3

Lance, Bert (1931–). American government official

1 If it ain't broke, don't fix it.
In *Nation's Business* May 1977, p. 27

Landor, Walter Savage (1775–1864). English poet

1 Fleas know not whether they are upon the body of a giant or upon one of ordinary size.
Imaginary Conversations of Literary Men and Statesmen (1824) 'Southey and Porson'

Lang, Andrew (1844–1912). Scottish man of letters

1 Politicians use statistics in the same way that a drunk uses lamp-posts – for support rather than illumination.
Speech (1910); quoted in Alan L. Mackay *The Harvest of a Quiet Eye* (1977)

Lang, Julia (1921–). British broadcaster

1 Are you sitting comfortably? Then I'll begin.
Listen with Mother (BBC radio programme for children, 1950–82) (sometimes 'Then we'll begin')

Langer, Susanne (1895–1985). American philosopher

1 Art is the objectification of feeling, and the subjectification of nature.
Mind (1967) vol. 1, pt 2, ch. 4

Langton, Stephen (d. 1228). Archbishop of Canterbury

1 *Veni, Sancte Spiritus,*
Come, Holy Spirit.
The 'Golden Sequence' for Whit Sunday (also attributed to several others, notably Pope Innocent III)

Larkin, Philip (Arthur) (1922–85). English poet

1 Nothing, like something, happens anywhere.
'I Remember, I Remember' (1954)

2 Life is first boredom, then fear.
'Dockery & Son' (1964)

3 Sexual intercourse began
In nineteen sixty-three
(Which was rather late for me) –
Between the end of the *Chatterly* ban.
And the Beatles' first LP.
'Annus Mirabilis' (1967)

4 They fuck you up, your mum and dad.
They may not mean to, but they do.
'This Be the Verse' (1974)

5 Man hands on misery to man.
It deepens like a coastal shelf.
Get out as early as you can,
And don't have any kids yourself.
'This Be the Verse' (1974)

6 A beginning, a muddle, and an end.
New Fiction no. 15, January 1978 (on the 'classic formula' for a novel)

7 Deprivation is for me what daffodils were for Wordsworth.
Required Writing (1983)

La Rochefoucauld, François, Duc de (1613–80). French moralist

1 *On n'est jamais si malheureux qu'on croit, ni si heureux qu'on espère.*
One is never as unhappy as one thinks, nor as happy as one hopes.
Sentences et maximes de morale (Dutch edition, 1664) maxim 128

2 The love of justice in most men is simply the fear of suffering injustice.
Réflexions, ou sentences et maximes morales (1665) no. 78

3 *Il y a de bons mariages, mais il n'y en a point de délicieux.*
There are good marriages, but no delightful ones.
Maximes (1678) no. 113

4 *L'hypocrisie est un hommage que le vice rend à la vertu.*
Hypocrisy is a tribute which vice pays to virtue.
Maximes (1678) no. 218

5 *C'est une grande habileté que de savoir cacher son habileté.*
The height of cleverness is to be able to conceal it.
Maximes (1678) no. 245

6 *La reconnaissance de la plupart des hommes n'est qu'une secrète envie de recevoir de plus grands bienfaits.*
In most of mankind gratitude is merely a secret hope for greater favours.
Maximes (1678) no. 298

Latimer, Hugh (c.1485–1555). English Protestant martyr

1 Be of good comfort Master Ridley, and play the man. We shall this day light such a candle by God's grace in England, as (I trust) shall never be put out.
Prior to being burned for heresy, 16 October 1555, in John Foxe *Actes and Monuments* (1570 edn) p. 1937

Lauder, Sir Harry (Hugh MacLennan) (1870–1950). Scottish music-hall entertainer

1 I love a lassie, a bonnie, bonnie lassie.
'I Love a Lassie' (1905 song)

2 Roamin' in the gloamin',
On the bonnie banks o' Clyde.
'Roamin' in the Gloamin'' (1911 song)

3 Keep right on to the end of the road.
'The End of the Road' (1924 song)

Laurel, Stan (Arthur Stanley Jefferson) and Hardy, Oliver (1890–1965; 1892–1957). American film comedians

1 Another nice mess you've gotten me into.
Another Fine Mess (film, 1930) and other Laurel and Hardy films; spoken by Oliver Hardy

Laurence, Margaret (1926–87). Canadian novelist

1 Privacy is a privilege not granted to the aged or the young.
The Stone Angel (1964) ch. 1

Lawrence, D(avid) H(erbert) (1885–1930). English novelist, essayist and poet

1 People are not fallen angels, they are merely people.
Letter to J. Middleton Murry and Katherine Mansfield, 17 February 1916

2 Morality which is based on ideas, or on an ideal, is an unmitigated evil.
Fantasia of the Unconscious (1922) ch. 7

3 Never trust the artist. Trust the tale. The proper function of a critic is to save the tale from the artist who created it.
Studies in Classic American Literature (1923) ch. 1

4 Evil, what is evil?
There is only one evil, to deny life.
'Cypresses' (1923)

5 A snake came to my water-trough
On a hot, hot day, and I in pyjamas
for the heat,
To drink there.
'Snake' (1923)

6 Damn all absolutes.
'The Novel' (1925)

7 You have to have something
vicious in you to be a creative
writer.
Book review, reprinted in *Phoenix* (1927)

8 The novel is the one bright book of
life.
Phoenix (1936) 'Why the novel matters'

Lazarus, Emma (1849–87).
American poet

1 Give me your tired, your poor,
Your huddled masses yearning to
breathe free,
The wretched refuse of your teeming shore,
Send these, the homeless, tempest-
tossed, to me:
I lift my lamp beside the golden
door.
'The New Colossus' (1883); inscription on
the Statue of Liberty, New York

Leacock, Stephen (Butler)
(1869–1944). English-born
Canadian humorist and economist

1 Advertising may be described as
the science of arresting human
intelligence long enough to get
money from it.
The Garden of Folly (1924) 'The Perfect
Salesman'

2 A sportsman is a man who, every
now and then, simply has to go out
and kill something. Not that he's
cruel. He wouldn't hurt a fly. It's
not big enough.
My Remarkable Uncle (1942)

Lévis, Duc de (1764–1830). French
soldier and writer

1 *Noblesse oblige.*
Nobility has its obligations.
Maximes et réflexions (1812 edn) 'Morale:
maximes et préceptes' no. 73

2 *Gouverner, c'est choisir.*
To govern is to choose.
Maximes et réflexions (1812 edn) 'Politique:
maximes de politique' no. 19

Lear, Edward (1812–88). English
artist and writer of humorous verse

1 The Dong with a Luminous Nose!
'The Dong with a Luminous Nose' (1871)

2 The lands where the Jumblies live.
'The Jumblies' (1871)

3 They went to sea in a sieve, they did
In a sieve they went to sea.
'The Jumblies' (1871)

4 The Owl and the Pussy-Cat went to
sea
In a beautiful pea-green boat.
'The Owl and the Pussy-Cat' (1871)

5 Oh lovely Pussy! O Pussy, my love,
What a beautiful Pussy you are.
'The Owl and the Pussy-Cat' (1871)

6 They sailed away for a year and a
day,
To the land where the Bong-tree
grows,
And there in a wood a Piggy-wig
stood
With a ring at the end of his nose.
'The Owl and the Pussy-Cat' (1871)

7 'Dear Pig, are you willing to sell for
one shilling
Your ring?' Said the Piggy, 'I will.'
'The Owl and the Pussy-Cat' (1871)

8 They dined on mince, and slices of
quince,
Which they ate with a runcible
spoon;
And hand in hand, on the edge of
the sand,
They danced by the light of the
moon.
'The Owl and the Pussy-Cat' (1871)

Leary, Timothy (1920–96).
American psychologist

1 If you take the game of life seriously, if you take your nervous
system seriously, if you take your

sense organs seriously, if you take the energy process seriously, you must turn on, tune in and drop out.
Lecture June 1966, in *The Politics of Ecstasy* (1968)

Leavis, F(rank) R(aymond)
(1895–1978). English literary critic

1 The common pursuit.
Title of book (1952)

Lebowitz, Fran(ces Ann) (1951–). American writer

1 Life is something to do when you can't get to sleep.
Metropolitan Life (1978)

2 Sleep is death without the responsibility.
Metropolitan Life (1978) 'Why I Love Sleep'

3 Perhaps the least cheering statement ever made on the subject of art is that life imitates it.
Metropolitan Life (1978) 'Arts'

4 Great people talk about ideas, average people talk about things, and small people talk about wine.
Social Studies (1981) 'People'

5 War is, undoubtedly, hell, but there is no earthly reason why it has to start so early in the morning.
Social Studies (1981) 'War Stories'

Leboyer, Frédérick (1918–). French gynaecologist and obstetrician

1 Making love is the sovereign remedy for anguish.
Birth without Violence (1991)

Le Carré, John (David John Moore Cornwell) (1931–). English novelist

1 The spy who came in from the cold.
Title of novel (1963)

2 A committee is an animal with four back legs.
Tinker, Tailor, Soldier, Spy (1974) pt 3, ch. 34

3 The only decent diplomat is a deaf Trappist.
A Perfect Spy (1986) ch. 3

Le Corbusier (Charles-Édouard Jeanneret) (1887–1965). French architect

1 *Une maison est une machine-à-habiter.*
A house is a machine for living in.
Vers une architecture (1923) p. ix

Lee, Harper (1926–). American novelist

1 Shoot all the bluejays you want, if you can hit 'em, but remember it's a sin to kill a mockingbird.
To Kill a Mockingbird (1960) ch. 10

Lee-Potter, Lynda (Lynda Berrison) (1934–2004). British journalist

1 Powerful men often succeed through the help of their wives. Powerful women only succeed in spite of their husbands.
In the *Daily Mail* 16 May 1984

Lehman, Ernest (1920–). American screenwriter

1 Sweet smell of success.
Title of book and film (1957)

Lenin (Vladimir Ilyich Ulyanov) (1870–1924). Russian revolutionary

1 One step forward, two steps back.
Title of book (1904)

2 Imperialism is the monopoly stage of capitalism.
Imperialism as the Last Stage of Capitalism (1916) ch. 7 'Briefest possible definition of imperialism'

3 While the State exists, there can be no freedom. When there is freedom there will be no State.
State and Revolution (1919) ch. 5

4 Liberty is precious – so precious that it must be rationed.
In Sidney and Beatrice Webb *Soviet Communism* (1936) p. 1036

5 Chess is the gymnasium of the mind.
Quoted in Colin Jarman *The Guinness Dictionary of Sports Quotations* (1990)

Lennon, John and McCartney, Paul (1940–1980; 1942–). English pop singers and songwriters

1 Money can't buy me love.
'Can't Buy Me Love' (1964 song)

2 It's been a hard day's night,
And I've been working like a dog.
'A Hard Day's Night' (1964 song)

3 She's got a ticket to ride, but she don't care.
'Ticket to Ride' (1965 song)

4 All the lonely people, where do they all come from?
'Eleanor Rigby' (1966 song)

5 Strawberry fields forever.
Title of song (1967)

6 Will you still need me, will you still feed me,
When I'm sixty four?
'When I'm Sixty Four' (1967 song)

7 I get by with a little help from my friends.
'With a Little Help From My Friends' (1967 song)

8 Give peace a chance.
Title of song (1969)

Leonardo da Vinci (1452–1519). Italian painter, sculptor, architect and engineer

1 Painting is poetry which is seen and not heard, and poetry is a painting which is heard but not seen.
Quoted in J. P. and Irma A. Richter *The Literary Works of Leonardo da Vinci* (2 vols., 1939)

2 He is a poor disciple who does not excel his master.
Quoted in Irma A. Richter (ed.) *Selections from the Notebooks of Leonardo da Vinci* (1977)

3 The span of a man's outspread arms is equal to his height.
Quoted in Irma A. Richter (ed.) *Selections from the Notebooks of Leonardo da Vinci* (1977)

Lerner, Alan Jay (1918–86). American songwriter

1 Why can't a woman be more like a man?
My Fair Lady (1956) 'A Hymn to Him'

2 The rain in Spain stays mainly in the plain.
My Fair Lady (1956) 'The Rain in Spain'

3 In Hertford, Hereford, and Hampshire,
Hurricanes hardly happen.
My Fair Lady (1956) 'The Rain in Spain'

4 I've grown accustomed to her face.
Title of song in *My Fair Lady* (1956)

Levant, Oscar (1906–72). American composer, pianist and writer

1 Chutzpah – that quality which enables a man who has murdered his mother and father to throw himself on the mercy of the court as an orphan.
The Unimportance of Being Oscar (1968)

Levenstein, Ros (NA). British advertising copywriter

1 I'm only here for the beer.
Slogan for Double Diamond beer, from 1971

Leverson, Ada (1865–1936). English novelist

1 You don't know a woman until you have had a letter from her.
Tenterhooks (1912) ch. 7

Levin, Bernard (1919–2004). English writer, journalist and critic

1 The musical equivalent of blanc-mange.
Of the music of Frederick Delius. *Enthusiasms* (1983)

Lewis, C(live) S(taples) (1898–1963). English novelist, literary scholar and theological writer

1 Often when I pray I wonder if I am not posting letters to a non-existent address.
Letter to Arthur Greeves, 24 December 1930

2 Gratitude looks to the past and love to the present: fear, avarice, lust and ambition look ahead.
The Screwtape Letters (1942) no. 15

3 Fatigue makes women talk more
and men less.
The Screwtape Letters (1942) no. 30

Lewis, (Harry) Sinclair (1885–
1951). American novelist

1 Our American professors like their
literature clear and cold and pure
and very dead.
Nobel Prize address, 12 December 1930

2 It can't happen here.
Title of novel (1935)

Lewis, John Spedan (1885–1963).
English shopkeeper and industrial
reformer

1 Never knowingly undersold.
Motto (from *c.*1920) of the John Lewis
Partnership, in *Partnership for All* (1948)
ch. 29

Leybourne, George (d. 1884).
English songwriter

1 He'd fly through the air with the
greatest of ease,
A daring young man on the flying
trapeze.
'The Flying Trapeze' (1868 song)

Liberace (Wladziu Valentino
Liberace) (1919–87). American
showman

1 When the reviews are bad I tell my
staff that they can join me as I cry
all the way to the bank.
Autobiography (1973) ch. 2 (a joke coined in
the mid-1950s)

Lichtenberg, Georg Christoph
(1742–99). German scientist and
philosopher

1 Doubt everything at least once,
even the proposition that two
times two equals four.
Aphorisms (*c.*1796) Notebook K (translated
by R. J. Hollingdale, 1990)

Liebermann, Max (1847–1935).
German painter and graphic artist

1 The art of drawing is the art of
omission.
Quoted in Paul Klee *On Modern Art* (1979)

Lincoln, Abraham (1809–65). 16th
President of the USA

1 What is conservatism? Is it not
adherence to the old and tried,
against the new and untried?
Speech, 27 February 1860, in R. P. Basler
(ed.) *Collected Works ...* (1953) vol. 3, p. 537

2 Fourscore and seven years ago our
fathers brought forth upon this
continent a new nation, conceived
in liberty, and dedicated to the
proposition that all men are created equal.
Address at the Dedication of the National
Cemetery at Gettysburg, 19 November
1863, in R. P. Basler (ed.) *Collected Works ...*
(1953) vol. 7, p. 23

3 We here highly resolve that the
dead shall not have died in vain,
that this nation, under God, shall
have a new birth of freedom; and
that government of the people, by
the people, and for the people,
shall not perish from the earth.
Address at the Dedication of the National
Cemetery at Gettysburg, 19 November
1863, in R. P. Basler (ed.) *Collected Works ...*
(1953) vol. 7, p. 23

4 You may fool all the people some of
the time; you can even fool some of
the people all of the time; but you
can't fool all of the people all the
time.
In Alexander K. McClure *Lincoln's Yarns and
Stories* (1904); also attributed to Phineas
Barnum

5 So you're the little woman who
wrote the book that made this great
war!
On meeting Harriet Beecher Stowe, author
of *Uncle Tom's Cabin* (1852); in Carl Sandburg *Abraham Lincoln: The War Years* (1936)
vol. 2, ch. 39

Lindner, R(obert) M(itchell)
(1914–56). American novelist

1 Rebel without a cause.
Title of book (1944) and film (1955) starring
James Dean

Linklater, Eric Robert (1889–
1974). Scottish journalist and writer

1 Authors and uncaptured criminals
… are the only people free from
routine.
Poet's Pub (1929) ch. 23

Linley, George (1798–1865).
English songwriter

1 'God bless the Prince of Wales!'
'God Bless the Prince of Wales' (1862 song);
translated from the Welsh original by J. C.
Hughes (1837–87)

Lippmann, Walter (1899–1974).
American journalist

1 There can be no higher law in
journalism than to tell the truth
and shame the devil.
Liberty and the News (1920) 'Journalism and
the Higher Law'

**Littlewood, Joan and Chilton,
Charles** (1914–2002; 1914–).

1 Oh what a lovely war!
Title of stage show (1963)

Livingstone Ken (Kenneth Robert
Livingstone) (1945–). British Labour
politician

1 If voting changed anything, they'd
abolish it.
Title of book (1987)

Livy (Titus Livius) (59 BC–AD 17).
Roman historian

1 *Vae victis!*
Down with the defeated!
Attributed to the Gallic King Brennus, who
captured Rome in 390 BC

Llewellyn, Richard (Richard
Llewellyn Lloyd) (1907–83). Welsh
novelist and playwright

1 How green was my valley.
Title of book (1939)

Lloyd George, David (Earl Lloyd-
George of Dwyfor) (1863–1945).
British Liberal politician and Prime
Minister

1 You cannot feed the hungry on
statistics.
Speech advocating tariff reform (1904)

2 At eleven o'clock this morning
came to an end the cruellest and
most terrible war that has ever
scourged mankind. I hope we may
say that thus, this fateful morning,
came to an end all wars.
Speech, *Hansard* 11 November 1918,
col. 2463

3 What is our task? To make Britain a
fit country for heroes to live in.
Speech at Wolverhampton, 23 November
1918, in *The Times* 25 November 1918

4 The world is becoming like a
lunatic asylum run by lunatics.
In the *Observer* 8 January 1933

5 A politician was a person with
whose politics you did not agree.
When you did agree, he was a
statesman.
Speech at Central Hall, Westminster, 2 July
1935, in *The Times* 3 July 1935

Locke, John (1632–1704). English
philosopher

1 Government has no other end but
the preservation of property.
Second Treatise on Civil Government (1681)

2 It is one thing to show a man that
he is in error, and another to put
him in possession of truth.
An Essay concerning Human Understanding
(1690) bk 4, ch. 7, sect. 11

Lodge, David (John) (1935–).
English novelist and critic

1 Literature is mostly about having
sex and not much about having
children. Life is the other way
round.
The British Museum Is Falling Down (1965)
ch. 4

2 Another law of academic life: *it is
impossible to be excessive in flattery of
one's peers.*
Small World (1984) pt 3, ch. 1

Logau, Friedrich von (1604–55).
German epigrammatist

1 *Gottes Mühlen mahlen langsam,
mahlen aber trefflich klein.*
Though the mills of God grind
slowly, yet they grind exceeding
small.
Sinngedichte (1654) 'Desz Dritten Tausend,
Andres Hundert' no. 24 (translated by
Longfellow)

London, Jack (1876–1916).
American novelist

1 The call of the wild.
Title of novel (1903)

Longfellow, Henry Wadsworth
(1807–82). American poet

1 Music is the universal language of
mankind.
Outre Mer (1835)

2 Lives of great men all remind us
We can make our lives sublime,
And, departing, leave behind us
Footprints on the sands of time.
'A Psalm of Life' (1838)

3 Under a spreading chestnut tree
The village smithy stands.
'The Village Blacksmith' (1839)

4 It was the schooner Hesperus,
That sailed the wintry sea.
'The Wreck of the Hesperus' (1839)

5 Dead he is not, but departed, – for
the artist never dies.
'Nuremberg' (1844) (on Albrecht Dürer)

6 I shot an arrow into the air,
It fell to earth, I knew not where.
'The Arrow and the Song' (1845)

7 By the shore of Gitche Gumee,
By the shining Big-Sea-Water,
Stood the wigwam of Nokomis.
The Song of Hiawatha (1855) 'Hiawatha's
Childhood'

8 From the waterfall he named her,
Minnehaha, Laughing Water.
The Song of Hiawatha (1855) 'Hiawatha and
Mudjekeewis'

9 A Lady with a Lamp shall stand
In the great history of the land.
'Santa Filomena' (1857) (on Florence
Nightingale)

10 Between the dark and the daylight,
When the night is beginning to
lower,
Comes a pause in the day's occu-
pations,
That is known as the Children's
Hour.
'The Children's Hour' (1859)

11 Listen, my children, and you shall
hear
Of the midnight ride of Paul
Revere,
On the eighteenth of April in Sev-
enty-five.
Tales of a Wayside Inn (1863) pt 1, 'The
Landlord's Tale: Paul Revere's Ride'

12 Ships that pass in the night, and
speak to each other in passing.
Tales of a Wayside Inn (1874) pt 3, 'The
Theologian's Tale: Elizabeth' pt 4

13 There was a little girl
Who had a little curl
Right in the middle of her fore-
head,
When she was good
She was very, very good,
But when she was bad she was
horrid.
Composed for his second daughter while a
baby, c.1850. See B. R. Tucker-Macchetta
The Home Life of Henry W. Longfellow (1882)
ch. 5

Longinus on the Sublime Greek
literary treatise of unknown
authorship and date

1 Sublimity is the echo of a noble
mind.
Sect. 9

Loos, Anita (c.1893–1981).
American writer

1 Gentlemen prefer blondes.
Title of novel (1925), and later a film (1953)

Louis, Joe (Joseph Louis Barrow)
(1914–81). American boxer

1 He can run. But he can't hide.
Of Billy Conn, before a title fight, 19 June
1946

Louis-Philippe (1773–1850). King of
France

1 The entente cordiale.
Speech, 27 December 1843; quoted in Collingham *The July Monarchy* (1988), p. 320

Louis XIV (1638–1715). King of France

1 *L'Etat c'est moi.*
I am the State.
Before the Parlement de Paris, 13 April 1655, in J. A. Dulaure *Histoire de Paris* (1834) vol. 6, p. 298 (attributed)

Louis XVI (1754–93). King of France

1 Louis XVI: Is this a revolt?
Duke of Rochefoucauld-Liancourt: No, sir, it's a revolution.
Exchange after the fall of the Bastille, 14 July 1789

Louis XVIII (1755–1824). King of France

1 *L'exactitude est la politesse des rois.*
Punctuality is the politeness of kings.
In *Souvenirs de J. Lafitte* (1844) bk 1, ch. 3 (attributed)

Lovelace, Richard (1618–58). English poet

1 Stone walls do not a prison make, Nor iron bars a cage.
'To Althea, From Prison' (1649)

Low, Sir David (1891–1963). British political cartoonist

1 Colonel Blimp.
Cartoon creation who expressed reactionary establishment opinions

Lowell, James Russell (1819–91). American poet and essayist

1 Books are the bees which carry the quickening pollen from one to another mind.
'Nationality in Literature', in the *North American Review* July 1849

2 Before Man made us citizens, great Nature made us men.
'On the Capture of Fugitive Slaves' (1854)

3 Every man feels instinctively that all the beautiful sentiments in the world weigh less than a single lovely action.
'Rousseau and the Sentimentalists', in the *North American Review* July 1867

4 The mind can weave itself warmly in the cocoon of its own thoughts, and dwell a hermit anywhere.
'On a Certain Condescension in Foreigners', in the *Atlantic Monthly* January 1869

5 There is no good in arguing with the inevitable. The only argument available with an east wind is to put on your overcoat.
'On Democracy', inaugural address on becoming president of the Birmingham and Midland Institute, 6 October 1884

6 Compromise makes a good umbrella but a poor roof.
'On Democracy', inaugural address on becoming president of the Birmingham and Midland Institute, 6 October 1884

Lowell, Robert (Traill Spence) (1917–77). American poet

1 Age is our reconciliation with dullness.
'Last Summer at Milgate' (1973)

2 We feel the machine slipping from our hands
As if someone else were steering;
If we see the light at the end of the tunnel,
It's the light of the oncoming train.
Day by Day (1977) 'Since 1939'

Lowndes, William (1652–1724). English politician

1 Take care of the pence, and the pounds will take care of themselves.
In Lord Chesterfield *Letters to his Son* (1774) 5 February 1750

Lowry, (Clarence) Malcolm (1909–57). English novelist

1 How alike are the groans of love to those of the dying.
Under the Volcano (1947) ch. 12

2 Dark as the grave wherein my
friend is laid.
Title of novel, published posthumously
(1968)

Lucan (Marcus Annaeus Lucanus)
(AD 39–65). Latin poet

1 *Stat magni nominis umbra.*
There stands the shade of a great
name.
Of Pompey. *Pharsalia*, bk 1, l. 135

Lucas, E(dward) V(errell) (1868–
1938). English essayist and
biographer

1 I have noticed that people who are
late are often so much jollier than
the people who have to wait for
them.
365 Days and One More (1926)

2 There can be no defence like elab-
orate courtesy.
Reading, Writing and Remembering (1932)
ch. 8

Lucas, George (1944–). American
film director and producer

1 May the force be with you.
Star Wars (film, 1977)

Lucretius (Titus Lucretius Carus)
(98–*c.*55 BC). Roman poet and
philosopher

1 *Nil posse creari*
De nilo.
Nothing can be created from
nothing.
De Rerum Natura, bk 1, line 155

2 *Vitaque mancipio, nulli datur, omni-*
bus usu.
To none is life given in freehold; to
all on lease.
De Rerum Natura, bk 3, line 971

3 *Ut quod ali cibus est aliis fuat acre*
venenum.
What is food to one may be literally
poison to others.
De Rerum Natura, bk 4, line 637

Luther, Martin (1483–1546).
German theologian

1 *Hier stehe ich. Ich kann nicht anders.*
Gott helfe mir. Amen.
Here I stand; I can do no other; God
help me; Amen.
Speech in defence of his doctrines at the
Diet of Worms, 18 April 1521

2 *Wer nicht liebt Wein, Weib und Ge-*
sang,
Der bleibt ein Narr sein Leben lang.
Who loves not woman, wine and
song
Remains a fool his whole life long.
Attributed

Lyly, John (*c.*1554–1606). English
poet and playwright

1 Night hath a thousand eyes.
The Maydes Metamorphosis (1600) act 3, sc. 1

Lyte, Henry Francis (1793–1847).
English curate

1 Abide with me.
'Abide with Me' (probably written in 1847)

Macaulay, Dame (Emilie) Rose
(1881–1958). English novelist and travel writer

1 You should always believe all you read in newspapers, as this makes them more interesting.
A Casual Commentary (1925) 'Problems of a Reader's Life'

MacDiarmid, Hugh (Christopher Murray Grieve) (1892–1978). Scottish poet, nationalist and communist

1 Scotland is not wholly surrounded by the sea – unfortunately.
Scottish Scene (1934) 'The Sea'

MacDonald, George (1824–1905). Scottish pastor, poet and novelist

1 Here lie I, Martin Elginbrodde:
Hae mercy o' my soul, Lord God;
As I wad do, were I Lord God,
And ye were Martin Elginbrodde.
David Elginbrod (1863) bk 1, ch. 13

2 To be trusted is a greater compliment than to be loved.
The Marquis of Lossie (published 1906)

MacLeish, Archibald (1892–1982). American poet

1 A poem should not mean
But be.
'Ars Poetica' (1926)

2 Anything can make us look, only art can make us see.
Poetry and Experience (1961) 'Riverside'

3 Poetry is the art of understanding what it is to be alive.
Recalled on his death

Macmahon, Comte de (1808–93). French military commander and President of the Third Republic

1 *J'y suis, j'y reste.*
Here I am, and here I stay.
At the taking of the Malakoff fortress during the Crimean War, 8 September 1855

Macmillan, Harold (1st Earl of Stockton) (1894–1986). British Conservative politician and Prime Minister

1 Let us be frank about it: most of our people have never had it so good.
Speech at Bedford, 20 July 1957, in *The Times* 22 July 1957 ('You Never Had It So Good' was also the US Democratic Party slogan during the 1952 election campaign)

2 The wind of change is blowing through this continent. Whether we like it or not, the growth of national consciousness is a political fact.
Speech to the South African Parliament, 3 February 1960

3 A man who trusts nobody is apt to be the kind of man whom nobody trusts.
In the *New York Herald Tribune* 17 December 1963

4 Tradition does not mean that the living are dead; it means that the dead are living.
In the *Manchester Guardian* 18 December 1963

MacNally, Leonard (1752–1820). Irish poet and playwright

1 Sweet lass of Richmond Hill.
'The Lass of Richmond Hill' (also attributed to others)

MacNeice, Louis (1907–63). British poet, born in Belfast

1 For this is Sunday morning, Fate's great bazaar.
'Sunday Morning' (1935)

2 It's no go the merrygoround, it's no go the rickshaw,
All we want is a limousine and a ticket for the peepshow.
'Bagpipe Music' (1938)

Magidson, Herb (1906–86). American songwriter

1 Music, maestro, please.
Title of song (1938)

Mahler, Gustav (1860–1911). Austrian composer, conductor and artistic director

1 *Endlich fortissimo!*
Fortissimo at last!
On seeing the Niagara Falls (1907); quoted in Charles Osborne *The Dictionary of Composers* (1977)

Mailer, Norman (Kingsley) (1923–). American novelist and journalist

1 The naked and the dead.
Title of novel (1948)

2 In America few people will trust you unless you are irreverent.
The Presidential Papers (1963) preface

3 Writing books is the closest men ever come to childbearing.
'Mr Mailer Interviews Himself', in the *New York Times Book Review* 17 September 1965

4 The surest way not to be remembered is to talk about the way you want to be.
Interview in *Playboy* August 1968

5 The horror of the Twentieth Century was the size of each event, and the paucity of its reverberation.
Of a Fire on the Moon (1970) pt 1, ch. 2

6 The true religion of America has always been America.
Interview in *Time Out*, 27 September–3 October 1984

Maine, Sir Henry (1822–88). English jurist

1 Except the blind forces of Nature, nothing moves in this world which is not Greek in its origin.
Village Communities (3rd edn, 1876) p. 238

Maistre, Josephe de (1753–1821). French writer and diplomat

1 *Toute nation a le gouvernement qu'elle mérite.*
Every country has the government it deserves.
Letters et opuscules inédits (1851) vol. 1, letter 53 (15 August 1811)

Malamud, Bernard (1914–86). American novelist and short-story writer

1 All biography is ultimately fiction.
Dubin's Lives (1979) p. 20

Mallarmé, Stéphane (1842–98). French poet

1 *Un coup de dés n'abolira jamais le hasard.*
A throw of the dice will never abolish chance.
Title of poem, in *Cosmopolis* May 1914

Mallory, George Leigh (1886–1924). English mountaineer

1 Because it's there.
When asked 'Why do you want to climb Mount Everest?'; quoted in the *New York Times* 18 March 1923

Malraux, André (1901–76). French novelist, essayist and art critic

1 *La condition humaine.*
The human condition.
Title of book (1933)

2 *L'art est un anti-destin.*
Art is a revolt against fate.
Les Voix du silence (1951) pt 4, ch. 7

Mamet, David (Alan) (1947–). American dramatist, screenwriter and director

1 The absence of the urge to create is decadence.
Writing in Restaurants (1986) 'Decadence'

2 All plays are about decay ... That is why the theater has always been essential to human psychic equilibrium.
Writing in Restaurants (1986) 'Decay: Some Thoughts for Actors'

3 A good film script should be able to do completely without dialogue.
In the *Independent* 11 November 1988

4 Film is the least realistic of art forms.
In the *Guardian* 16 February 1989

Mancroft, Lord (1914–87). British Conservative politician

1 Cricket – a game which the English, not being a spiritual people, have invented to give themselves some conception of eternity.
Bees in Some Bonnets (1979)

Mandale, W. R. (fl. 1850s). English writer

1 That's the way the money goes – Pop goes the weasel!
'Pop Goes the Weasel' (1853 song); also attributed to Charles Twiggs

Mandela, Nelson (1918–). South African statesman

1 No one is born hating another person because of the colour of his skin, or his background, or his religion. People must learn to hate, and if they can learn to hate, they can be taught to love, for love comes more naturally to the human heart than its opposite.
Long Walk to Freedom (1994)

Mankiewicz, Herman (1897–1953). American journalist, screenwriter and film producer

1 Old age ... it's the only disease you don't look forward to being cured of.
Citizen Kane (1941, with Orson Welles)

2 Rosebud.
Citizen Kane (1941, with Orson Welles)

Manley, Mrs (1663–1724). English novelist and playwright

1 No time like the present.
The Lost Lover (1696) act 4, sc. 1

Mann, Thomas (1875–1955). German novelist

1 *Unser Sterben ist mehr eine Angelegenheit der Weiterlebenden als unserer selbst.*
A man's dying is more the survivors' affair than his own.
The Magic Mountain (1924) ch. 6, sect. 8 (translated by H. T. Lowe-Porter)

Mao Zedong (Tse-tung) (1893–1976). Chinese statesman

1 Politics is war without bloodshed while war is politics with bloodshed.
Lecture, 1938, in *Selected Works* (1965) vol. 2, p. 153

2 Every Communist must grasp the truth, 'Political power grows out of the barrel of a gun.'
Speech, 6 November 1938, in *Selected Works* (1965) vol. 2, p. 224

3 All reactionaries are paper tigers.
Interview, 1946, in *Selected Works* (1961) vol. 4, p. 100

4 Letting a hundred flowers blossom and a hundred schools of thought contend is the policy for promoting progress in the arts and the sciences and a flourishing socialist culture in our land.
Speech in Peking (Beijing), 27 February 1957, in *Quotations of Chairman Mao* (1966) p. 302

5 The more books one reads, the more stupid one becomes.
Attributed, 1976; quoted in Ross Terrill *Mao: A Biography* (1980), ch. 22

Marie-Antoinette (1755–93). Queen consort of Louis XVI

1 *Qu'ils mangent de la brioche.*
Let them eat cake.
On being told that her people had no bread (attributed). Also used by others

Markham, Dewey 'Pigmeat' (1906–81). American songwriter and comedy writer

1 Here comes the judge.
Song title (1968) co-written with Dick Alen, Bob Astor and Sarah Harvey; often quoted as 'Here come de judge'

Marks, Leo (1920–2001). British writer

1 The life that I have is all that I have
And the life that I have is yours
The love that I have of the life that I have
Is yours and yours and yours.
Poem recited by Virginia McKenna as Violette Szabo in *Carve Her Name with Pride* (1958)

Marlowe, Christopher (1564–93). English playwright and poet

1 Our swords shall play the orators for us.
Tamburlaine the Great (1590) pt 1, act 1, sc. 2

2 Is it not passing brave to be a king,
And ride in triumph through Persepolis?
Tamburlaine the Great (1590) pt 1, act 2, sc. 5

3 Nature that framed us of four elements,
Warring within our breasts for regiment,
Doth teach us all to have aspiring minds.
Tamburlaine the Great (1590) pt 1, act 2, sc. 7

4 The sweet fruition of an earthly crown.
Tamburlaine the Great (1590) pt 1, act 2, sc. 7

5 Virtue is the fount whence honour springs.
Tamburlaine the Great (1590) pt 1, act 4, sc. 4

6 If all the pens that ever poets held
Had fed the feeling of their masters' thoughts.
Tamburlaine the Great (1590) pt 1, act 5, sc. 1

7 More childish valorous than manly wise.
Tamburlaine the Great (1590) pt 2, act 4, sc. 1

8 Holla, ye pampered jades of Asia!
What, can ye draw but twenty miles a day?
Tamburlaine the Great (1590) pt 2, act 4, sc. 3

9 Why, this is hell, nor am I out of it.
Doctor Faustus (c.1592) act 1, sc. 3

10 Was this the face that launched a thousand ships,
And burnt the topless towers of Ilium?
Sweet Helen, make me immortal with a kiss!
Doctor Faustus (c.1592) act 5, sc. 1

11 O I'll leap up to my God: who pulls me down?
See, see, where Christ's blood streams in the firmament.
Doctor Faustus (c.1592) act 5, sc. 2

12 Infinite riches in a little room.
The Jew of Malta (c.1592) act 1, sc. 1

13 Who ever loved that loved not at first sight?
Hero and Leander (1598) First Sestiad, l. 167

14 Come live with me, and be my love,
And we will all the pleasures prove.
'The Passionate Shepherd to his Love' (1599)

15 By shallow rivers, to whose falls,
Melodious birds sing madrigals.
'The Passionate Shepherd to his Love' (1599)

Marquis, Don(ald Robert Perry) (1878–1937). American novelist, playwright and poet

1 procrastination is the art of keeping up with yesterday.
archy and mehitabel (1927) 'certain maxims of archy'

2 an optimist is a guy that has never had much experience.
archy and mehitabel (1927) 'certain maxims of archy'

3 Writing a book of poetry is like dropping a rose petal down the Grand Canyon and waiting for the echo.
Quoted in E. Anthony *O Rare Don Marquis* (1962), ch. 6

Marryat, Frederick (1792–1848). English naval captain and novelist

1 As savage as a bear with a sore head.
The King's Own (1830) vol. 2, ch. 6

Martial (AD c.40–c.104). Spanish-born Latin epigrammatist

1 *Rus in urbe.*
Country in the town.
Epigrammata bk 12, no. 57

Marvell, Andrew (1621–78).
English poet

1 Had we but world enough, and
time,
This coyness, lady, were no crime.
'To His Coy Mistress' (1681) l. 1

2 My vegetable love should grow
Vaster than empires, and more
slow.
'To His Coy Mistress' (1681) l. 11

3 But at my back I always hear
Time's wingèd chariot hurrying
near.
'To His Coy Mistress' (1681) l. 21

4 Annihilating all that's made
To a green thought in a green
shade.
'The Garden' (1681) st. 6

5 Had it lived long, it would have
been
Lilies without, roses within.
'The Nymph Complaining for the Death of
her Fawn' (c.1650–2)

Marvell, Holt (Eric Maschwitz)
(1901–69). English songwriter

1 These foolish things
Remind me of you.
'These Foolish Things Remind Me of You'
(1935 song)

Marx, Groucho (1895–1977).
American film comedian

1 Either he's dead, or my watch has
stopped.
In *A Day at the Races* (film, 1937; script by
Robert Pirosh, George Seaton and George
Oppenheimer)

2 Please accept my resignation. I
don't want to belong to any club
that will accept me as a member.
Groucho and Me (1959) ch. 26

Marx, Karl (1818–83). German
political philosopher

1 Religion … is the opium of the
people.
*A Contribution to the Critique of Hegel's
Philosophy of Right* (1843–4) introduction

2 From each according to his abilities, to each according to his
needs.
Critique of the Gotha Programme (written
1875, but of earlier origin)

**Marx, Karl and Engels,
Friedrich** (1818–83; 1820–95). Co-
founders of modern Communism

1 A spectre is haunting Europe – the
spectre of Communism.
The Communist Manifesto (1848) opening
words

2 The history of all hitherto existing
society is the history of class
struggles.
The Communist Manifesto (1848) pt 1

3 The proletarians have nothing to
lose but their chains. They have a
world to win. Working men of all
countries, unite!
The Communist Manifesto (1848) *ad fin.*
(from the 1888 translation by Samuel
Moore, edited by Engels and commonly
quoted as 'Workers of the world, unite!')

Mary, Queen of Scots (1542–87).
Queen of Scotland 1542–67

1 *En ma fin git mon commencement.*
In my end is my beginning.
Motto embroidered with an emblem of her
mother, Mary of Guise, and quoted in a
letter from William Drummond of
Hawthornden to Ben Jonson in 1619

Mary Tudor (Mary I) (1516–58).
Queen of England from 1553

1 When I am dead and opened, you
shall find 'Calais' lying in my heart.
Holinshed's Chronicles vol. 4 (1808) p. 137

Masefield, John (Edward) (1878–
1967). English poet and novelist

1 I must go down to the seas again, to
the lonely sea and the sky,
And all I ask is a tall ship and a star
to steer her by.
'Sea Fever' (1902)

2 In this life he laughs longest who
laughs last.
The Widow in Bye Street (1912) ch. 4

Massinger, Philip (1583–1640).
English dramatist

1 He that would govern others, first
should be
The master of himself.
The Bondman (1623) act 1, sc. 3

Mathison, Melissa (1950–).
American screenwriter

1 E.T. phone home.
E.T. – the Extraterrestrial (film, 1982)

Maugham, W(illiam) Somerset
(1874–1965). English novelist

1 People ask you for criticism, but
they only want praise.
Of Human Bondage (1915) ch. 50

2 Money is like a sixth sense without
which you cannot make a complete use of the other five.
Of Human Bondage (1915) ch. 51

3 Impropriety is the soul of wit.
The Moon and Sixpence (1919) ch. 4

4 The Chinese are the aristocracy of
the East.
The Gentleman in the Parlour (1930)

Maupassant, Guy de (1850–93).
French writer

1 *La moindre chose contient un peu
d'inconnu. Trouvons-le.*
The least thing contains something
mysterious. Find it.
Pierre et Jean (1877) preface

McCarthy, Mary (1912–89).
American novelist and social
commentator

1 The happy ending is our national
belief.
'America the Beautiful', in *Commentary*,
September 1947

2 Every age has a keyhole to which its
eye is pasted.
'My Confession' (1953); collected in *On the
Contrary* (1961)

3 Every word she writes is a lie,
including 'and' and 'the'.
Quoting herself on Lillian Hellman in the
New York Times 16 February 1980, p. 12

McClellan, George B(rinton)
(1826–85). American soldier and
politician

1 All quiet along the Potomac.
Said at the time of the American Civil War
(attributed)

McCoy, Horace (1897–1955).
American novelist

1 They shoot horses don't they.
Title of novel (1935)

McEnroe, John (Patrick) (1959–).
American tennis player

1 You cannot be serious!
In protest at an umpire's decision at Wim-
bledon (early 1980s)

**McGoohan, Patrick, Markstein,
George and Tomblin, David**
(1928–; c.1930–87; 1931–). American
actor, German-born scriptwriter
and British director

1 I am not a number, I am a free man!
Number Six in *The Prisoner* (TV series, 1968)

McGough, Roger (1937–). English
poet and performer

1 Discretion is the better part of
Valerie (though all of her is nice).
'Discretion' (1969)

McGregor, Jimmy (1930–).
Scottish singer and songwriter

1 He's football crazy, he's football
mad.
'Football Crazy' (1960 song)

McLean, Don (1945–). American
songwriter

1 So, bye, bye, Miss American Pie,
Drove my Chevy to the levee
But the levee was dry.
'American Pie' (1972 song, on the death of
Buddy Holly)

McLuhan, (Herbert) Marshall
(1911–80). Canadian
communications theorist

1 The new electronic interdepend-
ence recreates the world in the
image of a global village.
The Gutenberg Galaxy (1962) p. 31

2 The medium is the message.
Understanding Media (1964) ch. 1 (title)

3 If the nineteenth century was the
age of the editorial chair, ours is the
century of the psychiatrist's couch.
Understanding Media (1964)

McMurtry, Larry Jeff (1936–).
American novelist

1 Self-parody is the first portent of
age.
Some Can Whistle (1989) pt 1, ch. 14

Mead, Margaret (1901–78).
American anthropologist

1 The greatest invention since the
novel.
Of television. Comment, 31 December 1974

Mead, Shepherd (1914–).
American advertising executive

1 How to succeed in business without really trying.
Title of book (1952)

Medawar, Sir Peter (Brian)
(1915–87). British zoologist and
immunologist

1 I cannot give any scientist of any
age better advice than this: the
intensity of a conviction that a
hypothesis is true has no bearing
over whether it is true or not.
Advice to a young scientist, attributed
(1879)

Melville, Herman (1819–91).
American novelist

1 Call me Ishmael.
Moby Dick (1851) ch. 1

2 There is a wisdom that is woe; but
there is a woe that is madness.
Moby Dick (1851) ch. 96

3 To produce a mighty book, you
must choose a mighty theme. No
great and enduring volume can
ever be written on the flea, though
many there be who have tried it.
Moby Dick (1851) ch. 104

Menander (342–*c*.292 BC). Greek
comic playwright

1 Whom the gods love dies young.
Dis Exapaton fragment 4, in F. H. Sandbach
(ed.) *Menandri Reliquiae Selectae* (1990)

Mencken, H(enry) L(ouis) (1880–
1956). American journalist,
language commentator and critic

1 Poetry is a comforting piece of fiction set to more or less lascivious
music.
Prejudices (1922) 3rd series, ch. 7

2 Faith may be defined briefly as an
illogical belief in the occurence of
the improbable.
Prejudices (1922) 3rd series, ch. 14

3 Hygiene is the corruption of
medicine by morality.
Prejudices (1922) 3rd series, 'The Physician'

4 The opera … is to music what a
bawdy house is to a cathedral.
Letter to Isaac Goldberg (1925)

5 When women kiss it always
reminds one of prize-fighters
shaking hands.
Chrestomathy (1949) ch. 30

6 Puritanism. The haunting fear that
someone, somewhere, may be
happy.
Chrestomathy (1949) ch. 30

7 Men have a much better time of it
than women. For one thing, they
marry later. For another thing, they
die earlier.
Chrestomathy (1949) ch. 30

8 Conscience: the inner voice which
warns us that someone may be
looking.
A Little Book in C major (1916) p. 42

Menzies, Sir Robert Gordon
(1894–1978). Australian statesman
1 What Great Britain calls the Far
East is to us the near north.
Quoted in the *Sydney Morning Herald* 27
April 1939

Mercer, David (1928–80). English
playwright
1 A suitable case for treatment.
Title of television play (1962) and film (1966)

Mercer, Johnny (1909–76).
American songwriter
1 Hooray for Hollywood.
Title of song which first appeared in the film
Hollywood Hotel (1937)
2 Make it one for my baby
And one more for the road.
'One For My Baby' (1943 song)

Meredith, George (1828–1909).
English novelist and poet
1 Kissing don't last: cookery do!
The Ordeal of Richard Feverel (1859) ch. 28
2 Cynicism is intellectual dandyism.
The Egoist (1879) ch. 7
3 There is nothing the body suffers
the soul may not profit by.
Diana of the Crossways (1885) ch. 43

Meredith, Owen (Edward Robert
Bulwer Lytton, 1st Earl of Lytton)
(1831–91). English poet and
statesman
1 Genius does what it must, and
Talent does what it can.
'Last Words of a Sensitive Second-Rate Poet'
(1868)

Metternich, Prince (Clemens
Lothar Wenzel) (1773–1859). Austrian
statesman
1 When Paris sneezes, Europe
catches cold.
Letter, 26 January 1830
2 Italy is a geographical expression.
In *Mémoires, Documents, etc. de Metternich
publiés par son fils* (1883) vol. 7, p. 415

Middleton, Thomas (c.1580–1627).
English playwright
1 Anything for a quiet life.
Title of play (written c.1620, possibly with
John Webster)

Mikes, George (1912–87).
Hungarian-born writer
1 On the Continent people have
good food; in England people have
good table manners.
How to be an Alien (1946)
2 Continental people have sex life;
the English have hot-water bottles.
How to be an Alien (1946)
3 An Englishman, even if he is alone,
forms an orderly queue of one.
How to be an Alien (1946)
4 Many continentals think life is a
game, the English think cricket is a
game.
How to be an Alien (1946)

Mill, John Stuart (1806–73).
English philosopher and
economist
1 If all mankind minus one were of
one opinion, and only one person
were of the contrary opinion,
mankind would no more be justified in silencing that one person
than he, if he had the power, would
be justified in silencing mankind.
On Liberty (1859) ch. 2
2 The liberty of the individual must
be thus far limited; he must not
make himself a nuisance to other
people.
On Liberty (1859) ch. 3
3 Liberty consists in doing what one
desires.
On Liberty (1859) ch. 5
4 Ask yourself whether you are
happy, and you cease to be so.
Autobiography (1873) ch. 5

Miller, Arthur (1915–2005).
American playwright
1 A good newspaper, I suppose, is a
nation talking to itself.
In the *Observer* 26 November 1961

2 A suicide kills two people, Maggie, that's what it's for!
After the Fall (1964) act 2

3 Without alienation, there can be no politics.
In *Marxism Today* January 1988

Miller, Henry (Valentine) (1891–1980). American novelist

1 Every man with a bellyful of the classics is an enemy of the human race.
Tropic of Cancer (1934)

2 Chaos is the score upon which reality is written.
Tropic of Cancer (1934)

3 Example moves the world more than doctrine.
The Cosmological Eye (1939) 'An Open Letter to Surrealists Everywhere'

4 Imagination is the voice of daring. If there is anything Godlike about God it is that. He dared to imagine everything.
Sexus (1945) ch. 14

5 I have always looked upon decay as being just as wonderful an expression of life as growth.
The Wisdom of the Heart (1947) 'Reflections on Writing'

6 All growth is a leap in the dark, a spontaneous unpremeditated act without benefit of experience.
The Wisdom of the Heart (1947) 'The Absolute Collective'

7 Life, as it is called, is for most of us one long postponement.
The Wisdom of the Heart (1947) 'The Enormous Womb'

8 In this age, which believes that there is a short cut to everything, the greatest lesson to be learned is that the most difficult way is, in the long run, the easiest.
The Books in My Life (1951) preface

Mills, Irving (1894–1985). American songwriter

1 It don't mean a thing If it ain't got that swing.
Title of song (1932)

Milne, A(lan) A(lexander) (1882–1956). English children's writer

1 They're changing guard at Buckingham Palace –
Christopher Robin went down with Alice.
When We Were Very Young (1924) 'Buckingham Palace'

2 Hush! Hush! Whisper who dares! Christopher Robin is saying his prayers.
When We Were Very Young (1924) 'Vespers'

3 How sweet to be a Cloud Floating in the Blue!
Winnie-the-Pooh (1926) ch. 1

4 I am a Bear of Very Little Brain, and long words Bother me.
Winnie-the-Pooh (1926) ch. 4

Milton, John (1608–74). English poet

1 Before the starry threshold of Jove's Court
My mansion is.
Comus (1637) l. 1

2 Above the smoke and stir of this dim spot,
Which men call earth.
Comus (1637) l. 5

3 What hath night to do with sleep?
Comus (1637) l. 122

4 Come, knit hands, and beat the ground,
In a light fantastic round.
Comus (1637) l. 143

5 A thousand fantasies
Begin to throng into my memory
Of calling shapes, and beckoning shadows dire,
And airy tongues, that syllable men's names
On sands, and shores, and desert wildernesses.
Comus (1637) l. 204

6 Sweet Echo, sweetest nymph that liv'st unseen
Within thy airy shell.
Comus (1637) l. 230

7 'Tis chastity, my brother, chastity:
She that has that, is clad in complete steel.
Comus (1637) l. 420

8 And filled the air with barbarous dissonance.
Comus (1637) l. 550

9 Beauty is Nature's coin.
Comus (1637) l. 739

10 Sabrina fair.
Comus (1637) l. 859 'Song'

11 Love Virtue, she alone is free.
Comus (1637) l. 1019

12 Yet once more, O ye laurels, and once more
Ye myrtles brown, with ivy never sere,
I come to pluck your berries harsh and crude.
'Lycidas' (1638) l. 1

13 For Lycidas is dead, dead ere his prime.
'Lycidas' (1638) l. 8

14 For we were nursed upon the self-same hill.
'Lycidas' (1638) l. 23

15 To sport with Amaryllis in the shade.
'Lycidas' (1638) l. 68

16 Fame is the spur that the clear spirit doth raise
(That last infirmity of noble mind)
To scorn delights, and live laborious days.
'Lycidas' (1638) l. 70

17 The hungry sheep look up, and are not fed.
'Lycidas' (1638) l. 125

18 Look homeward angel now, and melt with ruth.
'Lycidas' (1638) l. 163

19 At last he rose, and twitched his mantle blue:
Tomorrow to fresh woods, and pastures new.
'Lycidas' (1638) l. 192

20 Such sweet compulsion doth in music lie.
'Arcades' (1645) l. 68

21 Where more is meant than meets the ear.
'Il Penseroso' (1645) l. 120

22 Hence, loathèd Melancholy.
'L'Allegro' (1645) l. 1

23 Come, and trip it as ye go
On the light fantastic toe.
'L'Allegro' (1645) l. 33

24 Then to the spicy nut-brown ale.
'L'Allegro' (1645) l. 100

25 Warble his native wood-notes wild.
'L'Allegro' (1645) l. 125

26 New *Presbyter* is but old *Priest* writ large.
'On the New Forcers of Conscience under the Long Parliament' (1646)

27 Of man's first disobedience, and the fruit
Of that forbidden tree, whose mortal taste
Brought death into the world, and all our woe,
With loss of Eden.
Paradise Lost (1667) bk 1, l. 1

28 Things unattempted yet in prose or rhyme.
Paradise Lost (1667) bk 1, l. 15

29 That to the height of this great argument
I may assert eternal providence,
And justify the ways of God to men.
Paradise Lost (1667) bk 1, l. 24

30 A dungeon horrible, on all sides round
As one great furnace flamed, yet from those flames.
No light.
Paradise Lost (1667) bk 1, l. 61

31 Better to reign in hell, than serve in heaven.
Paradise Lost (1667) bk 1, l. 263

32 Thick as autumnal leaves that strew the brooks
In Vallombrosa, where the Etrurian shades.
High overarched imbower.
Paradise Lost (1667) bk 1, l. 302

33 With ruin upon ruin, rout on rout,
Confusion worse confounded.
Paradise Lost (1667) bk 2, l. 995

34 Flowers of all hue, and without
thorn the rose.
Paradise Lost (1667) bk 4, l. 256

35 Wherefore with thee
Came not all hell broke loose?
Paradise Lost (1667) bk 4, l. 917

36 Freely we serve,
Because we freely love, as in our
will
To love or not; in this we stand or
fall.
Paradise Lost (1667) bk 5, l. 538

37 The serpent subtlest beast of all the
field.
Paradise Lost (1667) bk 9, l. 86

38 O fairest of creation, last and best
Of all God's works.
Paradise Lost (1667) bk 9, l. 896

39 Yet I shall temper so
Justice with mercy.
Paradise Lost (1667) bk 10, l. 77

40 Some natural tears they dropped,
but wiped them soon;
The world was all before them,
where to choose
Their place of rest, and Providence
their guide:
They hand in hand, with wandering steps and slow,
Through Eden took their solitary
way.
Paradise Lost (1667) bk 12, l. 645

41 Ask for this great deliverer now,
and find him
Eyeless in Gaza at the mill with
slaves.
Samson Agonistes (1671) l. 40

42 Just are the ways of God,
And justifiable to men.
Samson Agonistes (1671) l. 293

43 And calm of mind, all passion
spent.
Samson Agonistes (1671) l. 1758

44 When I consider how my light is
spent,
E're half my days, in this dark world
and wide.
*Sonnet 16 'When I consider how my light is
spent' (1673)*

45 They also serve who only stand and
wait.
*Sonnet 16 'When I consider how my light is
spent' (1673)*

46 Methought I saw my late espousèd
saint
Brought to me like Alcestis from
the grave.
*Sonnet 19 'Methought I saw my late
espousèd saint' (1673)*

Missal Texts used in the service of
the Mass throughout the year

1 *Dominus vobiscum.*
Et cum spiritu tuo.
The Lord be with you.
And with thy spirit.
The Ordinary of the Mass

2 *In Nomine Patris, et Filii, et Spiritus
Sancti.*
In the Name of the Father, and of
the Son, and of the Holy Ghost.
The Ordinary of the Mass

3 *Introibo ad altare Dei.*
I will go unto the altar of God.
The Ordinary of the Mass

4 *Gloria Patri, et Filio, et Spiritui Sancto.*
*Sicut erat in principio, et nunc, et
semper, et in saecula saeculorum.*
Glory be to the Father, and to the
Son, and to the Holy Ghost. As it
was in the beginning, is now, and
ever shall be, world without end.
The Ordinary of the Mass 'The Doxology'

5 *Confiteor Deo omnipotenti.*
I confess to almighty God.
The Ordinary of the Mass

6 *Kyrie eleison … Christe eleison.*
Lord, have mercy upon us …
Christ, have mercy upon us.
The Ordinary of the Mass

7 *Gloria in excelsis Deo, et in terra pax hominibus bonae voluntatis.*
Glory be to God on high, and on earth peace to men of good will.
The Ordinary of the Mass

8 *Oremus.*
Let us pray.
The Ordinary of the Mass

9 *Sursum corda.*
Lift up your hearts.
The Ordinary of the Mass

10 *Deo gratias.*
Thanks be to God.
The Ordinary of the Mass

11 *Credo in unum Deum, Patrem omni-potentem, factorem coeli et terrae, visibilium omnium et invisibilium.*
I believe in one God, the Father almighty, maker of heaven and earth, and of all things visible and invisible.
The Ordinary of the Mass 'The Nicene Creed'

12 *Et incarnatus est de Spiritu Sancto, ex Maria Virgine; et homo factus est.*
And became incarnate by the Holy Ghost, of the Virgin Mary; and was made man.
The Ordinary of the Mass 'The Nicene Creed'

13 *Dignum et justum est.*
It is right and fitting.
The Ordinary of the Mass

14 *Sanctus, sanctus, sanctus, Dominus Deus Sabaoth. Pleni sunt coeli et terra gloria tua. Hosanna in excelsis. Benedictus qui venit in nomine Domini.*
Holy, holy, holy, Lord God of Hosts. Heaven and earth are full of thy glory. Hosanna in the highest. Blessed is he that cometh in the name of the Lord.
The Ordinary of the Mass

15 *Pater noster, qui es in coelis, sanctificetur nomen tuum.*
Our Father, who art in heaven, hallowed be thy name.
The Ordinary of the Mass

16 *Agnus Dei, qui tollis peccata mundi, miserere nobis. Agnus Dei, qui tollis peccata mundi, dona nobis pacem.*
Lamb of God, who takest away the sins of the world, have mercy on us. Lamb of God, who takest away the sins of the world, give us peace.
The Ordinary of the Mass

17 *Domine, non sum dignus ut intres sub tectum meum; sed tantum dic verbo, et sanabitur anima mea.*
Lord, I am not worthy that thou shouldst enter under my roof; but say only the word, and my soul shall be healed.
The Ordinary of the Mass

18 *Verbum caro factum est.*
The word was made flesh.
The Ordinary of the Mass

19 *Requiem aeternam dona eis, Domine: et lux perpetua luceat eis.*
Grant them eternal rest, O Lord; and let perpetual light shine on them.
Order of Mass for the Dead

20 *Dies irae, dies illa.*
That day, the day of wrath.
Order of Mass for the Dead 'Sequentia'

21 *Requiescant in pace.*
May they rest in peace.
Order of Mass for the Dead

22 *O felix culpa.*
O happy fault.
'Exsultet' on Holy Saturday

23 *In principio erat Verbum, et Verbum erat apud Deum, et Deus erat Verbum.*
In the beginning was the Word, and the Word was with God, and the Word was God.
The Ordinary of the Mass

24 *Ite missa est.*
Go, you are dismissed.
The Ordinary of the Mass (commonly translated as 'Go, the Mass is ended')

Mitchell, Margaret (1900–49). American novelist

1 I wish I could care what you do or where you go but I can't ... My dear, I don't give a damn.
Gone with the Wind (1936) ch. 57 (Rhett Butler to Scarlett). 'Frankly, my dear, I don't give a damn!' in the 1939 screen version by Sidney Howard

2 Death and taxes and childbirth!
There's never any convenient time
for any of them!
Scarlett O'Hara. *Gone With The Wind* (1936)
ch. 38

3 After all, tomorrow is another day.
Gone with the Wind (1936) *ad fin.*

Mitford, Nancy (Freeman)
(1904–73). English writer

1 Abroad is unutterably bloody and
foreigners are fiends.
Uncle Matthew speaking. *The Pursuit of Love*
(1945) ch. 15

Mizner, Wilson (1876–1933).
American dramatist

1 Be nice to people on your way up,
because you'll meet 'em on your
way down.
Alva Johnston *The Legendary Mizners* (1953)

2 If you steal from one author, it's
plagiarism; if you steal from many,
it's research.
Alva Johnston *The Legendary Mizners* (1953)

Mola, Emilio (d.1937). Spanish
general

1 *La quinta columna.*
The fifth column.
Speech, October 1936; said of the rebel
sympathizers at Madrid who would help
the four columns of nationalist rebels
besieging it

Molière (Jean-Baptiste Poquelin)
(1622–73). French comic playwright

1 *On ne meurt qu'une fois, et c'est pour
si longtemps!*
One dies only once, and it's for
such a long time!
Le Dépit amoureux (performed 1656, published 1662) act 5, sc. 3

2 *Hors de Paris, il n'y a pas de salut pour
honnêtes gens.*
Outside of Paris, there is no salva-
tion for gentlemen.
Les Précieuses ridicules (1659) sc. 9

3 *Les verrous et les grilles
Ne font pas la vertu des femmes et des
filles.*
Bolts and bars will not keep wives
and daughters chaste.
L'Ecole des maris (1661) act 1, sc. 2

4 *La naissance n'est rien où la vertu
n'est pas.*
Birth counts for little when virtue is
lacking.
Don Juan (1665) act 4, sc. 4

5 *Présentez toujours le devant au
monde.*
Always present your front to the
world.
L'Avare (1669) act 3, sc. 1

6 *Il faut manger pour vivre et non pas
vivre pour manger.*
One should eat to live, and not live
to eat.
L'Avare (1669) act 3, sc. 1

7 *Le scandale du monde est ce qui fait
l'offense,
Et ce n'est pas pécher que pécher en
silence.*
It is public scandal that constitutes
offence, and to sin in secret is not
to sin at all.
Le Tartuffe (1669) act 4, sc. 5

8 *Ils commencent ici par faire pendre un
homme et puis ils lui font son procès.*
Here [in Paris] they hang a man
first, and try him afterwards.
Monsieur de Pourceaugnac (1670) act 1, sc. 5

9 *Tout ce qui n'est point prose est vers; et
tout ce qui n'est point vers est prose.*
All that is not prose is verse; and all
that is not verse is prose.
Le Bourgeois Gentilhomme (1671) act 2, sc. 4

10 *Je vis de bonne soupe et non de beau
langage.*
Its good food and not fine words
that keeps me alive.
Les Femmes savantes (1672) act 2, sc. 7

11 *Un sot savant est sot plus qu'un sot
ignorant.*
A knowledgeable fool is a greater
fool than an ignorant fool.
Les Femmes savantes (1672) act 4, sc. 3

12 *Les livres cadrent mal avec le mariage.*
Reading and marriage don't go well
together.
Les Femmes savantes (1672) act 5, sc. 3

Montagu, Lady Mary Wortley
(1689–1762). English writer

1 Civility costs nothing and buys
everything.
Letter to her daughter Mary, Countess of
Bute, 30 May 1756, in Robert Halsband (ed.)
*Complete Letters of Lady Mary Wortley
Montagu* vol. 3 (1967)

Montaigne (Michel Eyquem de
Montaigne) (1533–92). French
moralist and essayist

1 *La plus grande chose du monde, c'est
de savoir être à soi.*
The greatest thing in the world is to
know how to be oneself.
Essais (1580) bk 1, ch. 39

2 *La gloire et le repos sont choses qui ne
peuvent loger en même gîte.*
Fame and tranquillity can never be
bedfellows.
Essais (1580) bk 1, ch. 39

3 *Que sais-je?*
What do I know?
Essais (1580) bk 2, ch. 12 (on the position of
the sceptic)

Montesquieu (Charles-Louis de
Secondat) (1689–1755). French
political philosopher

1 *Il faut pleurer les hommes à leur
naissance, et non pas à leur mort.*
Men should be bewailed at their
birth, and not at their death.
Lettres Persanes (1721) no. 40 (translated by J.
Ozell, 1722)

2 *Si les triangles faisoient un Dieu, ils lui
donneroient trois côtés.*
If the triangles were to make a God
they would give him three sides.
Lettres Persanes (1721) no. 59 (translated by J.
Ozell, 1722)

3 *L'amour de la démocratie est celui de
l'égalité.*
Love of democracy is love of
equality.
De l'esprit des lois (1748) vol. 5, ch. 3

4 *La liberté est le droit de faire tout ce
que les lois permettent.*
Freedom is the right to do anything
the laws permit.
De l'esprit des lois (1748) vol. 11, ch. 3

5 *Les Anglais sont occupés; ils n'ont pas
le temps d'être polis.*
The English are busy; they don't
have time to be polite.
Pensées et fragments inédits … vol. 2 (1901)
no. 1428

Montgomery, Robert (1807–55).
English clergyman and poet

1 The solitary monk who shook the
world.
Luther: a Poem (1842) ch. 3 'Man's Need and
God's Supply'

Moon, William Least Heat
(William Trogdon) (1939–).
American writer

1 Whoever the last true cowboy in
America turns out to be, he's likely
to be an Indian.
Blue Highways: A Journey Into America (1983)
pt 5, ch. 2

Moore, Clement (1779–1863).
American writer and poet

1 'Twas the night before Christmas,
when all through the house
Not a creature was stirring, not
even a mouse.
The Night Before Christmas (1822)

2 But I heard him exclaim, ere he
drove out of sight,
'Happy Christmas to all. And to all
a good night.'
The Night Before Christmas (1822)

Moore, Edward (1712–57). English
playwright

1 This is adding insult to injuries.
The Foundling (1748) act 5, sc. 5

2 I am rich beyond the dreams of
avarice.
The Gamester (1753) act 2, sc. 2

Moore, George (1852–1933).
Anglo-Irish novelist

1 Art must be parochial in the beginning to become cosmopolitan in the end.
Hail and Farewell: Ave (1911) p. 3

Moore, Thomas (1779–1852). Irish musician and songwriter

1 The harp that once through Tara's halls
The soul of music shed,
Now hangs as mute on Tara's walls
As if that soul were fled.
Irish Melodies (1807) 'The harp that once through Tara's halls'

2 The Minstrel Boy to the war is gone.
Irish Melodies (1807) 'The Minstrel Boy'

3 Rich and rare were the gems she wore,
And a bright gold ring on her wand she bore.
Irish Melodies (1807) 'Rich and rare were the gems she wore'

4 'Tis the last rose of summer
Left blooming alone;
All her lovely companions
Are faded and gone.
Irish Melodies (1807) ''Tis the last rose of summer'

5 Oft, in the stilly night,
Ere Slumber's chain has bound me,
Fond Memory brings the light
Of other days around me.
National Airs (1815) 'Oft in the Stilly Night'

Morell, Thomas (1703–84). English librettist

1 See, the conquering hero comes!
Sound the trumpets, beat the drums!
Judas Maccabeus (1747) 'A chorus of youths' and *Joshua* (1748) pt 3 (to music by Handel)

Morey, Larry American songwriter

1 Heigh ho, heigh ho
It's off to work we go.
First lines of the song 'Heigh-Ho' from the film *Snow White and the Seven Dwarfs* (1937)

2 Whistle while you work.
Title of song from the film *Snow White and the Seven Dwarfs* (1937)

Morley, Robert (1908–92). English actor

1 It is a great help for a man to be in love with himself. For an actor, it is absolutely essential.
In *Playboy* (1979)

Morris, Desmond (1928–). English anthropologist

1 The city is not a concrete jungle, it is a human zoo.
The Human Zoo (1969) introduction

Morris, George Pope (1802–64). American poet

1 Woodman, spare that tree!
'Woodman, Spare That Tree' (1830)

Morrison, Jim (1943–71). American rock singer and songwriter

1 C'mon, baby, light my fire.
'Light My Fire' (1967 song, with Robby Krieger)

Motley, John Lothrop (1814–77). American historian

1 Give us the luxuries of life, and we will dispense with its necessities.
In Oliver Wendell Holmes *Autocrat of the Breakfast-Table* (1857–8) ch. 6

Muggeridge, Malcolm (1903–90). British journalist

1 The orgasm has replaced the Cross as the focus of longing and the image of fulfilment.
Tread Softly (1966) p. 46

Muir, Frank (1920–98). English writer and broadcaster

1 The thinking man's crumpet.
Description of Joan Bakewell (attributed)

Mumford, Lewis (1895–1990). American sociologist and author

1 Every generation revolts against its fathers and makes friends with its grandfathers.
The Brown Decades (1931) p. 3

Murdoch, Dame (Jean) Iris (1919–99). Irish novelist and philosopher

1 All our failures are ultimately failures in love.
The Bell (1958)

2 One doesn't have to get anywhere in a marriage. It's not a public conveyance.
A Severed Head (1961) ch. 3

Murphy, Tom (Thomas) S. (1925–). American media company executive

1 If you hire mediocre people, they will hire mediocre people.
In *Fortune* 6 May 1991

Murray, Michael Director of Human Resources, Microsoft

1 If Microsoft were a car it would have a large gas pedal and a small but workable brake. It would not have a rear-view mirror.
In *Newsweek* 11 July 1994

Murrow, Ed (1908–65). American broadcaster and journalist

1 Anyone who isn't confused doesn't really understand the situation.
On the Vietnam War, in Walter Bryan *The Improbable Irish* (1969) ch. 1

Musset, Alfred de (1810–57). French poet and playwright

1 *Je suis venu trop tard dans un monde trop vieux.*
I have come too late into a world too old.
Rollo (1833)

Mussolini, Benito (1883–1945). Italian politician and Prime Minister

1 Better one day as a lion than a hundred years as a sheep.
Comment (c.1930); quoted in Denis Mack-Smith *Mussolini's Roman Empire* (1976), p. 47

2 A nation, to remain healthy, should make war every twenty-five years.
Comment (1934); quoted in Denis Mack-Smith *Mussolini's Roman Empire* (1976), p. 63

Nabokov, Vladimir (1899–1977). Russian-born American writer

1 Life is a great surprise. I do not see why death should not be an even greater one.
Pale Fire (1962)

2 Human life is but a series of footnotes to a vast, obscure unfinished masterpiece.
Pale Fire (1962) 'Commentary'

3 Solitude is the playfield of Satan.
Pale Fire (1962) 'Commentary'

4 Style and structure are the essence of a book; great ideas are hogwash.
Interview in the *Paris Review*, Summer 1967

5 Satire is a lesson, parody is a game.
Interview in *Wisconsin Studies in Contemporary Literature*, spring 1967

Nairne, Lady Caroline (1766–1845). Scottish songwriter

1 Will ye no come back again?
Song title

Napoleon I (1769–1821). French general and Emperor

1 *Du sublime au ridicule il n'y a qu'un pas.*
There is only one step from the sublime to the ridiculous.
To De Pradt, Polish ambassador, after the retreat from Moscow in 1812; in D. G. De Pradt *Histoire de l'Ambassade dans le grand-duché de Varsovie en 1812* (1815) p. 215

2 An army marches on its stomach.
Attributed, but also to Frederick the Great

3 *L'Angleterre est une nation de boutiquiers.*
England is a nation of shopkeepers.
In Barry E. O'Meara *Napoleon in Exile* (1822) vol. 2, p. 81

4 Not tonight, Josephine.
Attributed, but probably apocryphal

Nash, (Frederic) Ogden (1902–71). American humorous versifier

1 Candy
Is dandy
But liquor
Is quicker.
Hard Lines (1931) 'Reflections on Ice-Breaking'

2 I think that I shall never see
A billboard lovely as a tree.
Perhaps, unless the billboards fall,
I'll never see a tree at all.
Happy Days (1933) 'Song of the Open Road'

3 The camel has a single hump;
The dromedary, two;
Or else the other way around,
I'm never sure. Are you?
The Bad Parents' Garden of Verse (1936) 'The Camel'

4 God in His wisdom made the fly
And then forgot to tell us why.
Good Intentions (1942) 'The Fly'

Nathan, George (Jean) (1882–1958). American theatre critic

1 The test of a real comedian is whether you laugh at him before he opens his mouth.
Quoted in *American Mercury* September 1929

Necker, Germaine (Baronne de Staël) (1766–1817). French writer

1 *En France, on étudie les hommes; en Allemagne, les livres.*
In France, they study men; in Germany, books.
De l'Allemagne (1810)

2 *La poésie est le langage naturel de tous les cultes.*
Poetry is the natural language of all religions.
De l'Allemagne (1810)

Nelson, Lord Horatio (1758–1805). British admiral

1 Before this time to-morrow I shall have gained a peerage, or Westminster Abbey.
Before the battle of the Nile, in Robert Southey *Life of Nelson* (1813) ch. 5

2 I have only one eye, – I have a right to be blind sometimes … I really do not see the signal!
At the battle of Copenhagen, in Robert Southey *Life of Nelson* (1813) ch. 7

3 England expects that every man will do his duty.
At the battle of Trafalgar, in Robert Southey *Life of Nelson* (1813) ch. 9

4 Thank God, I have done my duty.
At the battle of Trafalgar, in Robert Southey *Life of Nelson* (1813) ch. 9

5 Kiss me, Hardy.
At the battle of Trafalgar, in Robert Southey *Life of Nelson* (1813) ch. 9

Newbolt, Sir Henry (1862–1938). English lawyer, poet and man of letters

1 There's a breathless hush in the Close to-night –
Ten to make and the match to win –.
A bumping pitch and a blinding light,
An hour to play and the last man in.
'Vitaï Lampada' (1897)

2 'Play up! play up! and play the game!'
'Vitaï Lampada' (1897)

Newley, Anthony and Bricusse, Leslie (1931–; 1931–). British songwriters

1 Stop the world, I want to get off.
Title of musical (1961)

Newman, John Henry (1801–90). English theologian and cardinal

1 Lead, kindly Light.
'Lead, kindly Light' (1834)

2 *We can believe what we choose.* We are answerable for what we choose to believe.
Letter to Mrs Froude, 27 June 1848

3 Praise to the Holiest in the height.
The Dream of Gerontius (1865)

4 If I am obliged to bring religion into after-dinner toasts (which indeed does not seem quite the thing) I shall drink – to the Pope, if you please – still, to Conscience first, and to the Pope afterwards.
A Letter Addressed to the Duke of Norfolk … (1875) sect. 5

Newton, John (1725–1807). English clergyman

1 Amazing grace!
Olney Hymns (1779) 'Amazing grace'

Newton, Sir Isaac (1642–1727). English mathematician and physicist

1 If I have seen further it is by standing on the shoulders of giants.
Letter to Robert Hooke, 5 February 1676, in H. W. Turnbull (ed.) *Correspondence of Isaac Newton* vol. 1 (1959) p. 416

2 *Actioni contrarium semper et aequalem esse reactionem.*
To every action there is always opposed an equal reaction.
Principia Mathematica (1687) Laws of Motion 3 (translated by Andrew Motte, 1729)

3 I don't know what I may seem to the world, but as to myself, I seem to have been only like a boy playing on the sea-shore and diverting myself in now and then finding a smoother pebble or a prettier shell than ordinary, whilst the great ocean of truth lay all undiscovered before me.
In Joseph Spence *Anecdotes* (ed. J. Osborn, 1966) no. 1259

4 In the absence of any other proof, the thumb alone would convince me of God's existence.
Attributed

Niemöller, Martin (1892–1984). German submarine commander

1 When Hitler attacked the Jews I was not a Jew, therefore, I was not concerned. And when Hitler attacked the Catholics, I was not a Catholic, and therefore, I was not concerned. And when Hitler attacked the unions and the industrialists, I was not a member of the unions and I was not concerned. Then, Hitler attacked me and the Protestant church – and there was nobody left to be concerned.
Children of Light and Darkness (1944) foreword

Nietzsche, Friedrich (1844–1900). German philosopher and writer

1 *Überzeugungen sind gefährlichere Feinde der Wahrheit als Lügen.*
Convictions are more dangerous enemies of truth than lies.
Menschliches, Allzumenschliches (1878) sect. 483

2 *Der Witz ist das Epigramm auf den Tod eines Gefühls.*
Wit is the epitaph of an emotion.
Menschliches, Allzumenschliches (1867–80) vol. 2, sect. 1, no. 202

3 *Moralität ist Heerden-Instinkt in Einzelnen.*
Morality is the herd-instinct in the individual.
Die fröhliche Wissenschaft (1882) bk 3, sect. 116

4 *Ich lehre euch den Übermenschen. Der Mensch ist Etwas, das überwunden werden soll.*
I teach you the superman. Man is something to be surpassed.
Also Sprach Zarathustra (1883) prologue, sect. 3

5 *Das Weib war der zweite Fehlgriff Gottes.*
Woman was God's second blunder.
Der Antichrist (1888) aphorism 48

6 Without music, life would be a mistake.
Die Götzen-Dämmerung (1889)

Nixon, Richard Milhous (1913–94). 37th President of the USA

1 There can be no whitewash at the White House.
Television speech on Watergate, 30 April 1973

2 American people don't believe anything until they see it on television.
In *Newsweek* 2 May 1994

Norden, Denis (1922–). English broadcaster and humorist

1 It's a funny kind of month, October. For the really keen cricket fan it's when you realise that your wife left you in May.
Quoted in *She* magazine, 1977

North, Christopher (Professor John Wilson) (1785–1854). Scottish literary critic

1 His Majesty's dominions, on which the sun never sets.
Blackwood's Magazine (April 1829) 'Noctes Ambrosianae' no. 42

2 Laws were made to be broken.
Blackwood's Magazine (May 1830) 'Noctes Ambrosianae' no. 49

3 Such accidents will happen in the best-regulated families.
Blackwood's Magazine (August 1834) 'Noctes Ambrosianae' no. 67

Norton, Caroline (née Sheridan) (1808–77). English poet and songwriter

1 Not lost but gone before.
'Not Lost but Gone Before'

Norworth, Jack (1879–1959).
American songwriter

1 Oh, shine on, shine on, harvest
moon

Up in the sky.
'Shine On, Harvest Moon' (1908 song)

Oates, Captain Lawrence (1880–1912). English polar explorer

1 I am just going outside and may be some time.
Last words, in *Scott's Last Expedition* (1913) ch. 20 (Scott's diary entry, 16–17 March 1912)

Ochs, Adolph S(imon) (1858–1935). American newspaper proprietor

1 All the news that's fit to print.
Motto of the *New York Times*, from 1896

Ogden, Frank (1920–). Canadian futurist

1 As the planet globalizes, groups tribalize.
Ogdenisms: The Frank Ogden Quote Book (1994)

2 My idea of long-range planning is lunch.
Ogdenisms: The Frank Ogden Quote Book (1994)

O Henry (William Sydney Porter) (1862–1910). American writer

1 Life is made up of sobs, sniffles, and smiles, with sniffles predominating.
The Four Million (1906) 'The Gift of the Magi'

2 If men knew how women pass the time when they are alone, they'd never marry.
The Four Million (1906) 'Memoirs of a Yellow Dog'

3 It was beautiful and simple as all truly great swindles are.
The Gentle Grafter (1908) 'The Octopus Marooned'

O'Keefe, Patrick (1872–1934). American advertising agent

1 Say it with flowers.
Slogan for the Society of American Florists, in *Florists' Exchange* 15 December 1917, p. 1268

Olivier, Laurence Baron (1907–89). English actor, producer and director

1 Acting is a masochistic form of exhibitionism. It is not quite the occupation of an adult.
Quoted in *Time Magazine* 3 July 1978

2 Shakespeare – the nearest thing in incarnation to the eye of God.
Quoted in *Kenneth Harris Talking To...*, 'Sir Laurence Olivier'

O'Neill, Eugene (1888–1953). American playwright

1 Life is for each man a solitary cell whose walls are mirrors.
Lazarus Laughed (1927) act 2, sc. 1

2 Life is perhaps most wisely regarded as a bad dream between two awakenings, and every day is a life in miniature.
Marco Millions (1928) act 2, sc. 2

3 A long day's journey into night.
Title of play (1939–41)

4 The iceman cometh.
Title of play (1946)

Oppenheimer, J(ulius) Robert (1904–67). American physicist

1 No man should escape our universities without knowing how little he knows.
In *Partisan Review*, Summer issue (1967)

Orbach, Susie (1946–). American psychotherapist

1 Fat is a feminist issue.
Title of book (1978)

Orczy, Baroness (Mrs Montague Barstow) (1865–1947). Hungarian-born novelist

1 We seek him here, we seek him there,
Those Frenchies seek him every-where.
Is he in heaven? – Is he in hell?
That demmed, elusive Pimpernel?
The Scarlet Pimpernel (1905) ch. 12

Orwell, George (Eric Arthur Blair) (1903–50). English novelist, essayist and journalist

1 I'm fat, but I'm thin inside. Has it ever struck you that there's a thin man inside every fat man, just as they say there's a statue inside every block of stone?
Coming up For Air (1939) pt 1, ch. 3

2 As I write, highly civilized human beings are flying overhead, trying to kill me.
The Lion and The Unicorn: Socialism and the English Genius (1941) pt 1, 'England Your England'

3 All propaganda is lies, even when one is telling the truth.
Diary entry, 14 March 1942

4 Four legs good, two legs bad.
Animal Farm (1945) ch. 3

5 All animals are equal but some animals are more equal than others.
Animal Farm (1945) ch. 10

6 The great enemy of clear language is insincerity.
'Politics and the English Language' (1946)

7 It was a bright cold day in April, and the clocks were striking thir-teen.
Nineteen Eighty-Four (1949) pt 1, ch. 1

8 Big brother is watching you.
Nineteen Eighty-Four (1949) pt 1, ch. 1

9 War is peace. Freedom is slavery. Ignorance is strength.
Nineteen Eighty-Four (1949) pt 1, ch. 1

10 *Doublethink* means the power of holding two contradictory beliefs in one's mind simultaneously, and accepting both of them.
Nineteen Eighty-Four (1949) pt 2, ch. 9

11 At 50, everyone has the face he deserves.
Notebook entry, 17 April 1949

Osborne, John (1929–94). English playwright

1 They spend their time mostly looking forward to the past.
Look Back in Anger (1956) act 2, sc. 1

2 Don't clap too hard – it's a very old building.
The Entertainer (1957) no. 7

O'Shaughnessy, Arthur (1844–81). English poet

1 We are the music makers,
We are the dreamers of dreams.
'Ode' (1874)

Osler, Sir William (1849–1919). Canadian-born physician

1 The greater the ignorance the greater the dogmatism.
Quoted in *Montreal Medical Journal*, September 1902

2 The natural man has only two primal passions, to get and beget.
Science and Immortality (1904) ch. 2

Otis, James (1725–83). American politician

1 Taxation without representation is tyranny.
Watchword (coined *c*.1761) of the American Revolution. *See Dictionary of American Biography* vol. 14, p. 102

Ovid (Publius Ovidius Naso) (43 BC–AD *c*.17). Roman poet

1 *Expedit esse deos, et, ut expedit, esse putemus.*
It is convenient that there be gods, and, as it is convenient, let us believe that there are.
Ars Amatoria bk 1, l. 637

2 *Ut desint vires, tamen est laudanda voluntas.*
Though the strength is lacking, yet the willingness is commendable.
Epistulae Ex Ponto bk 3, no. 4, l. 79

3 *Medio tutissimus ibis.*
You will go most safely by the middle way.
Metamorphoses bk 2, l. 137

4 *Video meliora, proboque;*
Deteriora sequor.
I see the better things, and approve; I follow the worse.
Metamorphoses bk 7, l. 20

5 *Tempus edax rerum.*
Time the devourer of everything.
Metamorphoses bk 15, l. 234

6 *Iam seges est ubi Troia fuit.*
Now there are cornfields where Troy once was.
Heroides bk 1, l. 42

Owen, Wilfred (1893–1918).
English poet

1 My subject is War, and the pity of War.
The Poetry is in the pity.
Preface (1918)

2 All a poet can do today is warn.
Preface (1918)

3 I am the enemy you killed, my friend.
'Strange Meeting' (1918)

Packard, Vance (1914–). American writer and journalist

1 The hidden persuaders.
Title of a study of the advertising industry (1957)

Pagnol, Marcel (1895–1974). French playwright and film-maker

1 *L'honneur, c'est comme les allumettes: ça ne sert qu'une fois.*
Honour is like a match, you can only use it once.
Marius (1946) act 4, sc. 5

Paine, Thomas (1737–1809). English political theorist

1 Government, even in its best state, is but a necessary evil; in its worst state, an intolerable one.
Common Sense (1776) ch. 1

2 My country is the world, and my religion is to do good.
The Rights of Man pt 2 (1792, ed. P. S. Foner, 1945) p. 414

3 Any system of religion that has any thing in it that shocks the mind of a child cannot be a true system.
The Age of Reason pt 1 (1794) p. 39

4 The sublime and the ridiculous are often so nearly related, that it is difficult to class them separately. One step above the sublime, makes

the ridiculous; and one step above the ridiculous, makes the sublime again.
The Age of Reason pt 2 (1795) p. 20

Palmer, Arnold (1929–). American golfer

1 Winning isn't everything, but wanting to is.
Quoted in Colin Jarman *The Guinness Dictionary of Sports Quotations* (1990)

Palmerston, Lord (Henry John Temple, 3rd Viscount Palmerston) (1784–1865). British Tory politician and Prime Minister

1 Die, my dear Doctor, that's the last thing I shall do!
Last words, in E. Latham *Famous Sayings and their Authors* (1904) p. 12

Pankhurst, Emmeline (née Goulden) (1858–1928). English suffragette

1 Women had always fought for men, and for their children. Now they were ready to fight for their own human rights.
My Own Story (1914) ch. 3

Parker, Dorothy (1893–1967). American critic and humorist

1 That woman speaks eighteen languages, and can't say No in any of them.
Quoted in Alexander Woollcott *While Rome Burns* (1934) 'Our Mrs Parker'

2 Men seldom make passes
At girls who wear glasses.
'News Item' (1937)

3 Sorrow is tranquillity remembered in emotion.
Here Lies (1939) 'Sentiment'

4 She ran the whole gamut of the emotions from A to B.
Of Katharine Hepburn at a Broadway first night (attributed)

Parker, Ross and Charles, Hugh (1914–74; 1907–95). British songwriters.

1 There'll always be an England
Song title (1979)

Parkinson, C(yril) N(orthcote)
(1909–93). English writer

1 Work expands so as to fill the time
available for its completion.
Parkinson's Law (1958) ch. 1

2 Time spent on any item of the
agenda will be in inverse proportion to the sum involved.
Parkinson's Law (1958) ch. 3

Parr-Davies, Harry (1914–55).
Welsh songwriter

1 Wish me luck, as you wave me
goodbye –
Cheerio, here I go, on my way.
Sung by Gracie Fields in *Shipyard Sally*
(1939)

Pascal, Blaise (1623–62). French
philosopher, mathematician,
physicist and moralist

1 *Dans une grande âme tout est grand.*
In a great soul everything is great.
Discours sur les passions de l'amour (attrib-
uted, *c.*1653)

2 *La dernière chose qu'on trouve en
faisant un ouvrage, est de savoir celle
qu'il faut mettre la première.*
The last thing one discovers in
composing a work is what to put
first.
Pensées (c.1654–62) no. 19

3 *Condition de l'homme: inconstance,
ennui, inquiétude.*
Man's condition. Inconstancy,
boredom, anxiety.
Pensées (c.1654–62) no. 127

4 *Notre nature est dans le mouvement;
le repos entier est la mort.*
Our nature consists in movement;
absolute rest is death.
Pensées (c.1654–62) no. 129

5 *Pesons le gain et la perte, en prenant
croix que Dieu est. Estimons ces deux
cas: si vous gagnez, vous gagnez tout;
si vous perdez, vous ne perdez rien.
Gagez donc qu'il est, sans hésiter.*
Let us weigh up the gain and loss
involved in calling heads that God
exists. Let us assess the two cases: if
you win you win everything, if you
lose you lose nothing. Do not
hesitate then; wager that he does
exist.
Pensées (c.1654–62) no. 233

6 *Tout notre raisonnement se réduit à
céder au sentiment.*
All our reasoning comes down to
surrendering to feeling.
Pensées (c.1654–62) no. 274

7 *Le cœur a ses raisons que la raison ne
connaît point.*
The heart has its reasons which
reason knows nothing of.
Pensées (c.1654–62) no. 277

8 *Le silence est la plus grande persécu-
tion: jamais les saints ne se sont tus.*
Silence is the greatest of all perse-
cutions: no saint was ever silent.
Pensées (c.1654–62) no. 920

Pasteur, Louis (1822–95). French
chemist

1 *Il n'existe pas de sciences appliquées,
mais seulement des applications de la
science.*
There are no such things as applied
sciences, only applications of science.
Speech, Lyons, 11 September 1872

Pater, Walter (1839–94). English
essayist and critic

1 All art constantly aspires towards
the condition of music.
Studies in the History of the Renaissance
(1873) 'The School of Giorgione'

Paterson, 'Banjo' (Andrew Barton
Paterson) (1864–1941). Australian
poet

1 'You'll come a-waltzing, Matilda,
with me.'
'Waltzing Matilda' (1903 song)

Patmore, Coventry (1823–96).
English poet

1 A woman is a foreign land.
The Angel in the House (1854) bk 2, *The Espousal*, canto 9, prelude 2, 'The Foreign Land'

2 Those who know God know that it is a quite a mistake to suppose that there are only five senses.
The Rod, the Root, and the Flower (1896) 'Aurea Dicta', no. 142

Paton, Alan (1903–88). South African writer

1 Cry, the beloved country.
Title of novel (1948)

Paul, Leslie (1905–85). Irish writer

1 Angry young man.
Title of book (1951); later associated with John Osborne's play *Look Back in Anger* (1956)

Payne, J(ohn) H(oward) (1791–1852). American actor, playwright and songwriter

1 Be it ever so humble, there's no place like home.
Clari, or, The Maid of Milan (1823 opera) 'Home, Sweet Home'

Peacock, Thomas Love (1785–1866). English novelist and poet

1 Marriage may often be a stormy lake, but celibacy is almost always a muddy horsepond.
Melincourt (1817) ch. 7

2 Sir, I have quarrelled with my wife; and a man who has quarrelled with his wife is absolved from all duty to his country.
Nightmare Abbey (1818) ch. 11

Peale, Norman Vincent (1898–1993). American religious broadcaster and writer

1 The power of positive thinking.
Title of book (1952)

Penn, William (1644–1718). English Quaker; founder of Pennsylvania.

1 Inquire often, but judge rarely, and thou wilt not often be mistaken.
Some Fruits of Solitude (1693)

Pepys, Samuel (1633–1703).
English diarist

1 And so to bed.
Diary 20 April 1660

2 Strange to see how a good dinner and feasting reconciles everybody.
Diary 9 November 1665

Perelman, S(idney) J(oseph) (1904–79). American humorist

1 Crazy like a fox.
Title of book (1944)

Peres, Shimon (1923–). Israeli statesman

1 Television has made dictatorship impossible, but democracy unbearable.
At a Davos meeting, in the *Financial Times* 31 January 1995

Pericles (c.490–429 BC). Athenian statesman

1 Famous men have the whole earth as their memorial.
Quoted in Thucydides *History of the Peloponnesian War*, 2.43

Persons, Ted (NA). American songwriter

1 Things ain't what they used to be.
Title of song (1941)

Peter, Laurence (1919–1990). Canadian writer

1 In a hierarchy every employee tends to rise to his level of incompetence.
The Peter Principle (1969) ch. 1

Petronius (Petronius Arbiter) (d. AD 65). Roman satirist

1 *Canis ingens, catena vinctus, in pariete erat pictus superque quadrata littera scriptum 'Cave canem.'*
A huge dog, tied by a chain, was

painted on the wall and over it was written in capital letters 'Beware of the dog.'
Satyricon 'Cena Trimalchionis' ch. 29, sect. 1

Phelps, Edward John (1822–1900). American lawyer and diplomat

1 The man who makes no mistakes does not usually make anything.
Speech at the Mansion House, London, 24 January 1889

Philby, Kim (Harold Adrian Russell Philby) (1912–88). British intelligence officer and Soviet spy

1 To betray, you must first belong.
In the *Sunday Times* 17 December 1967, p. 2

Philips, Ambrose (c.1675–1749). English poet

1 The flowers anew, returning seasons bring;
But beauty faded has no second spring.
The First Pastoral (1708) 'Lobbin' l. 47

Picasso, Pablo (1881–1973). Spanish painter, graphic artist, sculptor and ceramicist

1 There is no abstract art. You must always start with something. Afterward you can remove all traces of reality.
In an interview with Christian Zervos, editor of *Cahiers d'art* (1935), translated by Alfred H. Barr Jr in his *Picasso: Fifty Years of his Art* (1946)

2 I paint objects as I think them, not as I see them.
Quoted in John Golding *Cubism* (1959)

3 We all know that art is not truth. Art is a lie that makes us realize truth.
Quoted in Dore Ashton *Picasso on Art* (1972)

Pirandello, Luigi (1867–1936). Italian playwright and novelist

1 *Sei personaggi in cerca d'autore.*
Six characters in search of an author.
Title of play (1921)

Pirsig, Robert M(aynard) (1928–). American writer

1 The Buddha, the Godhead, resides quite as comfortably in the circuits of a digital computer or the gears of a cycle transmission as he does at the top of a mountain or in the petals of a flower.
Zen and the Art of Motorcycle Maintenance (1974) pt 1, ch. 1

Pitkin, W(alter) B(roughton) (1878–1953). American author

1 Life begins at forty.
Title of book (1932)

Pitt, William (Earl of Chatham) (1708–78). British Whig politician and Prime Minister

1 There is something behind the throne greater than the King himself.
Speech, *Hansard* (House of Lords) 2 March 1770

2 Where laws end, tyranny begins.
Speech to the House of Lords, 2 March 1770

3 The parks are the lungs of London.
In *Hansard* 30 June 1808

Planck, Max (Karl Ernst) (1858–1947). German physicist

1 Science cannot exist without some small portion of metaphysics.
The Universe in the Light of Modern Physics (1931) ch. 7

2 A new scientific truth does not triumph by convincing its opponents and making them see the light, but rather because its opponents eventually die, and a new generation grows up that is familiar with it.
A Scientific Autobiography (1949) p. 33

Plath, Sylvia (1932–63). American poet

1 Dying,
Is an art, like everything else.
'Lady Lazarus' (1963)

2 Is there no way out of the mind?
'Apprehensions' (1971)

Plato (c.428–c.348 BC). Greek philosopher

1 The wisest of you men is he who has realized, like Socrates, that in respect of wisdom he is really worthless.
Apology 23b (translated by H. Tredennick)

2 The unexamined life is not worth living.
Apology 38a (translated by H. Tredennick)

3 Men of sound sense have Law for their god, but men without sense Pleasure.
Epistulae 8. 354e (translated by R. G. Bury, 1925)

4 The most important stage of any enterprise is the beginning.
Republic 377b (translated by R. Waterfield, 1993)

5 Let no one ignorant of mathematics enter here.
(c.380 BC) Inscription over the door of the Academy at Athens

6 Is that which is holy loved by the gods because it is holy, or is it holy because it is loved by the gods?
Euthyphro 10

7 It is not living, but living well, which we ought to consider most important.
Crito 48b (translated by H. North Fowler, 1923)

8 Is virtue something that can be taught?
Meno 70a (translated by W. K. C. Guthrie)

Pliny the Elder (AD 23–79). Roman statesman and scholar

1 *Addito salis grano.*
With the addition of a grain of salt.
Historia Naturalis bk 23, sect. 149 (commonly quoted 'Cum grano salis [With a grain of salt]')

Poe, Edgar Allan (1809–49). American writer

1 Thy Naiad airs have brought me home,
To the glory that was Greece
And the grandeur that was Rome.
'To Helen' (1831)

2 While I nodded, nearly napping,
suddenly there came a tapping,
As of some one gently rapping,
rapping at my chamber door.
'The Raven' (1845) st. 1

3 Quoth the Raven, 'Nevermore'.
'The Raven' (1845) st. 17

4 All that we see or seem
Is but a dream within a dream.
'A Dream within a Dream' (1849)

Poincaré, Henri (1854–1912). French mathematician and philosopher of science

1 Science is built up of facts, as a house is built of stones; but an accumulation of facts is no more a science than a heap of stones is a house.
Science and Hypothesis (1905) ch. 9

Pompadour, Madame de (Antoinette Poisson, Marquise de Pompadour) (1721–64). Favourite of Louis XV of France

1 *Après nous le déluge.*
After us the deluge.
In Madame du Hausset *Mémoires* (1824) p. 19

Pompidou, Georges (1911–74). French politician and President

1 A statesman is a politician who places himself at the service of the nation. A politician is a statesman who places the nation at his service.
In the *Observer* 30 December 1973 'Sayings of the Year'

Pope, Alexander (1688–1744). English poet

1 Happy the man, whose wish and care
A few paternal acres bound,
Content to breathe his native air,
In his own ground.
'Ode on Solitude' (written c.1700)

2 Thus let me live, unseen, unknown;
Thus unlamented let me die;

Steal from the world, and not a stone
Tell where I lie.
'Ode on Solitude' (written c.1700)

3 Where'er you walk, cool gales shall fan the glade.
Pastorals (1709) 'Summer' l. 73

4 Some have at first for wits, then poets passed,
Turned critics next, and proved plain fools at last.
An Essay on Criticism (1711) l. 36

5 A little learning is a dangerous thing;
Drink deep, or taste not the Pierian spring.
An Essay on Criticism (1711) l. 215

6 Hills peep o'er hills, and Alps on Alps arise!
An Essay on Criticism (1711) l. 232

7 True wit is Nature to advantage dressed,
What oft was thought, but ne'er so well expressed.
An Essay on Criticism (1711) l. 297

8 Expression is the dress of thought.
An Essay on Criticism (1711) l. 318

9 As some to church repair,
Not for the doctrine, but the music there.
An Essay on Criticism (1711) l. 342

10 'Tis not enough no harshness gives offence,
The sound must seem an echo to the sense.
An Essay on Criticism (1711) l. 364

11 To err is human; to forgive, divine.
An Essay on Criticism (1711) l. 525

12 For fools rush in where angels fear to tread.
An Essay on Criticism (1711) l. 625

13 Belinda smiled, and all the world was gay.
The Rape of the Lock (1714) canto 2, l. 52

14 Here thou, great Anna! whom three realms obey,
Dost sometimes counsel take – and sometimes tea.
The Rape of the Lock (1714) canto 3, l. 7

15 At ev'ry word a reputation dies.
The Rape of the Lock (1714) canto 3, l. 16

16 The hungry judges soon the sentence sign,
And wretches hang that jury-men may dine.
The Rape of the Lock (1714) canto 3, l. 21

17 Coffee, (which makes the politician wise,
And see thro' all things with his half-shut eyes).
The Rape of the Lock (1714) canto 3, l. 117

18 How shall I lose the sin, yet keep the sense,
And love th'offender, yet detest th'offence?
'Eloisa to Abelard' (1717) l. 191

19 Welcome the coming, speed the parting guest.
Odyssey (1726) bk 15, l. 83

20 Nature, and Nature's laws lay hid in night.
God said, *Let Newton be!* and all was light.
'Epitaph: Intended for Sir Isaac Newton' (1730)

21 Trembling, hoping, ling'ring, flying,
Oh the pain, the bliss of dying!
'The Dying Christian to his Soul' (1730)

22 The ruling passion be it what it will,
The ruling passion conquers reason still.
Epistles to Several Persons (1733) 'To Lord Bathurst', l. 155

23 Of manners gentle, of affections mild;
In wit, a man; simplicity, a child.
'Epitaph: On Mr Gay in Westminster Abbey' (1733)

24 Laugh where we must, be candid where we can;
But vindicate the ways of God to man.
An Essay on Man Epistle 1 (1733) l. 15

25 Hope springs eternal in the human breast:
Man never Is, but always To be blest.
An Essay on Man Epistle 1 (1733) l. 95

26 Men would be angels, angels would
be gods.
An Essay on Man Epistle 1 (1733) l. 126

27 All are but parts of one stupendous
whole,
Whose body, Nature is, and God
the soul.
An Essay on Man Epistle 1 (1733) l. 267

28 And, spite of Pride, in erring Rea-
son's spite, One truth is clear,
'Whatever Is, is *right*.'
An Essay on Man Epistle 1 (1733) l. 289

29 The proper study of mankind is
man.
An Essay on Man Epistle 2 (1733) l. 2

30 An honest man's the noblest work
of God.
An Essay on Man Epistle 4 (1734) l. 248

31 Damned to everlasting fame!
An Essay on Man Epistle 4 (1734) l. 284

32 Shut, shut the door, good John!
fatigued I said,
Tie up the knocker, say I'm sick, I'm
dead.
'An Epistle to Dr Arbuthnot' (1735) l. 1

33 Damn with faint praise, assent with
civil leer,
And without sneering, teach the
rest to sneer.
'An Epistle to Dr Arbuthnot' (1735) l. 201 (of
Addison)

34 Unlearn'd, he knew no school-
man's subtle art,
No language, but the language of
the heart.
'An Epistle to Dr Arbuthnot' (1735) l. 398 (of
his own father)

35 Woman's at best a contradiction
still.
Epistles to Several Persons 'To a Lady' (1735)
l. 270

36 I am his Highness' dog at Kew;
Pray, tell me sir, whose dog are
you?
'Epigram Engraved on the Collar of a Dog
which I gave to his Royal Highness' (1738)

37 The worst of madmen is a saint run
mad.
Imitations of Horace Horace bk 1, Epistle 6
(1738) l. 27

38 While pensive poets painful vigils
keep,
Sleepless themselves, to give their
readers sleep.
The Dunciad (1742) bk 1, l. 93

39 Gentle Dullness ever loves a joke.
The Dunciad (1742) bk 2, l. 34

40 A brain of feathers, and a heart of
lead.
The Dunciad (1742) bk 2, l. 44

41 Thy hand, great Anarch! lets the
curtain fall;
And universal darkness buries all.
The Dunciad (1742) bk 4, l. 655

Popper, Sir Karl (Raimund)
(1902–94). Austrian-born English
philosopher

1 In so far as a scientific statement
speaks about reality, it must be
falsifiable: and in so far as it is not
falsifiable, it does not speak about
reality.
The Logic of Scientific Discovery, appendix to
1959 edition

2 Science starts only with problems.
Conjectures and Refutations (1960) ch. 10

3 Science may be described as the art
of systematic over-simplification.
Quoted in the *Observer* 1 August 1982

Porter, Cole (1891–1964). American
songwriter

1 Anything goes.
Anything Goes (1934) title song

2 I get a kick out of you.
Anything Goes (1934) 'I Get a Kick Out Of
You'

3 Miss Otis regrets (she's unable to
lunch today).
Title of song (1934)

4 My heart belongs to Daddy.
Title of song (1938)

5 Birds do it, bees do it,
Even educated fleas do it.
Let's do it, let's fall in love.
'Let's Do It' (1954 song; words added to the
1928 original)

6 Who wants to be a millionaire?
High Society (1955) 'Who wants to be a
millionaire'

Potter, Stephen (1900–69). British writer

1 The theory and practice of gamesmanship or the art of winning games without actually cheating.
Title of book (1947)

2 *How to be one up* – how to make the other man feel that something has gone wrong, however slightly.
Lifemanship (1950) p. 14

Pound, Ezra (1885–1972). American poet

1 All great art is born of the metropolis.
Letter to Harriet Monroe, 7 November 1913

2 Poetry must be read as music and not as oratory.
'Vers Libre and Arnold Dolmetsch', in the *Egoist*, July 1917

3 A man of genius has a right to any mode of expression.
Letter to J. B. Yeats, 4 February 1918

4 Great literature is simply language charged with meaning to the utmost possible degree.
How To Read (1931) pt 2

5 Literature is news that *stays* news.
The ABC of Reading (1934) ch. 2

6 Artists are the antennae of the race, but the bullet-headed many will never learn to trust their great artists.
Literary Essays (1954) 'Henry James'

Powell, Anthony (1905–2000). English novelist

1 A dance to the music of time.
Title of novel sequence (1951–75), after *Le 4 stagioni che ballano al suono del tempo* (title given by Giovanni Pietro Bellori to a painting by Nicolas Poussin)

2 Books do furnish a room.
Title of novel (1971)

3 Growing old is like being increasingly penalised for a crime you haven't committed.
Temporary Kings (1973) ch. 1

4 In this country it is rare for anyone, let alone a publisher, to take writers seriously.
In the *Daily Telegraph* 8 February 1979

Powell, (John) Enoch (1912–98). British Conservative and Ulster Unionist politician

1 History is littered with the wars which everybody knew would never happen.
Speech to Conservative Party Conference, 19 October 1967

2 As I look ahead, I am filled with much foreboding. Like the Roman, I seem to see 'the River Tiber foaming with much blood'.
Speech at Birmingham on racial tension in Britain, April 1968

Pratchett, Terry (1948–). English science-fiction writer

1 Most modern fantasy just rearranges the furniture in Tolkien's attic.
Stan Nicholls (ed.) *Wordsmiths of Wonder* (1993)

Priestley, J(ohn) B(oynton) (1894–1984). English playwright

1 The earth is nobler than the world we have put upon it.
Johnson Over Jordan (1939) act 3

2 An inspector calls.
Title of play (1947)

Prior, Matthew (1664–1721). English poet

1 From ignorance our comfort flows, The only wretched are the wise.
'To the Hon. Charles Montague' (1692) st. 9

2 They never taste who always drink; They always talk, who never think.
'Upon this Passage in Scaligerana' (1740)

Procter, Adelaide Ann (1825–64). English writer of popular verse

1 Seated one day at the organ, I was weary and ill at ease.
'A Lost Chord' (1858)

2 But I struck one chord of music,
Like the sound of a great Amen.
'A Lost Chord' (1858)

Protagoras (b. *c.*485 BC). Greek
sophist

1 [That] man is the measure of all
things.
In Plato *Theaetetus* 160d

Proudhon, Pierre-Joseph (1809–
65). French social reformer

1 *La propriété c'est le vol.*
Property is theft.
Qu'est-ce que la propriété? (1840) ch. 1

Proust, Marcel (1871–1922). French
novelist

1 *A la recherche du temps perdu.*
In search of lost time.
Title of novel (1918, translated by C. K. Scott-
Moncrieff and S. Hudson as 'Remembrance
of things past')

2 *Le bonheur est dans l'amour un état
anormal.*
In love, happiness is abnormal.
A la recherche du temps perdu (1918) 'A
l'ombre des jeunes filles en fleur'

3 *L'adolescence est le seul temps où l'on
ait appris quelque chose.*
Adolescence is the only time when
we can learn something.
A la recherche du temps perdu (1918) 'A
l'ombre des jeunes filles en fleur'

4 *On devient moral dès qu'on est malheureux.*
We become moral once we are
miserable.
A la recherche du temps perdu (1918) 'A
l'ombre des jeunes filles en fleur'

5 *L'amour, c'est l'espace et le temps
rendus sensibles au cœur.*
Love is space and time made tender
to the heart.
A la recherche du temps perdu (1923) 'La
Prisonnière'

6 *L'adultère introduit l'esprit dans la
lettre que bien souvent le mariage eût
laissée morte.*
Adultery introduces some energy
into an otherwise dead marriage.
A la recherche du temps perdu (1923) 'La
Prisonnière'

7 *Laissons les jolies femmes aux
hommes sans imagination.*
Leave the pretty women for the
men without imagination.
A la recherche du temps perdu (1925) 'Al-
bertine disparue'

8 *Le bonheur est salutaire pour les corps,
mais c'est le chagrin qui développe les
forces de l'esprit.*
Happiness is healthy for the body,
but it is sorrow which enhances the
forces of the mind.
A la recherche du temps perdu (1927) 'Le
Temps retrouvé'

9 *Le style, pour l'écrivain aussi bien que
pour le peintre, est une question non de
technique mais de vision.*
For the writer as well as for the
painter, style is not a question of
technique, but of vision.
A la recherche du temps perdu (1927) 'Le
Temps retrouvé'

Publilius Syrus (1st century BC).
Writer of Latin mimes

1 *Inopi beneficium bis dat qui dat cel-
eriter.*
He gives the poor man twice as
much good who gives quickly.
Sententiae no. 274 (proverbially '*Bis dat qui
cito dat* [He gives twice who gives soon]')

Punch (1841–1992). English
humorous weekly periodical

1 Advice to persons about to marry. –
'Don't.'
Vol. 8, p. 1 (1845)

2 You pays your money and you
takes your choice.
Vol. 10, p. 17 (1846)

3 Never do to-day what you can put
off till to-morrow.
Vol. 17, p. 241 (1849)

4 There was an old owl lived in an
  oak
  The more he heard, the less he
  spoke;
  The less he spoke, the more he
  heard.
  O, if men were all like that wise
  bird!
  Vol. 68, p. 155 (1875)

5 It's worse than wicked, my dear, it's
  vulgar.
  Almanac (1876)

6 Don't look at me, Sir, with – ah – in
  that tone of voice.
  Vol. 87, p. 38 (1884)

7 I'm afraid you've got a bad egg, Mr
  Jones.
  Oh no, my Lord, I assure you! Parts
  of it are excellent!
  Vol. 109, p. 222 (1895)

8 Look here, Steward, if this is coffee,
  I want tea; but if this is tea, then I
  wish for coffee.
  Vol. 123, p. 44 (1902)

9 Sometimes I sits and thinks, and
  then again I just sits.
  Vol. 131, p. 297 (1906)

Putnam, Israel (1718–90).
American general

1 Men, you are all marksmen – don't
  one of you fire until you see the
  white of their eyes.
  At Bunker Hill, 1775, in R. Frothingham *History of the Siege of Boston* (1873) ch. 5 n. (also attributed to William Prescott, 1726–95)

Puzo, Mario (1920–99). American
novelist

1 I'll make him an offer he can't refuse.
  The Godfather (1969) ch. 1

Pyrrhus (319–272 BC). King of
Epirus from 306 BC

1 One more such victory and we are
  lost.
  On defeating the Romans at Asculum, 279 BC, in Plutarch *Parallel Lives* 'Pyrrhus' ch. 21, sect. 9

Quarles, Francis (1592–1644).
English poet

1 He teaches to deny that faintly
  prays.
  A Feast for Worms (1620) sect. 7, Meditation
  7, l. 2

2 I wish thee as much pleasure in the
  reading, as I had in the writing.
  Emblems (1635) 'To the Reader'

3 Be wisely worldly, be not worldly
  wise.
  Emblems (1635) bk 2, no. 2, l. 46

4 Man is Heaven's masterpiece.
  Emblems (1635) bk 2, no. 6, epigram 6

5 He that begins to live, begins to die.
  Hieroglyphics of the Life of Man (1638) no. 1,
  epigram 1

Quintilian (Marcus Fabius
Quintilianus) (*c.*35–*c.*100 AD).
Spanish-born Roman rhetorician

1 *Mendaces memorem esse oportere.*
  Liars need to have good memories.
  Institutio Oratoria, 4.2.9.1

Rabelais, François (*c*.1494–*c*.1553). French humanist, satirist and physician

1 *Natura vacuum abhorret.*
Nature abhors a vacuum.
Gargantua (1532) bk 1, ch. 5

2 *Du cheval donné toujours regardait en la gueule.*
Always look a gift horse in the mouth.
Gargantua (1532) bk 1, ch. 11

3 *Ignorance est mère de tous les maux.*
Ignorance is the mother of all evils.
Cinquième Livre (1564) pt 7

4 *Tirez le rideau, la farce est jouée.*
Bring down the curtain, the farce is played out.
Attributed last words

Rado, James and Ragni, Gerome (1939–; 1942–). American songwriters

1 This is the dawning of the age of Aquarius.
Hair (1967) 'Aquarius'

Raine, Craig (1944–). English poet

1 The mind is a museum to be looted at night.
'The Grey Boy' (1984)

Raleigh, Sir Walter (1552–1618). English explorer and courtier

1 If all the world and love were young,
And truth in every shepherd's tongue
These pretty pleasures might me move
To live with thee and be thy love.
'The Nymph's Reply to the Shepherd' (attributed, *c*.1592)

2 Fain would I climb, yet fear I to fall.
Line written on a window-pane, in Thomas Fuller *History of the Worthies of England* (1662) 'Devonshire' p. 261

Raphael, Frederic (1931–). British novelist and screenwriter

1 City of perspiring dreams.
Of Cambridge. *The Glittering Prizes* (1976) ch. 3

Ravetch, Irving and Frank, Harriet (1920–; 1917–). American screenwriters

1 The long hot summer.
Title of film (1958) based on stories by William Faulkner

Read, Sir Herbert (1893–1968). English poet and art historian

1 This is the happy warrior,
This is he.
Naked Warriors (1919) 'The Scene of War, 4. The Happy Warrior'

2 Art is … pattern informed by sensibility.
The Meaning of Art (1955) ch. 1

Reagan, Ronald (Wilson) (1911–2004). 40th President of the USA

1 Politics is supposed to be the second oldest profession. I have come to realize that it bears a very close resemblance to the first.
At a conference in Los Angeles, 2 March 1977

2 Recession is when your neighbour loses his job. Depression is when you lose yours.
Election campaign speech, Jersey City, 1 September 1980

Reardon, Ray (1932–). Welsh snooker player

1 I cannot remember anyone ever asking 'Who came second?' Can you?
Quoted in Colin Jarman *The Guinness Dictionary of Sports Quotations* (1990)

Reed, Henry (1914–86). English poet and playwright

1 Today we have naming of parts.
'Lessons of the War: 1, Naming of Parts' (1946)

Reich, Charles A. (1928–). American jurist

1 The greening of America.
Title of book (1970)

Reid, Keith (1946–). English pop singer and songwriter

1 Her face, at first … just ghostly Turned a whiter shade of pale.
'A Whiter Shade of Pale' (1967 song)

Reisner, Dean (1918–2002). American screenwriter

1 You've got to ask yourself a question. Do I feel lucky. Well do you punk?
Dirty Harry (film, 1971); spoken by Clint Eastwood

Reith, Lord (John Charles Walsham Reith, Baron Reith of Stonehaven) (1889–1971). British politician and first general manager of the BBC (1922–7)

1 He who prides himself on giving what he thinks the public wants is often creating a fictitious demand for lower standards which he will then satisfy.
Memo to Crawford Committee (1926)

Remarque, Erich Maria (1898–1970). German novelist

1 All quiet on the western front.
English title of *Im Westen nichts Neues* (1929 novel)

Rendall, Montague John (1862–1950). Member of the first BBC Board of Governors

1 Nation shall speak peace unto nation.
Motto of the BBC

Reuther, Walter (1907–70). American labour leader

1 If it looks like a duck, walks like a duck and quacks like a duck, then it just may be a duck.
As a test, during the McCarthy era, of Communist affiliations

Revlon, Charles Haskell (1906–75). American cosmetics salesman

1 In the factory, we make cosmetics; in the store we sell hope.
Quoted in Andrew P. Tobias *Fire and Ice* (1976), ch. 8

Reynolds, Frederic (1764–1841). English playwright

1 It is better to have written a damned play, than no play at all – it snatches a man from obscurity.
The Dramatist (1789) act 1, sc. 1

Reynolds, Malvina (1900–78). American songwriter

1 Little boxes on the hillside … And they're all made out of ticky-tacky And they all look just the same.
'Little Boxes' (1962 song); the reference is to houses built to the south of San Francisco

Reynolds, Sir Joshua (1723–92). English painter

1 Few have been taught to any purpose who have not been their own teachers.
Discourses on Art (ed. R. Wark, 1975) no. 2 (11 December 1769)

2 A mere copier of nature can never produce anything great.
Discourses on Art (ed. R. Wark, 1975) no. 3 (14 December 1770)

3 Genius … is the child of imitation.
Discourses on Art (ed. R. Wark, 1975) no. 6 (10 December 1774)

Rhodes, Cecil (1853–1902). South African statesman

1 So little done, so much to do.
Said on the day of his death, in Lewis Michell *Life of Rhodes* (1910) vol. 2, ch. 39

Rice-Davies, Mandy (1944–). English courtesan

1 He would, wouldn't he?
At the trial of Stephen Ward, 29 June 1963, on being told that Lord Astor claimed that her allegations concerning himself were untrue; in the *Guardian* 1 July 1963

Rich, Adrienne (1929–). American poet

1 Love only what you do,
And not what you have done.
The Diamond Cutters and Other Poems (1955)
'The Diamond Cutters'

2 All wars are useless to the dead.
Leaflets (1969) 'Implosions'

Richards, Frank (Charles Hamilton) (1876–1961). English writer for boys

1 The fat greedy owl of the Remove.
'Billy Bunter' in the *Magnet* (1909) vol. 3, no. 72 'The Greyfriars Photographer'

Richelieu, Duc de (Cardinal Armand Jean du Plessis) (1585–1642). French statesman

1 Secrecy is the first essential in the affairs of State.
Testament Politique (1688)

Rimbaud, (Jean Nicolas) Arthur (1854–91). French poet

1 *Le poète est vraiment voleur de feu.*
The poet is the true fire-stealer.
Letter to Paul Demeny, 15 May 1871

2 *Je me crois en enfer, donc j'y suis.*
I believe myself to be in hell;
therefore I am.
Une saison en enfer (1873) 'Mauvais sang'

Ritz, César (1850–1918). Swiss hotel proprietor

1 *Le client n'a jamais tort.*
The customer is never wrong.
In R. Nevill and C. E. Jerningham *Piccadilly to Pall Mall* (1908) p. 94

Rivarol, Antoine de (1753–1801). French man of letters

1 *Ce qui n'est pas clair n'est pas français.*
What is not clear is not French.
Discours sur l'universalité de la langue française (1784)

Robbe-Grillet, Alain (1922–). French novelist

1 *On n'échappe pas à son sort.*
One cannot escape destiny.
Les Gommes (1953)

Robin, Leo (1895–1984). American songwriter

1 Thanks for the memory.
Title of song (with Ralph Rainger, 1937)

2 Diamonds are a girl's best friend.
'Diamonds are a Girl's Best Friend' from the 1949 film *Gentlemen Prefer Blondes* (music by Jule Styne)

Roddenberry, Gene (1921–91). American scriptwriter, producer and director

1 Space – the final frontier.
Introductory voiceover to *Star Trek* (1966)

2 To boldly go where no man has gone before.
The mission of the starship *Enterprise*.
Introductory voiceover to *Star Trek* (1966)

3 Beam us up, Mr Scott.
Star Trek 'Gamesters of Triskelion' (1966); usually quoted as 'Beam me up, Scotty'

Rogers, Will (1879–1935). American actor and humorist

1 Well, all I know is what I read in the papers.
In the *New York Times* 30 September 1923

2 Half our life is spent trying to find something to do with the time we have rushed through life trying to save.
Letter in the *New York Times* 29 April 1930

3 I don't make jokes – I just watch the government and report the facts.
Quoted in 'A Rogers Thesaurus' in the *Saturday Review* 25 August 1962

Roland, Mme (Marie-Jeanne
Philipon) (1754–93). French
revolutionary

1 *O liberté! O liberté! que de crimes on
commet en ton nom!*
O liberty! O liberty! what crimes are
committed in thy name!
In A. de Lamartine *Histoire des Girondins*
(1847) bk 51, ch. 8

Roosevelt, Franklin D(elano)
(1882–1945). 32nd President of the
USA

1 I pledge you, I pledge myself, to a
new deal for the American people.
Speech to the Democratic Convention in
Chicago, 2 July 1932, accepting the presidential nomination; in *Public Papers* (1938)
vol. 1, p. 647

2 The only thing we have to fear is
fear itself.
Inaugural address, 4 March 1933, in *Public
Papers* (1938) vol. 2, p. 11

3 In the field of world policy, I would
dedicate this nation to the policy of
the good neighbour.
Inaugural address, 4 March 1933

Rossetti, Christina (Georgina)
(1830–94). English poet

1 Remember me when I am gone
away,
Gone far away into the silent land.
'Remember' (1862)

2 In the bleak mid-winter.
'Mid-Winter' (1875)

Rostand, Edmond (1868–1918).
French playwright

1 *Le seul rêve intéresse,
Vivre sans rêve, qu'est-ce?*
The dream, alone, is of interest.
What is life, without a dream?
La Princesse lointaine (1895) act 1, sc. 4

Rostand, Jean (1894–1977). French
biologist

1 *Vous tuez un homme, vous êtes un
assassin; vous en tuez mille, vous êtes
un conquérant ; vous les tuez tous,
vous êtes un dieu.*
Kill a man, and you are an assassin.
Kill millions of men, and you are a
conqueror. Kill everyone, and you
are a god.
Pensées d'un biologiste (1939)

Rosten, Leo (Calvin) (1908–97).
American writer, humorist and
anthologist

1 Any man who hates dogs and
babies can't be all bad.
Speech at a Hollywood dinner in honour of
W. C. Fields 16 February 1939

2 The only reason for being a professional writer is that you just
can't help it.
In D. L. Kirkpatrick (ed.) *Contemporary
Novelists* (1976)

Roth, Philip (1933–). American
Jewish novelist

1 Satire is moral outrage transformed
into comic art.
Reading Myself and Others (1975) 'On *Our
Gang*'

2 The road to hell is paved with
works-in-progress.
In the *New York Times Book Review* 15 July
1979

Rouget de Lisle, Claude-Joseph
(1760–1836). French soldier

1 *Allons, enfants de la patrie,
Le jour de gloire est arrivé …
Aux armes, citoyens!
Formez vos battaillons!*
Come, children of our country, the
day of glory has arrived … To arms,
citizens! Form your battalions!
'La Marseillaise' (25 April 1792)

Rousseau, Jean Jacques (1712–78).
French political philosopher,
educationist and writer

1 *L'homme est né libre, et partout il est
dans les fers.*
Man is born free, yet everywhere he
is in chains.
Du contrat social (1762) bk 1, ch. 1

2 *J'aime mieux être homme à paradoxes
qu'homme à préjugés.*
I would rather be a man of paradoxes than of prejudices.
Emile ou de l'éducation (1762) pt 2

Rowe, Nicholas (1674–1718).
English playwright

1 Is this that haughty, gallant, gay
Lothario?
The Fair Penitent (1703) act 5, sc. 1

Rowland, Helen (1875–1950).
American writer

1 A husband is what is left of a lover,
after the nerve has been extracted.
A Guide to Men (1922) p. 19

Rowland, Richard (c.1881–1947).
American film producer

1 The lunatics have taken charge of
the asylum.
On the take-over of United Artists by
Charles Chaplin, Mary Pickford, Douglas
Fairbanks and D. W. Griffith, in Terry Ram-
saye *A Million and One Nights* (1926) vol. 2,
ch. 79

Rushdie, Salman (1947–). British
novelist

1 Most of what matters in your life
takes place in your absence.
Midnight's Children (1981) 'Alpha and
Omega' bk 2

Rusk, Dean (1909–94). US politician; Secretary of State, 1961–9

1 We're eyeball to eyeball, and I
think the other fellow just blinked.
On the Cuban missile crisis, 24 October
1962, in the *Saturday Evening Post* 8
December 1962

Ruskin, John (1819–1900). English
art and social critic

1 When we build, let us think that we
build for ever.
Seven Lamps of Architecture (1849) 'The
Lamp of Memory' sect. 10

2 Remember that the most beautiful
things in the world are the most
useless; peacocks and lilies for
instance.
The Stones of Venice (1851–3) vol. 1, ch. 2

3 The purest and most thoughtful
minds are those which love colour
the most.
The Stones of Venice (1851–3) vol. 2, ch. 5

4 No person who is not a great
sculptor or painter can be an
architect. If he is not a sculptor or
painter, he can only be a *builder*.
Lectures on Architecture and Painting (1854)
Lectures 1 and 2 (addenda)

5 All violent feelings … produce in
us a falseness in all our impressions
of external things, which I would
generally characterize as the
'Pathetic Fallacy'.
Modern Painters (1856) vol. 3, pt 4, ch. 12

6 Mountains are the beginning and
the end of all natural scenery.
Modern Painters (1856) vol. 4, pt 5, ch. 20

7 Fine art is that in which the hand,
the head, and the heart of man go
together.
The Two Paths (1859) Lecture 2

8 Soldiers of the ploughshare as well
as soldiers of the sword.
Unto this Last (1862) Essay 3, p. 102

9 Government and co-operation are
in all things the laws of life;
anarchy and competition the laws
of death.
Unto this Last (1862) Essay 3, p. 102

10 There is no wealth but life.
Unto this Last (1862) Essay 4, p. 156

11 All books are divisible into two
classes, the books of the hour, and
the books of all time.
Sesame and Lilies (1865) p. 16 'Of Kings'
Treasuries'

12 Be sure that you go to the author to
get at his meaning, not to find
yours.
Sesame and Lilies (1865) p. 24 'Of Kings'
Treasuries'

13 Labour without joy is base. Labour without sorrow is base. Sorrow without labour is base. Joy without labour is base.
Time and Tide (1867) Letter 5

14 Life without industry is guilt, and industry without art is brutality.
Lectures on Art (1870) Lecture 3 'The Relation of Art to Morals' sect. 95

Russell, Bertrand (3rd Earl Russell) (1872–1970). British philosopher and mathematician

1 Mathematics may be defined as the subject in which we never know what we are talking about, nor whether what we are saying is true.
Mysticism and Logic (1918) ch. 4

2 To fear love is to fear life, and those who fear life are already three parts dead.
Marriage and Morals (1929) ch. 19

3 One of the symptoms of approaching nervous breakdown is the belief that one's work is terribly important, and that to take a holiday would bring all kinds of disaster.
The Conquest of Happiness (1930) ch. 5

4 Of all forms of caution, caution in love is perhaps the most fatal to true happiness.
The Conquest of Happiness (1930) ch. 12

5 The scientific attitude of mind involves a sweeping away of all other desires in the interest of the desire to know.
Interview in the *New Statesman* 24 May 1930

Russell, Lord John (1792–1878). British Whig politician and Prime Minister

1 A proverb is one man's wit and all men's wisdom.
In R. J. Mackintosh *Sir James Mackintosh* (1835) vol. 2, ch. 7

2 If peace cannot be maintained with honour, it is no longer peace.
Speech at Greenock, 19 September 1853, in *The Times* 21 September 1853, p. 7

Rutherford, Ernest (Baron Rutherford of Nelson) (1871–1937). British physicist

1 All science is either physics or stamp collecting.
In J. B. Birks *Rutherford at Manchester* (1962) p. 108

Ryle, Gilbert (1900–76). English philosopher

1 The dogma of the Ghost in the Machine.
The Concept of Mind (1949) ch. 1 (on the mental-conduct concepts of Descartes)

Sacks, Oliver (1933–). American neurologist and writer

1 The man who mistook his wife for a hat.
Title of book (1985)

Saint-Exupéry, Antoine de (1900–44). French author and aviator

1 *L'expérience nous montre qu'aimer ce n'est point nous regarder l'un l'autre mais regarder ensemble dans la même direction.*
Life has taught us that love does not consist in gazing at each other but in looking together in the same direction.
Terre des hommes (1939)

2 *Les grandes personnes ne comprennent jamais rien toutes seules, et c'est fatigant, pour les enfants, de toujours et toujours leur donner des explications.*
Adults never understand anything for themselves, and it is tiresome for children to be always and forever explaining things to them.
Le Petit Prince (1943)

3 *On ne voit bien qu'avec le cœur. L'essentiel est invisible pour les yeux.*
Only with the heart can a person see rightly; what is essential is invisible to the eye.
Le Petit Prince (1943)

4 *La vie crée l'ordre, mais l'ordre ne crée pas la vie.*
Life creates order, but order does not create life.
Lettre à un otage (1944)

Saki (Hector Hugh Munro) (1870–1916). Scottish writer

1 The cook was a good cook, as cooks go; and as good cooks go, she went.
Reginald (1904) 'Reginald on Besetting Sins'

2 I always say beauty is only sin deep.
Reginald (1904) 'Reginald's Choir Treat'

3 The young have aspirations that never come to pass, the old have reminiscences of what never happened.
Reginald (1904) 'Reginald at the Carlton'

4 All decent people live beyond their incomes nowadays, and those who aren't respectable live beyond other peoples'.
Chronicles of Clovis (1911) 'The Match-Maker'

Salinger, J(erome) D(avid) (1919–). American novelist and short-story writer

1 I'd just be the catcher in the rye.
The Catcher in the Rye (1951) ch. 22

Salvianus (c.400–c.470 AD). Christian writer from Gaul

1 *Quot curiales, tot tyranni.*
As many councillors, so many tyrants.
De Gubernatione Dei, 5.18.27

Sampson, Anthony (1926–2004). British journalist

1 Members [of civil service orders] rise from CMG (known sometimes in Whitehall as 'Call Me God') to the KCMG ('Kindly Call Me God') to – for a select few governors and super-ambassadors – the GCMG ('God Calls Me God').
Anatomy of Britain (1962) ch. 18

Samuel, Herbert Louis (1st Viscount Samuel) (1870–1963). British Liberal statesman and writer

1 A library is thought in cold storage.
A Book of Quotations (1947) p. 10

2 Hansard is history's ear, already listening.
House of Lords, December 1949

Sand, George (Amandine Aurore Lucile Dupin, Baronne Dudevant) (1804–76). French novelist

1 *Nulle créature humaine ne peut commander à l'amour.*
No human being can give orders to love.
Jacques (1833)

2 *Le vrai est trop simple, il faut y arriver toujours par le compliqué.*
Truth is too simple; it must always be arrived at in a complicated manner.
Letter to Armand Barbès, May 1867

Sandburg, Carl (1878–1967). American poet

1 Pile the bodies high at Austerlitz and Waterloo. Shovel them under and let me work –
I am the grass; I cover all.
Cornhuskers (1918) 'Grass'

2 Poetry is the opening and closing of a door, leaving those who look through to guess about what is seen during a moment.
'Poetry Considered' in the *Atlantic Monthly* March 1923

3 Sometime they'll give a war and nobody will come.
The People, Yes (1936)

4 A baby is God's opinion that life should go on.
Remembrance Rock (1948) ch. 2

5 Slang is a language that rolls up its sleeves, spits on its hands and goes to work.
In the *New York Times* 13 February 1959

Santayana, George (1863–1952). Spanish-born US philosopher and writer

1 Those who cannot remember the past are condemned to repeat it.
The Life of Reason (1905) vol. 1, ch. 12

2 An artist is a dreamer consenting to dream of the actual world.
The Life of Reason (1905) vol. 4, ch. 3

3 For an idea ever to be fashionable is ominous, since it must afterwards be always old-fashioned.
Winds of Doctrine (1913) 'Modernism and Christianity'

4 There is no cure for birth and death save to enjoy the interval.
Soliloquies in England (1922) 'War Shrines'

5 A building without ornamentation is like a heaven without stars.
Quoted in the *Christian Science Monitor* 14 December 1990

Sargent, John Singer (1856–1925). American painter

1 Every time I paint a portrait I lose a friend.
In N. Bentley and E. Esar *Treasury of Humorous Quotations* (1951)

Saroyan, William (1908–81). American playwright and novelist

1 The daring young man on the flying trapeze.
Title of story collection (1934)

Sartre, Jean-Paul (1905–80). French philosopher and writer

1 *Je suis condamné à être libre.*
I am condemned to be free.
L'Etre et le néant (1943) pt 4, ch. 1

2 *Pas besoin de gril, l'Enfer, c'est les Autres.*
No need of a gridiron, Hell is other people.
Huis Clos (1944) sc. 5

3 *Un homme n'est rien d'autre qu'une série d'entreprises.*
Man is no other than a series of undertakings.
L'Existentialisme est un humanisme (1946)

4 *L'homme n'est rien d'autre que ce qu'il se fait. Tel est le premier principe de l'existentialisme.*
Man is nothing else but that which he makes of himself. That is the first principle of existentialism.
L'Existentialisme est un humanisme (1946)

5 *Comme tous les songe-creux, je con-*
fondis le désenchantement avec la
vérité.
Like all dreamers, I mistook disen-
chantment for truth.
Les Mots (1964) 'Ecrire'

Sassoon, Siegfried (1886–1967).
English poet

1 Soldiers are citizens of death's grey
land.
Drawing no dividend from time's
tomorrows.
'Dreamers' (1918)

2 'He's a cheery old card,' grunted
Harry to Jack
As they slogged up to Arras with
rifle and pack.
But he did for them both by his
plan of attack.
'The General' (1918)

3 But the past is just the same, – and
War's a bloody game.
'Aftermath' (1919)

Sayers, Dorothy L(eigh) (1893–
1957). English detective-story writer

1 Plain lies are dangerous.
'The Psychology of Advertising' in the
Spectator 19 November 1937

Scalpone, Al (NA). American
advertising copywriter

1 The family that prays together
stays together.
Motto devised for the Roman Catholic
Family Rosary Crusade, 1947

Schelling, Friedrich von (1775–
1854). German philosopher

1 *Architektur ist überhaupt die erstarrte*
Musik.
Architecture in general is frozen
music.
Philosophie der Kunst (1809) in *Werke* (1916)
vol. 3, p. 24

Schiller, Friedrich von (1759–
1805). German poet and playwright

1 *Freude, schöner Götterfunken,*
Tochter aus Elysium.
Joy, beautiful radiance of the gods,
daughter of Elysium.
'An die Freude' (1785)

2 *Alle anderen Dinge müssen; der*
Mensch ist das Wesen, welches will.
All other things must; man is the
being who wills.
Über das Erhabene (1794)

3 *Mitt der Dummheit kämpfen Götter*
selbst vergebens.
Even the gods themselves struggle
in vain against stupidity.
Die Jungfrau von Orléans (1801) act 3, sc. 6

Schnabel, Artur (1882–1951).
Austrian-born pianist

1 The notes I handle no better than
many pianists. But the pauses
between the notes – ah, that is
where the art resides!
In the *Chicago Daily News* 11 June 1958

2 I know two kinds of audiences only
– one coughing, and one not
coughing.
My Life and Music (1961) pt 2, ch. 10

Schopenhauer, Artur (1788–
1860). German philosopher

1 *Das Ganze der Erfahrung gleicht einer*
Geheimschrift und die Philosophie der
Entzifferung derselben.
The whole of experience is like a
cryptograph, and philosophy is
like the deciphering of it.
Die Welt als Wille und Vorstellung (1844),
vol. 2, ch. 17

2 *Jede Trennung gibt einen Vorgesch-*
mack des Todes – und jedes Wieder-
sehn einen Vorgeschmack der Aufer-
stehung.
Every parting is a foretaste of death,
and every reunion a foretaste of
resurrection.
Parerga und Paralipomena (1851) ch. 26

Schumacher, E(rnst)
F(riedrich) (1911–77). British
economist and public servant

1 Small is Beautiful: a Study of Economics as if People Mattered.
Title of book (1973)

Schumpeter, Joseph Alois (1883–1950). Austrian-born American economist

1 Bureaucracy is not an obstacle to democracy but an inevitable complement to it.
Capitalism, Socialism and Democracy (1942) ch. 18

Schwartz, Eugene M. (1927–). American art collector

1 Collecting is the only socially commendable form of greed.
In the *New York Times* 7 September 1995

Schwarzenegger, Arnold (1947–). Austrian-born American actor (and later politician)

1 I'll be back.
The Terminator (film, 1984)

Schweitzer, Albert (1875–1965). German medical missionary, theologian, musician and philosopher

1 An optimist is a person who sees a green light everywhere, while the pessimist sees only the red stop-light. The truly wise person is colour-blind.
Quoted in CBS News tribute, 14 January 1965

Scott, C(harles) P(restwich) (1846–1932). British journalist; editor of the *Manchester Guardian*, 1872–1929

1 Comment is free, but facts are sacred.
Manchester Guardian 5 May 1921

Scott, Sir Walter (1771–1832). Scottish novelist and poet

1 And come he slow, or come he fast, It is but Death who comes at last.
Marmion (1808) canto 2, st. 30

2 O, young Lochinvar is come out of the west,
Through all the wide Border his steed was the best.
Marmion (1808) canto 5, st. 12 ('Lochinvar' st. 1)

3 And dar'st thou then
To beard the lion in his den,
The Douglas in his hall?
Marmion (1808) canto 6, st. 14

4 O what a tangled web we weave,
When first we practise to deceive!
Marmion (1808) canto 6, st. 17

5 When pain and anguish wring the brow,
A ministering angel thou!
Marmion (1808) canto 6, st. 30

6 Yet seemed that tone, and gesture bland,
Less used to sue than to command.
The Lady of the Lake (1810) canto 1, st. 21

7 Time rolls his ceaseless course.
The Lady of the Lake (1810) canto 3, st. 1

8 But with the morning cool repentance came.
Rob Roy (1817) ch. 12

9 The hour is come, but not the man.
The Heart of Midlothian (1818) ch. 4, title

Seaton, George (George Stenius) (1911–79). American screenwriter and director

1 For those who believe in God no explanation is necessary. For those who do not believe in God no explanation is possible.
Prologue to *The Song of Bernadette* (film, 1943)

Seeger, Pete (1919–). American folk singer and songwriter

1 Where have all the flowers gone?
Title of song (1961)

Selden, John (1584–1654). English historian and antiquary

1 'Tis not the drinking that is to be blamed, but the excess.
Table Talk (1689) 'Humility'

2 Pleasure is nothing else but the intermission of pain.
Table Talk (1689) 'Pleasure'

3 Preachers say, Do as I say, not as I do.
Table Talk (1689) 'Preaching'

Seneca (Lucius Annaeus Seneca, 'The Younger') (c.4 BC–c.65 AD). Roman Stoic philosopher, statesman and tragedian

1 *Utrumque enim vitium est, et omnibus credere et nulli.*
It is equally unsound to trust everyone and to trust no one.
Epistulae 3.4

2 *Homines dum docent discunt.*
Men learn while they teach.
Epistulae 7.8

Service, Robert W(illiam) (1874–1958). Canadian poet

1 A promise made is a debt unpaid, and the trail has its own stern code.
'The Cremation of Sam McGee' (1907)

2 Back of the bar, in a solo game, sat Dangerous Dan McGrew.
'The Shooting of Dan McGrew' (1907)

3 Ah! the clock is always slow;
It is later than you think.
'It Is Later Than You Think' (1921)

Shadwell, Thomas (c.1642–92). English playwright

1 Sighs are the natural language of the heart.
Psyche (1675) act 3

2 And wit's the noblest frailty of the mind.
A True Widow (1679) act 2, sc. 1.

3 The haste of a fool is the slowest thing in the world.
A True Widow (1679) act 3, sc. 1

4 Every man loves what he is good at.
A True Widow (1679) act 5, sc. 1

Shakespeare, William (1564–1616). English playwright

1 Our remedies oft in ourselves do lie
Which we ascribe to heaven.
All's Well That Ends Well (1603–4) act 1, sc. 1, l. 212

2 A young man married is a man that's marred.
All's Well That Ends Well (1603–4) act 2, sc. 3, l. c.315

3 No legacy is so rich as honesty.
All's Well That Ends Well (1603–4) act 3, sc. 5, l. 12

4 ... Praising what is lost
Makes the remembrance dear.
All's Well That Ends Well (1603–4) act 5, sc. 3, l. 19

5 The triple pillar of the world transformed
Into a strumpet's fool.
Antony and Cleopatra (1606–7) act 1, sc. 1, l. 12

6 CLEOPATRA: I'll set a bourn how far to be beloved.
ANTONY: Then must thou needs find out new heaven, new earth.
Antony and Cleopatra (1606–7) act 1, sc. 1, l. 16

7 In nature's infinite book of secrecy
A little I can read.
Antony and Cleopatra (1606–7) act 1, sc. 2, l. 9

8 On the sudden
A Roman thought hath struck him.
Antony and Cleopatra (1606–7) act 1, sc. 2, l. c.90

9 The nature of bad news infects the teller.
Antony and Cleopatra (1606–7) act 1, sc. 2, l. c.103

10 In time we hate that which we often fear.
Antony and Cleopatra (1606–7) act 1, sc. 3, l. 12

11 Eternity was in our lips and eyes,
Bliss in our brows bent.
Antony and Cleopatra (1606–7) act 1, sc. 3, l. 35

12 Give me to drink mandragora ...
Antony and Cleopatra (1606–7) act 1, sc. 5, l. 4

13 My salad days,
When I was green in judgment,
cold in blood.
Antony and Cleopatra (1606–7) act 1, sc. 5,
l. 73

14 For her own person,
It beggared all description.
Antony and Cleopatra (1606–7) act 2, sc. 2,
c.205

15 The barge she sat in, like a burnished throne,
Burned on the water.
Antony and Cleopatra (1606–7) act 2, sc. 2, l.
c.199

16 Age cannot wither her, nor custom stale
Her infinite variety.
Antony and Cleopatra (1606–7) act 2, sc. 2, l.
c.243

17 I' the east my pleasure lies.
Antony and Cleopatra (1606–7) act 2, sc. 3,
l. 40

18 I will praise any man that will praise me.
Antony and Cleopatra (1606–7) act 2, sc. 6, l.
c.88

19 We have kissed away
Kingdoms and provinces.
Antony and Cleopatra (1606–7) act 3, sc. 10,
l. 7

20 He wears the rose
Of youth upon him.
Antony and Cleopatra (1606–7) act 3, sc. 11,
l. 20

21 O! my fortunes have
Corrupted honest men.
Antony and Cleopatra (1606–7) act 4, sc. 5,
l. 16

22 I am dying, Egypt, dying.
Antony and Cleopatra (1606–7) act 4, sc. 13,
l. 18

23 And there is nothing left remarkable
Beneath the visiting moon.
Antony and Cleopatra (1606–7) act 4, sc. 13,
l. 67

24 Let's do it after the high Roman fashion,
And make death proud to take us.
Antony and Cleopatra (1606–7) act 4, sc. 13,
l. 87

25 His legs bestrid the ocean; his reared arm
Crested the world.
Antony and Cleopatra (1606–7) act 5, sc. 2,
l. 81

26 I wish you all joy of the worm.
Antony and Cleopatra (1606–7) act 5, sc. 2, l.
c.260

27 Give me my robe, put on my crown; I have
Immortal longings in me.
Antony and Cleopatra (1606–7) act 5, sc. 2, l.
c.282

28 O, how full of briers is this working-day world!
As You Like It (1599) act 1, sc. 3, l. c.12

29 Under the greenwood tree
Who loves to lie with me.
As You Like It (1599) act 2, sc. 5, l. 1

30 A motley fool.
As You Like It (1599) act 2, sc. 7, l. 12

31 And thereby hangs a tale.
As You Like It (1599) act 2, sc. 7, l. 28

32 All the world's a stage,
And all the men and women merely players:
They have their exits and their entrances;
And one man in his time plays many parts,
His acts being seven ages.
As You Like It (1599) act 2, sc. 7, l. 139

33 Jealous in honour, sudden, and quick in quarrel,
Seeking the bubble reputation
Even in the cannon's mouth.
As You Like It (1599) act 2, sc. 7, l. 151

34 Sans teeth, sans eyes, sans taste, sans everything.
As You Like It (1599) act 2, sc. 7, l. 166

35 Blow, blow, thou winter wind,
Thou art not so unkind
As man's ingratitude.
As You Like It (1599) act 2, sc. 7, l. 174

36 Most friendship is feigning, most loving, mere folly.
As You Like It (1599) act 2, sc. 7, l. 182

37 It is as easy to count atomies as to resolve the propositions of a lover.
As You Like It (1599) act 3, sc. 2, l. c.246

38 Time travels in divers paces with divers persons.
As You Like It (1599) act 3, sc. 2, l. c.301

39 Honesty coupled to beauty is to have honey a sauce to sugar.
As You Like It (1599) act 3, sc. 3, l. 26

40 Dead shepherd, now I find thy saw of might:
'Who ever loved that loved not at first sight?'
As You Like It (1599) act 3, sc. 5, l. 82

41 Can one desire too much of a good thing?
As You Like It (1599) act 4, sc. 1, l. 115

42 Men are April when they woo, December when they wed.
As You Like It (1599) act 4, sc. 1, l. 139

43 Oh! how bitter a thing it is to look into happiness through another man's eyes.
As You Like It (1599) act 5, sc. 2, l. c.48

44 It was a lover and his lass.
As You Like It (1599) act 5, sc. 3, l. 18

45 Sweet lovers love the spring.
As You Like It (1599) act 5, sc. 3, l. 23

46 A living dead man.
The Comedy of Errors (1594) act 5, sc. 1, l. 238

47 What is the city but the people?
Coriolanus (1608) act 3, sc. 1, l. 198

48 Boldness be my friend!
Arm me, audacity.
Cymbeline (1609–10) act 1, sc. 6, l. 18

49 O, for a horse with wings!
Cymbeline (1609–10) act 3, sc. 2, l. c.49

50 How hard it is to hide the sparks of nature!
Cymbeline (1609–10) act 3, sc. 3, l. 79

51 Fear no more the heat o' the sun,
Nor the furious winter's rages.
Cymbeline (1609–10) act 4, sc. 2, l. 258

52 Golden lads and girls all must,
As chimney-sweepers, come to dust.
Cymbeline (1609–10) act 4, sc. 2, l. 262

53 He that sleeps feels not the toothache.
Cymbeline (1609–10) act 5, sc. 4, l. c.176

54 You come most carefully upon your hour.
Hamlet (1601) act 1, sc. 1, l. 6

55 For this relief much thanks; 'tis bitter cold.
Hamlet (1601) act 1, sc. 1, l. 8

56 Not a mouse stirring.
Hamlet (1601) act 1, sc. 1, l. 10

57 This bodes some strange eruption to our state.
Hamlet (1601) act 1, sc. 1, l. 69

58 But, look, the morn, in russet mantle clad,
Walks o'er the dew of yon high eastern hill.
Hamlet (1601) act 1, sc. 1, l. 166

59 A little more than kin, and less than kind.
Hamlet (1601) act 1, sc. 2, l. 65

60 I am too much i' the sun.
Hamlet (1601) act 1, sc. 2, l. 67

61 Cast thy nighted colour off.
Hamlet (1601) act 1, sc. 2, l. 68

62 But I have that within which passeth show;
These but the trappings and the suits of woe.
Hamlet (1601) act 1, sc. 2, l. 85

63 Frailty, thy name is woman!
Hamlet (1601) act 1, sc. 2, l. 146

64 A truant disposition.
Hamlet (1601) act 1, sc. 2, l. 169

65 The funeral baked meats
Did coldly furnish forth the marriage tables.
Hamlet (1601) act 1, sc. 2, l. 180

66 In the dead vast and middle of the night.
Hamlet (1601) act 1, sc. 2, l. 198

67 A countenance more in sorrow than in anger.
Hamlet (1601) act 1, sc. 2, l. 231

68 Foul deeds will rise,
Though all the earth o'erwhelm them, to men's eyes.
Hamlet (1601) act 1, sc. 2, l. 256

69 Neither a borrower, nor a lender be.
Hamlet (1601) act 1, sc. 3, l. 73

70 To thine own self be true,
And it must follow, as the night the day,
Thou canst not then be false to any man.
Hamlet (1601) act 1, sc. 3, l. 76

71 Springes to catch woodcocks.
Hamlet (1601) act 1, sc. 3, l. 115

72 But to my mind, – though I am native here,
And to the manner born, – it is a custom
More honoured in the breach than the observance.
Hamlet (1601) act 1, sc. 4, l. 14

73 Angels and ministers of grace defend us!
Hamlet (1601) act 1, sc. 4, l. 65

74 Something is rotten in the state of Denmark.
Hamlet (1601) act 1, sc. 4, l. 90

75 Murder most foul, as in the best it is;
But this most foul, strange, and unnatural.
Hamlet (1601) act 1, sc. 5, l. 27

76 O villain, villain, smiling, damnèd villain!
My tables, – meet it is I set it down,
That one may smile, and smile, and be a villain.
Hamlet (1601) act 1, sc. 5, l. 106

77 There are more things in heaven and earth, Horatio,
Than are dreamt of in your philosophy.
Hamlet (1601) act 1, sc. 5, l. 166

78 To put an antic disposition on.
Hamlet (1601) act 1, sc. 5, l. 172

79 The time is out of joint; O cursèd spite,
That ever I was born to set it right!
Hamlet (1601) act 1, sc. 5, l. 188

80 By indirections find directions out.
Hamlet (1601) act 2, sc. 1, l. 66

81 Brevity is the soul of wit.
Hamlet (1601) act 2, sc. 2, l. 90

82 More matter with less art.
Hamlet (1601) act 2, sc. 2, l. 95

83 POLONIUS: What do you read, my lord?
HAMLET: Words, words, words.
Hamlet (1601) act 2, sc. 2, *c*.195

84 Though this be madness, yet there is method in't.
Hamlet (1601) act 2, sc. 2, *c*.211

85 There is nothing either good or bad, but thinking makes it so.
Hamlet (1601) act 2, sc. 2, l. 251

86 It goes so heavily with my disposition that this goodly frame, the earth, seems to me a sterile promontory; this most excellent canopy, the air, look you, this brave o'erhanging firmament, this majestical roof fretted with golden fire, why, it appears no other thing to me but a foul and pestilent congregation of vapours. What a piece of work is a man! How noble in reason! how infinite in faculty! in form, in moving, how express and admirable! in action how like an angel! in apprehension how like a god! the beauty of the world! the paragon of animals! And yet, to me, what is this quintessence of dust?
Hamlet (1601) act 2, sc. 2, *c*.316

87 The play, I remember, pleased not the million; 'twas caviare to the general.
Hamlet (1601) act 2, sc. 2, *c*.465

88 Good my lord, will you see the players well bestowed?
Do you hear, let them be well used; for they are the abstracts and brief chronicles of the time.
Hamlet (1601) act 2, sc. 2, *c*.553

89 O, what a rogue and peasant slave am I.
Hamlet (1601) act 2, sc. 2, l. *c*.584

90 What's Hecuba to him or he to Hecuba
That he should weep for her?
Hamlet (1601) act 2, sc. 2, l. *c*.593

91 The play's the thing
Wherein I'll catch the conscience of the king.
Hamlet (1601) act 2, sc. 2, l. *c*.641

92 To be, or not to be: that is the question.
Hamlet (1601) act 3, sc. 1, l. 56

93 To die, to sleep;
To sleep: perchance to dream: ay, there's the rub;
For in that sleep of death what dreams may come
When we have shuffled off this mortal coil,
Must give us pause.
Hamlet (1601) act 3, sc. 1, l. 64

94 Death,
The undiscovered country from whose bourn
No traveller returns.
Hamlet (1601) act 3, sc. 1, l. 78

95 Thus conscience doth make cowards of us all.
Hamlet (1601) act 3, sc. 1, l. 83

96 Get thee to a nunnery.
Hamlet (1601) act 3, sc. 1, l. c.124

97 O! what a noble mind is here o'er-thrown.
Hamlet (1601) act 3, sc. 1, l. c.159

98 Madness in great ones must not unwatched go.
Hamlet (1601) act 3, sc. 1, l. 191

99 Speak the speech, I pray you, as I pronounced it to you, trippingly on the tongue.
Hamlet (1601) act 3, sc. 2, l. 1

100 Playing, whose end, both at the first and now, was and is, to hold, as 'twere, the mirror up to nature;
Hamlet (1601) act 3, sc. 2, l. c.23

101 The lady doth protest too much, methinks.
Hamlet (1601) act 3, sc. 2, l. c.242

102 KING: What do you call the play?
HAMLET: The Mouse-trap.
Hamlet (1601) act 3, sc. 2, l. c.247

103 I will speak daggers to her, but use none.
Hamlet (1601) act 3, sc. 2, l. c.385

104 My words fly up, my thoughts remain below:
Words without thoughts never to heaven go.
Hamlet (1601) act 3, sc. 3, l. 97

105 A king of shreds and patches.
Hamlet (1601) act 3, sc. 4, l. 102

106 I must be cruel only to be kind.
Hamlet (1601) act 3, sc. 4, l. 178

107 For 'tis the sport to have the engineer
Hoist with his own petar.
Hamlet (1601) act 3, sc. 4, l. 206

108 Diseases desperate grown,
By desperate appliances are relieved,
Or not at all.
Hamlet (1601) act 4, sc. 2, l. 9

109 A man may fish with the worm that hath eat of a king, and eat of the fish that hath fed of that worm.
Hamlet (1601) act 4, sc. 3, l. 27

110 We go to gain a little patch of ground,
That hath in it no profit but the name.
Hamlet (1601) act 4, sc. 4, l. 18

111 How all occasions do inform against me.
Hamlet (1601) act 4, sc. 4, l. 32

112 Some craven scruple
Of thinking too precisely on the event.
Hamlet (1601) act 4, sc. 4, l. 40

113 We know what we are, but not what we may be.
Hamlet (1601) act 4, sc. 5, l. c.42

114 When sorrows come, they come not single spies,
But in battalions.
Hamlet (1601) act 4, sc. 5, l. c.78

115 There's such divinity doth hedge a king,
That treason can but peep to what it would.
Hamlet (1601) act 4, sc. 5, l. c.123

116 There's rosemary, that's for remembrance.
Hamlet (1601) act 4, sc. 5, l. c.174

117 Where th'offence is, let the great axe fall.
Hamlet (1601) act 4, sc. 5, l. 216

118 There is a willow grows aslant a brook,
That shows his hoar leaves in the glassy stream.
Hamlet (1601) act 4, sc. 7, l. 167

119 Alas, poor Yorick. I knew him, Horatio; a fellow of infinite jest, of most excellent fancy.
Hamlet (1601) act 5, sc. 1, l. c.201

120 Let Hercules himself do what he may,
The cat will mew, and dog will have his day.
Hamlet (1601) act 5, sc. 1, l. 288

121 There's a divinity that shapes our ends,
Rough-hew them how we will.
Hamlet (1601) act 5, sc. 2, l. 10

122 The readiness is all.
Hamlet (1601) act 5, sc. 2, l. c.235

123 Good night, sweet prince,
And flights of angels sing thee to thy rest.
Hamlet (1601) act 5, sc. 2, l. 312

124 Absent thee from felicity awhile,
Hamlet (1601) act 5, sc. 2, l. c.361

125 The rest is silence.
Hamlet (1601) act 5, sc. 2, l. c.372

126 What, in thy quips and thy quiddities?
Henry IV, Part 1 (1597) act 1, sc. 2, l. c.50

127 'Tis no sin for a man to labour in his vocation.
Henry IV, Part 1 (1597) act 1, sc. 2, l. c.116 (referring to thieving)

128 If all the year were playing holidays,
To sport would be as tedious as to work.
Henry IV, Part 1 (1597) act 1, sc. 2, l. c.226

129 I know a trick worth two of that.
Henry IV, Part 1 (1597) act 2, sc. 1, l. c.40

130 Out of this nettle, danger, we pluck this flower, safety.
Henry IV, Part 1 (1597) act 2, sc. 3, l. c.11

131 A plague of all cowards, still say I.
Henry IV, Part 1 (1597) act 2, sc. 4, l. c.175

132 Instinct is a great matter, I was a coward on instinct.
Henry IV, Part 1 (1597) act 2, sc. 4, l. c.304

133 Banish plump Jack and banish all the world.
Henry IV, Part 1 (1597) act 2, sc. 4, l. c.533

134 And all the courses of my life do show
I am not in the roll of common men.
Henry IV, Part 1 (1597) act 3, sc. 1, l. c.42

135 I can teach thee, coz, to shame the devil,
By telling truth: 'Tell truth, and shame the devil'.
Hotspur to Glyndwr *Henry IV, Part* 1 (1597) act 3, sc. 1, l. 55

136 That would set my teeth nothing on edge,
Nothing so much as mincing poetry.
Henry IV, Part 1 (1597) act 3, sc. 1, l. c.132

137 The skipping king, he ambled up and down
With shallow jesters and rash bavin wits.
Henry IV, Part 1 (1597) act 3, sc. 2, l. 60

138 I am as vigilant as a cat to steal cream.
Henry IV, Part 1 (1597) act 4, sc. 2, l. 58

139 Greatness knows itself.
Henry IV, Part 1 (1597) act 4, sc. 3, l. 74

140 I have a truant been to chivalry.
Henry IV, Part 1 (1597) act 5, sc. 1, l. 94

141 Two stars keep not their motion in one sphere.
Henry IV, Part 1 (1597) act 5, sc. 4, l. 65

142 But thought's the slave of life, and life time's fool.
Henry IV, Part 1 (1597) act 5, sc. 4, l. c.81

143 The better part of valour is discretion, in the which better part I have saved my life.
Henry IV, Part 1 (1597) act 5, sc. 4, l. c.118

144 He hath eaten me out of house and home.
Henry IV, Part 2 (1597) act 2, sc. 1, l. 75

145 Is it not strange that desire should
so many years outlive performance?
Henry IV, Part 2 (1597) act 2, sc. 4, l. c.283

146 Uneasy lies the head that wears a
crown.
Henry IV, Part 2 (1597) act 3, sc. 1, l. 31

147 We have heard the chimes at midnight.
Henry IV, Part 2 (1597) act 3, sc. 2, l. c.231

148 Against ill chances men are ever
merry,
But heaviness foreruns the good
event.
Henry IV, Part 2 (1597) act 4, sc. 2, l. 81

149 Thy wish was father, Harry, to that
thought.
Henry IV, Part 2 (1597) act 4, sc. 5, l. 91

150 I know thee not, old man: fall to
thy prayers.
Henry IV, Part 2 (1597) act 5, sc. 5, l. c.52

151 O! for a Muse of fire, that would
ascend
The brightest heaven of invention;
A kingdom for a stage, princes to
act
And monarchs to behold the
swelling scene.
Henry V (1599) chorus, l. 1

152 Can this cockpit hold
The vasty fields of France? or may
we cram
Within this wooden O the very
casques
That did affright the air at Agin-
court?
Henry V (1599) chorus, l. 11

153 Consideration like an angel came,
And whipped the offending Adam
out of him.
Henry V (1599) act 1, sc. 1, l. 28

154 For his nose was as sharp as a pen,
and a' babbled of green fields.
Henry V (1599) act 2, sc. 3, l. c.15

155 Once more unto the breach, dear
friends, once more;
Or close the wall up with our English dead!
Henry V (1599) act 3, sc. 1, l. 1

156 Cry 'God for Harry! England and
Saint George!'
Henry V (1599) act 3, sc. 1, l. 34

157 Men of few words are the best men.
Henry V (1599) act 3, sc. 2, l. c.40

158 The royal captain of this ruined
band.
Henry V (1599) act 4, chorus, l. 29

159 A little touch of Harry in the night.
Henry V (1599) act 4, chorus, l. 47

160 There is some soul of goodness in
things evil,
Would men observingly distil it
out.
Henry V (1599) act 4, sc. 1, l. 4

161 We few, we happy few, we band of
brothers;
For he to-day that sheds his blood
with me
Shall be my brother; be he ne'er so
vile
This day shall gentle his condition:
And gentlemen in England, now a-
bed
Shall think themselves accursed
they were not here,
And hold their manhoods cheap
whiles any speaks
That fought with us upon Saint
Crispin's day.
Henry V (1599) act 4, sc. 3, l. 35

162 Expect Saint Martin's summer,
halcyon days.
Henry VI, Part 1 (1592) act 1, sc. 2, l. 131

163 The first thing we do let's kill all the
lawyers.
Henry VI, Part 2 (1592) act 4, sc. 2, l. 78

164 And Adam was a gardener.
Henry VI, Part 2 (1592) act 4, sc. 2, l. c.146

165 Ignorance is the curse of God,
Knowledge the wing wherewith we
fly to heaven.
Henry VI, Part 2 (1592) act 4, sc. 7, l. 72

166 O tiger's heart wrapped in a woman's hide!
Henry VI, Part 3 (1592) act 1, sc. 4, l. 137

167 The common people swarm like
summer flies.
Henry VI, Part 3 (1592) act 2, sc. 6, l. 8

168 Hasty marriage seldom proveth well.
Henry VI, Part 3 (1592) act 4, sc. 1, l. 18

169 Fearless minds climb soonest unto crowns.
Henry VI, Part 3 (1592) act 4, sc. 8, l. 62

170 Suspicion always haunts the guilty mind.
Henry VI, Part 3 (1592) act 5, sc. 6, l. 11

171 Men's evil manners live in brass; their virtues
We write in water.
Henry VIII (1613) act 4, sc. 2, l. 45

172 Beware the ides of March.
Julius Caesar (1599) act 1, sc. 2, l. 18

173 Why, man, he doth bestride the narrow world
Like a Colossus.
Julius Caesar (1599) act 1, sc. 2, l. 134

174 The fault, dear Brutus, is not in our stars,
But in ourselves, that we are underlings.
Julius Caesar (1599) act 1, sc. 2, l. 139

175 Yond Cassius has a lean and hungry look;
He thinks too much: such men are dangerous.
Julius Caesar (1599) act 1, sc. 2, l. 193

176 It was Greek to me.
Julius Caesar (1599) act 1, sc. 2, l. c.288

177 Cowards die many times before their deaths;
The valiant never taste of death but once.
Julius Caesar (1599) act 2, sc. 2, l. 32

178 *Et tu, Brute?*
Then fall, Caesar!
Julius Caesar (1599) act 3, sc. 1, l. 77

179 O! pardon me, thou bleeding piece of earth,
That I am meek and gentle with these butchers.
Julius Caesar (1599) act 3, sc. 1, l. 254

180 Let slip the dogs of war.
Julius Caesar (1599) act 3, sc. 1, l. 273

181 Friends, Romans, countrymen, lend me your ears;
I come to bury Caesar, not to praise him.
Julius Caesar (1599) act 3, sc. 2, l. 79

182 But Brutus says he was ambitious;
And Brutus is an honourable man.
Julius Caesar (1599) act 3, sc. 2, l. c.92

183 Ambition should be made of sterner stuff.
Julius Caesar (1599) act 3, sc. 2, l. c.98

184 If you have tears, prepare to shed them now.
Julius Caesar (1599) act 3, sc. 2, l. c.174

185 This was the most unkindest cut of all.
Julius Caesar (1599) act 3, sc. 2, l. c.188

186 A friend should bear his friend's infirmities.
Julius Caesar (1599) act 4, sc. 3, l. 85

187 There is a tide in the affairs of men,
Which, taken at the flood, leads on to fortune;
Omitted, all the voyage of their life
Is bound in shallows and in miseries.
Julius Caesar (1599) act 4, sc. 3, l. 217

188 My life is run his compass.
Julius Caesar (1599) act 5, sc. 3, l. 25

189 This was the noblest Roman of them all.
Julius Caesar (1599) act 5, sc. 5, l. 68

190 Mad world! mad kings! mad composition!
King John (1596) act 2, sc. 1, l. 561

191 Strong reasons make strange actions.
King John (1596) act 3, sc. 4, l. 182

192 Nothing will come of nothing.
King Lear (1605–6) act 1, sc. 1, l. c.92

193 Time shall unfold what pleated cunning hides.
King Lear (1605–6) act 1, sc. 1, l. c.280

194 Now, gods, stand up for bastards!
King Lear (1605–6) act 1, sc. 2, l. 22

195 Thou whoreson Z, thou unnecessary letter.
King Lear (1605–6) act 2, sc. 2, l. 63.

196 O reason not the need!
King Lear (1605–6) act 2, sc. 4, l. 264

197 Blow, winds, and crack your cheeks! rage! blow!
King Lear (1605–6) act 3, sc. 2, l. 1

198 I am a man
More sinned against than sinning.
King Lear (1605–6) act 3, sc. 2, l. c.57

199 He that has a little tiny wit,
With hey, ho, the wind and the rain,
Must make content with his fortunes fit,
Though the rain it raineth every day.
King Lear (1605–6) act 3, sc. 2, l. c.74

200 That way madness lies.
King Lear (1605–6) act 3, sc. 4, l. 21

201 Poor Tom's a-cold.
King Lear (1605–6) act 3, sc. 4, l. c.151

202 As flies to wanton boys, are we to the gods;
They kill us for their sport.
King Lear (1605–6) act 4, sc. 1, l. 36

203 It is the stars,
The stars above us, govern our conditions.
King Lear (1605–6) act 4, sc. 3, l. c.34

204 Every inch a king.
King Lear (1605–6) act 4, sc. 6, l. c.111

205 Let copulation thrive.
King Lear (1605–6) act 4, sc. 6, l. c.117

206 The wheel is come full circle.
King Lear (1605–6) act 5, sc. 3, l. c.176

207 Thou'lt come no more,
Never, never, never, never, never!
King Lear (1605–6) act 5, sc. 3, l. c.309

208 They have been at a great feast of languages, and stolen the scraps.
Love's Labour's Lost (1595) act 5, sc. 1, l. c.39

209 A light heart lives long.
Love's Labour's Lost (1595) act 5, sc. 2, l. 18

210 When shall we three meet again
In thunder, lightning, or in rain?
When the hurly-burly's done,
When the battle's lost and won.
Macbeth (1606) act 1, sc. 1, l. 1

211 Fair is foul, and foul is fair:
Hover through the fog and filthy air.
Macbeth (1606) act 1, sc. 1, l. 11

212 A drum! a drum!
Macbeth doth come.
Macbeth (1606) act 1, sc. 3, l. 30

213 The weird sisters.
Macbeth (1606) act 1, sc. 3, l. 32

214 What! can the devil speak true?
Macbeth (1606) act 1, sc. 3, l. 107

215 Time and the hour runs through the roughest day.
Macbeth (1606) act 1, sc. 3, l. 147

216 Yet I do fear thy nature;
It is too full o' the milk of human kindness.
Macbeth (1606) act 1, sc. 5, l. c.17

217 But screw your courage to the sticking-place,
And we'll not fail.
Macbeth (1606) act 1, sc. 7, l. 62

218 Is this a dagger which I see before me,
The handle toward my hand?
Macbeth (1606) act 2, sc. 1, l. 33

219 The attempt and not the deed,
Confounds us.
Macbeth (1606) act 2, sc. 2, l. 12

220 A little water clears us of this deed.
Macbeth (1606) act 2, sc. 2, l. 68

221 There's daggers in men's smiles.
Macbeth (1606) act 2, sc. 3, l. 139

222 We have scotched the snake, not killed it.
Macbeth (1606) act 3, sc. 2, l. 13

223 Never shake
Thy gory locks at me.
Macbeth (1606) act 3, sc. 4, l. 50

224 Double, double toil and trouble;
Fire burn and cauldron bubble.
Macbeth (1606) act 4, sc. 1, l. 10

225 By the pricking of my thumbs,
Something wicked this way comes.
Macbeth (1606) act 4, sc. 1, l. 44

226 MACBETH: How now, you secret,
black, and midnight hags!
What is't you do?
WITCHES: A deed without a name.
Macbeth (1606) act 4, sc. 1, l. 48

227 Out, damned spot!
Macbeth (1606) act 5, sc. 1, l. c.38

228 All the perfumes of Arabia will not
sweeten this little hand.
Macbeth (1606) act 5, sc. 1, l. c.55

229 To-morrow, and to-morrow, and
to-morrow,
Creeps in this petty pace from day
to day.
Macbeth (1606) act 5, sc. 5, l. 18

230 Out, out, brief candle!
Life's but a walking shadow, a poor
player,
That struts and frets his hour upon
the stage,
And then is heard no more; it is a
tale
Told by an idiot, full of sound and
fury,
Signifying nothing.
Macbeth (1606) act 5, sc. 5, l. 22

231 Lay on, Macduff;
And damned be him that first cries,
'Hold, enough!'
Macbeth (1606) act 5, sc. 7, l. 62

232 Virtue is bold, and goodness never
fearful.
Measure for Measure (1604) act 3, sc. 1, l. 210

233 Death's a great disguiser.
Measure for Measure (1604) act 4, sc. 2, l.c.185

234 What news on the Rialto?
The Merchant of Venice (1596–8) act 1, sc. 3, l. c.38

235 Truth will come to light; murder
cannot be hid long.
The Merchant of Venice (1596–8) act 2, sc. 2, l. c.86

236 Love is blind, and lovers cannot see
The pretty follies that themselves
commit.
The Merchant of Venice (1596–8) act 2, sc. 6, l. 36

237 The portrait of a blinking idiot.
The Merchant of Venice (1596–8) act 2, sc. 9, l. 54

238 Let him look to his bond.
The Merchant of Venice (1596–8) act 3, sc. 1, l. c.51

239 Hath not a Jew eyes?
The Merchant of Venice (1596–8) act 3, sc. 1, l. c.63

240 If you prick us, do we not bleed? if
you tickle us, do we not laugh? if
you poison us, do we not die? and if
you wrong us, shall we not
revenge?
The Merchant of Venice (1596–8) act 3, sc. 1, l. c.68

241 Tell me where is fancy bred.
Or in the heart or in the head?
The Merchant of Venice (1596–8) act 3, sc. 2, l. 63

242 The quality of mercy is not
strained,
It droppeth as the gentle rain from
heaven
Upon the place beneath.
The Merchant of Venice (1596–8) act 4, sc. 1, l. c.182

243 Take thou thy pound of flesh.
The Merchant of Venice (1596–8) act 4, sc. 1, l. 305

244 In such a night as this.
The Merchant of Venice (1596–8) act 5, sc. 1, l. 1

245 So shines a good deed in a naughty
world.
The Merchant of Venice (1596–8) act 5, sc. 1, l. 90

246 Why, then the world's mine oyster,
Which I with sword will open.
The Merry Wives of Windsor (1597) act 2, sc. 2, l. 2

247 I cannot tell what the dickens his
name is.
The Merry Wives of Windsor (1597) act 3, sc. 2, l. 16

248 The course of true love never did
run smooth.
A Midsummer Night's Dream (1595–6) act 1, sc. 1, l. 134

249 Ill met by moonlight, proud Titania.
A Midsummer Night's Dream (1595–6) act 2, sc. 1, l. 60

250 I'll put a girdle round about the earth
In forty minutes.
A Midsummer Night's Dream (1595–6) act 2, sc. 1, l. 175

251 I know a bank where the wild thyme blows.
A Midsummer Night's Dream (1595–6) act 2, sc. 1, l. 249

252 What angel wakes me from my flowery bed?
A Midsummer Night's Dream (1595–6) act 3, sc. 1, l. c.135

253 Lord, what fools these mortals be!
A Midsummer Night's Dream (1595–6) act 3, sc. 2, l. 115

254 And, as imagination bodies forth
The forms of things unknown, the poet's pen
Turns them to shapes, and gives to airy nothing
A local habitation and a name.
A Midsummer Night's Dream (1595–6) act 5, sc. 1, l. 14

255 Time goes on crutches till love have all his rites.
Much Ado About Nothing (1598–9) act 2, sc. 1, l. c.334

256 Men were deceivers ever.
Much Ado About Nothing (1598–9) act 2, sc. 3, l. c.66

257 Comparisons are odorous.
Much Ado About Nothing (1598–9) act 3, sc. 5, l. 15

258 Patch grief with proverbs.
Much Ado About Nothing (1598–9) act 5, sc. 1, l. 17

259 There was never yet philosopher
That could endure the toothache patiently.
Much Ado About Nothing (1598–9) act 5, sc. 1, l. 35

260 But I will wear my heart upon my sleeve
For daws to peck at: I am not what I am.
Othello (1602–4) act 1, sc. 1, l. 64

261 To suckle fools and chronicle small beer.
Othello (1602–4) act 2, sc. 1, l. 163

262 Thy honesty and love doth mince this matter.
Othello (1602–4) act 2, sc. 3, l. c.249

263 Not poppy, nor mandragora,
Nor all the drowsy syrups of the world,
Shall ever medicine thee to that sweet sleep
Which thou owedst yesterday.
Othello (1602–4) act 3, sc. 3, l. 331

264 This denoted a foregone conclusion.
Othello (1602–4) act 3, sc. 3, l. 429

265 It is the cause, it is the cause, my soul;
Let me not name it to you, you chaste stars!
Othello (1602–4) act 5, sc. 2, l. 1

266 Put out the light, and then put out the light.
Othello (1602–4) act 5, sc. 2, l. 7

267 Then, must you speak
Of one that loved not wisely but too well.
Othello (1602–4) act 5, sc. 2, l. 342

268 Killing myself to die upon a kiss.
Othello (1602–4) act 5, sc. 2, l. 356

269 We were not born to sue, but to command.
Richard II (1595) act 1, sc. 1, l. 196

270 How long a time lies in one little word!
Four lagging winters and four wanton springs
End in a word: such is the breath of kings.
Richard II (1595) act 1, sc. 3, l. 206

271 I was a journeyman to grief?
Richard II (1595) act 1, sc. 3, l. 274

272 There is no virtue like necessity.
Richard II (1595) act 1, sc. 3, l. 278

273 They say the tongues of dying men
Enforce attention, like deep harmony.
Richard II (1595) act 2, sc. 1, l. 5

274 This precious stone set in the silver sea.
Richard II (1595) act 2, sc. 1, l. 46

275 This blessèd plot, this earth, this realm, this England,
This nurse, this teeming womb of royal kings.
Richard II (1595) act 2, sc. 1, l. 50

276 Grace me no grace, nor uncle me no uncle.
Richard II (1595) act 2, sc. 3, l. 87

277 The caterpillars of the commonwealth.
Richard II (1595) act 2, sc. 3, l. 166

278 Not all the water in the rough rude sea
Can wash the balm from an anointed king.
Richard II (1595) act 3, sc. 2, l. 54

279 Let's talk of graves, of worms, and epitaphs.
Richard II (1595) act 3, sc. 2, l. 145

280 The purple testament of bleeding war.
Richard II (1595) act 3, sc. 3, l. 94

281 I have been studying how I may compare
This prison where I live unto the world.
Richard II (1595) act 5, sc. 5, l. 1

282 I wasted time, and now doth time waste me.
Richard II (1595) act 5, sc. 5, l. 49

283 Now is the winter of our discontent
Made glorious summer by this sun of York.
Richard III (1591) act 1, sc. 1, l. 1

284 Was ever woman in this humour wooed?
Was ever woman in this humour won?
Richard III (1591) act 1, sc. 2, l. 229

285 So wise so young, they say, do never live long.
Richard III (1591) act 3, sc. 1, l. 79

286 I am not in the giving vein to-day.
Richard III (1591) act 4, sc. 2, l. 115

287 An honest tale speeds best being plainly told.
Richard III (1591) act 4, sc. 4, l. 359

288 A horse! a horse! my kingdom for a horse!
Richard III (1591) act 5, sc. 4, l. 7

289 From forth the fatal loins of these two foes
A pair of star-crossed lovers take their life.
Romeo and Juliet (1595) prologue

290 The two hours' traffick of our stage.
Romeo and Juliet (1595) prologue

291 Did my heart love till now? Forswear it, sight,
For I ne'er saw true beauty till this night.
Romeo and Juliet (1595) act 1, sc. 5, l. 51

292 But, soft! what light through yonder window breaks?
It is the east, and Juliet is the sun.
Romeo and Juliet (1595) act 2, sc. 1, l. 1

293 O Romeo, Romeo! wherefore art thou Romeo?
Romeo and Juliet (1595) act 2, sc. 1, l. 33

294 What's in a name? that which we call a rose
By any other name would smell as sweet.
Romeo and Juliet (1595) act 2, sc. 1, l. 43

295 Parting is such sweet sorrow
That I shall say good-night till it be morrow.
Romeo and Juliet (1595) act 2, sc. 1, l. 185

296 I am the very pink of courtesy.
Romeo and Juliet (1595) act 2, sc. 4, l. c.63

297 A plague o' both your houses!
Romeo and Juliet (1595) act 3, sc. 1, l. c.112

298 I am Fortune's fool.
Romeo and Juliet (1595) act 3, sc. 1, l. c.142

299 Whiter than new snow on a raven's back.
Romeo and Juliet (1595) act 3, sc. 2, l. 19

300 Adversity's sweet milk, philosophy.
Romeo and Juliet (1595) act 3, sc. 3, l. 54

301 Thank me no thankings, nor proud me no prouds.
Romeo and Juliet (1595) act 3, sc. 5, l. 153

302 'Tis an ill cook that cannot lick his own fingers.
Romeo and Juliet (1595) act 4, sc. 2, l. 6

303 Kiss me Kate, we will be married o' Sunday.
The Taming of the Shrew (1592) act 2, sc. 1, l. 318

304 You taught me language, and my profit on't
Is I know how to curse.
The Tempest (1611) act 1, sc. 2, l. 365

305 Full fathom five thy father lies;
Of his bones are coral made.
The Tempest (1611) act 1, sc. 2, l. 394

306 Misery acquaints a man with strange bedfellows.
The Tempest (1611) act 2, sc. 2, l. c.42

307 Thought is free.
The Tempest (1611) act 3, sc. 2, l. c.134

308 The isle is full of noises.
The Tempest (1611) act 3, sc. 2, l. c.135

309 Our revels now are ended. These our actors,
As I foretold you, were all spirits and
Are melted into air, into thin air.
The Tempest (1611) act 4, sc. 1, l. 148

310 We are such stuff
As dreams are made on, and our little life
Is rounded with a sleep.
The Tempest (1611) act 4, sc. 1, l. 156

311 I'll break my staff,
Bury it certain fathoms in the earth,
And, deeper than did ever plummet sound,
I'll drown my book.
The Tempest (1611) act 5, sc. 1, l. 54

312 Where the bee sucks, there suck I
In a cowslip's bell I lie.
The Tempest (1611) act 5, sc. 1, l. 88

313 O brave new world,
That has such people in't.
The Tempest (1611) act 5, sc. 1, l. 183

314 We have seen better days.
Timon of Athens (c.1607) act 4, sc. 2, l. 27

315 Time hath, my lord, a wallet at his back,
Wherein he puts alms for oblivion.
Troilus and Cressida (1602) act 3, sc. 3, l. 145

316 If music be the food of love, play on;
Give me excess of it, that, surfeiting,
The appetite may sicken, and so die.
Twelfth Night (1601) act 1, sc. 1, l. 1

317 Many a good hanging prevents a bad marriage.
Twelfth Night (1601) act 1, sc. 5, l. c.20

318 Better a witty fool than a foolish wit.
Twelfth Night (1601) act 1, sc. 5, l. c.32

319 One would think his mother's milk were scarce out of him.
Twelfth Night (1601) act 1, sc. 5, l. c.170

320 Make me a willow cabin at your gate,
And call upon my soul within the house.
Twelfth Night (1601) act 1, sc. 5, l. c.289

321 O mistress mine! where are you roaming?
Twelfth Night (1601) act 2, sc. 3, l. c.42

322 Dost thou think, because thou art virtuous, there shall be no more cakes and ale?
Twelfth Night (1601) act 2, sc. 3, l. c.124

323 Come away, come away, death,
And in sad cypress let me be laid.
Twelfth Night (1601) act 2, sc. 4, l. 51

324 She sat like patience on a monument,
Smiling at grief.
Twelfth Night (1601) act 2, sc. 4, l. c.116

325 But be not afraid of greatness: some men are born great, some achieve greatness, and some have greatness thrust upon them.
Twelfth Night (1601) act 2, sc. 5, l. c.158

326 Then westward ho!
Twelfth Night (1601) act 3, sc. 1, l. c.133

327 Why, this is very midsummer madness.
Twelfth Night (1601) act 3, sc. 4, l. c.62

328 More matter for a May morning.
Twelfth Night (1601) act 3, sc. 4, l. c.158

329 There is no darkness but ignorance.
Twelfth Night (1601) act 4, sc. 2, l. 43

330 Thus the whirligig of time brings in his revenges.
Twelfth Night (1601) act 5, sc. 1, l. c.388

331 When that I was and a little tiny boy,
With hey, ho, the wind and the rain;
A foolish thing was but a toy,
For the rain it raineth every day.
Twelfth Night (1601) act 5, sc. 1, l. c.401

332 Who is Silvia? what is she,
That all our swains commend her?
The Two Gentlemen of Verona (1592–3) act 4, sc. 2, l. 40

333 I saw his heart in's face.
The Winter's Tale (1610–11) act 1, sc. 2, l. 447

334 A sad tale's best for winter.
The Winter's Tale (1610–11) act 2, sc. 1, l. 27

335 Exit, pursued by a bear.
The Winter's Tale (1610–11) act 3, sc. 3 (stage direction)

336 A snapper-up of unconsidered trifles.
The Winter's Tale (1610–11) act 4, sc. 2, l. c.25

337 Though I am not naturally honest, I am so sometimes by chance.
The Winter's Tale (1610–11) act 4, sc. 3, l. c.734

338 Shall I compare thee to a summer's day?
Sonnet 18

339 Rough winds do shake the darling buds of May.
Sonnet 18

340 Like as the waves make towards the pebbled shore,
So do our minutes hasten to their end.
Sonnet 60

341 No longer mourn for me when I am dead.
Sonnet 71

342 That time of year thou mayst in me behold
When yellow leaves, or none, or few, do hang

Upon those boughs which shake against the cold,
Bare ruined choirs, where late the sweet birds sang.
Sonnet 73

343 Time's thievish progress to eternity.
Sonnet 77

344 Lilies that fester smell far worse than weeds.
Sonnet 94

345 When in the chronicle of wasted time
I see descriptions of the fairest wights.
Sonnet 106

346 Let me not to the marriage of true minds
Admit impediments.
Sonnet 116

347 If this be error, and upon me proved,
I never writ, nor no man ever loved.
Sonnet 116

348 Love comforteth like sunshine after rain.
Venus and Adonis (1593) l. 799

349 Item, I give unto my wife my second-best bed, with the furniture.
Will, 1616

350 Good friend, for Jesu's sake forbear
To dig the dust enclosed here.
Blest be the man that spares these stones,
And curst be he that moves my bones.
Epitaph on his tomb, probably composed by himself

Shankly, Bill (1914–81). British football manager

1 Some people think football is a matter of life and death … I can assure them it is much more serious than that.
In the *Sunday Times* 4 October 1981, but originally said in the late 1960s

Shaw, George Bernard (1856–1950). Irish playwright

1 'Do you know what a pessimist is?'
'A man who thinks everybody is as
nasty as himself, and hates them
for it.'
An Unsocial Socialist (1887), ch. 5

2 We don't bother much about dress
and manners in England, because,
as a nation, we don't dress well and
we've no manners.
You Never Can Tell (1896) act 1

3 The great advantage of a hotel is
that it's a refuge from home life.
You Never Can Tell (1896) act 2

4 There are no secrets better kept
than the secrets everybody guesses.
Mrs Warren's Profession (1898) act 3

5 You're not a man, you're a
machine.
Arms and the Man (1898) act 3

6 The worst sin towards our fellow
creatures is not to hate them, but to
be indifferent to them: that's the
essence of inhumanity.
The Devil's Disciple (1901) act 2

7 Martyrdom ... the only way in
which a man can become famous
without ability.
The Devil's Disciple (1901) act 3

8 There is no love sincerer than the
love of food.
Man and Superman (1903) act 1

9 Marriage is the most licentious of
human institutions.
Man and Superman (1903) act 3

10 Hell is full of musical amateurs:
music is the brandy of the damned.
Man and Superman (1903) act 3

11 Liberty means responsibility. That
is why most men dread it.
Man and Superman (1903) 'Maxims: Liberty
and Equality'

12 He who can, does. He who cannot,
teaches.
Man and Superman (1903) 'Maxims: Education'

13 Marriage is popular because it
combines the maximum of temptation with the maximum of
opportunity.
Man and Superman (1903) 'Maxims: Marriage'

14 Decency is Indecency's conspiracy
of silence.
Man and Superman (1903) 'Maxims:
Decency'

15 Life levels all men: death reveals
the eminent.
Man and Superman (1903) 'Maxims: Fame'

16 The golden rule is that there are no
golden rules.
Man and Superman (1903) 'Maxims: The
Golden Rule'

17 There are only two qualities in the
world: efficiency and inefficiency,
and only two sorts of people: the
efficient and the inefficient.
John Bull's Other Island (1907) act 4

18 The greatest of evils and the worst
of crimes is poverty.
Major Barbara (1907) preface

19 He knows nothing; and he thinks
he knows everything. That points
clearly to a political career.
Major Barbara (1907) act 3

20 Fashions, after all, are only induced
epidemics.
The Doctor's Dilemma (1911) 'Preface on
Doctors: Fashions and Epidemics'

21 Science becomes dangerous only
when it imagines that it has
reached its goal.
The Doctor's Dilemma (1911) preface, 'The
Latest Theories'

22 All professions are conspiracies
against the laity.
The Doctor's Dilemma (1911) act 1

23 Assassination is the extreme form
of censorship.
The Showing-Up of Blanco Posnet (1911)
'Limits to Toleration'

24 It is impossible for an Englishman
to open his mouth without making
some other Englishman hate or
despise him.
Pygmalion (1916) preface

25 There are only two classes in good
   society in England: the equestrian
   classes and the neurotic classes.
   Heartbreak House (1919) act 3

26 I enjoy convalescence. It is the part
   that makes illness worth while.
   Back to Methuselah (1921) pt 2

27 A government which robs Peter to
   pay Paul can always depend on the
   support of Paul.
   Everybody's Political What's What? (1944)
   ch. 30

28 A perpendicular expression of a
   horizontal desire.
   Of dancing. Quoted in the *New Statesman*
   23 March 1962

Shelley, Percy Bysshe (1792–1822).
English poet

1 I met a traveller from an antique
   land
   Who said: Two vast and trunkless
   legs of stone
   Stand in the desert.
   'Ozymandias' (1819)

2 'My name is Ozymandias, king of
   kings:
   Look on my works, ye Mighty, and
   despair!'
   Nothing beside remains. Round
   the decay
   Of that colossal wreck, boundless
   and bare
   The lone and level sands stretch far
   away.
   'Ozymandias' (1819)

3 That orbèd maiden, with white fire
   laden,
   Whom mortals call the Moon.
   'The Cloud' (1819)

4 I am the daughter of Earth and
   Water,
   And the nursling of the Sky;
   I pass through the pores of the
   ocean and shores;
   I change, but I cannot die.
   'The Cloud' (1819)

5 O, Wind,
   If Winter comes, can Spring be far
   behind?
   'Ode to the West Wind' (1819) l. 69

6 Hail to thee, blithe Spirit!
   Bird thou never wert.
   'To a Skylark' (1819)

7 He gave man speech, and speech
   created thought,
   Which is the measure of the universe.
   Prometheus Unbound (1820) act 2, sc. 4, l. 72

8 A traveller from the cradle to the
   grave
   Through the dim night of this
   immortal day.
   Prometheus Unbound (1820) act 4, l. 551

9 And the jessamine faint, and the
   sweet tuberose,
   The sweetest flower for scent that
   blows.
   'The Sensitive Plant' (1820) pt 1, l. 37

10 Poets are the unacknowledged
   legislators of the world.
   A Defence of Poetry (1821)

11 Life, like a dome of many-coloured
   glass,
   Stains the white radiance of Eternity,
   Until Death tramples it to fragments.
   Adonais (1821) st. 52

12 Let there be light! said Liberty,
   And like sunrise from the sea,
   Athens arose!
   Hellas (1822) l. 682

Shenstone, William (1714–63).
English poet and essayist

1 The charm dissolves; th' aerial
   music's past;
   The banquet ceases, and the vision
   flies.
   'Elegy 11. He complains how soon the
   pleasing novelty of life is over' (1764)

2 A fool and his words are soon
   parted.
   Works … (1764) vol. 2 'On Reserve'

Sheridan, Philip Henry (1831–88).
American Union cavalry
commander in the Civil War

1 The only good Indian is a dead
   Indian.
   At Fort Cobb, January 1869 (attributed)

Sheridan, Richard Brinsley (1751–1816). Anglo-Irish playwright

1 Conscience has no more to do with gallantry than it has with politics.
The Duenna (1775) act 2, sc. 4

2 Too civil by half.
The Rivals (1775) act 3, sc. 4

3 You had no taste when you married me.
The School for Scandal (1777) act 2, sc. 1

4 An unforgiving eye, and a damned disinheriting countenance!
The School for Scandal (1777) act 4, sc. 1

5 There is no trusting appearances.
The School for Scandal (1777) act 5, sc. 2

6 A man may surely be allowed to take a glass of wine by his own fireside.
Said while watching his theatre, the Drury Lane, burn down; in T. Moore *Life of Sheridan* (1825) vol. 2, p. 20

Sherman, Sidney (1805–73). American soldier

1 Remember the Alamo!
Battle cry at San Jacinto, 21 April 1836

Shirley, James (1596–1666). English playwright

1 The glories of our blood and state
Are shadows, not substantial things;
There is no armour against fate;
Death lays his icy hand on kings:
Sceptre and crown
Must tumble down,
And in the dust be equal made.
With the poor crooked scythe and spade.
The Contention of Ajax and Ulysses (1659) act 1, sc. 3

Sidney, Algernon (1622–83). English politician

1 Liars ought to have good memories.
Discourses Concerning Government (published 1689)

Sidney, Sir Philip (1554–86). English soldier, poet and courtier

1 Dumb swans, not chattering pies, do lovers prove;
They love indeed who quake to say they love.
Astrophil and Stella (1591) sonnet 54

2 Comedy is an imitation of the common errors of our life.
The Defence of Poetry (1595)

3 Thy necessity is yet greater than mine.
On giving his water-bottle to a dying soldier on the battlefield of Zutphen, 1586; in Sir Fulke Greville *Life of Sir Philip Sidney* (1652) ch. 12 (commonly quoted 'thy need is greater than mine')

Sieyès, Emmanuel Joseph (1748–1836). French abbot and statesman

1 *J'ai vécu.*
I survived.
When asked what he had done during the French Revolution. See F. A. M. Mignet *Notice historique sur la vie et les travaux de M. le Comte de Sieyès* (1836)

Sillitoe, Alan (1928–). English writer

1 The loneliness of the long-distance runner.
Title of novel (1959)

Simon, Paul (1941–). American singer and songwriter

1 And here's to you, Mrs Robinson
Jesus loves you more than you will know.
'Mrs Robinson' (1967 song, from the film *The Graduate*)

2 Like a bridge over troubled water
I will lay me down.
'Bridge over Troubled Water' (1970 song)

Simonides (c.556–468 BC). Greek poet

1 Painting is silent poetry, poetry is eloquent painting.
In Plutarch *Moralia* 'De Gloria Atheniensium' sect. 3

Simpson, Harold (NA). American songwriter

1 Down in the forest something stirred.
'Down in the Forest' (1906 song)

Sims, George R(obert) (1847–1922). English journalist and playwright

1 It is Christmas Day in the workhouse.
'In the Workhouse – Christmas Day' (1879)

Sitwell, Sir (Francis) Osbert (1892–1969). English writer

1 In reality, killing time
Is only the name for another of the multifarious ways
By which Time kills us.
'Milordo Inglese' (1958)

Skelton, Robin (1925–97). Canadian poet and aphorist

1 Death is the only mystery we all solve.
A Devious Dictionary (1991)

2 Never believe what you cannot doubt.
A Devious Dictionary (1991)

3 Anything said off the cuff has usually been written on it first.
A Devious Dictionary (1991)

4 It requires less skill to love than to be loved.
A Devious Dictionary (1991)

5 When one hears of progress one should ask for whom.
A Devious Dictionary (1991)

6 Kneel to nobody; bow to everyone.
A Devious Dictionary (1991)

7 More dreams are destroyed in bed than are ever found there.
A Devious Dictionary (1991)

8 Procrustes was an editor.
A Devious Dictionary (1991)

Skinner, B(urrhus) F(rederic) (1904–90). American psychologist

1 Education is what survives when what has been learned has been forgotten.
In the New Scientist 21 May 1964

2 The real question is not whether machines think but whether men do.
Contingencies of Reinforcement (1969) ch. 9

Smart, Christopher (1722–71). English poet

1 For sincerity is a jewel which is pure and transparent, eternal and inestimable.
Jubilate Agno (c.1758–63) Fragment B, l. 40

2 For Charity is cold in the multitude of possessions, and the rich are covetous of their crumbs.
Jubilate Agno (c.1758–63) Fragment B, l. 154

Smiles, Samuel (1812–1904). English writer

1 The spirit of self-help is the root of all genuine growth in the individual.
Self-Help (1859) ch. 1

2 The shortest way to do many things is to do only one thing at once.
Self-Help (1859) ch. 9

Smith, Adam (1723–90). Scottish economist and philosopher

1 To found a great empire for the sole purpose of raising up a people of customers, may at first sight appear a project fit only for a nation of shopkeepers. It is, however, a project altogether unfit for a nation of shopkeepers; but extremely fit for a nation whose government is influenced by shopkeepers.
An Inquiry into the Nature and Causes of the Wealth of Nations (1776) bk 4, ch. 7, pt 3

2 Consumption is the sole end and purpose of all production.
An Inquiry into the Nature and Causes of the Wealth of Nations (1776) bk 4, ch. 8

3 The discipline of colleges and universities is in general contrived, not for the benefit of the students, but

for the interest, or more properly speaking, for the ease of the masters.
An Inquiry into the Nature and Causes of the Wealth of Nations (1776) bk 5, ch. 1, pt 3

4 Science is the great antidote to the poison of enthusiasm and superstition.
An Inquiry into the Nature and Causes of the Wealth of Nations (1776) bk 5, ch. 1, pt 3, article 3

5 There is no art which one government sooner learns of another than that of draining money from the pockets of the people.
An Inquiry into the Nature and Causes of the Wealth of Nations (1776) bk 5, ch. 2

Smith, Dodie (1896–1990). English novelist and playwright

1 The family – that dear octopus from whose tentacles we never quite escape.
Dear Octopus (1938) p. 120

Smith, Logan Pearsall (1865–1946). American-born British writer

1 The denunciation of the young is a necessary part of the hygiene of older people, and greatly assists the circulation of their blood.
Afterthoughts (1931) 'Age and Death'

2 An improper mind is a perpetual feast.
Afterthoughts (1931) 'Life and Human Nature'

3 There is more felicity on the far side of baldness than young men can possibly imagine.
Afterthoughts (1931) 'Age and Death'

4 When they come downstairs from their Ivory Towers, Idealists are very apt to walk straight into the gutter.
Afterthoughts (1931) 'Other People'

5 A best-seller is the gilded tomb of a mediocre talent.
Afterthoughts (1931) 'Art and Letters'

Smith, Samuel Francis (1808–95). American poet and divine

1 My country, 'tis of thee,
Sweet land of liberty,
Of thee I sing:
Land where my fathers died,
Land of the pilgrims' pride,
From every mountain-side
Let freedom ring.
'America' (1831)

Smith, Stevie (Florence Margaret Smith) (1902–71). English poet and novelist

1 I was much too far out all my life
And not waving but drowning.
'Not Waving but Drowning' (1957)

Smith, Sydney (1771–1845). English clergyman and essayist

1 I have no relish for the country; it is a kind of healthy grave.
Letter to Miss G. Harcourt, 1838, in *Letters of Sidney Smith* (1953)

2 My definition of marriage … it resembles a pair of shears, so joined that they cannot be separated; often moving in opposite directions, yet always punishing anyone who comes between them.
In Lady Holland *Memoir* (1855) vol. 1, ch. 11

3 No furniture so charming as books.
In Lady Holland *Memoir* (1855) vol. 1, ch. 9.

4 As the French say, there are three sexes – men, women, and clergymen.
In Lady Holland *Memoir* (1855) vol. 1, ch. 9

5 Poverty is no disgrace to a man, but it is confoundedly inconvenient.
In J. Potter Briscoe (ed.) *Sydney Smith: His Wit and Wisdom* (1900) p. 89

6 I never read a book before reviewing it; it prejudices a man so.
In H. Pearson *The Smith of Smiths* (1934) ch. 3

7 What a pity it is that we have no amusements in England but vice and religion!
In H. Pearson *The Smith of Smiths* (1934) ch. 10

8 Death must be distinguished from dying, with which it is often confused.
In H. Pearson *The Smith of Smiths* (1934) ch. 11

Smith, Walter Chalmers (1824–1908). Scottish clergyman

1 Immortal, invisible, God only wise.
'Immortal, invisible, God only wise' (1867 hymn)

Smollett, Tobias (1721–71). Scottish novelist

1 I think for my part one half of the nation is mad – and the other not very sound.
The Adventures of Sir Launcelot Greaves (1762) ch. 6

2 I am pent up in frowzy lodgings, where there is not room enough to swing a cat.
Humphry Clinker (1771) vol. 1 (letter from Matthew Bramble, 8 June)

Snow, C(harles) P(ercy) (Baron Snow of Leicester) (1905–80). English novelist and scientist

1 The official world, the corridors of power.
Homecomings (1956) ch. 22

Socrates (469–399 BC). Greek philosopher

1 How many things I can do without!
On looking at objects for sale, in Diogenes Laertius *Lives of the Philosophers* bk 2, ch. 25

2 I know nothing except the fact of my ignorance.
In Diogenes Laertius *Lives of the Philosophers* bk 2, sect. 32

3 The unexamined life is not worth living.
In Plato *Apology* 38a

4 This sense of wonder is the mark of the philosopher. Philosophy indeed has no other origin.
Quoted in Plato *Theaetetus* 150c

5 There is only one good, knowledge, and only one evil, ignorance.
Quoted in Diogenes Laertius *Vitae Philosophorum* 2.31

Solzhenitsyn, Alexander (1918–). Russian novelist

1 You only have power over people as long as you don't take *everything* away from them. But when you've robbed a man of *everything* he's no longer in your power – he's free again.
The First Circle (1968) ch. 17

Somoza, (García) Anastasio (1925–80). Nicaraguan dictator

1 You won the elections. But I won the count.
In the *Guardian*, 17 June 1977

Sondheim, Stephen (1930–). American songwriter

1 Where are the clowns?
Send in the clowns.
A Little Night Music (1973) 'Send in the Clowns'

Sontag, Susan (1933–2004). American critic and theorist

1 Interpretation is the revenge of the intellect upon art.
In the *Evergreen Review* December 1964

2 Perversity is the muse of modern literature.
Against Interpretation (1966) 'Camus' Notebooks'

3 What pornography is really about, ultimately, isn't sex but death.
In *Partisan Review* spring 1967

4 The camera makes everyone a tourist in other people's reality, and eventually in one's own.
In the *New York Review of Books* 18 April 1974

5 The most interesting ideas are heresies.
Interview in *Salmagundi*, fall–winter 1975

Soper, Donald (Baron Soper) (1903–98). British Methodist minister

1 It is, I think, good evidence of life after death.
On the quality of debate in the House of Lords, in the *Listener* 17 August 1978

Sophocles (*c.*496–406 BC). Greek playwright

1 There are many wonderful things, and nothing is more wonderful than man.
Antigone l. 333

2 Remember there is no success without hard work.
Electra l. 945

Soule, John L. B. (1815–91). American journalist

1 Go West, young man, go West!
Terre Haute [Indiana] *Express* (1851) editorial

Southey, Robert (1774–1843). English poet and writer

1 You are old, Father William, the young man cried.
'The Old Man's Comforts' (1799)

2 Now tell us all about the war, And what they fought each other for.
'The Battle of Blenheim' (1800)

3 Curses are like young chickens, they always come home to roost.
The Curse of Kehama (1810) motto

4 Your true lover of literature is never fastidious.
The Doctor (1812) ch. 17

5 My name is Death: the last best friend am I.
'The Lay of the Laureate' (1816) st. 87

Spark, Dame Muriel (née Camberg) (1918–). Scottish writer

1 Parents learn a lot from their children about coping with life.
The Comforters (1957) ch. 6

2 I am putting old heads on your young shoulders … all my pupils are the crème de la crème.
The Prime of Miss Jean Brodie (1961) ch. 1

3 One's prime is elusive. You little girls, when you grow up, must be on the alert to recognise your prime at whatever time of your life it may occur. You must live it to the full.
The Prime of Miss Jean Brodie (1961) ch. 1

4 Give me a girl at an impressionable age, and she is mine for life.
The Prime of Miss Jean Brodie (1961) ch. 1

Sparrow, John (1906–92). Warden of All Souls College, Oxford, 1952–77

1 That indefatigable and unsavoury engine of pollution, the dog.
Letter to *The Times* 30 September 1975

Spencer, Herbert (1820–1903). English philosopher

1 Opinion is ultimately determined by the feelings, and not by the intellect.
Social Statics (1850) pt 4, ch. 30, sect. 8

2 Science is organized knowledge.
Education (1861) ch. 2

Spender, Sir Stephen (1909–95). English poet and critic

1 Pylons, those pillars
Bare like nude, giant girls that have no secret.
'Pylons' (1933)

2 The poet shares with other artists the faculty of seeing things as though for the first time.
Life and the Poet (1942)

3 Poetry cannot take sides except with life.
Life and the Poet (1942)

Spenser, Edmund (*c.*1552–99). English poet

1 And he that strives to touch the stars,
Oft stumbles at a straw.
The Shepherd's Calendar (1579) 'July' l. 99

2 A gentle knight was pricking on the plain.
The Faerie Queen (1596) bk 1, canto 1, st. 1

3 And painful pleasure turns to pleasing pain.
The Faerie Queen (1596) bk 3, canto 10, st. 60

4 Dan Chaucer, well of English undefiled,
On Fame's eternal beadroll worthy to be filed.
The Faerie Queen (1596) bk 4, canto 2, st. 32

5 O sacred hunger of ambitious minds.
The Faerie Queen (1596) bk 5, canto 12, st. 1

6 Sweet Thames, run softly, till I end my song.
Prothalamion (1596) l. 37

7 I was promised on a time,
To have reason for my rhyme;
From that time unto this season,
I received nor rhyme nor reason.
'Lines on his Pension' (Attributed)

Spielberg, Steven (1947–).
American film director

1 Close encounters of the third kind.
Title of film (1977)

Spinoza, Baruch (Benedict de Spinoza) (1632–77). Dutch philosopher

1 *Summum Mentis bonum est Dei cognitio, et summa Mentis virtus Deum cognoscere.*
The greatest good of the mind is the knowledge of God, and the greatest virtue of the mind is to know God.
Ethics (1677) bk 4, prop. 28

Stanley, Sir Henry Morton (1841–1904). British explorer

1 Dr Livingstone, I presume?
How I Found Livingstone (1872) ch. 11

Stead, William Thomas (1849–1912). English journalist and reformer

1 An editor is the uncrowned king of an educated democracy.
'Government by Journalism', in the *Contemporary Review* May 1886

2 The duty of a journalist is the duty of a watchman.
'Government by Journalism', in the *Contemporary Review* May 1886

Steele, Sir Richard (1672–1729). Irish-born essayist and playwright

1 Every man is the maker of his own fortune
In the *Tatler* no. 52 (9 August 1709)

2 Reading is to the mind what exercise is to the body.
In the *Tatler* no. 147 (18 March 1710)

3 A woman seldom writes her mind but in her postscript.
In the *Spectator* no. 79 (31 May 1711)

4 There are so few who can grow old with a good grace.
In the *Spectator* no. 263 (1 January 1712)

Stefansson, Vilhjalmur (1879–1962). Canadian Arctic explorer and author

1 What is the difference between unethical and ethical advertising? Unethical advertising uses falsehoods to deceive the public; ethical advertising uses truth to deceive the public.
Discovery (published 1964)

Steffens, (Joseph) Lincoln (1866–1936). American journalist

1 I have seen the future and it works.
On his visit to post-Revolutionary Russia (1919), in *Autobiography*

Stein, Gertrude (1874–1946). American writer

1 You are all a lost generation.
Said of the young who served in the First World War; Hemingway subsequently used it as his epigraph to *The Sun Also Rises* (1926)

2 In the United States there is more space where nobody is than where anybody is. That is what makes America what it is.
The Geographical History of America (1936)

3 Nature is commonplace. Imitation is more interesting.
Quoted in Sir Charles Spencer Chaplin *My Autobiography* (1964)

Steinbeck, John (1902–68). American novelist

1 I know this – a man got to do what he got to do.
The Grapes of Wrath (1939) ch. 18

2 A journey is like a marriage. The certain way to be wrong is to think you control it.
Travels with Charley in search of America (1962) pt 1

3 A good writer always works at the impossible.
Recalled on his death

Stendhal (Henri Beyle) (1783–1842). French writer

1 *La politique au milieu des intérêts d'imagination, c'est un coup de pistolet au milieu d'un concert.*
Politics mixed with the imagination is like a shot fired in the middle of a concert.
Le Rouge et le noir (1830) bk 2, ch. 22

2 *Les gens qu'on honore ne sont que des fripons qui ont eu le bonheur de n'être pas pris en flagrant délit.*
Respected people are only rascals who have had the good fortune not to be caught in the act.
Le Rouge et le noir (1830) bk 2, ch. 44

Sterne, Laurence (1713–68). Irish-born English novelist

1 Writing, when properly managed (as you may be sure I think mine is) is but a different name for conversation.
Tristram Shandy (1759–67) bk 2, ch. 11

2 As an Englishman does not travel to see Englishmen, I retired to my room.
A Sentimental Journey (1768) 'Preface. In the Desobligeant'

3 There are worse occupations in this world than feeling a woman's pulse.
A Sentimental Journey (1768) 'The Pulse, Paris'

Stevens, Wallace (1879–1955). American poet

1 The only emperor is the emperor of ice-cream.
Harmonium (1923) 'The Emperor of Ice-Cream'

2 I do not know which to prefer,
The beauty of inflections
Or the beauty of innuendoes,
The blackbird whistling
Or just after.
Harmonium (1923) 'Thirteen Ways of Looking at a Blackbird' pt 5

3 Poetry is a means of redemption.
Opus Posthumous (1957) Aphorisms, 'Adagia'

4 The poet is the priest of the invisible.
Opus Posthumous (1957) Aphorisms, 'Adagia'

5 Literature is based not on life but on propositions about life, of which this is one.
Opus Posthumous (1957) Aphorisms, 'Adagia'

6 Ethics are no more a part of poetry than they are of painting.
Opus Posthumous (1957) Aphorisms, 'Adagia'

7 The poet makes silk dresses out of worms.
Opus Posthumous (1957) Aphorisms, 'Adagia'

8 Authors are actors, books are theatres.
Opus Posthumous (1957) Aphorisms, 'Adagia'

Stevenson, Adlai (1900–65). American Democratic politician

1 If they [the Republicans] will stop telling lies about the Democrats, we will stop telling the truth about them.
Speech during 1952 Presidential campaign; in J. B. Martin *Adlai Stevenson and Illinois* (1976) ch. 8

2 Let's talk sense to the American people. Let's tell them the truth, that there are no gains without pains.
Speech of acceptance at the Democratic National Convention, Chicago, Illinois, 26 July 1952; in *Speeches* (1952) p. 20

3 It is often easier to fight for principles than to live up to them.
Speech, New York, 27 August 1952

4 In America any boy may become President.
Speech in Indianapolis, 26 September 1952; in *Major Campaign Speeches ... 1952* (1953) p. 174

5 A free society is a society where it is safe to be unpopular.
Speech in Detroit, 7 October 1952; in *Major Campaign Speeches ... 1952* (1953) p. 218

6 An independent is a guy who wants to take the politics out of politics.
The Art of Politics

Stevenson, Robert Louis (1850–94). Scottish novelist

1 Marriage is like life in this – that it is a field of battle, and not a bed of roses.
Virginibus Puerisque (1881) title essay, pt 1

2 Books are good enough in their own way, but they are a mighty bloodless substitute for life.
Virginibus Puerisque (1881) 'An Apology for Idlers'

3 Politics is perhaps the only profession for which no preparation is thought necessary.
Familiar Studies of Men and Books (1882) 'Yoshida-Torajiro'

4 Fifteen men on the dead man's chest
Yo-ho-ho, and a bottle of rum!
Treasure Island (1883) ch. 1

5 Pieces of eight!
Treasure Island (1883) ch. 10

6 A child should always say what's true,
And speak when he is spoken to,
And behave mannerly at table:
At least as far as he is able.
A Child's Garden of Verses (1885) no.5, 'Whole Duty of Children'

7 Here he lies where he longed to be;
Home is the sailor, home from sea,
And the hunter home from the hill.
Underwoods (1887) 'Requiem'

8 Over the sea to Skye.
Songs of Travel (1896) 'Sing me a song of a lad that is gone'

Stinnett, Caskie (1911–98). American writer

1 A diplomat ... is a person who can tell you to go to hell in such a way that you actually look forward to the trip.
Out of the Red (1960)

Stinson, Joseph C. (1947–). American screenwriter

1 Go ahead, make my day.
Sudden Impact (film, 1983); spoken by Clint Eastwood

St Laurent, Louis (1882–1973). Prime Minister of Canada

1 Socialists are Liberals in a hurry.
Attributed

Stoppard, Tom (1937–). Czech-born British playwright

1 Eternity's a terrible thought. I mean, where's it all going to end?
Rosencrantz and Guildenstern are Dead (1967) act 2

2 The bad end unhappily, the good unluckily. That is what tragedy means.
Rosencrantz and Guildenstern are Dead (1967) act 2

3 It's not the voting that's democracy; it's the counting.
Jumpers (1972)

4 War is capitalism with the gloves off.
Travesties (1974)

5 Ambushing the audience is what theatre is all about.
In *Newsweek* 16 January 1984

Stowe, Harriet Beecher (1811–96). American novelist

1 I s'pect I growed. Don't think nobody never made me.
Topsy, in *Uncle Tom's Cabin* (1852) ch. 20

Strachey, Lytton (1880–1932). English biographer

1 Ignorance is the first requisite of the historian.
Eminent Victorians (1918) preface

2 Discretion is not the better part of biography.
In Michael Holroyd *Lytton Strachey* vol. 1 (1967) preface

Summerskill, Edith (1901–80). British Labour politician

1 Nagging is the repetition of unpalatable truths.
Speech to the Married Women's Association, 14 July 1960

Sun Tzu (fl. *c*.500 BC).

1 All warfare is based on deception.
The Art of War, ch. 1, 'Laying Plans', sect. 18 (translated by James Clavell, 1981)

2 Know the enemy and know yourself; in a hundred battles, you will never be defeated.
Art of War, ch. 3 (translated by Yuan Shibang, 1987)

3 There is no place where espionage is not possible.
Art of War, ch. 13 (translated by Yuan Shibang, 1987)

Surtees, R(obert) S(mith) (1805–64). English sporting journalist and novelist

1 Three things I never lends – my 'oss, my wife, and my name.
Hillingdon Hall (1845) ch. 33

2 There is no secret so close as that between a rider and his horse.
Mr Sponge's Sporting Tour (1853) ch. 31

Swaffer, Hannen (1879–1962). British journalist

1 Freedom of the press in Britain means freedom to print such of the proprietor's prejudices as the advertisers don't object to.
In Tom Driberg *Swaff* (1974) ch. 2

Swift, Jonathan (Dean Swift) (1667–1745). Anglo-Irish poet and satirist

1 Satire is a sort of glass, wherein beholders do generally discover everybody's face but their own.
The Battle of the Books (1704) preface

2 Laws are like cobwebs, which may catch small flies, but let wasps and hornets break through.
A Critical Essay upon the Faculties of the Mind (1709)

3 There is nothing in this world constant, but inconstancy.
A Critical Essay upon the Faculties of the Mind (1709)

4 We have just enough religion to make us hate, but not enough to make us love one another.
Thoughts on Various Subjects (1711)

5 We are so fond of one another, because our ailments are the same.
Journal to Stella 1 February 1711

6 Proper words in proper places, make the true definition of a style.
Letter to a Young Gentleman lately entered into Holy Orders (9 January 1720)

7 Every man desires to live long; but no man would be old.
Thoughts on Various Subjects (1727 edn)

8 Walls have tongues, and hedges ears.
'A Pastoral Dialogue between Richmond Lodge and Marble Hill' (written 1727) l. 8

9 Hail, fellow, well met,
'My Lady's Lamentation' (written 1728) l. 165

10 So, naturalists observe, a flea
Hath smaller fleas that on him prey;
And these have smaller fleas to bite 'em,
And so proceed *ad infinitum*.
Thus every poet, in his kind,
Is bit by him that comes behind.
'On Poetry' (1733) l. 337

11 She wears her clothes, as if they were thrown on her with a pitchfork.
Polite Conversation (1738) Dialogue 1

Swinburne, Algernon Charles (1837–1909). English poet

1 Before the beginning of years
There came to the making of man
Time with a gift of tears,
Grief with a glass that ran.
Atalanta in Calydon (1865) chorus 'Before the beginning of years'

2 Thou hast conquered, O pale Galilean; the world has grown grey from Thy breath;
We have drunken of things Lethean, and fed on the fullness of death.
'Hymn to Proserpine' (1866)

Synge, John Millington (1871–1909). Irish playwright

1 Oh my grief, I've lost him surely. I've lost the only Playboy of the Western World.
The Playboy of the Western World (1907) act 3 ad fin.

Szasz, Thomas (1920–). Hungarian-born psychiatrist

1 A teacher should have maximal authority and minimal power.
The Second Sin (1973) 'Education'

2 The stupid neither forgive nor forget; the naïve forgive and forget; the wise forgive but do not forget.
The Second Sin (1973) 'Personal Conduct'

3 If you talk to God, you are praying; if God talks to you, you have schizophrenia.
The Second Sin (1973) 'Schizophrenia'

4 Two wrongs don't make a right, but they make a good excuse.
The Second Sin (1973) 'Social Relations'

Szent-Györgyi, Albert von (1893–1986). Hungarian-born biochemist

1 Discovery consists of seeing what everybody has seen and thinking what nobody has thought.
In Irving Good (ed.) *The Scientist Speculates* (1962) p. 15

Tacitus, Cornelius (Publius or Gaius Cornelius Tacitus) (AD 55–c.120). Roman historian and orator

1 *Solitudinem faciunt pacem appellant.*
They make a wilderness and they call it peace.
Speech of the British chief Calgacus before the battle of Mons Graupius, referring to the Romans. *Agricola* ch. 30

2 *Elegantiae arbiter.*
The arbiter of taste.
Of Petronius. *Annals* bk 16, ch. 18

Taylor, A(lan) J(ohn) P(ercivale) (1906–90). British historian

1 Human blunders, usually, do more to shape history than human wickedness.
The Origins of the Second World War (1961) ch. 10

2 History gets thicker as it approaches recent times.
English History 1914–45 (1965) Bibliography

Taylor, Elizabeth (1932–). English-born American film actress

1 Success is a great deodorant.
ABC TV broadcast, 6 April 1977

2 Some of my best leading men have been horses and dogs.
Attributed

Taylor, Jeremy (1613–67). English divine

1 *Si fueris Romae, Romano vivito more; si fueris alibi, vivito sicut ibi.*
If you are at Rome, live in the Roman style; if you are elsewhere, live as they live elsewhere.
Ductor Dubitantium (1660) bk 1, ch. 1, rule 5 (usually quoted: 'When in Rome, do as the Romans do')

Tebbit, Norman (1931–). British Conservative politician

1 I grew up in the Thirties with our unemployed father. He did not riot, he got on his bike and looked for work.
Speech at Conservative Party Conference, 15 October 1981, in the *Daily Telegraph* 16 October 1981

Temple, William (1881–1944). Archbishop of Canterbury (1942–4)

1 It is a mistake to suppose that God is only, or even chiefly, concerned with religion.
R. V. C. Bodley *In Search of Serenity* (1955)

Tennyson, Alfred, Lord (1809–92). English poet

1 Alone and warming his five wits, The white owl in the belfry sits.
'Song–The Owl' (1830)

2 Music that gentlier on the spirit lies,
Than tired eyelids upon tired eyes.
'The Lotos-Eaters' (1832) Choric Song, st. 1, l. 46

3 The Lady of Shalott.
'The Lady of Shalott' (1832, revised 1842) pt 2

4 She left the web, she left the loom,
She made three paces through the room,
She saw the water-lily bloom,
She saw the helmet and the plume,
She looked down to Camelot.
Out flew the web and floated wide;
The mirror cracked from side to side.
'The Lady of Shalott' (1832, revised 1842) pt 3

5 Break, break, break,
On thy cold grey stones, O Sea!
'Break, Break, Break' (1842)

6 And the stately ships go on
To their haven under the hill.
'Break, Break, Break' (1842)

7 A sight to make an old man young.
'The Gardener's Daughter' (1842) l. 140

8 Kind hearts are more than coronets,
And simple faith than Norman blood.
'Lady Clara Vere de Vere' (1842) st. 7

9 In the spring a young man's fancy
lightly turns to thoughts of love.
'Locksley Hall' (1842) l. 19

10 This is truth the poet sings,
That a sorrow's crown of sorrow is
remembering happier things.
'Locksley Hall' (1842) l. 75

11 But the jingling of the guinea helps
the hurt that Honour feels.
'Locksley Hall' (1842) l. 105

12 Science moves, but slowly slowly,
creeping on from point to point.
'Locksley Hall' (1842) l. 134

13 Knowledge comes, but wisdom
lingers.
'Locksley Hall' (1842) l. 141

14 Ah! when shall all men's good
Be each man's rule, and universal
peace
Lie like a shaft of light across the
land?
'The Golden Year' (1846) l. 47

15 Sweet and low, sweet and low,
Wind of the western sea.
The Princess (1847) pt 3, song (added 1850)

16 Now sleeps the crimson petal, now
the white.
The Princess (1847) pt 7, l. 161, song (added 1850)

17 Sweet is every sound,
Sweeter thy voice, but every sound
is sweet;
Myriads of rivulets hurrying
through the lawn,

The moan of doves in immemorial
elms,
And murmuring of innumerable
bees.
The Princess (1847) pt 7, l. 203, song (added 1850)

18 Never morning wore
To evening, but some heart did
break.
In Memoriam A. H. H. (1850) canto 6

19 And ghastly through the drizzling
rain
On the bald street breaks the blank
day.
In Memoriam A. H. H. (1850) canto 7

20 'Tis better to have loved and lost
Than never to have loved at all.
In Memoriam A. H. H. (1850) canto 27

21 Nature, red in tooth and claw.
In Memoriam A. H. H. (1850) canto 56

22 So many worlds, so much to do,
So little done, such things to be.
In Memoriam A. H. H. (1850) canto 73

23 God's finger touched him, and he
slept.
In Memoriam A. H. H. (1850) canto 85

24 He seems so near and yet so far.
In Memoriam A.H.H. (1850) canto 97

25 Ring out, wild bells, to the wild sky.
In Memoriam A. H. H. (1850) canto 106

26 Ring out the thousand wars of old,
Ring in the thousand years of
peace.
In Memoriam A. H. H. (1850) canto 106

27 Come not, when I am dead,
To drop thy foolish tears upon my
grave.
'Come not, when I am dead' (1850)

28 Half a league, half a league,
Half a league onward,
All in the valley of Death
Rode the six hundred.
'The Charge of the Light Brigade' (1854)

29 Their's not to make reply,
Their's not to reason why,
Their's but to do and die.
'The Charge of the Light Brigade' (1854)

30 Cannon to right of them,
Cannon to left of them,
Cannon in front of them
Volleyed and thundered.
'The Charge of the Light Brigade' (1854)

31 Into the jaws of Death,
Into the mouth of Hell.
'The Charge of the Light Brigade' (1854)

32 For men may come and men may
go,
But I go on for ever.
'The Brook' (1855) l. 33

33 Come into the garden, Maud.
Maud (1855) pt 1, sect. 22, st. 1

34 I come from haunts of coot and
hern,
I make a sudden sally
And sparkle out among the fern,
To bicker down a valley.
'The Brook' (1855) l. 23

35 The woods decay, the woods decay
and fall,
The vapours weep their burthen to
the ground,
Man comes and tills the field and
lies beneath,
And after many a summer dies the
swan.
'Tithonus' (1860, revised 1864) l. 1

36 Man dreams of fame while woman
wakes to love.
Idylls of the King 'Merlin and Vivien' (1869)
l. 458

37 So all day long the noise of battle
rolled
Among the mountains by the
winter sea.
Idylls of the King 'The Passing of Arthur'
(1869) l. 170

38 Authority forgets a dying king.
Idylls of the King 'The Passing of Arthur'
(1869) l. 289

39 For man is man and master of his
fate.
Idylls of the King 'The Marriage of Geraint'
(1869) l. 355

40 The old order changeth, yielding
place to new,
And God fulfils himself in many
ways,
Lest one good custom should corrupt the world.
Idylls of the King 'The Passing of Arthur'
(1869) l. 408

41 The greater man, the greater courtesy.
Idylls of the King 'The Last Tournement' (1871)
l. 628

Terence (Publius Terentius Afer)
(c.190–159 BC). Roman comic
playwright

1 Fortis fortuna adiuvat.
Fortune assists the brave.
Phormio l. 203

Teresa (of Calcutta), Mother
(1910–97). Roman Catholic nun and
missionary

1 I see God in every human being.
When I wash the leper's wounds I
feel I am nursing the Lord himself.
In 1977

Tertullian (Quintus Septimius
Florens Tertullianus) (c.160–c.220 AD).
Christian theologian

1 Certum est quia impossibile est.
It is certain because it is impossible.
De Carne Christi ch. 5

Thackeray, William Makepeace
(1811–63). English novelist

1 How to live well on nothing a year.
Vanity Fair (1847–8) ch. 36 (title)

2 Come, children, let us shut up the
box and the puppets, for our play is
played out.
Vanity Fair (1847–8) ch. 67

3 Remember, it is as easy to marry a
rich woman as a poor woman.
Pendennis (1848–50) ch. 28

4 'Tis strange what a man may do,
and a woman yet think him an
angel.
The History of Henry Esmond (1852) bk 1, ch. 7

5 Business first; pleasure afterwards.
The Rose and the Ring (1855) ch. 1

Thatcher, Margaret (Baroness Thatcher) (1925–). British Conservative politician and Prime Minister

1 In politics, if you want anything said, ask a man. If you want anything done, ask a woman.
In *People* 15 September 1975

2 Any woman who understands the problems of running a home will be nearer to understanding the problems of running a country.
Interview in the *Observer* 8 May 1979

3 To those who wait with bated breath for that favourite media catchphrase, the U-turn, I have only this to say. You turn if you want to. The lady's not for turning.
Address to the Conservative Party Conference, 1980

4 I don't mind how much my Ministers talk – as long as they do what I say.
In *The Times* (1987)

5 If one leads a country such as Britain – a strong country that has taken a lead in world affairs in good times and bad, that is always reliable, then you must have a touch of iron about you.
In *The Times* (1987)

Thomas, Brandon (1856–1914). English playwright

1 I'm Charley's aunt from Brazil – where the nuts come from.
Charley's Aunt (1892) act 1

Thomas, Dylan (1914–53). Welsh poet

1 Man be my metaphor.
'If I Were Tickled by The Rub of Love' (1934)

2 Light breaks where no sun shines.
'Light Breaks Where No Sun Shines' (1934)

3 And death shall have no dominion.
'And death shall have no dominion' (1936).

4 The hand that signed the paper felled a city.
'The Hand That Signed the Paper Felled a City' (1936)

5 After the first death, there is no other.
'A Refusal to Mourn the Death, by Fire, of a Child in London' (1946)

6 Do not go gentle into that good night,
Old age should burn and rave at close of day;
Rage, rage against the dying of the light.
'Do Not Go Gentle into that Good Night' (1952)

7 The land of my fathers. My fathers can have it.
Of Wales. In *Adam* December 1953

8 To begin at the beginning: It is spring, moonless night in the small town, starless and bible-black.
Under Milk Wood (1954), opening lines

9 Before you let the sun in, mind it wipes its shoes.
Under Milk Wood (1954)

10 Oh I'm a martyr to music.
Under Milk Wood (1954)

11 A good poem is a contribution to reality. The world is never the same once a good poem has been added to it.
Quite Early One Morning (1954) 'On Poetry'

12 I've had eighteen straight whiskies. I think that's the record.
Attributed; supposedly said just before his death

Thomas, Edward (1878–1917). English nature writer and poet

1 A merely great intellect can produce great prose, but not poetry, not one line.
Letter to Gordon Bottomley, 26 February 1908

2 The Past is a strange land, most strange.
'Parting' (1915)

3 Yes; I remember Adlestrop –
The name, because one afternoon Of heat the express-train drew up there
Unwontedly. It was late June.
'Adlestrop' (1915)

4 The sorrow of true love is a great sorrow
And true love parting blackens a bright morrow.
'Last Poem' (1917)

Thomas, R(onald) S(tuart)
(1913–2000). Welsh poet

1 The poem in the rock and
The poem in the mind
Are not one.
It was in dying
I tried to make them so.
'The Epitaph' (1972)

Thomas Aquinas, St (*c.*1225–74).
Italian Dominican friar and Doctor of the Church

1 *Ergo necesse est devenire ad aliquod primum movens, quod a nullo movetur; et hoc omnes intelligunt Deum.*
Therefore it is necessary to arrive at a prime mover, put in motion by no other; and this everyone understands to be God.
Summa Theologicae (*c.*1265) pt 3, qu. 2, art. 3

2 *Ars autem deficit ab operatione naturae.*
Art pales when compared to the workings of nature.
Summa Theologia (*c.*1272), bk 3, question 66, article 4

Thompson, Francis (1859–1907).
English poet

1 And upon thy so sore loss
Shall shine the traffic of Jacob's ladder
Pitched betwixt Heaven and Charing Cross.
'The Kingdom of God' (1913)

2 Look for me in the nurseries of heaven.
'To My Godchild Francis M.W.M.' (1913)

Thomson, James (1700–48).
Scottish poet

1 Rule, Britannia, rule the waves;
Britons never will be slaves.
Alfred: a Masque (1740) act 2

Thoreau, Henry David (1817–62).
American writer

1 The lawyer's truth is not Truth, but consistency or a consistent expediency.
Civil Disobedience (1849)

2 It takes two to speak the truth, – one to speak, and another to hear.
A Week on the Concord and Merrimack Rivers (1849) 'Wednesday'

3 Read the best books first, or you may not have a chance to read them at all.
A Week on the Concord and Merrimack Rivers (1849) 'Sunday'

4 As if you could kill time without injuring eternity.
Walden, or Life in the Woods (1854) 'Economy'

5 There is no odor so bad as that which arises from goodness tainted.
Walden, or Life in the Woods (1854) 'Economy'

6 Every generation laughs at the old fashions, but follows religiously the new.
Walden, or Life in the Woods (1854) 'Economy'

7 Our life is frittered away by detail … Simplify, simplify.
Walden, or Life in the Woods (1854) 'Where I lived, and what I lived for' in *Writings* (1906 edn) vol. 2, p. 101

8 We do not enjoy poetry unless we know it to be poetry.
Journal, 1 October 1856

Thurber, James (1894–1961).
American humorist and cartoonist

1 The war between men and women.
Cartoon series title in the *New Yorker* 20 January–28 April 1934

2 Well, if I called the wrong number, why did you answer the phone?
Cartoon caption in the *New Yorker* 5 June 1937

3 Early to rise and early to bed makes a male healthy and wealthy and dead.
'The Shrike and the Chipmunks' in the *New Yorker* 18 February 1939

4 It is better to have loafed and lost than never to have loafed at all.
Fables of Our Time (1939) 'The Courtship of Arthur and Al'

5 Seeing is deceiving. It's eating that's believing.
Further Fables for Our Time (1956)

Tillich, Paul (Johannes) (1886–1965). German pastor, theologian and philosopher

1 Faith comprises both itself and doubt of itself.
Biblical Religion and the Search for Ultimate Reality (1955)

2 Faith is the state of being ultimately concerned.
Dynamics of Faith (1957)

Tocqueville, Alexis de (1805–59). French historian and politician

1 *Il n'y a qu'un journal qui puisse venir déposer au même moment dans mille esprits la même pensée.*
Only a newspaper can place at the same time in a thousand minds the same thought.
De la Démocratie en Amérique (1835), vol. 2, pt 2, ch. 6

2 *On voit que l'histoire est une galerie de tableaux où il y a peu d'originaux et beaucoup de copies.*
History is a gallery of pictures in which there are few originals and many copies.
L'Ancien régime (1856, ed. J. P. Mayer, 1951) p. 133

Tolkien, J(ohn) R(onald) R(euel) (1892–1973). English writer and philologist

1 In a hole in the ground there lived a hobbit.
The Hobbit (1937) ch. 1

2 One Ring to rule them all, One Ring to find them One Ring to bring them all and in the darkness bind them.
In the Land of Mordor where the Shadows lie.
The Fellowship of the Ring (1954) epigraph

Tolstoy, Leo (1828–1910). Russian novelist

1 *Notre corps est une machine à vivre.*
Our body is a machine for living.
War and Peace (1865–9) bk 10, ch. 29 (translated by A. and L. Maude).

2 All happy families resemble one another, but each unhappy family is unhappy in its own way.
Anna Karenina (1875–7) pt 1, ch. 1 (translated by A. and L. Maude)

Toscanini, Arturo (1867–1957). Italian conductor

1 God tells me how he wants this music played – and you get in his way.
To players in his orchestra (1930); quoted in Howard Tubman *Etude*

Toynbee, Arnold Joseph (1889–1975). English economic historian and social reformer

1 No annihilation without representation.
Advocating greater British representation at the United Nations (1947)

2 Civilisation is a movement and not a condition; a voyage and not a harbour.
Quoted in *Reader's Digest* October 1958

Trevelyan, G(eorge) M(acaulay) (1876–1962). English historian

1 Disinterested intellectual curiosity is the life-blood of real civilization.
English Social History (1942) introduction

Trinder, Tommy (1909–89). British comedian

1 Overpaid, overfed, oversexed, and over here.
Of American troops in Britain during the Second World War (attributed)

Trollope, Anthony (1815–82). English novelist

1 There is no road to wealth so easy and respectable as that of matrimony.
Doctor Thorne (1858) ch. 16

2 Those who have courage to love should have courage to suffer.
The Bertrams (1859) ch. 27

3 As for conceit, what man will do any good who is not conceited? Nobody holds a good opinion of a man who has a low opinion of himself.
Orley Farm (1862) ch. 22

4 Love is like any other luxury. You have no right to it unless you can afford it.
The Way We Live Now (1875) ch. 84

5 Equality would be a heaven, if we could attain it.
The Prime Minister (1876) ch. 68

6 I hold that gentleman to be the best dressed whose dress no one observes.
Thackeray (1879) ch. 9

7 Three hours a day will produce as much as a man ought to write.
Autobiography (1883) ch. 15

Trotsky, Leon (Lev Davidovich Bronstein) (1879–1940). Russian revolutionary

1 You have played out your role. Go where you belong: to the dustheap of history.
To the Mensheviks, at the first Congress of Soviets (1917)

2 The end may justify the means, as long as there is something that justifies the end.
An Introduction to his Thought

Truman, Harry S. (1884–1972). 33rd President of the USA

1 Every segment of our population, and every individual, has a right to expect from his Government a Fair Deal.
Speech to Congress, 6 September 1945

2 If you can't stand the heat you better get out of the kitchen.
Address to the Aero Club of Washington, 27 December 1952

3 It's a recession when your neighbour loses his job; it's a depression when you lose yours.
In the *Observer* 13 April 1958

4 Wherever you have an efficient government you have a dictatorship.
Lecture at Columbia University, 28 April 1959, in *Truman Speaks* (1960) p. 51

5 The buck stops here.
Motto on a sign on his desk

Turgenev, Ivan (1818–83). Russian novelist

1 Nature is not a temple, but a workshop, and man's the workman in it.
Fathers and Sons (1862) ch. 9 (translated by Rosemary Edmonds)

2 Whatever a man prays for, he prays for a miracle.
Every prayer reduces itself to this: Great God, grant that twice two be not four.
Poems in Prose (1881) 'Prayer'

Twain, Mark (Samuel Langhorne Clemens) (1835–1910). American writer

1 I must have a prodigious quantity of mind; it takes me as much as a week to make it up.
The Innocents Abroad (1869) ch. 7

2 They spell it Vinci and pronounce it Vinchy; foreigners always spell better than they pronounce.
The Innocents Abroad (1869) ch. 19

3 Travel is fatal to prejudice.
The Innocents Abroad (1869) conclusion

4 Nothing helps scenery like ham and eggs.
Roughing It (1872) ch. 17

5 All kings is mostly rapscallions.
The Adventures of Huckleberry Finn (1884) ch. 23

6 Cauliflower is nothing but cabbage with a college education.
Pudd'nhead Wilson (1894) ch. 5

7 As to the Adjective: when in doubt, strike it out.
Pudd'nhead Wilson (1894) ch. 11

8 If you pick up a starving dog and make him prosperous, he will not bite you. This is the principal difference between a dog and a man.
Pudd'nhead Wilson (1894) ch. 16

9 Few things are harder to put up with than the annoyance of a good example.
Pudd'nhead Wilson (1894) ch. 19

10 When in doubt, tell the truth.
Following the Equator (1897) ch. 2

11 Truth is the most valuable thing we have. Let us economize it.
Following the Equator (1897) ch. 7

12 Man is the Only Animal that Blushes. Or needs to.
Following the Equator (1897) ch. 27

13 The man with a new idea is a crank until the idea succeeds.
Following the Equator (1897) ch. 32

14 There are several good protections against temptations, but the surest is cowardice.
Following the Equator (1897) ch. 36

15 The report of my death was an exaggeration.
In the *New York Journal* 2 June 1897 (usually quoted 'Reports of my death have been greatly exaggerated')

16 A classic … something that everybody wants to have read and nobody wants to read.
Speech on 'The Disappearance of Literature' at the Nineteenth Century Club, 20 November 1900

17 Always do right. This will gratify some people, and astonish the rest.
Speech, Brooklyn, 16 February 1901

18 The man who is a pessimist before 48 knows too much; if he is an optimist after it, he knows too little.
Notebooks December 1902

19 Scientists have odious manners, except when you prop up their theory; then you can borrow money off them.
The Bee (published 1917)

20 I don't know anything that mars good literature so completely as too much truth.
'The Savage Club Dinner'; quoted in Albert Bigelow Paine (ed.) *Mark Twain's Speeches* (1923)

21 I have been told that Wagner's music is better than it sounds.
Autobiography (published 1924)

22 Familiarity breeds contempt – and children.
Notebooks (1935)

23 Education consists mainly in what we have unlearned.
Notebooks (1935)

24 Golf is a good walk spoiled.
Attributed; quoted in Michael Hobbs *The Golf Quotations Book* (1992)

Tynan, Kenneth (1927–80).
English theatre critic

1 A novel is a static thing that one moves through; a play is a dynamic thing that moves past one.
Curtains (1961)

2 A critic is a man who knows the way but can't drive the car.
In the *New York Times Magazine* 9 January 1966, p. 27

3 A neurosis is a secret you don't know you're keeping.
In Kathleen Tynan *Life of Kenneth Tynan* (1987) ch. 19

Unamuno, Miguel de (1864–1936). Spanish philosopher and writer

1 Science is a cemetery of dead ideas.
The Tragic Sense of Life (1913)

Updike, John (1932–). American novelist, short-story writer and critic

1 A healthy male adult bore consumes *each year* one and a half times his own weight in other people's patience.
Assorted Prose (1965) 'Confessions of a Wild Bore'

2 Sex is like money; only too much is enough.
Couples (1968) ch. 5

3 Facts are generally overesteemed. For most practical purposes, a thing is what men think it is.
Buchanan Dying (1974) act 1

4 Americans have been conditioned to respect newness, whatever it costs them.
A Month of Sundays (1975) ch. 18

5 America is a vast conspiracy to make you happy.
Problems (1980) 'How to Love America and Leave It at the Same Time'

Ustinov, Sir Peter (1921–2004). Russian-born actor, director and writer

1 Laughter would be bereaved if snobbery died.
In the *Observer* 13 March 1955

2 Laughter … the most civilized music in the world.
Dear Me (1977) ch. 3

Valéry, Paul (1871–1945). French poet and critic

1 *Un poème n'est jamais achevé – c'est toujours un accident qui le termine, c'est-à-dire qui le donne au public.*
A poem is never finished; it is always an accident that puts a stop to it, that gives it to the public.
Littérature (1930)

2 *Il faut n'appeler Science que l'ensemble des recettes qui réussissent toujours. – Tout le reste est littérature.*
Science means simply the aggregate of all the recipes that are always successful. All the rest is literature.
Moralités (1932)

3 *Dieu créa l'homme, et ne le trouvant pas assez seul, il lui donne une compagne pour lui faire mieux sentir sa solitude.*
God created man and, finding him not sufficiently alone, gave him a companion to make him feel his solitude more keenly.
Tel Quel 1, 'Moralités' (1941)

4 *La politique est l'art d'empêcher les gens de se mêler de ce qui les regarde.*
Politics is the art of preventing people from taking part in affairs which concern them.
Tel Quel 2, 'Rhumbs' (1943)

Vanbrugh, Sir John (1664–1726). English architect and playwright

1 Thinking is to me the greatest fatigue in the world.
The Relapse (1696) act 2, sc. 1

2 Much of a muchness.
The Provoked Husband (1728) act 1, sc. 1

van Damm, Vivian (c.1889–1960). British theatre manager

1 We never closed.
On the Windmill Theatre, London, during the Second World War; in *Tonight and Every Night* (1952) ch. 18

Vaughan, Henry (1622–95). English poet

1 I saw Eternity the other night, Like a great ring of pure and endless light.
Silex Scintillans (1650–5) 'The World'

Vaughan Williams, Ralph (1872–1958). British composer

1 I don't know whether I like it, but it's what I meant.
Of his Fourth Symphony; quoted in Ian Crofton and Donald Fraser *A Dictionary of Musical Quotations* (1985)

Victoria, Queen (1819–1901). Queen of the United Kingdom from 1837

1 We are not amused.
Attributed, in Caroline Holland *Notebooks of a Spinster Lady* (1919) ch. 21, 2 January 1900

Vidal, Gore (1925–). American novelist and critic

1 Whenever a friend succeeds, a little something in me dies.
In the *Sunday Times Magazine* 16 September 1973

2 For certain people, after fifty, litigation takes the place of sex.
Quoted in the *Evening Standard* (1981)

3 American men do not read novels because they feel guilty when they read books which do not have facts in them.
In the *Saturday Review* 18 June 1984

Villiers, George (2nd Duke of Buckingham) (1628–87). English courtier and writer

1 Ay, now the plot thickens very much upon us.
The Rehearsal (1672) act 3, sc. 2

Villon, François (b. 1431). French poet

1 *Mais où sont les neiges d'antan?*
But where are the snows of yester-year?
Le Grand Testament (1461) 'Ballade des dames du temps jadis' (translated by D. G. Rossetti)

Virgil (Publius Vergilius Maro) (70–19 BC). Roman poet

1 *Arma virumque cano.*
I sing of arms and the man.
Aeneid bk 1, l. 1

2 *Quidquid id est, timeo Danaos et dona ferentes.*
Whatever it may be, I fear the Greeks, even when bearing gifts.
Spoken by Laocoon, a Trojan prince and priest of Apollo, warning the city against the wooden horse left by the Greeks. *Aeneid* bk 2, l. 49

3 *Dis aliter visum.*
The gods thought otherwise.
Aeneid bk 2, l. 428

4 *Quis fallere possit amantem?*
Who could deceive a lover?
Aeneid bk 4, l. 296

5 *Audentis Fortuna iuvat.*
Fortune assists the bold.
Aeneid bk 10, l. 284 (often quoted 'Fortune favours the brave')

6 *Latet anguis in herba.*
There's a snake hidden in the grass.
Eclogues no. 3, l. 93

7 *Omnia vincit Amor: et nos cedamus Amori.*
Love conquers all things: let us too give in to Love.
Eclogues no. 10, l. 69

8 *Ultima Thule.*
Farthest Thule.
Georgics no. 1, l. 30

9 *Sed fugit interea, fugit inreparabile tempus.*
But meanwhile it is flying, irre-trievable time is flying.
Georgics no. 3, l. 284 (usually quoted '*tempus fugit* [time flies]')

Voltaire (François-Marie Arouet) (1694–1778). French writer and philosopher

1 *Il faut, dans le gouvernement, des bergers et des bouchers.*
Governments need both shepherds and butchers.
'The Piccini Notebooks' (c.1735–50) in T. Besterman (ed.) *Voltaire's Notebooks* (2nd edn, 1968) vol. 2, p. 517

2 *Dans ce meilleur des mondes possibles ... tout est au mieux.*
In this best of possible worlds ... all is for the best.
Candide (1759) ch. 1 (usually quoted 'All is for the best in the best of all possible worlds')

3 *Dans ce pays-ci il est bon de tuer de temps en temps un amiral pour en-courager les autres.*
In this country [England] it is thought well to kill an admiral from time to time to encourage the others.
Candide (1759) ch. 23

4 *La superstition met le monde entier en flammes; la philosophie les éteint.*
Superstition sets the whole world in flames; philosophy quenches them.
Dictionnaire philosophique (1764) 'Superstition'

5 *Le mieux est l'ennemi du bien.*
The best is the enemy of the good.
Contes (1772) 'La Begueule' l. 2

6 *On doit des égards aux vivants; on ne doit aux morts que la vérité.*
We owe respect to the living; to the dead we owe only truth.
'Première Lettre sur Oedipe' in *Oeuvres* (1785) vol. 1, p. 15 n

7 *Si Dieu n'existait pas, il faudrait l'inventer.*
 If God did not exist, it would be necessary to invent him.
 Épîtres no. 96 'A l'Auteur du livre des trois imposteurs'

8 I disapprove of what you say, but I will defend to the death your right to say it.
 Attributed to Voltaire, but first written by S. G. Tallentyre; in *The Friends of Voltaire* (1907) p. 199

9 *Dieu n'est pas pour les gros bataillons, mais pour ceux qui tirent le mieux.*
 God is on the side not of the big battalions, but of the best shots.
 In *Voltaire's Notebooks* (1952)

10 The art of medicine consists of amusing the patient while Nature cures the disease.
 Attributed

Walcott, Derek (1930–). West Indian poet and dramatist

1 Who knows who his grandfather is, much less his name?
The Star-Apple Kingdom (1980) 'The Schooner *Flight*', pt 5

2 The fate of poetry is to fall in love with the world, in spite of History.
In the *New York Times* 8 December 1992

3 The process of poetry is one of excavation and of self-discovery.
In the *New York Times* 8 December 1992

Walker, Alice (1944–). American writer

1 Anybody can observe the Sabbath, but making it holy surely takes the rest of the week.
In Search of Our Mothers' Gardens, 'To the Editors of *Ms.* Magazine' (1983)

Wallace, Edgar (1875–1932). English thriller writer

1 What is a highbrow? He is a man who has found something more interesting than women.
In the *New York Times* 24 January 1932, sect. 8, p. 6

Wallace, George (1919–98). American Democratic politician

1 Segregation now, segregation tomorrow and segregation forever!
Inaugural speech as Governor of Alabama, January 1963, in *Birmingham World* 19 January 1963

Wallas, Graham (1858–1932). British politicial scientist

1 The little girl had the making of a poet in her who, being told to be sure of her meaning before she spoke, said, 'How can I know what I think till I see what I say?'
The Art of Thought (1926) ch. 4

Waller, Edmund (1606–87). English poet

1 Poets that lasting marble seek Must carve in Latin or in Greek.
'Of English Verse' (1645)

Walpole, Horace (4th Earl of Orford) (1717–97). English writer and politician

1 This world is a comedy to those that think, a tragedy to those that feel.
Letter to Anne, Countess of Upper Ossory, 16 August 1776

Walton, Izaak (1593–1683). English writer

1 Angling may be said to be so like the mathematics, that it can never be fully learnt.
The Compleat Angler (1653) 'Epistle to the Reader'

2 Good company and good discourse are the very sinews of virtue.
The Compleat Angler (1653) pt 1, ch. 2

3 An excellent angler, and now with God.
Of Sir George Hastings, *The Compleat Angler* (1653) pt 1, ch. 4

4 No man can lose what he never had.
The Compleat Angler (1653) pt 1, ch. 5

Warhol, Andy (1928–87).
American graphic artist, painter
and film-maker

1 In the future everybody will be
world famous for fifteen minutes.
Quoted in Andy Warhol, Kasper König,
Pontus Hultén and Olle Granath (eds.) *Andy
Warhol* (1968)

2 When you think about it, department stores are kind of like
museums.
America (1985)

Warren, Robert Penn (1905–89).
American writer

1 The urge to write poetry is like
having an itch. When the itch
becomes annoying enough, you
scratch it.
In the *New York Times* 16 December 1969

Washington, George (1732–99).
1st President of the USA

1 We have, therefore, to resolve to
conquer or die.
General orders, 2 July 1776, in J. C. Fitzpatrick
(ed.) *Writings of George Washington* vol. 5
(1932) p. 211

2 The time is now near at hand
which must probably determine
whether Americans are to be free-
men or slaves
General orders, 2 July 1776

3 I can't tell a lie, Pa; you know I can't
tell a lie. I did cut it with my
hatchet.
In M. L. Weems *Life of George Washington*
(10th edn, 1810) ch. 2

Watts, Isaac (1674–1748). English
hymn-writer

1 When I survey the wondrous cross.
Hymns and Spiritual Songs (1707) 'Crucifixion
to the World, by the Cross of Christ'

2 For Satan finds some mischief still
For idle hands to do.
Divine Songs for Children (1715) 'Against
Idleness and Mischief'

3 Our God, our help in ages past.
The Psalms of David Imitated (1719) Psalm 90
('Our God' altered to 'O God' by John
Wesley, 1738)

Waugh, Evelyn (1903–66). English
novelist

1 That's the public-school system all
over. They may kick you out but
they never let you down.
Decline and Fall (1928) pt 1, ch. 3

2 I have often observed in women of
her type a tendency to regard all
athletics as inferior forms of fox-
hunting.
Decline and Fall (1928) pt 1, ch. 10

3 Instead of this absurd division into
sexes, they ought to class people as
static and dynamic.
Decline and Fall (1928) pt 2, ch. 7

4 I came to the conclusion many
years ago that almost all crime is
due to the repressed desire for aesthetic expression.
Decline and Fall (1928) pt 3, ch. 1

5 Any one who has been to an English public school will always feel
comparatively at home in prison.
Decline and Fall (1928) pt 3, ch. 4

6 All this fuss about sleeping
together. For physical pleasure I'd
sooner go to my dentist any day.
Vile Bodies (1930) ch. 6

7 Up to a point, Lord Copper.
Scoop (1938) bk 1, ch. 1

8 News is what a chap who doesn't
care much about anything wants to
read. And it's only news until he's
read it. After that it's dead.
Scoop (1938) bk 1, ch. 5

9 We are all American at puberty; we
die French.
Diary note, 18 July 1961

10 Punctuality is the virtue of the
bored.
Michael Davie (ed.) *Diaries of Evelyn Waugh*
(1976) 'Irregular Notes 1960–65', 26 March
1962

11 Manners are especially the need of
the plain. The pretty can get away
with anything.
In the *Observer* 15 April 1962

12 One can write, think and pray
exclusively of others; dreams are all
egocentric.
Diary entry, 5 October 1962

13 All fictional characters are flat.
'The Art of Fiction 30: Evelyn Waugh', in the
Paris Review, no. 8, summer/fall 1963

14 Only when one has lost all curiosity has one reached the age to write
an autobiography.
A Little Learning (1964), opening words

15 With a thorough knowledge of the
Bible, Shakespeare and Wisden,
you cannot go far wrong.
A Little Learning (1964)

Weatherly, Frederick (1848–
1929). English songwriter

1 Roses are flowering in Picardy.
'Roses of Picardy' (1916 song)

Webb, Sidney (Baron Passfield)
(1859–1947). English socialist

1 Marriage is the waste-paper basket
of the emotions.
In Bertrand Russell *Autobiography* (1967)
vol. 1, ch. 4

Weber, Max (1864–1920). German
sociologist

1 *Die protestantische Ethik und der
Geist des Kapitalismus.*
The protestant ethic and the spirit
of capitalism.
Archiv für Sozialwissenschaft Sozialpolitik
vol. 20 (1904–5) (title of article)

Webster, John (c.1580–c.1625).
English playwright

1 Love mixed with fear is sweetness.
The Duchess of Malfi (1623) act 3, sc. 2

2 Cover her face; mine eyes dazzle:
she died young.
The Duchess of Malfi (1623) act 4, sc. 2

3 I know death hath ten thousand
several doors
For men to take their exits.
The Duchess of Malfi (1623) act 4, sc. 2

4 Other sins only speak; murder
shrieks out.
The Duchess of Malfi (1623) act 4, sc. 2

5 We are merely the stars' tennis-
balls, struck and bandied
Which way please them.
The Duchess of Malfi (1623) act 5, sc. 4

6 Cowardly dogs bark loudest.
The White Devil (1612) act 3, sc. 2

7 They that sleep with dogs shall rise
with fleas.
The White Devil (1612) act 5, sc. 1

8 We think caged birds sing, when
indeed they cry.
The White Devil (1612) act 5, sc. 4

9 I have heard grief named the eldest
child of sin.
The White Devil (1612) act 5, sc. 4

Weil, Simone (1909–43). French
philosophical writer and mystic

1 The future is made of the same stuff
as the present.
On Science, Necessity, and the Love of God
(1941)

Weissmuller, Johnny (1904–84).
American film actor

1 Me Tarzan, you Jane.
Summing up his role in *Tarzan, the Ape Man*
(film, 1932); these words do not occur in the
film or the original book, by Edgar Rice
Burroughs

Weldon, Fay (1931–). English
writer

1 Every time you open your ward-
robe, you look at your clothes and
you wonder what you are going to
wear. What you are really saying is
'Who am I going to be today?'
In the *New Yorker* 26 June 1995

Welles, Orson (1915–85). American
actor and film director

1 In Italy for thirty years under the
Borgias they had warfare, terror,
murder, bloodshed – they pro-
duced Michelangelo, Leonardo da
Vinci and the Renaissance. In
Switzerland they had brotherly

love, five hundred years of democracy and peace and what did that produce …? The cuckoo clock.
The Third Man (film, 1949); words added by Welles to Graham Greene's script

2 The biggest electric train set any boy ever had!
Of the RKO studios, in Peter Noble *The Fabulous Orson Welles* (1956) ch. 7

3 There are only two emotions in a plane: boredom and terror.
In *The Times* 6 May 1985

4 Every actor in his heart believes everything bad that's printed about him.
Attributed

Wellesley, Arthur (1st Duke of Wellington) (1769–1852). British soldier and statesman

1 Up guards and at them!
Attributed, at the Battle of Waterloo, 18 June 1815

2 The battle of Waterloo was won on the playing fields of Eton.
Attributed

3 Publish and be damned.
To the publisher of the *Memoirs* of the courtesan Hariette Wilson, attempting blackmail (attributed)

4 If you believe that, you'll believe anything.
Attributed

Wells, H(erbert) G(eorge) (1866–1946). English novelist

1 Lies are the mortar that bind the savage individual man into the social masonry.
Love and Mr Lewisham (1900) ch. 23

2 In the country of the blind the one-eyed man is king.
'The Country of the Blind' (1904)

3 Moral indignation is jealousy with a halo.
The Wife of Sir Isaac Harman (1914) ch. 9

4 Cynicism is humour in ill-health.
'The Story of The Last Trump' (1915)

5 Human history becomes more and more a race between education and catastrophe.
The Outline of History (1920) vol. 2, ch. 41

Werefkin, Marianne (1860–1938). Russian-born painter

1 There is no history of art – there is the history of artists.
Lettres à un inconnu (1901–05)

Wesker, Arnold (1932–). English playwright

1 You breed babies and you eat chips with everything.
Chips with Everything (1962) act 1, sc. 2

Wesley, Charles (1707–88). English Methodist preacher and hymn-writer

1 Soldiers of Christ, arise,
And put your armour on.
Hymns and Sacred Poems (1749) 'The Whole Armour of God'

2 Forth in thy name, O Lord, I go,
My daily labour to pursue.
Hymns and Sacred Poems (1749) 'Forth in Thy Name'

Wesley, John (1703–91). English preacher; founder of Methodism

1 I look upon all the world as my parish.
Journal (ed. N. Curnock) 11 June 1739

2 I design plain truth for plain people.
Sermons on Several Occasions (1746) in *Works* (Centenary edn) vol. 1, p. 104

3 Beware you be not swallowed up in books! An ounce of love is worth a pound of knowledge.
Quoted in R. Southey *Life of Wesley* (1820) ch. 16

Wesley, Samuel (1662–1735). English clergyman and poet

1 Style is the dress of thought.
'An Epistle to a Friend concerning Poetry' (1700)

West, Mae (1892–1980). American film actress

1 Beulah, peel me a grape.
I'm No Angel (film, 1933)

2 Why don't you come up sometime, and see me?
She Done Him Wrong (film, 1933); usually quoted 'Why don't you come up and see me sometime?'

3 It's not the men in my life that counts – it's the life in my men.
I'm No Angel (film, 1933)

4 A man in the house is worth two in the street.
Belle of the Nineties (film, 1934)

5 I always say, keep a diary and some day it'll keep you.
Every Day's a Holiday (film, 1937)

6 Is that a gun in your pocket, or are you just glad to see me?
In Joseph Weintraub *Peel Me a Grape* (1975) p. 47 (usually quoted 'Is that a pistol in your pocket …')

Wharton, Edith (née Jones) (1861–1937). American novelist

1 An unalterable and unquestioned law of the musical world required that the German text of French operas sung by Swedish artists should be translated into Italian for the clearer understanding of English-speaking audiences.
The Age of Innocence (1920)

2 Blessed are the pure in heart for they have so much more to talk about.
In *John O'London's Weekly* 10 April 1932

Whately, Richard (1787–1863). English philosopher, theologian and Archbishop of Dublin

1 Honesty is the best policy; but he who is governed by that maxim is not an honest man.
Apophthegms (1854)

Whistler, James McNeill (1834–1903). American-born painter

1 Nature is usually wrong.
Mr Whistler's 'Ten O'Clock' (1885) p. 14

2 A picture is finished when all trace of the means used to bring about the end has disappeared.
The Gentle Art of Making Enemies (1890)

3 Poor lawyers, like poor paintings, are dear at any price.
On the cost and quality of some of the lawyers he had hired. Quoted in Arthur Jerome Eddy *Recollections and Impressions of J. A. M. Whistler* (1903)

4 OSCAR WILDE: How I wish I had said that.
WHISTLER: You will, Oscar, you will.
In R. Ellman *Oscar Wilde* (1987) pt 2, ch. 5

White, E(lwyn) B(rooks) (1899–1985). American writer and parodist

1 Democracy is the recurrent suspicion that more than half the people are right more than half the time.
In the *New Yorker* 3 July 1944

2 Commuter – one who spends his life
In riding to and from his wife;
A man who shaves and takes a train,
And then rides back to shave again.
Poems and Sketches (1982) 'The Commuter'

Whitehead, Alfred North (1861–1947). English philosopher and mathematician

1 Knowledge does not keep any better than fish.
'The Aims of Education; a plea for reform' (1916) address as president of the Mathematical Association

2 Familiar things happen, and mankind does not bother about them. It requires a very unusual mind to undertake the analysis of the obvious.
Science and the Modern World (1925)

3 The worship of God is not a rule of safety – it is an adventure of the spirit, a flight after the unattainable. The death of religion comes with the repression of the high hope of adventure.
Science and the Modern World (1925)

4 Religion is what a man does with his solitariness.
Religion in the Making (1926)

5 The safest general characterization of the European philosophical tradition is that it consists of a series of footnotes to Plato.
Process and reality (1929) pt 2, ch. 1, sect. 1

6 Life is an offensive, directed against the repetitious mechanism of the Universe.
Adventures of Ideas (1933) pt 1, ch. 5

7 There are no whole truths; all truths are half-truths. It is trying to treat them as whole truths that plays the devil.
Dialogues (1954) prologue

8 What is morality in any given time or place? It is what the majority then and there happen to like, and immorality is what they dislike.
Dialogues (1954) 30 August 1941

9 Art is the imposing of a pattern on experience, and our aesthetic enjoyment is recognition of the pattern.
Dialogues (1954) 10 June 1943

Whitelaw, William (1st Viscount Whitelaw) (1918–). Scottish Conservative politician

1 He is going round the country stirring up apathy.
Of Harold Wilson during the general election campaign (attributed, 1974)

2 A short, sharp shock.
At the Conservative Party Conference, 10 October 1979, on more effective measures against young offenders

Whiting, William (1825–78). English teacher; master of the Quiristers of Winchester College

1 O hear us when we cry to thee, For those in peril on the sea.
'Eternal Father, Strong to Save' (1869 hymn)

Whitman, Walt(er) (1819–92). American poet

1 I sing the body electric.
Title of poem (1855)

2 I celebrate myself, and sing myself.
'Song of Myself' (written 1855) pt 1

3 And I will show that nothing can happen more beautiful than death.
Leaves of Grass (1860) 'Proto-Leaf', later renamed 'Starting From Paumanok'

4 Pioneers! O pioneers!
'Pioneers! O Pioneers!' (1881)

5 When lilacs last in the dooryard bloomed.
'When lilacs last in the dooryard bloomed' (1881) st. 1

Whittier, John Greenleaf (1807–92). American poet

1 For of all sad words of tongue or pen,
The saddest are these: 'It might have been!'
'Maud Muller' (1854)

2 'Shoot, if you must, this old grey head,
But spare your country's flag,' she said.
'Barbara Frietchie' (1863)

3 Dear Lord and Father of mankind, Forgive our foolish ways!
'The Brewing of Soma' (1872)

Whittington, Robert

1 A man for all seasons.
Of Sir Thomas More, in *Vulgaria* (1521) pt 2 'De constructione nominum'

Wilcox, Ella Wheeler (1855–1919). American poet

1 Laugh and the world laughs with you;
Weep, and you weep alone.
'Solitude', the *Sun* (New York) 25 February 1883

Wilde, Oscar (1854–1900). Anglo-Irish playwright and poet

1 Over the piano was printed a notice: 'Please do not shoot the pianist. He is doing his best.'
Impressions of America: Leadville (1883)

2 The one duty we owe to history is to rewrite it.
Intentions (1891) 'The Critic as Artist' pt 1

3 All art is immoral.
Intentions (1891) 'The Critic as Artist' pt 2

4 A little sincerity is a dangerous thing, and a great deal of it is absolutely fatal.
Intentions (1891) 'The Critic as Artist' pt 2

5 Life imitates Art far more than Art imitates Life.
Intentions (1891) 'The Decay of Lying'

6 There is no such thing as a moral or an immoral book. Books are well written, or badly written.
The Picture of Dorian Gray (1891) preface

7 There is only one thing in the world worse than being talked about, and that is not being talked about.
The Picture of Dorian Gray (1891) ch. 1

8 A man cannot be too careful in the choice of his enemies.
The Picture of Dorian Gray (1891) ch. 1

9 Murder is always a mistake … One should never do anything that one cannot talk about after dinner.
The Picture of Dorian Gray (1891) ch. 19

10 I can resist everything except temptation.
Lady Windermere's Fan (1892) act 1

11 We are all in the gutter, but some of us are looking at the stars.
Lady Windermere's Fan (1892) act 3

12 CECIL GRAHAM: What is a cynic?
LORD DARLINGTON: A man who knows the price of everything and the value of nothing.
Lady Windermere's Fan (1892) act 3

13 Experience is the name every one gives to their mistakes.
Lady Windermere's Fan (1892) act 3

14 The play was a great success, but the audience was a disaster.
Attributed comment after the poor reception of *Lady Windermere's Fan* (1892)

15 MRS ALLONBY: They say, Lady Hunstanton, that when good Americans die they go to Paris.
LADY HUNSTANTON: Indeed? And when bad Americans die, where do they go to?
LORD ILLINGWORTH: Oh, they go to America.
A Woman of No Importance (1893) act 1

16 The English country gentleman galloping after a fox – the unspeakable in full pursuit of the uneatable.
A Woman of No Importance (1893) act 1

17 Children begin by loving their parents; after a time they judge them; rarely, if ever, do they forgive them.
A Woman of No Importance (1893) act 2

18 After a good dinner one can forgive anybody, even one's own relations.
A Woman of No Importance (1893) act 2

19 The truth is rarely pure, and never simple.
The Importance of Being Earnest (1895) act 1

20 In married life three is company and two none.
The Importance of Being Earnest (1895) act 1

21 Ignorance is like a delicate exotic fruit; touch it and the bloom is gone.
The Importance of Being Earnest (1895) act 1

22 To lose one parent, Mr Worthing, may be regarded as a misfortune; to lose both looks like carelessness.
The Importance of Being Earnest (1895) act 1

23 All women become like their mothers. That is their tragedy. No man does. That's his.
The Importance of Being Earnest (1895) act 1
(also in dialogue form in *A Woman of No Importance* (1893) act 2)

24 The good ended happily, and the bad unhappily. That is what fiction means.
The Importance of Being Earnest (1895) act 2

25 Fashion is what one wears oneself. What is unfashionable is what other people wear.
An Ideal Husband (1895) act 3

26 Yet each man kills the thing he
loves,
By each let this be heard,
Some do it with a bitter look,
Some with a flattering word.
The Ballad of Reading Gaol (1898) pt 1, st. 7

27 How else but through a broken
heart
May Lord Christ enter in?
The Ballad of Reading Gaol (1898) pt 5, st. 14

28 I have nothing to declare except
my genius.
At the New York Custom House, in Frank
Harris *Oscar Wilde* (1918) p. 75

29 I am dying, as I have lived, beyond
my means.
Accepting some champagne just before his
death (attributed)

30 Either that wallpaper goes or I do.
On his deathbed in a Paris hotel bedroom
(attributed)

31 Work is the curse of the drinking
classes.
In H. Pearson *Life of Oscar Wilde* (1946) ch. 12

Wilder, Thornton (1897–1975).
American novelist and playwright

1 Marriage is a bribe to make a
housekeeper think she's a house-
holder.
The Merchant of Yonkers (1939) act 1

2 Literature is the orchestration of
platitudes.
In *Time* 12 January 1953

Wilensky, Robert (1951–).
American academic

1 We've all heard that a million
monkeys banging on a million
typewriters will eventually reproduce the entire works of Shakespeare. Now, thanks to the Internet, we know this is not true.
In *The Mail on Sunday* 16 February 1997

William III (William of Orange)
(1650–1702). King of Great Britain
and Ireland from 1688

1 Every bullet has its billet.
In John Wesley *Journal* (1827) 6 June 1765

William of Ockam (c.1285–1349).
English Franciscan friar and
philosopher

1 *Entia non sunt multiplicanda praeter
necessitatem.*
No more things should be pre-
sumed to exist than are absolutely
necessary.
'Occam's Razor', philosophical principle
attributed to Occam but earlier in origin;
not found in this form in his writings

William of Wykeham (1324–
1404). English prelate and
statesman

1 Manners maketh man.
Motto (proverbial since the mid-fourteenth
century)

Williams, Robin (1952–).
American comedian and film actor

1 Cricket is baseball on valium.
Quoted in Colin Jarman *The Guinness Dictionary of Sports Quotations* (1990)

Williams, Tennessee (Thomas
Lanier Williams) (1911–83). American
playwright

1 What is the victory of a cat on a hot
tin roof? – I wish I knew … Just
staying on it, I guess, as long as she
can.
Cat on a Hot Tin Roof (1955) act 1

2 You can be young without money
but you can't be old without it.
Cat on a Hot Tin Roof (1955) act 1

3 Life is all memory except for the
one present moment that goes by
you so quick you hardly catch it
going.
The Milk Train Doesn't Stop Here Anymore
(1963) sc. 3

Williams, William Carlos (1883–
1963). American poet

1 All writing is a disease. You can't
stop it.
Quoted in *Newsweek* 7 January 1957

2 Anything is good material for
poetry. Anything.
Paterson (1958) bk 5

Wilmot, John (Earl of Rochester) (1647–80). English poet

1 Since 'tis nature's law to change, Constancy alone is strange.
'A Dialogue between Strephon and Daphne' l. 31 (published 1691)

2 A merry monarch, scandalous and poor.
'A Satire on King Charles II' (1697)

3 Here lies a great and mighty king Whose promise none relies on; He never said a foolish thing, Nor ever did a wise one.
'The King's Epitaph' in C. E. Doble et al. *Thomas Hearne: Remarks and Collections* (1885–1921) 17 November 1706

Wilson, Edmund (1895–1972). American literary critic, social commentator and novelist

1 In a sense, one can never read the book that the author originally wrote, and one can never read the same book twice.
The Triple Thinkers (1938) introduction

Wilson, Harold (Baron Wilson of Rievaulx) (1916–95). British Labour politician and Prime Minister

1 All the little gnomes in Zurich and other finance centres.
Speech, House of Commons, 12 November 1956

2 A week is a long time in politics.
Comment to lobby correspondents, October 1964

Wilson, Sir Angus (1931–91). English writer

1 All fiction is for me a kind of magic and trickery – a confidence trick, trying to make people believe something is true that isn't.
In the *Paris Review* (1957) no. 17

2 The impulse to write a novel comes from a momentary unified vision of life.
The Wild Garden (1963)

Wilson, Woodrow (1856–1924). 28th President of the USA

1 No nation is fit to sit in judgement upon any other nation.
Speech in New York, 20 April 1915; in *Selected Addresses* (1918) p. 79

2 It must be a peace without victory … Only a peace between equals can last.
Speech to US Senate, 22 January 1917, in *Messages and Papers* (1924) vol. 1, p. 352

3 The world must be made safe for democracy.
Speech to Congress, 2 April 1917, in *Selected Addresses* (1918) p. 195

Wilton, Robb (1881–1957). British radio comedian

1 The day war broke out.
Preamble to radio monologues in the role of a Home Guard, from c.1940

Winner, Michael (1935–). British director

1 A team effort is a lot of people doing what I say.
Attributed

Wittgenstein, Ludwig (1889–1951). Austrian-born British philosopher

1 *Was sich überhaupt sagen lässt, lässt sich klar sagen; und wovon man nicht reden kann, darüber muss man schweigen.*
What can be said at all can be said clearly; and whereof one cannot speak thereof one must be silent.
Tractatus Logico-Philosophicus (1921) preface

2 *Die Welt ist die Gesamtheit der Tatsachen, nicht der Dinge.*
The world is the totality of facts, not of things.
Tractatus Logico-Philosophicus (1921) prop. 1.1

3 *Der Tod ist kein Ereignis des Lebens. Den Tod erlebt man nicht.*
Death is not an event in life: we do not live to experience death.
Tractatus Logico-Philosophicus (1921) prop. 6.4311

4 *Der Philosoph behandelt eine Frage
wie eine Krankheit.*
The philosopher's treatment of a
question is like the treatment of an
illness.
Philosophische Untersuchungen (1953) sect.
255

**Wodehouse, Sir P(elham)
G(renville)** (1881–1975). Anglo-
American writer

1 It is a good rule in life never to
apologize. The right sort of people
do not want apologies, and the
wrong sort take a mean advantage
of them.
The Man Upstairs (1914) title story

2 To my daughter Leonora without
whose never-failing sympathy and
encouragement this book would
have been finished in half the time.
The Heart of a Goof (1926) dedication

3 It is no use telling me that there are
bad aunts and good aunts. At the
core, they are all alike. Sooner or
later, out pops the cloven hoof.
The Code of the Woosters (1938) ch. 2

Wogan, Terry (1938–). Irish
broadcaster

1 Television contracts the imagination and radio expands it.
In the *Observer* 30 December 1984 'Sayings
of the Year'

Wolfe, Charles (1791–1823). Irish
poet

1 Not a drum was heard, not a
funeral note,
As his corse to the rampart we
hurried.
'The Burial of Sir John Moore at Corunna'
(1817)

Wolfe, Tom (Thomas Kennerley)
(1931–). American journalist and
novelist

1 Radical chic invariably favors rad-
icals who seem primitive, exotic
and romantic.
Radical Chic (1970)

2 A cult is a religion with no political
power.
In Our Time (1980) ch. 2

3 The bonfire of the vanities.
Title of novel (1987)

4 A liberal is a conservative who has
been arrested.
The Bonfire of the Vanities (1987) ch. 24

Wollstonecraft, Mary (1759–97).
English feminist; mother of Mary
Shelley

1 I do not wish them [women] to
have power over men; but over
themselves.
A Vindication of the Rights of Woman (1792)
ch. 4

2 Minute attention to propriety
stops the growth of virtue.
Collected Letters (ed. R. Wardle, 1979) p. 141

Wolstenholme, Kenneth (1921–
2002). English sports commentator

1 They think it's all over – it is now.
World Cup Final, 30 July 1966

Wood, Mrs Henry (née Ellen Price)
(1814–87). English novelist

1 Dead! and … never called me
mother.
East Lynne (dramatized by T. A. Palmer,
1874, the words are not in the novel of 1861)

Woods, Harry (1889–1968).
American actor and songwriter

1 But we'll travel along
Singin' a song,
Side by side.
'Side by Side' (1927 song)

Woolf, Virginia (1882–1941).
English novelist

1 One of those comfortably padded
lunatic asylums which are known,
euphemistically, as the stately
homes of England.
The Common Reader (1925) 'Lady Dorothy
Nevill'

2 Life is not a series of gig lamps
symmetrically arranged; life is a
luminous halo, a semi-transparent

envelope surrounding us from the beginning of consciousness to the end.
The Common Reader (1925) 'Modern Fiction'

3 A good essay must have this permanent quality about it; it must draw its curtain round us, but it must be a curtain that shuts us in not out.
The Common Reader (1925) 'The Modern Essay'

4 So that is marriage, Lily thought, a man and a woman looking at a girl throwing a ball.
To the Lighthouse (1927) pt 1, ch. 13

5 A woman must have money and a room of her own if she is to write fiction.
A Room of One's Own (1929) ch. 1

6 One cannot think well, love well, sleep well, if one has not dined well.
A Room of One's Own (1929) ch. 1

7 Literature is strewn with the wreckage of men who have minded beyond reason the opinions of others.
A Room of One's Own (1929) ch. 3

Woollcott, Alexander (1887–1943). American writer and broadcaster

1 A broker is a man who takes your fortune and runs it into a shoestring.
Quoted in Samuel Adams *Alexander Woollcott* (1945) ch. 15

2 All the things I really like to do are either illegal, immoral or fattening.
Quoted in R. Drennan *Wit's End* (1968)

3 The scenery was beautiful, but the actors got in front of it.
Play review

Wordsworth, William (1770–1850). English poet

1 I heard a thousand blended notes,
While in a grove I sate reclined,
In that sweet mood when pleasant thoughts
Bring sad thoughts to the mind.
'Lines Written in Early Spring' (1798) st. 1

2 His little, nameless, unremembered, acts
Of kindness and of love.
'Lines composed a few miles above Tintern Abbey' (1798) l. 26

3 One impulse from a vernal wood
May teach you more of man,
Of moral evil and of good,
Than all the sages can.
'The Tables Turned' (1798)

4 A slumber did my spirit seal.
'A slumber did my spirit seal' (1800)

5 Thrice welcome, darling of the Spring
Even yet thou are to me
No bird, but an invisible thing,
A voice, a mystery.
'To the Cuckoo' (1807) st. 4

6 Poetry is the spontaneous overflow of powerful feelings: it takes its origin from emotion recollected in tranquillity.
Lyrical Ballads (2nd edn, 1802) Preface

7 Who is the happy Warrior? Who is he
Whom every man in arms should wish to be?
'Character of the Happy Warrior' (1807)

8 Earth has not anything to show more fair:
Dull would he be of soul who could pass by
A sight so touching in its majesty:
This City now doth like a garment wear
The beauty of the morning; silent, bare,
Ships, towers, domes, theatres, and temples lie
Open unto the fields, and to the sky;
All bright and glittering in the smokeless air.
'Composed upon Westminster Bridge' (1807)

9 Dear God! the very houses seem
asleep;
And all that mighty heart is lying
still!
'Composed upon Westminster Bridge'
(1807)

10 We must be free or die, who speak
the tongue
That Shakespeare spake; the faith
and morals hold
Which Milton held.
'It is not to be thought of that the Flood'
(1807)

11 I travelled among unknown men,
In lands beyond the sea.
'I travelled among unknown men' (1807)

12 Milton! thou shouldst be living at
this hour:
England hath need of thee.
'Milton! thou shouldst be living at this hour'
(1807)

13 My heart leaps up when I behold
A rainbow in the sky.
'My heart leaps up when I behold' (1807)

14 The Child is father of the Man;
And I could wish my days to be
Bound each to each by natural
piety.
'My heart leaps up when I behold' (1807)

15 The rainbow comes and goes,
And lovely is the rose.
'Ode. Intimations of Immortality' (1807) st. 1

16 But yet I know, where'er I go,
That there hath passed away a glory
from the earth.
'Ode. Intimations of Immortality' (1807) st. 1

17 Whither is fled the visionary
gleam?
Where is it now, the glory and the
dream?
'Ode. Intimations of Immortality' (1807) st. 4

18 Our birth is but a sleep and a for-
getting.
'Ode. Intimations of Immortality' (1807) st. 5

19 Not in entire forgetfulness,
And not in utter nakedness,
But trailing clouds of glory do we
come
From God, who is our home:
Heaven lies about us in our infancy!

Shades of the prison-house begin to
close
Upon the growing boy.
'Ode. Intimations of Immortality' (1807) st. 5

20 To me the meanest flower that
blows can give
Thoughts that do often lie too deep
for tears.
'Ode. Intimations of Immortality' (1807) st. 11

21 Behold her, single in the field,
Yon solitary Highland lass!
'The Solitary Reaper' (1807)

22 O blithe new-comer! I have heard,
I hear thee and rejoice:
O Cuckoo! Shall I call thee bird,
Or but a wandering voice?
'To the Cuckoo' (1807) st. 1

23 The world is too much with us; late
and soon,
Getting and spending, we lay waste
our powers.
'The world is too much with us' (1807)

24 Bliss was it in that dawn to be alive,
But to be young was very heaven!
'The French Revolution, as it Appeared to
Enthusiasts' (1809); also *The Prelude* (1850)
bk 9, l. 108

25 I wandered lonely as a cloud
That floats on high o'er vales and
hills,
When all at once I saw a crowd,
A host, of golden daffodils;
Beside the lake, beneath the trees,
Fluttering and dancing in the
breeze.
'I wandered lonely as a cloud' (1815 edn)

26 Not choice
But habit rules the unreflecting
herd.
'Grant that by this unsparing hurricane'
(1822)

Wotton, Sir Henry (1568–1639).
English poet and diplomat

1 An ambassador is an honest man
sent to lie abroad for the good of his
country.
Written in the album of Christopher Fleck-
more in 1604

Wragg, Ted (1938–). English educator

1 Nobody loves a bad teacher.
Education: an Action Guide for Parents (1986)

Wriston, Walter Bigelow (1919–). American banker

1 When you retire … you go from who's who to who's that.
In the *New York Times* 21 April 1985

Wylie, Betty Jane (1931–). Canadian writer

1 First deal with your own tears; tomorrow do something about acid rain.
Successfully Single (1986)

2 Poverty isn't being broke; poverty is never having enough.
Everywoman's Money Book (1989, with Lynne MacFarlane)

Xenophon (c.428–c.354 BC). Greek historian

1 The sea! the sea!
   Anabasis bk 4, ch. 7, sect. 24

7 And therefore I have sailed the seas
and come
To the holy city of Byzantium.
'Sailing to Byzantium' (1928)

8 The innocent and the beautiful
Have no enemy but time.
'In Memory of Eva Gore Booth and Con
Markiewicz' (1933)

9 Think like a wise man but express
yourself like the common people.
*Letters on Poetry from W. B. Yeats to Dorothy
Wellesley* (1940) 21 December 1935

10 Cast a cold eye
On life, on death.
Horseman, pass by!
'Under Ben Bulben' (1938) st. 6

Yeames, W(illiam) F(rederick)
(1835–1918). British painter

1 And when did you last see your
father?
Title of painting (1878), now in the Walker
Art Gallery, Liverpool

Yeats, W(illiam) B(utler) (1865–
1939). Irish poet

1 I will arise and go now, and go to
Innisfree,
And a small cabin build there, of
clay and wattles made.
'The Lake Isle of Innisfree' (1893)

2 A pity beyond all telling,
Is hid in the heart of love.
'The Pity of Love' (1893)

3 Tread softly because you tread on
my dreams.
'He Wishes for the Cloths of Heaven' (1899)

4 And pluck till time and times are
done,
The silver apples of the moon,
The golden apples of the sun.
'Song of Wandering Aengus' (1899)

5 In dreams begins responsibility.
Responsibilities (1914) epigraph

6 Lord, what would they say
Did their Catullus walk that way?
'The Scholars' (1919)

Yeltsin, Boris (1931–). Russian
statesman, President of the Russian
Federation (1991–9)

1 Europe is in danger of plunging
into a cold peace.
In *Newsweek* 19 December 1994

Young, Edward (1683–1765).
English poet and playwright

1 Be wise with speed;
A fool at forty is a fool indeed.
The Love of Fame (1725–8) Satire 2, l. 282

2 Procrastination is the thief of time.
Night Thoughts (1742–5) 'Night 1' l. 393

3 The course of Nature is the art of
God.
Night Thoughts (1742–5) 'Night 9' l. 1267

Yourcenar, Marguerite
(Marguerite de Crayencour) (1903–
87). French novelist

1 *Les trois quarts de nos exercices intel-
lectuels ne sont plus que broderies sur
le vide.*
Three quarters of our intellectual
performances are no more than
decorations over a void.
Mémoires d'Hadrien (1958)

Zangwill, Israel (1864–1926).
Jewish spokesman and writer

1 America is God's Crucible, the
great Melting-Pot where all the
races of Europe are melting and re-
forming!
The Melting Pot (1908) act 1

Zemeckis, Robert and Gale, Bob
(1952–; 1951–). American film
producers

1 Back to the future.
Title of a film (1985)

Zola, Emile (1840–1902). French
novelist

1 *J'accuse.*
I accuse.
Title of an open letter to the President of the
French Republic regarding the Dreyfus
affair; in *L'Aurore* 13 January 1898

Index

The organization of this Index is strictly alphabetical – letter-by-letter and not word-by-word. So, for example, *seal* and *search* are located between *sea* and *sea-shore*. Word variants are grouped together under their basic form: for example, quotations containing the words *see*, *seeing*, *sees*, *saw*, and *seen* are grouped together under the headword *see*, and you will find instances of *teeth* located under *tooth*. The only exceptions are when a quotation is primarily remembered by a word which has an irregular grammatical form (such as *better* or *worse*) or which is historically distinctive in some way (such as *unkindest*).

References to authors are by surname only, except where two authors share the same surname, in which case first names are included. Anonymous items are referred to as Anon and classified according to original language. References to biblical quotations are listed in their alphabetical place as New Testament, Old Testament or Apocrypha.

Abbreviations

adj.	adjective
adv.	adverb
interj.	interjection
n.	noun
prep.	preposition
pron.	pronoun
v.	verb

bandy (v.) Johnson 19;
Webster 5
bang (n.) Eliot, T. S. 17
banish Shakespeare 133
bank (n.) Anon (English) 61;
Burns, Robert 7; Hope, Bob 1;
Lauder 2; Liberace 1;
Shakespeare 251
banner Key 1
banquet Shenstone 1
bar (n.) Hardy 6; Lovelace 1;
Molière 1; Service 2
Barabbas Campbell, Thomas
3
barbarous Milton 8
bare Shakespeare 342; Shelley
2; Wordsworth 8
bargain (n.) Dickens 12;
Franklin 3
barge (n.) Shakespeare 15
bark (v.) Auden 6; Webster 6
Barkis Dickens 13
barn New Testament 18
barrel Mao Zedong 2
barren Campbell, Thomas 1
base (adj.) Dryden 7; Ruskin
13
baseball Barzun 2; Williams,
Robin 4
based (v.) Lawrence 2
basket Conrad 2; Webb 1
bastard Anon (English) 33;
Hillary 1; Shakespeare 194
Bates, Charley Dickens 6
battalion Rouget de Lisle 1;
Shakespeare 114; Voltaire 9
batter Donne 8
battle de Gaulle 1;
Goldsmith 12; Hussein 1;
Old Testament 79;
Shakespeare 210; Stevenson,
Robert Louis 1; Sun Tzu 2;
Tennyson 37; Wellesley 2
bavin Shakespeare 137
bawdy Mencken 4
bazaar MacNeice 1
be MacLeish 1; Shakespeare
94
beach Churchill, Winston 4;
Eliot, T. S. 6
Beachy Head Chesterton 9
beacon Huxley, T. H. 2
Beale, Miss Anon (English)
16
beam (n.) New Testament 23
beam (v.) Dickens 11;
Roddenberry 3
beamish Carroll 16
bean Bossidy 1
beans Epstein 4

bear (n.) Marryat 1; Milne 4;
Shakespeare 335
bear (v.) Chapman 1;
Churchill, Winston 5;
Emerson 14; Kempis 5;
Moore, Thomas 3; Old
Testament 33; Shakespeare
186
beard (n.) Drake 1
beard (v.) Scott, Walter 3
beast Coleridge 7; Fields,
W. C. 1; Milton 37; Old
Testament 9
beastie Anon (English) 27;
Burns, Robert 2
beastly Coward 6
beat (adj.) Kerouac, Jack 1
beat (v.) Carroll 13; Halm 1;
Milton 4; Morell 1; Old
Testament 96
beating (n.) Bright 1
Beatles Larkin 3
beautiful (adj.) Alexander,
Cecil Frances 1; Anon
(English) 43; Anouilh 1;
Constable, John 1; Foster 3;
Huxley, T. H. 4; Lear 4, 5;
Lowell, James Russell 3;
O. Henry 3; Ruskin 2; Schiller
1; Schumacher 1; Whitman
3; Woollcott 3
beautiful (n.) Yeats 8
beauty Arnold, Samuel
James 1; Arras 1; Bacon 17;
Byron 5; Congreve 7; Donne
2; Farquhar 4; Hume 7; Hunt,
Leigh 3; James, Henry 9;
Keats 5, 20; Milton 9; Philips
1; Saki 2; Shakespeare 39, 86,
291; Stevens 2; Wordsworth
8
because Mallory 1
beckoning Milton 5
become de Beauvoir 1
bed Alexander, Cecil Frances
3; Anon (English) 7;
Benchley 2; Breton 1; Davies,
Robertson 1; Hillingdon 1;
Kyd 2; New Testament 103;
Pepys 1; Shakespeare 252,
349; Skelton 7; Stevenson,
Robert Louis 1; Thurber 3
bedfellow Montaigne 2;
Shakespeare 306
bedpan Kuhn 1
bedroom Campbell, Mrs
Patrick 1; Hoffnung 1
bee Lowell, James Russell 1;
Porter 5; Shakespeare 312;
Tennyson 17

beechen Campbell, Thomas
1
beer Calverley 1; Gladstone
3; Levenstein 1; Shakespeare
261
Beethoven Berry 1
before Norton 1;
Roddenberry 2
beget Osler 2
beggar (v.) Shakespeare 14
begin Bacon 3; Balzac 6;
Dryden 10; Lang, Julia 1;
Larkin 3; Pitkin 1; Pitt 2;
Quarles 5; Thomas, Dylan 8;
Yeats 5
beginning (n.) Aristotle 3;
Churchill, Winston 8;
Dryden 3; Eliot, T. S. 28;
Godard 2; Larkin 6; Mary,
Queen of Scots 1; Missal 4,
23; Moore, George 1; New
Testament 93, 150; Old
Testament 1; Plato 4; Ruskin
6; Swinburne 1; Thomas,
Dylan 8; Woolf 2
behave Stevenson, Robert
Louis 6
behind (prep.) Lamb,
Charles 2; New Testament
42; Pitt 1; Shelley 5
behold Bunyan 5; New
Testament 18, 23, 117;
Shakespeare 151, 342;
Wordsworth 13
beholder Swift 1
being (n.) Kundera 1; New
Testament 120; Schiller 2
belfry Tennyson 1
belief Cupitt 1; Emerson 14;
Hume 6; Kaufman 2;
McCarthy 1; Mencken 2;
Orwell 10
believe Anouilh 2; Anselm 1;
Bacon 8; Browne 2; Dick 1;
Emerson 14; Horace 6;
Krutch 1; Macaulay 1; Missal
11; Newman 2; New
Testament 71, 102, 104;
Nixon 2; Ovid 1; Rimbaud 2;
Seaton 1; Skelton 2; Thurber
5; Welles 4; Wellesley 4;
Wilson, Angus 1
Belinda Pope 13
bell Anon (English) 28;
Cummings 2; Donne 14;
Ginsberg 1; Hood 3; Keats 26;
Shakespeare 312; Tennyson
25
belle Keats 13
bellyful Miller, Henry 1

cosmetics Revlon 1
cosmic Bucke 1
cosmopolitan Moore, George 1
cost (v.) Anon (English) 32; Montagu 1; Updike 4
costly Adams, Henry Brooks 2
couch McLuhan 3
cough (n.) Anon (English) 34
cough (v.) Schnabel 2
councillor Salvianus 1
counsel Pope 14
counsellor Old Testament 86
count (n.) Somoza 1
count (v.) Browning, Elizabeth Barrett 2; Chargaff 1; Emerson 15; Getty 1; Hanrahan 1; Molière 4; Shakespeare 37
countenance Cervantes 1; Shakespeare 67; Sheridan, Richard Brinsley 4
counter Hobbes 1
counterfeited (adj.) Goldsmith 7
counting (n.) Stoppard 3
country (n.) Anon (English) 23; Bierce 3; Burke, Edmund 7; Byron 4; Chesterton 11; Churchill, Charles 3; Collins, William 1; Cowper 10; de Gaulle 3; Disraeli 20; Erasmus 1; Gladstone 1; Hartley 1; Homer 4; Horace 13; Huxley, Aldous 10; Johnson 8; Kennedy, John F. 2; Lloyd George 3; Maistre 1; Martial 1; New Testament 37; Paine 2; Paton 1; Peacock 2; Powell, Anthony 4; Rouget de Lisle 1; Shakespeare 94; Smith, Samuel Francis 1; Smith, Sydney 1; Thatcher 2, 5; Wells 2; Whitelaw 1; Whittier 2; Wotton 1
country (adj.) Wilde 16
countryman Shakespeare 181
couple Fielding 6
courage Crane, Stephen 1; Kennedy, Robert F. 1; Shakespeare 217; Trollope 2
course (n.) Scott, Walter 7; Shakespeare 134, 248; Young 3
court Levant 1; Milton 1
courtesy Lucas, E. V. 2; Shakespeare 296; Tennyson 41

courtmartial (v.) Behan 1
cousin Gilbert 2
cover (v.) New Testament 149; Webster 2
covet Old Testament 34
covetous Smart 2
cow Beaumont and Fletcher 2; Betjeman 1
coward Connell 1; Shakespeare 95, 131, 132, 177
cowardice Twain 14
cowardly Webster 6
cowboy Moon 1
cowering (adj.) Burns, Robert 2
cowslip Shakespeare 312
coyness Marvell, Andrew 1
crack (v.) Shakespeare 197; Tennyson 4
cradle Browning, Robert 5; Shelley 8
craft (n.) Chaucer 11; La Bruyère 2
cragged Donne 1
cram Shakespeare 152
crank Twain 13
craven Shakespeare 112
crazy Epstein 4; McGregor 1; Perelman 1
cream Shakespeare 138
create Anon (English) 10; Brecht 3; Dostoevsky 1; Jefferson 1; Lawrence 3; Lincoln 2; Lucretius 1; Mamet 1; Old Testament 1, 3; Saint-Exupéry 4; Valéry 3
creation Hugo 2; Jefferson 1; Milton 38
creative Lawrence 7
creativity Koestler 2
creator Anon (English) 10
creature Alexander, Cecil Frances 1; Faulkner 2; Moore, Clement 1
credit (n.) Cowper 15; Darwin, Francis 1
credulity Lamb, Charles 5
creep (v.) Bowen 1; Shakespeare 229; Tennyson 12
crème de la crème Spark 2
crest (v.) Shakespeare 25
crew Coleridge 5
cricket Cardus 1; Mancroft 1; Mikes 4; Norden 1; Williams, Robin 1
crime Allen, Woody 1; Corneille 2; Farquhar 1, 3; Gibbon 2; Gilbert 10;

Marvell, Andrew 1; Powell, Anthony 3; Roland 1; Shaw 18; Waugh 4
criminal (n.) Linklater 1
crimson Tennyson 16
crisis Kissinger 5
critic Disraeli 17; Lawrence 3; Pope 4; Tynan 2
critical Herbert, A. P. 3
criticism Arnold, Matthew 7; Johnson 38; Maugham 1
crocodile Bacon 36
Cromwell Amery 1; Bedford and Sullivan 1
crooked Herbert, George 7; Kant 1; Shirley 1
cross (n.) Baring-Gould 1; Bennard 1; Hayes 1; Kempis 5; Muggeridge 1; New Testament 78; Watts 1
cross (v.) Auden 5
crow (v.) New Testament 63
crowd (n.) Gray, Thomas 13; Wordsworth 16
crowded Diana 1
crown (n.) Bagehot 1; Carroll 13; Marlowe 4; Shakespeare 27, 146, 169; Shirley 1; Tennyson 10
crown (v.) Bates, Katherine Lee 1; Goldsmith 6
crucible Zangwill 1
crucify Alexander, Cecil Frances 4
crude Milton 12
cruel Cromwell 3; Eliot, T. S. 10; Leacock 2; Shakespeare 106
cruelty Bunyan 4
crumb Smart 2
crumpet Muir 1
crust Ellis 1; Keats 14
crutch Shakespeare 255
cry (n.) Berkeley 1
cry (v.) Liberace 1; New Testament 2; Old Testament 65, 88; Paton 1; Webster 8; Whiting, William 1
cryptograph Schopenhauer 1
cube Fermat 1
cuccu [cuckoo] Anon (English) 1
cuckoo Kesey 1; Wordsworth 22
cuckoo clock Welles 1
cuff Skelton 3
cult Wolfe, Tom 2
cultural Hirsch, E. D. 1

46, 341; Sheridan, Philip
Henry 1; Stevenson, Robert
Louis 4; Tennyson 27;
Thurber 3; Unamuno 1;
Waugh 8; Wood 1
dead (n.) Book of Common
Prayer 17; Cather 1; Crabbe 2;
Dryden 22; Huxley, Aldous 8;
Lincoln 3; Macmillan 4;
Mailer 1; New Testament 29,
92, 135; Rich 2; Shakespeare
66, 155; Voltaire 6
deadly Kipling 21
deaf (adj.) Le Carré 3
deal (n.) Roosevelt, Franklin
D. 1
Dean, Nellie Armstrong,
Harry 1
dear (adj.) Book of Common
Prayer 16; Shakespeare 4, 174;
Smith, Dodie 1; Whistler 3
death Anon (English) 40;
Anouilh 1; Auden 8; Barthes
1; Behan 1; Berger 2;
Bhagavadgita 1; Bonhoeffer
2; Book of Common Prayer
11, 15; Bright 1; Browne 5;
Browning, Robert 16;
Cervantes 3; Dickinson,
Emily 1; Donne 6, 7, 11; Eliot,
George 1; Eliot, T. S. 7, 23;
Forster 4; Franklin 9;
Galsworthy 1; Hawthorne 1;
Hemingway 4, 6; Henry,
Patrick 1; Hobbes 4; Holland
1; Jarry 1; Keats 24, 25; La
Bruyère 7; Lebowitz 2;
Milton 27; Mitchell,
Margaret 2; Montesquieu 1;
Nabokov 1; New Testament
4, 126, 136; Old Testament 59,
85; Pascal 4; Ruskin 9;
Santayana 4; Sassoon 1;
Schopenhauer 2; Scott,
Walter 1; Shakespeare 24, 92,
93, 177, 233, 323; Shankly 1;
Shaw 15; Shelley 11; Shirley
1; Skelton 1; Smith, Sydney
8; Sontag 3; Soper 1; Southey
5; Swinburne 2; Tennyson
28, 31; Thomas, Dylan 3, 5;
Twain 15; Voltaire 8;
Webster 3; Whitehead 3;
Whitman 3; Wittgenstein 3;
Yeats 10
deathless Donne 3
debt New Testament 14;
Service 1
debtor New Testament 14
decadence Mamet 1

decay (n.) Donne 16; Mamet
2; Miller, Henry 5; Shelley
2
decay (v.) Tennyson 35
deceive Baruch 1; Scott,
Walter 4; Stefansson 1;
Thurber 5; Virgil 4
deceiver Shakespeare 256
December Anderson,
Maxwell 1; Shakespeare 42
decency Dillon 2; Shaw 14
decent Hope, Anthony 2; Le
Carré 3
deception Sun Tzu 1
decipher Schopenhauer 1
decisive Cartier-Bresson 1
deck (n.) Hemans 1
declare Book of Common
Prayer 7; Wilde 28
decline (v.) Babington 5
decoration Yourcenar 1
dedicated Davies, Ray 1
deed Eliot, George 2; Eliot,
T. S. 24; Goethe 7;
Shakespeare 68, 219, 220, 226,
245
deep (adj.) Arnold, Matthew
1; Carlyle, Thomas 11; Frost
2; James, Henry 7; Saki 2;
Shakespeare 273, 311;
Wordsworth 20
deep (n.) Book of Common
Prayer 17; Old Testament 1,
64
deepen Larkin 5
deer Higley 1
defaced (adj.) Bacon 5
defeat (n.) Churchill,
Winston 13, 16
defeat (v.) Sun Tzu 2
defeated (n.) Livy 1
defence Charles I 1; Dillon 2;
Lucas, E. V. 2
defend Chesterton 3;
Shakespeare 73; Voltaire 8
defiance Churchill, Winston
13
definite Goldwyn 4
definition Swift 6
defy Bacon 27
degradation James, Alice 1
delay (n.) Dryden 6
delete Anon (English) 57
delicate Wilde 21
delight (n.) Anon (English) 5;
Blake, William 5; Milton 16
delightful La Rochefoucauld
3
deliver Anon (English) 27;
New Testament 14

deliverer Milton 41
deluge Pompadour 1
delusion Inge 5
demand Reith 1
democracy Chesterton 14;
Cooper 1; Montesquieu 3;
Peres 1; Schumpeter 1; Stead
1; Stoppard 3; Welles 1;
White, E. B. 1; Wilson,
Woodrow 3
Democrat Stevenson, Adlai 1
demon Faulkner 2
demonic Baudelaire 3
den New Testament 52; Scott,
Walter 3
Denmark Shakespeare 74
denote Shakespeare 264
dentist Waugh 6
denunciation Smith, Logan
Pearsall 1
deny Disraeli 26; Goethe 4;
Huxley, T. H. 3; Lawrence 4;
New Testament 63, 78;
Quarles 1
deodorant Taylor, Elizabeth
1
depart Amery 1; Cromwell 1;
Longfellow 2; New
Testament 76
departed (adj.) Book of
Common Prayer 16; Byron 3;
Longfellow 5
department store Warhol 2
depend Disraeli 20; Joad 1;
Shaw 27
dependence Hobbes 2
deplorable Doyle, Arthur
Conan 12
deposit (n.) Connolly 4
depression Reagan 2;
Truman 3
deprivation Larkin 7
depth Bacon 15
depths Old Testament 65
descend Churchill, Winston
11
description Shakespeare 14,
345
desert (adj.) Gray, Thomas
11; Milton 5
desert (n.) Old Testament 88;
Shelley 1
deserve Dryden 25; Maistre 1;
Orwell 11
design (v.) Issigonis 1, 2;
Wesley, John 2
desire (n.) Bacon 21; Blake,
William 15; Butler, Samuel
(1835) 6; Drayton 1; Eliot, T. S.
10; Russell, Bertrand 5;

know more ⊕

PENGUIN POCKET REFERENCE

THE PENGUIN POCKET ENGLISH DICTIONARY

This pocket edition of the bestselling *Penguin English Dictionary* is the perfect reference book for everyday use. Compiled by Britain's foremost lexicographers, up to date and easy to use, it is the ideal portable companion for quick reference.

– Includes a wealth of words, phrases and clear definitions, with more information than other comparable dictionaries

– Covers standard and formal English, as well as specialist terms, slang and jargon

– Provides invaluable guidance on correct usage, commonly confused words and grammar and spelling

www.penguin.com

know more

PENGUIN POCKET REFERENCE

THE PENGUIN POCKET SPANISH DICTIONARY
JOSEPHINE RIQUELME-BENEYTO

The Penguin Pocket Spanish Dictionary is an invaluable and handy wordfinder for students and travellers alike. Covering both English–Spanish and Spanish–English, it offers clear definitions in an easy-to-use format, ensuring that you find the word you need quickly and efficiently.

- Includes over 36,000 entries

- Gives entry-by-entry guidance on pronunciation

- Lists irregular verbs in both languages

know more ⟨🐧⟩

PENGUIN POCKET REFERENCE

THE PENGUIN POCKET FRENCH DICTIONARY
ROSALIND FERGUSSON

The Penguin Pocket French Dictionary is an invaluable and handy wordfinder for students and travellers alike. Covering both English–French and French–English, it offers clear definitions in an easy-to-use format, ensuring that you find the word you need quickly and efficiently.

- Includes over 35,000 entries

- Gives entry-by-entry guidance on pronunciation

- Lists irregular verbs in both languages

know more

PENGUIN POCKET REFERENCE

THE PENGUIN POCKET BOOK OF FACTS
EDITED BY DAVID CRYSTAL

The Penguin Pocket Book of Facts is a goldmine of information, figures and statistics on every conceivable subject – from the world's highest mountains and longest rivers to the gods of mythology, and from time zones to Nobel Prize winners. The ultimate one-stop factfinder, this is the essential book for browsers, crossword and trivia addicts, and for anyone who needs to check facts at home or at work.

– Up-to-date information about everything from astronomy to zoology

– Easy to use

– Illustrated throughout with maps and diagrams

www.penguin.com

know more (P)

PENGUIN POCKET REFERENCE

THE PENGUIN POCKET DICTIONARY OF BABIES' NAMES
DAVID PICKERING

The Penguin Pocket Dictionary of Babies' Names is essential reading for all expectant parents wishing to choose the perfect name for their child. It gives the meanings and stories behind thousands of names from all parts of the world – ranging from the most well-known choices to more unusual names.

- Gives variations and shortened forms for each name

- Highlights names popularized by books, films and celebrities

- Lists the most popular girls' and boys' names from 1700 to the present

- Shows how tastes for names have changed in the twenty-first century

know more

PENGUIN WRITERS' GUIDES

HOW TO PUNCTUATE
GEORGE DAVIDSON

HOW TO WRITE BETTER ENGLISH
ROBERT ALLEN

HOW TO WRITE EFFECTIVE EMAILS
R. L. TRASK

IMPROVE YOUR SPELLING
GEORGE DAVIDSON

WRITING FOR BUSINESS
CHRIS SHEVLIN

The Penguin Writers' Guides series provides authoritative, succinct and easy-to-follow guidance on specific aspects of written English. Whether you need to brush up your skills or get to grips with something for the first time, these invaluable guides will help you find the best way to communicate clearly and effectively.

Get your message across

PENGUIN ONLINE

News, reviews and previews of forthcoming books

read about your favourite authors

•

investigate over 12,000 titles

•

browse our online magazine

•

enter one of our literary quizzes

•

win some fantastic prizes in our competitions

•

e-mail us with your comments and book reviews

•

instantly order any Penguin book

'To be recommended without reservation ... a rich and rewarding online experience' *Internet Magazine*

www.penguin.com